ROBERT HOOKE

Memorial to Hooke in Westminster Abbey. The memorial has been carved into a black marble lozenge which is part of the pavement that Dr Richard Busby paid for and Robert Hooke laid for him. The memorial is to the north of and close by Busby's grave in the Lantern, at the foot of the steps to the Sacrarium. The memorial was dedicated on 3 March 2004.

(By kind permission of the Dean and Chapter of Westminster)

Robert Hooke

Tercentennial Studies

Edited by
MICHAEL COOPER
City University, London
and
MICHAEL HUNTER
Birkbeck, University of London

ASHGATE

Published by
Ashgate Publishing Limited
Gower House
Croft Road
Aldershot
Hants GU11 3HR
England

Ashgate Publishing Company
Suite 420
101 Cherry Street
Burlington
VT 05401-4405
USA

Ashgate website: http://www.ashgate.com

British Library Cataloguing in Publication Data
Robert Hooke : tercentennial studies
   1. Hooke, Robert, 1635–1703 2.Scientists – Great Britain – Biography 3.Scholars –
   Great Britain – Biography 4.Science – Great Britain – History – 17th century
   I.Cooper, M. A. R. (Michael Alan Ralph) II.Hunter, Michael Cyril William
   509.2

Library of Congress Cataloging-in-Publication Data
Robert Hooke : tercentennial studies / edited by Michael Cooper and Michael Hunter.
    p. cm.
   Includes bibliographical references and index.
   ISBN 0-7546-5365-X (alk. paper)
 1. Hooke, Robert, 1635–1703. 2. Science – Great Britain – History – 17th century. 3.
Scientists – Great Britain – Intellectual life – 17th century. 4. Hooke, Robert,
1635–1703 – Influence. I. Cooper, Michael, 1935– II. Hunter, Michael Cyril William.

   Q143.H7R63 2006
   509.2–dc22

2005017266

ISBN 0 7546 5365 X

Typeset by IML Typographers, Birkenhead, Merseyside
Printed and bound in Great Britain by MPG Books Ltd, Bodmin, Cornwall

Contents

List of Figures and Tables

Figures

Tables

List of Contributors

Jim Bennett Museum of the History of Science, University of Oxford

Douwe Draaisma Department of Theory and History of Psychology, University of Groningen

Ellen Tan Drake College of Oceanic and Atmospheric Sciences, Oregon State University

Mordechai Feingold Humanities and Social Sciences, California Institute of Technology

Ofer Gal Ben Gurion University and University of Sydney

John Hennessy Department of Physics and Astronomy, University of Leicester

Jacques Heyman Department of Engineering, University of Cambridge

Lisa Jardine Queen Mary, University of London

S. H. Joseph Department of Mechanical Engineering, University of Sheffield

Hentie Louw School of Architecture, Planning and Landscape, University of Newcastle upon Tyne

Allan Mills Department of Physics and Astronomy, University of Leicester

Hideto Nakajima Department of History, Philosophy and Social Studies of Science and Technology, Tokyo Institute of Technology

Michael Nauenberg Department of Physics, University of California, Santa Cruz

Robert D. Purrington Department of Physics, Tulane University, New Orleans

Edward Smith Westminster School

Alison Stoesser Architectural Historian

Stephen Watson Department of Physics and Astronomy, University of Leicester

Nick Wilding Italian Academy for Advanced Studies in America at Columbia University

Introduction

Robert Hooke was undoubtedly one of the leading figures of the Scientific Revolution, a polymath who made seminal contributions to many fields, from natural philosophy and technology to architecture and civic design. As we enter the twenty-first century, there are signs that Hooke is at last gaining the recognition that he was long denied. Between September 2002 and September 2003, no fewer that four books entirely devoted to him were published.[1] Two more followed in 2005,[2] and he has also been the subject of a flood of articles and contributions to books over the past 25 years, as will be apparent from the comprehensive bibliography appended to this book.

We have come a long way from the state of affairs when virtually the only satisfactory treatments of Hooke were Margaret 'Espinasse's spirited, if rather partial, study of 1956 and E. N. da C. Andrade's generous but brief appraisal in his Wilkins lecture of 1949 (though both remain worth reading, as do such incisive post-war studies as those of Koyré and Patterson that will be referred to below).[3] A significant turning point was represented by the volume to which this one is in many ways the successor, *Robert Hooke: New Studies*, edited by Michael Hunter and Simon Schaffer, published in 1989 and based on a conference held at the Royal Society in 1987 under the auspices of the British Society for the History of Science. A quarter of a century later, the 'Hooke 2003' conference from which the current volume has stemmed was again held at the Royal Society, this time under the aegis of Gresham College, the Royal Academy of Engineering and the Royal Society itself. In the intervening years, it could be argued that 'Hooke studies' have gained momentum, and the main themes in these may be summarized here by way of background to this volume's contents.

It is perhaps appropriate to begin with Hooke's most famous work *Micrographia* (1665), which continues to attract attention at both a scholarly and a more popular level. Indeed, it was one of the first works, either by Hooke or any of his contemporaries, to be made available on CDRom.[4] A meticulously annotated edition of the work was published in 1989, though in Spanish rather than English, so for English readers a fully annotated version of the book remains a desideratum.[5] The making of the book has been the subject of two studies, by John Harwood (in *Robert Hooke: New Studies*) and Michael

Aaron Dennis, while its setting in terms of the microscopy of the period has been explored by various authors.[6] *Micrographia* also receives attention, for instance, in Adrian Johns's recent *The Nature of the Book* (1998), while no general work on the science of the period seems complete without a commentary on the book and the reproduction of some of its striking engraved images of the microscopical observations that Hooke made.[7] Not least because of these, it seems likely that this will continue to be the work by Hooke that engages the widest audience.

Micrographia, of course, also describes and illustrates instruments other than the microscope, thus linking it to the virtuosity as an instrument-maker that Hooke displayed throughout his career. Here, the acknowledged master is Jim Bennett, author of a number of studies over the years, of which the latest, and in some ways the most significant, appears in the present volume. Hooke's engagement with practical mechanics was considered by many then (and by some now) to be an occupation proper for the less educated in society. But Hooke was not alone in regarding it as an appropriate undertaking for a highly educated man – his rival Christiaan Huygens would be another case in point. Indeed, as Bennett argues below, Hooke's mechanical experiments were both ingenious and ingenuous – in the sense of transparency – while he also brings out the moral purpose that Hooke regarded practical mechanics as having. The significance of John Wilkins in imbuing Hooke's sense of moral purpose in mechanics has been underlined in another recent publication.[8] It is in *Micrographia* that we find Hooke setting out his firm belief in experimenting with instruments for measuring and observing natural phenomena. Such experiments can not only produce useful knowledge, but also reveal the beauty and magnificence of the natural world, both near at hand at the end of a microscope or far away through a long telescope. Hideto Nakajima shows below that Hooke did much more important work in observational astronomy than has been generally thought. Hooke's sense of wonder at the natural world and the discovery of knowledge that can bring great benefits to mankind were strong incentives to pursue experimental natural philosophy, as they have been to many scientists ever since.

Given Hooke's publication of meticulous technical drawings and verbal descriptions of many of his scientific instruments and other experimental apparatus, it is somewhat surprising that so few recent writers on Hooke have made and used one of his devices for its intended purpose, or even as a teaching or learning aid (the main exception is Michael Wright's reconstruction of Hooke's longitude timekeeper).[9] In this book however, there are three papers whose authors have done just that. Michael Nauenberg reports on his repeating of Hooke's gravitational experiments with pendulums and spheres rolling in inverted cones; Steve Joseph reports on various investigations into motion, air and combustion; and Allan Mills and his colleagues describe their reconstruction of Hooke's mechanism for driving his equatorial quadrant. Collectively these papers show not only the misunderstandings and misconceptions that have arisen from reliance solely on texts, but, rather more importantly, how understanding of physical phenomena can come through, literally, hands-on engagement with apparatus and instruments. Anyone who has performed even the simple act of taking a heavy pendulum bob hanging from a ceiling and setting it in motion along a curved path (as Hooke did at a meeting of the Royal Society in 1666) can feel both the force attracting the bob towards the centre of motion and the effort needed to set it in motion at right angles to the central force. Hooke's understanding of natural phenomena came from interaction between his senses and his intellect – a combination which made him one of the world's most ingenious and prescient experimental scientists.

Hooke also used *Micrographia* for imaginative speculation about many of the phenomena that he had observed both during experiments, and when going about his daily mundane tasks. In particular, he publicly divulged the germ of his ideas about the geological history of the world and the significance of fossils, and this is an aspect of his scientific work which has received extensive study over the past 30 years. A pioneer was David Oldroyd, who initially used Hooke's writings on this subject, and particularly the 'Discourse of Earthquakes' in his *Posthumous Works*, to exemplify his scientific method more generally, subsequently going on to study Hooke's reaction to the criticism to which his geological views were subjected in the 1680s. Further contributions were made by Yushi Ito and Rhoda Rappaport, both of whom tried to understand Hooke's ideas in relation to their context, with Rappaport taking a particular interest in the audience to which he delivered his lectures on the subject at the Royal Society; this contextualist thrust subsequently matured into her study of the entire period of earth science in which Hooke participated in her aptly-entitled monograph *When Geologists were Historians* (1997). Meanwhile, Hooke's geology became the subject of a book-length study in its own right in 1996, in the form of Ellen Tan Drake's *Restless Genius*, an edition of the geological lectures from *Posthumous Works* with a lengthy introduction surveying Hooke's life, his work in this field, and his place in the history of geology.

A further theme that has attracted a good deal of attention

comprises Hooke's pronouncements on scientific method, not least in writings published in his *Posthumous Works* (1705). Interest in this topic, and particularly in Hooke's elusive 'philosophical algebra', goes back to a seminal article by Mary Hesse published in 1966. It was taken up by David Oldroyd in the 1972 article already referred to, while Oldroyd made a further significant contribution on the basis of hitherto unknown manuscript material in 1987. A further exhaustive study of this aspect of Hooke unfortunately remains available only through microfilm: this is Patri Pugliese's 1982 Harvard PhD thesis on Hooke, Chapters 1 and 2 of which deal at length with his methodological statements. In terms of how the organisation of science might be used to forward the method that seemed to him appropriate, Hooke's views receive extensive attention in a paper on conflicting strategies in the early Royal Society as a whole published by Michael Hunter and Paul Wood in 1986, while this broader context also provides the rationale of William T. Lynch's recent account of Hooke in his *Solomon's Child: Method in the Early Royal Society of London* (2001), based in this case mainly on the early sections of *Micrographia*. Discussion of such topics seems set to continue, though, partly due to the extent to which they have been the subject of recent treatment elsewhere, they are dealt with only tangentially here.[10]

There has also been interest in a more miscellaneous range of aspects of Hooke's science, not least those that formed the subject of the tireless series of presentations that he made to the Royal Society as Curator of Experiments and Cutlerian Lecturer from 1662 onwards, many of them published in his *Posthumous Works*. Indeed, his contribution to the early Royal Society (revaluated in relation to the history of the Cutlerian Lectureship in a 1989 study by Michael Hunter) is here taken up by Robert Purrington, who considers Hooke's relations with that body in the last decade of his career. Of the writings that emanated from Hooke's presentations to the Society, those that dealt with perception and memory were the subject of studies by Bernard Singer and J. J. MacIntosh in the 1970s and 1980s, followed by Lotte Mulligan and Jamie Kassler in the 1990s, while in the current volume, they are taken up by Douwe Draaisma and Nick Wilding. Other such topics are not dealt with here, partly because of the attention that they have received elsewhere. For instance, Hooke's views on the structure of the human body, developed in the context of his presentations to the early Royal Society on the basis of notions formed during his association with the seminal Oxford group of physiologists in the 1650s (the subject of Robert G. Frank's classic study of 1980) have recently formed the subject of an intriguing revaluation of his views on the possibility of human flight.[11]

If on such topics there has been a degree of continuity, other aspects of Hooke's achievement have come to the fore in recent years after hitherto being almost entirely neglected. Perhaps the most significant is Hooke's activity as a surveyor for the City of London in the aftermath of the Great Fire, for which the profuse documentation in the City of London archives had been completely unknown until investigated by Michael Cooper, first in a series of articles in the late 1990s and latterly in a book. This has illustrated a significant part of Hooke's activity in the 1660s and 1670s – complementing and competing with the demands of his work as Curator of Experiments to the Royal Society – to the implications of which for our overall evaluation of him we will return later in this introduction.

By comparison, Hooke's architectural work is only slowly attracting the attention that it deserves, perhaps partly because so many of the important buildings he is known to have designed no longer survive. However, a striking reassessment of Hooke from this point of view has recently been offered by Giles Worsley, who suggests on the basis of personal and professional links and stylistic analogies that Hooke might have been the architect of various major houses of the late seventeenth century, the responsibility for the design of which has always been problematic, including Petworth (Sussex) and Boughton (Northamptonshire).[12] In addition, the current volume contains a study by Alison Stoesser which traces influences on Hooke's architecture and which importantly supplements the pioneering work of M. I. Batten, published in the *Journal of the Walpole Society* in 1936–7. Here, too, Jacques Heyman shows how, in order to meet the exigencies of rebuilding London after the Great Fire, Hooke and his friend and colleague Sir Christopher Wren transformed traditional construction procedures, directed by a master-craftsman, into a recognisably modern practice involving architect, engineer and surveyor. Further pursuing this theme of the introduction of new methods and procedures into building construction, Hentie Louw discusses Hooke as a scientist–architect, arguing that he was more interested in finding practical solutions to technical problems in building, at which he excelled, than in combining a rational consistency with artistic creativity in his architectural designs.

Other themes have been the subject of controversy. Some of these are of relatively recent origin, in at least two cases going back to contributions to *Robert Hooke: New Studies*. One of these is the view that, so far from being the quintessential mechanistic philosopher that he had often been taken to be, Hooke was, in fact, deeply influenced by magical ideas, particularly notions originating in the tradition of natural magic. This was the claim made by John Henry in that volume, and a parallel claim has been made by Penelope Gouk, initially in a study of another neglected aspect of Hooke, his ideas on music, which was subsequently developed into a chapter in her book-length study of music and natural magic in English natural philosophy in Hooke's period, in which he is presented as a more ambivalent figure than had usually been presumed.[13] There has already been an article-length response to Henry's ideas by Mark Ehrlich, in which a more mechanistic reading is offered of many of the findings that Henry adduced, and it seems likely that the initial case was overstated, even if the entire state of affairs in the late seventeenth century now seems more complex from this point of view than it once did.[14]

The second, relatively new, area of controversy concerns Hooke's status, and the extent to which this affected his intellectual persona and his relationship with his scientific peers. Again, this goes back to *Robert Hooke: New Studies* and to Steven Shapin's challenging paper, 'Who was Robert Hooke?'. Subsequently, this was developed into a broader study of the significance of status in underwriting intellectual credit in the period in Shapin's *A Social History of Truth* (1994). Whatever truth there may be in Shapin's claims about the valorization of the leisured amateur as the role model of science in the period, these had an unfortunate effect from the point of view of Hooke, who was unfairly singled out for attention as a man who had difficulties because of his relatively lowly status. This impression was reinforced by other studies published in the aftermath of Shapin's, by Stephen Pumfrey and Rob Iliffe, with such more provocative titles as 'Ideas above his station' or 'In the warehouse'. Indeed, it is revealing that by 1995 even a popular guidebook to scientific sites in Britain picked up on this aspect of Hooke's career.[15] Fortunately, in this volume Mordechai Feingold is able to illustrate many of the false presumptions underlying such evaluations of Hooke's status. Insofar as Shapin extended his case to imply that Hooke was not only of subservient status but also of questionable morality, evidence has been presented by Michael Cooper in his book on Hooke's activities as City Surveyor of his civic virtue in being scrupulously fair, fearsomely efficient and astonishingly hard-working in responding to the needs of thousands of individual citizens anxious to rebuild their homes and resume their trades and businesses in the aftermath of London's Great Fire. It is hoped that the record will now be set straight as far as Hooke's reputation and character are concerned.

Third, there is the perennial issue of Hooke's contribution to Newton's discoveries in celestial mechanics, which has bedevilled his reputation ever since his own time but which shows no sign of abating. Since the time of W. W. Rouse Ball's pioneering study of 1893, scholars have been aware that, at the very least, Newton was less than generous in his acknowledgment of Hooke's contribution to the intellectual breakthrough which led to the *Principia*. This controversy has continued ever since, with the contributions of a succession of scholars from Koyré and Patterson in the post-war years, through Lohne and Westfall in the 1960s, to Pugliese's contribution to *Robert Hooke: New Studies*. Subsequently, matters have been reinvigorated, particularly by the contributions of Michael Nauenburg, and readers can sample his work for themselves in the pages that follow. It now seems likely that Hooke did sow in Newton's mind some of the critical notions on which his synthesis depended, including the combination of radial and tangential velocities to explain the elliptical motion of the planets.

On the other hand it could be argued that even now (saving the contribution here by Ofer Gal) the controversy has been framed within almost wholly Newtonian terms of reference. Somewhere in the contradictory views of Nauenberg and Gal on the Newton/Hooke dispute – which have since been the subject of further debate* – can be located a view of nature on Hooke's part which is neither mechanistic nor magical, but far more complicated – a synthesis of his cosmological and his equally seminal geological ideas. It still remains a desideratum to realize the percipient suggestion made by Louise Patterson in 1950 'that from Hooke's point of view the gravitation theory was subordinate to a larger scheme of natural philosophy of which that theory was part' – in particular, his search for a hypothesis that would describe the material world 'not merely as a self-regulating mechanism but also as an evolving mechanism'.[16]

This call for a broader synthesis is arguably the key to how Hooke studies as a whole should develop. It might be thought that the current challenge is the lack of a collected and annotated edition of Hooke's writings, matching the recent edition of the works of his mentor, Boyle. This would, of course, be highly desirable, as would a proper scrutiny of neglected parts of Hooke's manuscript corpus, perhaps particularly volume 20 of the Royal Society's Classified Papers. On the other hand, as far as his published works are concerned, the various facsimile reprints issued in the twentieth century have made these widely available. What is far more important is the need for change in the way Hooke is interpreted and an end to the scholarly compartmentalization from which he has suffered: this has arguably underestimated his achievement by obscuring links

*See *Physics Today*, February and August 2004, and *Early Science and Medicine*, **10** (2005), 510–43.

between its different parts. To an extent, such integration has been the objective of the various biographies of the man that have appeared in recent years. Stephen Inwood, in particular, makes a point of trying to do justice to the sheer range of activities in which Hooke was involved at any one time, in implicit contrast to the single-mindedness that Newton could afford in his more academic setting – though there are times when even Inwood baulks at the sheer profusion of Hooke's commitments. More significant is the need to bring together the different components of Hooke's intellectual life, as exemplified by Louise Patterson's agenda, outlined in the previous paragraph, or by some of the best of the other studies noted in this introduction. In this way, we may at last learn to do justice to the true contribution to the making of science and the modern world of this extraordinary man.

Michael Cooper
Michael Hunter

Acknowledgements

We would like to express our gratitude, and that of more than 100 people who attended the 'Hooke 2003' conference held at the Royal Society in July 2003, to the following institutions who generously donated funds or services, without which the conference could not have taken place: Gresham College; The Royal Society; and The Royal Academy of Engineering.

In connection with the production of this volume, we are grateful to: Gresham College for support in the form of a grant towards the costs of editing and indexing; and the Library and Archive staff of the Royal Society for general help and co-operation.

Illustrations are reproduced by kind permission of: The Dean and Chapter of Westminster (Frontispiece); The British Library (Figures 1.2, 1.11, 1.12, part of 2.3); The Master and Fellows of Trinity College, Cambridge (Figures 1.4, 1.6); Bibliothèque Nationale, Paris (Figure 3.2); The President and Council of the Royal Society (front cover and Figure 3.5); Kerry Downes (Figure 11.1); Koen Ottenheym (Figure 11.2); Guildhall Library, Corporation of London (Figures 11.3, 11.7, 11.9, 11.10); English Heritage National Monuments Record (Figure 14.2); The Dean and Chapter of Westminster (Figure 14.3); and Westminster City Archives (Figure 14.4).

We also acknowledge the permission of Birkhauser Publishing Ltd to include Michael Nauenberg's chapter which appeared in the March 2005 issue of *Physics in Perspective*.

PART 1
CELESTIAL MECHANICS
AND ASTRONOMY

Chapter 1

Robert Hooke's Seminal Contribution to Orbital Dynamics

Michael Nauenberg

Preamble

During the second half of the seventeenth century, the outstanding problem in astronomy was to understand the physical basis for Kepler's three empirical laws describing the observed orbital motion of a planet around the Sun. In the middle 1660s Robert Hooke (1635–1703) proposed that a planet's motion is determined by compounding its tangential velocity with the change in radial velocity impressed by the gravitational attraction of the Sun, and he described his physical concept to Isaac Newton in a correspondence in 1679. Newton denied having heard of Hooke's novel concept of orbital motion, but shortly after their correspondence he implemented it by a geometric construction from which he deduced the physical origin of Kepler's area law, which later became Proposition I, Book I, of his *Principia* in 1687.[1] Three years earlier, Newton had deposited a preliminary draft of it, his *De Motu Corporum in Gyrum* (*On the Motion of Bodies*), at the Royal Society of London, which Hooke apparently was able to examine a few months later. Shortly thereafter he applied Newton's construction in a novel way to obtain the path of a body under the action of an attractive central force that varies linearly with the distance from its centre of motion (Hooke's Law). I show that Hooke's construction corresponds to Newton's for his proof of Kepler's area law in his *De Motu*. Hooke's understanding of planetary motion was based on his observations with mechanical analogues. I also repeated two of his experiments and demonstrate the accuracy of his observations. My results thus cast new light on the significance of Hooke's contributions to the development of orbital dynamics, which in the past have either been neglected or misunderstood.

Introduction

One of the most fascinating questions in the history of science concerns the role that Robert Hooke played in the development of dynamics and the theory of gravitation during the seventeenth century, which culminated in Isaac Newton's masterpiece, the *Principia* in 1687.[2] Hooke was one of the most prolific and inventive scientists of all times, and he made fundamental contributions to virtual all branches of science;[3] one third of the 15 volumes of Robert T. Gunther's *Early Science in Oxford* are dedicated to his work.[4]

Despite Hooke's profound influence, however, particularly on Newton's development of orbital dynamics, he was nearly completely forgotten after his death in 1703, and remained unknown until around the turn of the twentieth century. Ernst Mach, in his influential book first published in 1883, *The Science of Mechanics*, devoted only a few lines to Hooke, although he perceptively stated that 'Hooke really approached nearest to Newton's conception, though he never completely reached the latter's altitude of view'.[5] Ten years later, W. W. Rouse Ball published some of the correspondence between Hooke and Newton,[6] and the subsequent discovery of two additional letters of Hooke, which were published by Jean Pelseneer and Alexandre Koyré,[7] initiated a reappraisal of Hooke's contributions to mechanics that continues to the present time.[8] René Dugas, in contrast to Mach, recognized Hooke's crucial role in his book of 1958, *Mechanics in the Seventeenth Century*,[9] but some recent accounts of the development of mechanics still ignore Hooke's significant contributions. Most physicists and mathematicians still remain unaware of them, as can be seen by reading modern textbooks or journals that cover classical mechanics, where Hooke is mentioned only in connection with his eponymous law of elasticity.[10]

During the past few years, however, a number of books and articles have appeared that describe Hooke's many contributions to science, and also his major role in the reconstruction of London after the Great Fire of 1666.[11] There now appears to be consensus among historians of science that Hooke's physical explanation for the orbital motion of planets – 'compounding the celestiall motions of the planetts of a direct motion by the tangent & an attractive motion towards the centrall body'[12] – had an influence on Newton's work that culminated in the publication of his *Principia*. Hooke communicated his ideas on orbital motion to Newton in a letter in 1679 and, according to one of Newton's most outstanding biographers, Richard S. Westfall:

Newton's papers reveal no similar understanding of circular motion before this letter. Every time he had considered it, he had spoken of a tendency to recede from the center, what [Christiaan] Huygens [1629–95] called centrifugal force; and like others who spoke in such terms, he had looked upon circular motion as a state of equilibrium between two equal and opposing forces, one away from the center and one toward it. Hooke's statement treated circular motion as a disequilibrium in which an unbalanced force deflects a body that would otherwise continue in a straight line. It was not an inconsiderable lesson for Newton to learn.[13]

But there is considerable confusion in the literature as to exactly what the 'lesson' was that Newton learned from Hooke. In a letter to Edmond Halley on 20 June 1686,[14] Newton vehemently denied that he had learned anything from Hooke, although he admitted, in one of his unpublished autobiographical manuscripts, that:

> In the end of the year 1679 in answer to a Letter from Dr Hook ... I found now that whatsoever was the law of the forces wch kept the Planets in their Orbs, the areas described by a Radius drawn from them to the Sun would be proportional to the times in wch they were described. And by the help of these two Propositions I found that their Orbs would be such Ellipses as Kepler had described.[15]

To understand the influence of Hooke's concept of orbital motion on Newton, we must know how Newton viewed orbital dynamics prior to Hooke's letter to him in 1679. Newtonian scholars commonly conclude that Newton's crucial step thereafter was to switch from a traditional view of circular motion as giving rise to a centrifugal force or tendency to recede from the centre, to the concept of a centripetal force directed toward the centre. As I have shown elsewhere,[16] this is misleading in view of Newton's already profound, albeit incomplete, understanding of orbital motion at that time.

In the following sections, I first describe Newton's early development of orbital dynamics as based on his 'Waste Book' of 1664 and on his letter of 13 December 1679 to Hooke. I then present Hooke's formulation of the physical principles of orbital motion for central forces and analyse his diagram of 1685 for the motion of a body under the action of a central force that varies linearly with the distance.[17] I show graphically that it implements his dynamical principles in a way very similar to Newton's description of his proof of Kepler's area law in his *De Motu Corporum in Gyrum* (*On the Motion of Bodies*) of 1684,[18] the preliminary draft of his *Principia*. I next present further background on the development of Hooke's physical ideas for orbital motion, which were based on mechanical analogues. I

repeated Hooke's experiments on a conical pendulum and on a ball
rolling inside an inverted cone, finding both to agree with Hooke's
observations. I close with a summary and conclusions.

Newton's Theory of Orbital Motion Prior to Hooke's Letter of 1679

René Descartes illustrated the traditional view of circular motion in
1644 by considering a stone rotating in a sling (Figure 1.1).[19]

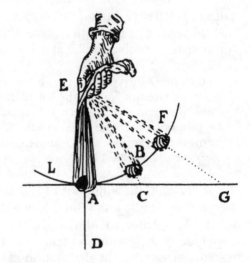

Figure 1.1 Descartes's 1644
illustration of the traditional
view of circular motion as a
'tendency to recede from the
centre'.

If the stone is freed at point *A*, then it would move along the tangent
to the circle from point *A* to point *C*, but instead the sling constrains it
to move along a circular path to point *B*. The 'tendency' of the stone to
recede radially is felt by the person's hand at the centre, because the
stone exerts a force that depends on its weight and velocity and on the
length of the sling. The magnitude of this force was not known
quantitatively until Huygens and somewhat later Newton showed that it
is proportional to the radial acceleration,[20] which is equal to the square
of the velocity of the stone divided by the length of the sling.

Prior to 1679, Newton based his description of the orbital motion of a
body under the action of a central force on a generalization of the
properties of circular motion,[21] compounding its orbital velocity along
the tangent with a change of velocity perpendicular to this direction,
whereas Hooke considered its *total* change in velocity directed toward
the centre of force. Newton thought of orbital motion in this way at
least as early as 1664, when he wrote in his 'Waste Book': 'If the body

... moved in an Ellipsis, then its force in each point (if its motion [velocity] in that point bee given) may bee found by a tangent circle of Equall crookednesse with that point of the Ellipsis'.[22]

Newton equated force with acceleration, and by a 'circle of Equall crookednesse' (his word for curvature) he meant the osculating circle (as Gottfried Leibniz called it 30 years later) at a point on the ellipse. Newton evidently was applying his concept of radial acceleration for circular motion, with the radius being the radius of curvature at a point on the ellipse. For non-circular motion, there is a component of acceleration perpendicular to the orbit, but then the centre of curvature and the centre of force do not coincide and the velocity along the orbit is not constant, because there is a component of the force tangential to the orbit that produces a tangential acceleration. Thus, Newton required, as he stated, that the motion or velocity at a point on the ellipse 'bee given'. Newton discovered how to calculate this velocity by Kepler's area law (or what we now call conservation of angular momentum), which was the essential missing link in his analysis, only after he received Hooke's letters of 1679.

Further evidence that the lesson that Newton learned from Hooke was not simply to switch from a centrifugal to a centripetal representation of force (as some Newtonian scholars have claimed) can be found in a letter Newton wrote to Hooke on 13 December 1679.[23] In its corner he drew a diagram (Figure 1.2) that shows he was

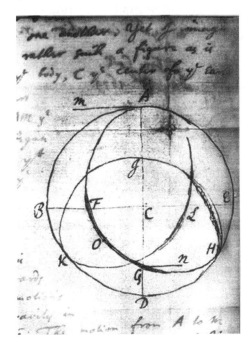

Figure 1.2   Newton's diagram in his letter to Hooke dated 13 December 1679 showing the orbit of a body moving under the action of a constant force directed towards the centre located at C.
(British Library)

able to compute 'by points *quam proximè*' (approximately) the orbit of a body under the action of a constant central force (see Appendix).

His text indicates that he also understood very well the changes that would occur in this orbit if the force increases toward the centre, as I have discussed in detail elsewhere.[24] Moreover, Newton continued to argue in terms of his concept of centrifugal force long after 1679. For example, following some arguments with John Flamsteed, the first Astronomer Royal, Newton explained in a letter to James Crompton[25] in April 1681 that the orbit of a comet around the Sun is determined by 'the *vis centrifuga* [centrifugal force] at *C* [perihelion] overpow'ring the attraction & forcing the Comet there notwithstanding the attraction, to begin to recede from the Sun'.[26] In fact, Newton never abandoned his concept of orbital dynamics based upon his curvature approach,[27] and in Book 3, Proposition 28, of his *Principia* he applied it in combination with Kepler's area law to obtain a remarkable solution of the effect of solar perturbation on the motion of the Moon around the Earth.[28] But he did not explain his curvature approach in the first edition of his *Principia* of 1687; it appeared as an alternate method for solving this problem only in the second and third editions of 1713 and 1726. As a consequence, his early curvature approach has been regarded erroneously as his more mature development of orbital dynamics.[29]

In Newton's curvature approach, Kepler's area law (or conservation of angular momentum) had remained hidden;[30] he discovered its physical origin (that the acting force must be directed toward a fixed centre) only after implementing Hooke's way of 'compounding' velocities geometrically for a general orbit.[31] Newton had considered an approach similar to Hooke's in his earliest work on dynamics, as shown in his 'Waste Book' of 1664 (Figure 1.3)[32] but he evidently did not consider extending it to arbitrary motion until after Hooke prompted him to do so.

Kepler's area law was crucial to Newton's development of orbital dynamics, because it permitted him to express the time variable in purely geometrical terms, stating that 'the areas which bodies [planets] made to move in orbits describe by radii drawn to an unmoving centre of force lie in unmoving planes and are proportional to the times'.[33] Newton's proof of Kepler's area law is one of the cornerstones of his *Principia*, which he presented in Book 1, Proposition 1, Theorem I.

Hooke's Formulation of the Principles of Orbital Dynamics

Hooke's profound physical intuition, which was guided by his numerous experiments (thought to be on the order of several

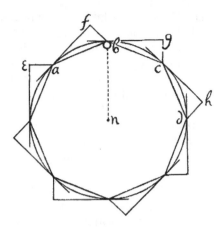

Figure 1.3 The diagram in Newton's 1664 'Waste Book' showing an octagon inscribed in a circle with centre at n to describe orbital motion. The tangential displacements or velocities af, bg, ... are compounded with the corresponding deflections fb, gc, ... , or impressed velocities in the normal direction, to give the total displacements ab, bc, ... along the orbit .
(Whiteside 1991, p. 13)

hundred)[34] led him during the middle 1660s to a correct *qualitative* formulation of the principles of dynamics as applied to celestial mechanics. He stated that the orbital motion of a planet is determined by 'compounding' its inertial motion along a straight line with an attractive motion toward the Sun impressed by the gravitational attraction of the Sun. Furthermore, in 1674 he formulated the concept of universal gravitational attraction,[35] and he later deduced the inverse-square law based on his conjecture that gravity originates in periodic pulses from matter, in analogy to the emission of light and sound.[36] While crediting Hooke with some of these ideas and acknowledging his influence on Newton, historians of science generally have concluded, with few exceptions,[37] that Hooke was unable to obtain a *quantitative* or *mathematical* formulation of his principles of dynamics.

This judgment echoes the charges Newton levelled against Hooke in a letter to Halley of 20 June 1686:

Borel[38] did something in it & wrote modestly, he [Hooke] has done nothing & yet written in such a way as if he knew & had sufficiently hinted all but what remained to be determined by the drudgery of calculations & observations, excusing himself from that labour by reason of his other business: whereas he should rather have excused himself by reason of his inability. For tis plain by his words he knew not how to go about it. Now is not this very fine? Mathematicians that find out, settle & do all the business must content themselves with being nothing but dry calculators & drudges & another that does nothing but pretend & grasp at all things must carry away all the invention as well of those that were to follow him as of those that went before ... For as Borell wrote long before him that by a tendency of the Planets towards the sun like that of gravity or magnetism the Planets would move in Ellipses, so Bullialdus[39] wrote that all force respecting the Sun as its center & depending on matter must be reciprocally in a duplicate ratio of the distance from the centre ... .[40]

Newton's diatribe followed after he had heard that Hooke had claimed that Newton had plagiarized from him the discovery of the inverse-square law of the gravitational force. Halley, in his capacity as editor of the *Principia*, had tactfully written to Newton on 22 May 1686:

Mr Hook has some pretensions upon the invention of the rule of the decrease of Gravity, being reciprocally as the squares of the distances from the Center. He sais you had the notion from him, though he owns the Demonstration of the Curves generated therby to be wholly your own; how much of this is so, you know best ...[41]

Newton also had criticized Hooke's claim that the inverse-square law implied that the planets move in elliptical orbits around the Sun, pointing out that Hooke had concluded incorrectly that their velocities in such orbits vary inversely with their distances from the Sun. What Newton conveniently forgot in his effort to discredit Hooke is that in Hooke's letter to him in 1679, Hooke had correctly described some of the principles of orbital motion that led Newton to his discovery of Kepler's area law, and to a deeper understanding of orbital dynamics.[42] Newton later referred to Hooke in his *System of the World* (the less mathematical treatment of Book III of the *Principia*), lumping him together with other well-known natural philosophers whose speculations about the motion of the planets were *wrong*: 'The later philosophers *pretend* [my italics] to account for it either by the action of certain vortices, as Kepler and Descartes; or by some other principle of impulse or attraction, as Borelli, Hooke, and others of our nation'.[43]

Actually, Hooke arrived at his remarkable physical insights in dynamics by careful observations of *mechanical analogues* of celestial motion, by applying mathematical reasoning, and not merely by guessing. With the notable exceptions of Johannes Lohne and V.I. Arnol'd,[44] many Newtonian scholars have repeated the misconception that Hooke's discoveries of the principles of mechanics and the inverse-square law of gravitational force were pure guesses, or somehow based on incorrect mathematical reasoning. A. Rupert Hall, for example, has stated that, 'Other philosophers of mechanics, such as Marcus Marci[45] and Robert Hooke, were just as deeply embroiled in imprecise notions and perilous analogies as was Borelli';[46] and further, that:

> One sees his [Newton's] point: Hooke had been *almost* as vague as Borelli, and certainly could never have produced dynamical demonstrations applicable to planetary motion: yet we may allow that the idea of a terrestrial projectile becoming a satellite in elliptical orbit was Hooke's own, though a 'guess' indeed as Newton rightly called it.[47]

This sentiment, that Hooke did not have any sound basis for his physical principles, echoes the words of the eighteenth-century French mathematician Alexis-Claude Clairaut who, although considered to be a supporter of Hooke, stated that Hooke's examples 'serve to show what a distance there is between a truth that is glimpsed and a truth that is demonstrated'.[48]

From the outset however, Hooke's dynamical principles were grounded on careful experiments and observations of mechanical systems that could serve as analogues of celestial dynamics. The best-documented example is that of the motion of a circular or conical pendulum,[49] but there also is evidence that he studied the dynamics of balls rolling inside various surfaces of revolution. These mechanical systems serve as approximate *analogue models* for different central attractive forces. Indeed, for a long time Hooke had been applying the maxim 'That Nature seems to take similar Ways for producing similar Effects; without granting of which we cannot reason or make any Conclusion from similar Operations'.[50] He cautions, however, that *'Omne simile non est idem* [Everything that looks the same is not equal]'.[51]

Recently, Pugliese has reproduced a remarkable diagram (Figure 1.4)[52] which is part of an unfinished and unpublished manuscript that Hooke wrote, entitled 'The Laws of Circular Motion', which is deposited in the Wren Library, Trinity College, Cambridge. This diagram shows a graphical construction of a segment of an orbit for a body moving in a central field of force, and on a page associated with it is inscribed the date 1 September 1685. This date, as we shall see, is important in relating it to Newton's *De Motu*,[53] the preliminary draft of his *Principia*, which was registered by Halley at the Royal Society in November 1684. Hooke's graphical construction shows a body

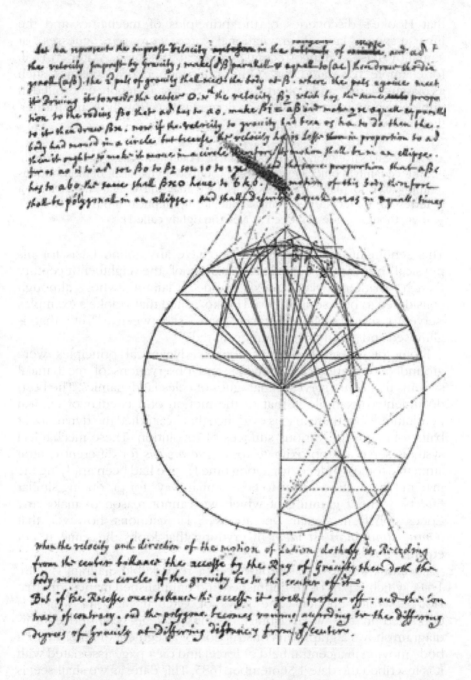

let ha represents the impress velocity ... in the ... of ..., and ad to the velocity imprest by gravity, make (dβ) parallel & equal to (ac) & ... draw the dia gonall (aβ). the ... pull of gravity that ... the body at β. where the ... pull ... meet ... Driving it towards the center O. wth the velocity βz which has the same ... propor tion to the radius βo that ad has to ao. make βi = aβ ... making ie equal & parallel to it then draw βie. now if the velocity to gravity had been of ha to do then the body had moved in a circle but because the velocity ... is lesse than in proportion to ad then it ought to make it move in a circle ... by ... motion shall be in an ellipse. for as ai to ad so βo to βz so io to z ... the same proportion that aβ has to abo the same shall βxo have to 6 k δ. ... motion of this body therefore shall be polygonall in an ellipse. and shall ... equal areas ... equall times

when the velocity and direction of the motion of ... doth ... its Receding from the center ballance the recesse by the Ray of Gravity then doth the body move in a circle if the gravity be to the center of it. But if the Recesse over ballance the recesse it goes farther off: and the con trary if contrary. and the polygons becomes various according to the differing degrees of gravity at differing distances from the center.

Figure 1.4 Hooke's September 1685 geometrical construction and graphical evaluation of orbital motion in a central field of force which varies linearly with distance.

moving under the action of an attractive force that varies linearly with the distance from the centre of its orbit, and in the handwritten text associated with it he states that its orbit is that of an *ellipse*. Pugliese has analysed it only for the special case of circular motion implying that Hooke failed to generalize his construction to non-circular motion, implying that 'Hooke claims, but certainly does not demonstrate, [its orbit] to be elliptical'. Pugliese asserted earlier that, 'There can be no doubt that Hooke could not have taken this [dynamical] principle so far [as Newton]', and he concluded that Hooke 'does not seem to have ever come to a full appreciation of the magnitude of the step from his ideas to Newton's achievement'.[54]

Pugliese's comments and conclusions thus seem to reinforce the conventional wisdom among historians of science about Hooke's mathematical limitations. I have carried out a detailed analysis of Hooke's diagram, however, which leads to very different conclusions.[55] Hooke's graphical solution for the orbit of a body moving in a central field of force that varies linearly with the distance from the centre of its orbit is based precisely on the same *geometrical* construction that Newton developed the preceding year in Theorem 1 of his *De Motu*, and which two years later became Proposition 1 in Book 1 of his *Principia*. Hooke's geometrical construction is effectively the *mathematical formulation* of the principles of dynamics that he had been proposing during the previous 20 years. Moreover, contrary to Pugliese's assertion, I have shown that Hooke in his diagram gives several different graphical demonstrations that the vertices of the resulting polygonal orbit lie on an *ellipse*, and that this is an *exact property* of his construction, which is equivalent to an affine transformation of a circle into an ellipse.[56]

While the extent to which members of the Royal Society were aware of Newton's *De Motu* is uncertain,[57] at least two letters exist indicating that Hooke appears to have seen it shortly after it was registered at the Royal Society in November 1684. Thus, a month later Flamsteed wrote to Newton that, 'I am obliged by your kind concession of the perusall of your papers, tho I beleive I shall not get a sight of them till our common freind [friend] Mr Hooke & the rest of the towne have beene first satisfied'.[58] And on 29 June 1686, Halley wrote to Newton that 'it [*De Motu*] has been enterd upon the Register books of the Society as all this past Mr Hook was acquainted with it ...'.[59]

Assuming that Hooke saw and read Newton's *De Motu*, he would have recognized that Newton had implemented geometrically Hooke's dynamical principle of *compounding* a tangential velocity with an impressed radial acceleration due to a centre of attraction.[60]

Thus, Newton had drawn a diagram on the first page of his *De Motu*
(Figure 1.5) that describes a geometrical construction that embodies
Hooke's dynamical principles for a body undergoing a sequence of
impulses under the action of a central force.

In it, the trajectory *ABCDEF* is determined by the initial tangential
velocity described by the length *AB* and by the impressed deflections
cC, *dD*, *eE*, and *fF* corresponding to impulses at B, C, D, E that are
directed toward the centre of force at *S*, or as Newton wrote:

> Let the time be divided into equal intervals, and in the first interval of time
> suppose the body by reason of its innate force describes the line *AB*.
> Likewise in the second interval of time if nothing were to impede it
> suppose it would continue straight on to *c* covering a length *Bc* equal to
> the line *AB*, so that the radii *AS*, *BS*, *cS* being drawn to the center [*S*] the
> areas *ASB*, *BSc* would be made equal. But actually when the body comes
> to *B* let the centripetal force act [on it] with a single great impulse, forcing
> the body to deviate from the line *Bc* and continue on in the line *BC*.[61]

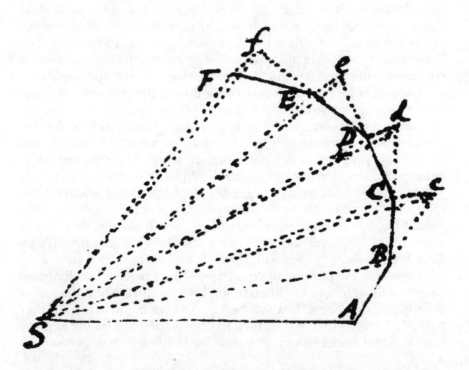

Figure 1.5 The first page of Newton's 1684 manuscript *De Motu*,
showing the diagram associated with his proof of Kepler's area law.
(Whiteside 1989, p. 3)

Newton applied this geometrical construction to prove Kepler's area law, that 'All bodies circulating about a centre [of force] sweep out areas proportional to the times'.[62]

Whether or not Hooke had seen Newton's *De Motu*, he gave his own description of the geometrical construction in his 1685 diagram (Figures 1.4 and 1.6) in a handwritten text above it in the same physical terms that he had used for the past 20 years:

> Let *ha* represent the imprest velocity in the tangent of an ellipse and *aδ* the velocity imprest by Gravity. Make (*δβ*) parallel and equal to (*ac*), then draw the diagonall (*aβ*). The second puls of gravity [referring to Hooke's theory of periodic gravitational pulses] shall meet the body at *β* where the puls againe meets it, driving it towards the center *o* with the velocity *βγ* which has the same proportion to the radius *βo* that *aδ* has to *ao*.[63]

Hooke's description is similar to Newton's and not merely a translation from Latin into English, quoted above. Furthermore, Hooke proceeds in his geometrical construction in a way quite different from Newton by applying it in a *novel* way to obtain the orbit of a body moving in an attractive central field of force that varies linearly with distance. We can see this more clearly by deleting some of Hooke's auxiliary lines and enlarging the result, as shown in Figure 1.6.

We see that Hooke's diagram corresponds to Newton's, taking into account that Hooke's proceeds clockwise with the initial velocity of the body directed along *ha*, while Newton's proceeds counter-clockwise with its initial velocity directed along *AB*.

Background to Hooke's Physical Principles of Orbital Motion

I now turn to how Hooke developed his understanding of orbital dynamics and discuss further aspects of his correspondence with Newton in 1679, as well as Halley's and Newton's correspondence in 1686.

On 23 May 1666 Hooke gave a remarkable lecture to the members of the newly founded Royal Society, entitled 'A Statement of Planetary Movements as a Mechanical Problem',[64] in which he proposed that the Keplerian elliptical orbits of planets around the Sun could be obtained by *compounding* an inertial straight-line motion with an *inflection* toward the centre of the Sun due to an attractive property of the Sun. This was the first published account in which some of the essential dynamical principles of planetary motion were stated clearly and unambiguously, nearly two decades before Newton implemented

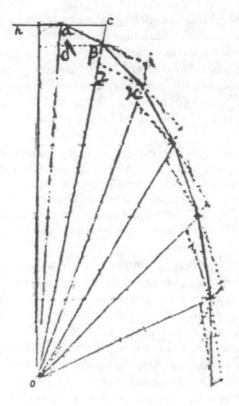

Figure 1.6   An enlargement of the upper part of Hooke's September 1685 diagram (shown in Figure 1.4) with some auxiliary lines deleted to show more clearly its correspondence with Newton's diagram (shown in Figure 1.5).

them in mathematical form in his celebrated *Principia*. Hooke's paper, which was registered by the Royal Society, begins with his statement:

> I have often wondered, why the planets should move about the sun according to Copernicus's supposition, being not included in any solid orbs (which the ancients possibly for this reason might embrace) nor tied to it, as their centre, by any visible strings; and neither depart from it beyond such a degree, nor yet move in a straight line, as all bodies, that have one single impulse, ought to do ... .[65]

Hooke then dismisses a theory, partly due to Borelli,[66] which was in vogue at the time, that the impressed force is due to a medium of variable density acting on the planetary body, and states his own idea that:

the second cause of inflecting a direct motion into a curve may be from an attractive body placed in the centre; whereby it continually endeavours to attract or draw it to itself. For if such a principle be supposed, all the phenomena of the planets seem possible to be explained by the common principle of mechanic motions; and possibly the prosecuting [of] this speculation may give us a true hypothesis of their motion, and from some few observations, their motions may be so far brought to a certainty, that we may be able to calculate them to the greatest exactness and certainty that can be desired.

This inflexion of a direct motion into a curve by a supervening attractive principle I shall endeavour to explicate from some experiments with a pendulous body: not that I suppose the attraction of the sun to be exactly according to the same degrees, as they are in a pendulum … .[67]

Hooke proposed that a conical pendulum, by projecting its motion onto a plane perpendicular to its axis of suspension, could serve as a *mechanical analogue* to demonstrate the principles of planetary orbital motion. His analogue model generalized Descartes's demonstration of circular motion of a stone revolving on a sling (Figure 1.1). Hooke discussed the theory of the conical pendulum, pointing out that the effective radial force on its bob

is greater and greater, according as it is farther and farther removed from the centre, which seems to be otherwise in the attraction of the sun … But however it be, the compounding this motion with a direct or straight motion just crossing it, may serve to explicate this hypothesis, though all the appearances of it are not exactly the same.[68]

Evidently, Hooke was well aware of the shortcomings of the conical pendulum as a model for planetary orbital motion.

At the time, Hooke was Curator of the newly founded Royal Society, and one of his main tasks was to present weekly scientific experiments. He gave a demonstration to the members of 'a pendulum fastened to the roof of the room with a large wooden ball of lignum vitae on the end of it'.[69] This would have given an impressive demonstration of nearly closed elliptical orbits as projected onto a plane normal to its axis of suspension, as I verified by repeating Hooke's experiment. I suspended a weight from the ceiling of a room, attached a pen to it, and traced its motion on a sheet of paper on the floor, as shown in Figure 1.7,[70] which also confirmed Hooke's careful observation that 'the progression of the auges [apsides] are very evident'.[71]

Later, in a letter that Hooke wrote to Newton on 6 December 1679,[72] he made a drawing (Figure 1.8) of a similar orbit of a body revolving

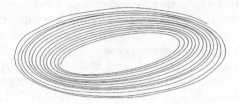

Figure 1.7 The trajectory of a conical pendulum as determined experimentally by the author.

around the centre of the Earth 'supposing then the earth were cast into two half globes', which clearly shows a 'progression of the auges'.[73]

Nevertheless, in the literature on the Newton-Hooke correspondence, Hooke's diagram has invariably been reproduced incorrectly as a symmetrical figure,[74] which leaves out the 'progression of the auges'. Hooke, moreover, demonstrated mathematically that in this case the horizontal force on the bob increases linearly with the distance from its axis of suspension.[75]

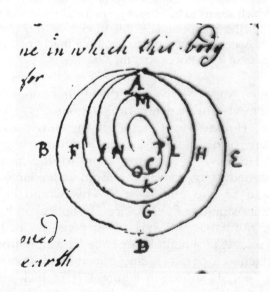

Figure 1.8 Hooke's drawing for the trajectory of a body moving inside the Earth, supposing that it was divided into two half globes. (Koyré 1952, p. 330)

The pendulum's axis intersects the centre of its elliptical motion, while the centre of force for the motion of a planet is at a focal point of its elliptical orbit. Furthermore, the period of the pendulum is nearly independent of the size of its orbit, as Hooke discovered for the oscillation of springs.[76] This is in striking contrast to the dependence of the periods of planets on their distances from the Sun, which obey Kepler's third law, that is, the square of their periods vary with the cube of the major axes of their elliptical orbits. But, as noted above, Hooke was well aware of the shortcoming of his model for planetary motion. He also attached a smaller pendulum to it to model, although less successfully, the motion of the Moon around the Earth. This is particularly significant, because it shows that Hooke understood the universal character of the gravitational force, which he later enunciated explicitly. He also proposed and carried out several other inconclusive experiments to determine how the gravitational force varies with the distance both above and below the surface of the Earth.[77]

Hooke developed his ideas further in his Cutlerian Lectures, which he delivered at the regular meetings of the Royal Society. His first lecture, which he delivered in 1670, was on *An Attempt to Prove the Motion of the Earth from Observations* by observing stellar parallax[78] and thus to 'furnish the Learned with an *experimentum crucis* to determine between the *Tychonick* and the *Copernican* Hypotheses'.[79] Two years earlier, in October 1668,[80] he had begun to erect a zenith telescope in his quarters in Gresham College in London (Figure 1.9), and in 1670 he began to make observations of the star Gamma Draconis as it passed directly overhead.[81]

Now, at the end of his lecture in 1670, which he did not publish until 1674,[82] Hooke restated his *principles* of dynamics and formulated the principle of universal gravitational attraction:

At which time also I shall explain a System of the World differing in many particulars from any yet known, answering in all things to the common Rules of Mechanical Motions: This depends on three Suppositions. First, That all Cœlestial Bodies whatsoever, have an attraction or gravitating power towards their own Centers, whereby they attract not only their own parts, and keep them from flying from them, as we may observe the Earth to do, but that they do also attract all the other Cœlestial Bodies that are within the sphere of their activity; and consequently that not only the Sun and Moon have an influence upon the body and motion of the Earth, and the Earth upon them, but that [Mercury] also [Venus], [Mars], [Saturn], and [Jupiter] by their attractive powers,[83] have a considerable influence upon its motion as in the same manner the corresponding attractive power of the Earth hath a considerable influence upon every one of their motions

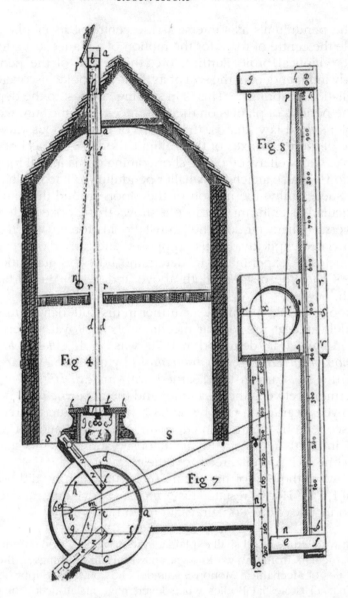

Figure 1.9 Hooke's zenith telescope which was designed to follow the star Gamma Draconis as it passed directly above his lodgings in Gresham College. In addition to the telescope and its housing ('Fig 4'), the drawing shows an ingenious micrometer ('Fig 7') designed by Hooke to measure accurately the deviations of an observed star from the zenith marked by the intersection at 'e' of the cross hairs 'ab' (longitude) and 'cd' (latitude).

(Gunther 1931, plate following p. vii)

also. The second supposition is this, That all bodies whatsoever that are put into a direct and simple motion, will so continue to move forward in a streight line, till they are by some other effectual powers deflected and bent into a Motion, describing a Circle, Ellipsis, or some other more compounded Curve Line. The third supposition is, That these attractive powers are so much the more powerful in operating by how much the nearer the body wrought upon is to their own Centers. Now what these several degrees are I have not yet experimentally verified ... .[84]

In light of Newton's later unkind description of Hooke, as quoted in my introduction, we must remember that Hooke was a very busy employee of the Royal Society, at whose weekly meetings he performed several experiments of his own as well as those ordered by the committee.[85] He did not have the advantage of inherited wealth like his early mentor, Robert Boyle, or of a well-paid academic chair like Newton, which would have given him the freedom to follow his own intellectual pursuits. Instead, Hooke supplemented his income by serving as one of the main surveyors for the reconstruction of the City of London after the Great Fire in 1666,[86] by designing buildings and private houses, and by attempting to patent his inventions.

Hooke discussed his ideas with Newton in letters to him in 1679. By then Hooke had become Secretary of the Royal Society, and his avowed purpose in his first letter was to again establish contact with Newton, with whom he had a strained relationship since their earlier controversy on optics, and to elicit Newton's reaction to his current physical hypotheses. Thus, he wrote to Newton on 24 November 1679:

> For my own part I shall take it as a great favour if you shall please to communicate by Letter your objections against any hypothesis or opinion of mine, And particularly if you will let me know your thoughts of that of compounding the celestiall motions of the planetts of a direct motion by the tangent & an attractive motion towards the centrall body.[87]

It appears, from this letter and from his later correspondence with Newton, that one of Hooke's principal reasons for now writing to Newton was that he had been unable to make progress in expressing his physical principles of celestial mechanics mathematically, and he wanted to solicit help from Newton, whose great mathematical abilities were known to several members of the Royal Society. Hooke's diary shows that he had approached other mathematicians earlier for help without success. He now also discussed with Newton the motion of a body inside the Earth, which was mostly of concern to him insofar as it clarified the orbital dynamics for central forces, which he had been studying with mechanical analogues for the past 14 years. Thus, Newton responded on 13 December 1679, sending Hooke a drawing of the orbit of a body moving under the action of a constant radial force (Figure 1.2),[88] to which Hooke replied on 6 January 1680:

> Your Calculation of the Curve by a body attracted by an æquall power at all Distances from the center Such as that of a ball Rouling in an inverted Concave Cone is right and the two auges [apsides] will not unite by about a third of a Revolution.[89]

Newton's letter of 13 December must have come as a great revelation to Hooke. In his response quoted above, Hooke showed that he had previously observed the orbit of a ball rolling inside an inverted cone, and that he knew that the effective radial force acting on it is constant. He also realized that Newton had developed a method for calculating such an orbit. But almost all historians of science have ignored Hooke's insightful observations.[90]

I repeated Hooke's experiment of a ball rolling inside an inverted cone and took a stroboscopic picture of its trajectory (Figure 1.10) which can be seen to correspond, as Hooke had observed 326 years ago, to the theoretical trajectory Newton drew (Figure 1.2), although the angle between successive apsides is somewhat different.

Hooke continued:

> But my supposition is that the Attraction always is in a duplicate proportion to the Distance from the Center Reciprocall, and Consequently that the Velocity will be in a subduplicate proportion to the Attraction and Consequently as Kepler Supposes Reciprocall to the Distance.[91]

Here Hooke announced for the first time his belief that the gravitational force depends inversely on the square of the distance of a planet from the Sun. He erred, however, in saying that Kepler took its velocity to depend inversely on the radial distance. Newton later pounced on Hooke's error, claiming that Hooke did not understand orbital motion under a central inverse-square force, but ignoring that Hooke in his letter went further and supposed correctly:

> that with Such an [inverse-square] attraction the auges [apsides] will unite in the same part of the Circle and that the neerest point of accesse to the center will be opposite to the furthest Distant. Which I conceive doth very Intelligibly and truly make out all the Appearances of the Heavens.[92]

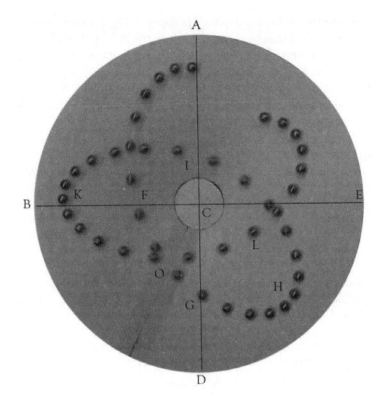

Figure 1.10   Stroboscopic photograph taken by the author of the trajectory of a ball revolving inside an inverted cone. The angle between successive 'auges' (apsides) depends on the cone's angle of aperture, but Hooke did not mention it. I chose an angle of 60° which brings the trajectory in approximate agreement with Newton's diagram (Figure 1.2).

Nowhere, however, is there any evidence in Hooke's letter that he knew at this time how to demonstrate his conjecture mathematically. Instead, he goes on, stating that:

> (though in truth I agree with You that the Explicating the Curve in which a body Descending to the Center of the Earth, would circumgyrate were a Speculation of noe Use yet) the finding out the proprietys of a Curve made by two such principles will be of great Concerne to Mankind ... . This Curve truly Calculated will shew the error of those many lame shifts [*ad hoc* approximations] made use of by astronomers to approach the true motion of the planets with their tables.[93]

Finally, in a letter to Newton on 17 January 1680, Hooke again stated that 'I doubt not but that by your excellent method you will easily find out what that Curve must be, and its proprietys, and suggest a physicall Reason of this proportion'.[94]

Hooke's remarks indicate that at this time he did not know how to calculate the orbital motion of a planet in an attractive central field of force; his remarkable physical understanding and hypothesis were based on *mechanical analogue* models. However, asking Newton for mathematical help turned out to be a capital mistake for Hooke, while very fortunate for Newton. Newton formulated Hooke's problem mathematically and solved it for various central forces, including the inverse-square force, but he never acknowledged Hooke's seminal physical concept or even replied to Hooke's letter of 17 January. Two months earlier however, Newton had written to Hooke that:

> I did not before the receipt of your last letter [sent four days earlier], so much as heare ([that] I remember) of your Hypotheses of compounding the celestial motion of the Planets, of a direct motion by the tang[en]t to the curve ...
>
> If I were not so unhappy as to be unacquainted with your Hypotheses above-mentioned ...[95]

Newton went on to congratulate Hooke 'that so considerable a discovery as you made of the earth's annual parallax is seconded by Mr. Flamstead's Observations'.[96] Hooke, however, had not told Newton anything in his last letter about his own apparent discovery of the Earth's parallax, but only had commented briefly that Flamsteed 'hath confirmed the paralax of the orb of the earth'.[97]

Thus, it appears that Newton was familiar with Hooke's tract on *An Attempt to Prove the Motion of Earth from Observations*,[98] as Newton later admitted to Halley in a letter of 27 July 1686.[99] Hooke himself was not convinced of Newton's denials and later wrote in an unpublished memorandum that, 'Newton pretends he knew not Hooke's Hypoth. as by his Answer to the former dated Nov. 28, 1679 ...'.[100] Hooke also scribbled this telling comment on the margin of Newton's letter to him of that date.

Five years earlier, in 1674, Hooke had published his hypotheses,[101] which evidently were read by some of the leading scientists at the time, such as Christiaan Huygens and Giovanni Domenico Cassini, Director of the Paris Observatory, who had sent their comments to the *Philosophical Transactions*.[102] Also, as noted above, Hooke communicated his ideas directly to Newton in 1679. A decade later, on 15 February 1689, Hooke noted in his diary that, 'At Hallys

[Halley's] met Newton; vainly pretended claim yet acknowledged my information. Interest has no conscience: A posse ad esse non valet consequentia [It is not valid to infer from the plausible to the actual]'.[103]

Hooke had mentioned to Newton in a letter of 6 January 1680, without giving any supporting arguments, that:

> my supposition is that the Attraction always is in a duplicate proportion to the Distance from the center Reciprocall … [It] truly makes out all the Appearances of the Heavens … not that I believe there really is such an attraction to the very Center of the Earth …[104]

In fact, Hooke had conjectured correctly on physical grounds that:

> I rather Conceive that the more the body approaches the Center, the lesse will it be Urged by the attraction – possibly somewhat like the Gravitation on a pendulum or a body moved in a Concave Sphære where the power Continually Decreases the neerer the body inclines to a horizontall motion …[105]

Newton later also conveniently forgot these remarks and charged that 'what he [Hooke] told me of the duplicate proportion was erroneous, namely that it reacht down from hence to the center of the earth'.[106] Nevertheless, in letters that Newton wrote to Halley in the summer of 1686 that were intended primarily to deny Hooke credit for any of the fundamental ideas in his *Principia*,[107] Newton admitted that Hooke's letters of 1679 had stimulated him to consider again the fundamental problems of celestial mechanics. Newton had engaged in a bitter invective against Hooke after he had heard rumours that Hooke had accused him of plagiarism, but after he had calmed down following a soothing letter from Halley,[108] he responded to Halley on 14 July 1686, that:

> This is true, that his [Hooke's] Letters occasioned my finding the method of determining Figures, wch when I had tried in the Ellipsis, I threw the calculation by being upon other studies & so it rested for about 5 yeares till upon your request I sought for [that] paper, & not finding it did it again & reduced it into the Propositions shewed you by Mr. Paget[109] …[110]

Two weeks later, on 27 July 1686, Newton again wrote to Halley:

> And thô his correcting my Spiral occasioned my finding the Theorem by wch I afterward examined the Ellipsis; yet I am not beholden to him for any light into [that] business but only for the diversion he gave me from my other studies to think on these things & for his dogmaticalnes in

writing as if he had found the motion in the Ellipsis, wch inclined me to try it after I saw by what method it was to be done.[111]

However, seven years earlier, in his letter to Hooke of 13 December 1679, Newton had concluded with the comment that:

Your acute Letter having put me upon considering thus far the species of this curve, I might add something about its description by points *quam proximè*. But the thing being of no great moment I rather beg your pardon for having troubled you thus far with this second scribble ...[112]

Newton's computational method 'by points *quam proximè*' has long been puzzling, but I have shown that it was based on his development of the calculus of *curvature* between 1664 and 1671.[113] The earliest extant documentary evidence that Newton applied to orbital motion Hooke's idea of *compounding* the tangential velocity of a body with its radial velocity as impressed by an attractive central force (an idea that Newton claimed repeatedly that he could not remember having heard from Hooke) is in Newton's *De Motu* of 1684, five years after his correspondence with Hooke. This supports my arguments that Hooke had contributed in a fundamental way to Newton's understanding of the dynamical principles that he incorporated in his *Principia*. Significantly, in *De Motu* Newton did not discuss his curvature method which had been his approach to orbital dynamics prior to his 1679 correspondence with Hooke. Newton later recalled that:

In the end of the year 1679 in answer to a Letter from Dr Hook ... I found now that whatsoever was the law of the forces wch kept the Planets in their Orbs, the areas described by a Radius drawn from then to the Sun would be proportional to the times in wch they were described. And by the help of these two Propositions I found that their Orbs would be such Ellipses as Kepler had described.[114]

In 1684 Hooke declared to Christopher Wren (1632–1723) and Edmond Halley, two of his friends at the Royal Society, that on the principle of an inverse-square gravitational force 'all the Laws of celestiall motions were to be demonstrated, and that he himself had done it ...'.[115] However, despite a subsequent challenge by Wren, who offered a prize of a 40-shilling book for such a demonstration, Hooke apparently failed to produce a *calculation* for such planetary motion.[116] Unfortunately, Hooke never published his remarkable graphical solution of 1685 (Figure 1.4) for the motion of a body under the action of an attractive radial force that varies linearly with distance.

Summary and Conclusions

Hooke's fundamental idea was to determine planetary motion by compounding the planet's tangential velocity with a change in its radial velocity impressed by the gravitational attractive force of the Sun. He gained his profound physical understanding of orbital dynamics by observing mechanical analogues like the motion of a conical pendulum and the motion of a ball rolling inside various surfaces of revolution. I verified Hooke's observations by repeating two of his experiments, one that showed the projection of the trajectory of a conical pendulum onto a plane perpendicular to its axis of symmetry (Figure 1.7), and another one that showed the projection of the trajectory of a ball revolving inside an inverted cone (Figure 1.10). Both experiments demonstrate that Hooke's descriptions of these trajectories were fairly accurate.

Hooke also analysed mathematically the radial forces that act on these bodies toward the axis of symmetry of their motions.[117] My analysis of Hooke's diagram of 1685 (Figure 1.4), which gave a geometrical construction and graphical evaluation of the path of a body in an attractive radial field of force that depends linearly on the distance, offers new evidence that Hooke came much closer to formulating his principles of dynamics *mathematically* than has been thought previously.[118] In the mid-1660s Hooke developed these principles, demonstrating them with *mechanical analogues*, and not simply by guessing them as historians of science have assumed. Indeed, he applied precisely the same rules of reasoning that Newton later included in Book III of his *Principia*. However, prior to the recent publication of Hooke's diagram of 1685, there was no concrete evidence of the extent to which Hooke had been able to formulate his dynamical principles in mathematical form and apply them to the approximate evaluation of the orbital motion of a body in an attractive central field of force. Hooke apparently was able to accomplish this only after he had seen Newton's *De Motu* of 1684, in which Newton gave an equivalent geometrical construction (Figure 1.3). However, Newton applied his construction only to obtain a proof of Kepler's area law whereas Hooke applied his construction to determine graphically that the orbit of a body moving under the action of an attractive central force that varies linearly with the distance is an ellipse.

The key to a mathematical formulation of the physical principles of orbital motion, which had long eluded Hooke, is to start with the approximation that the central force on a body acts in instantaneous periodic impulses instead of continuously. Hooke actually conjectured that the gravitational attraction originates in periodic pulses, in analogy to the emission of light and sound,[119] and he deduced from this idea that the strength of gravity varies inversely with the square of the distance from the centre of attraction. Newton's letter of 13 December 1679 indicated to Hooke that Newton was capable of evaluating, at least approximately, the orbital motion of a body in an attractive central field of force. But in the absence of the infinitesimal calculus that Newton and Leibniz developed, Hooke could have solved the problem of orbital dynamics by a discrete graphical method only approximately.

Among Hooke's unpublished manuscripts in the library of the Royal Society in London I found a handwritten document that is part of a translation[120] into English of the treatise of 1696 by Guillaume-François-Antoine Marquis de l'Hôpital on the *Analysis of infinitesimal small quantities to describe curved lines.*[121] This was the first textbook that was published on the differential calculus and was based on lectures by Jean Bernoulli, whom l'Hôpital had hired as his tutor. Assuming that Hooke received and read l'Hôpital's textbook, he must have understood the significance of this mathematical development, which Newton did not discuss in any detail in his *Principia.* Hooke also may have been familiar with Leibniz's work on the differential calculus of 1684,[122] but this is unknown, because Hooke's diaries during the crucial period 1682–87 have been lost. I also did not find evidence among Hooke's manuscripts at the Royal Society that he investigated orbital motion during this period. The differential calculus, of course, was precisely the mathematical tool that Hooke had been lacking, but he unfortunately had gone to Newton for mathematical help. One might speculate that had Hooke corresponded with Leibniz or Huygens rather than with Newton in 1679, the development of orbital dynamics might have taken a different path.

Among Hooke's unpublished manuscripts in the Wren Library at Trinity College, Cambridge, there is a memorandum entitled 'A True state of the Case and Controversy between Sr Isaac Newton & Dr Robert Hooke as to the Priority of that Noble Hypothesis of Motion of the Planets about the Sun as their Centre'.[123] In it Hooke accurately recounts his main contributions to the theory of mechanics and gravitation that he had communicated to Newton in his correspondence in 1679, but he does not mention his unpublished graphical computation of 1685 and related work. Hooke's memorandum makes it clear that he understood quite well the extent and significance of his contributions to celestial mechanics relative to those of Newton. After Hooke's death in 1703, Richard Waller pencilled in the margin of the manuscript of Hooke's diary the enigmatic comment that, 'Dr. Hook who was as I could prove were it a proper time the first Inventor or if you please first Hinter of those things about which Magni Nominis Heroes have contested for priority'.[124] Many documents of Hooke's contributions have been lost, some of which may have pertained to his work on orbital dynamics.[125] But as I have shown, we already have ample evidence that the development of orbital dynamics was due to Hooke's as well as to Newton's contributions, and to their inadvertent collaboration through their timely and momentous correspondence in 1679.

Appendix

Newton's diagram (Figure 1.2) in his letter to Hooke of 13 December 1679 appears to be a freehand sketch of the orbit of a body supposed to be moving under the action of a central force that is independent of the distance from the centre C, but this cannot be a mere sketch because the initial segment *AFOGH* of the orbit is almost exactly symmetric under reflection-symmetry. Evidently Newton must have discovered this symmetry which is due to the invariance of dynamics under reversal of the direction of time.

This symmetry suggests how Newton might have constructed his diagram. Thus, if he had a theoretical method to calculate the segment of the orbit *AFO* from the farthermost point *A* from the centre of force at *C* to its nearest point *O*, he could have used this segment as a template to obtain continuations of the orbit by sequential mirror reflections. One then would expect that the segments *AFO* and *OGH* are mirror images with respect to the line *OC*. This is not the case, however, because under a reflection and rotation that leaves the segment *AFOGH* unchanged, the image of *C* shifts by a small amount into the first quadrant *ACB* while the image of *O* shifts toward the point *F* on the curve *AFO*. Thus, it is not clear where the centre of force *C* is, and whether Newton had calculated the segment *AFO* or the segment *OGH* to use as a template to obtain continuations of the orbit by mirror reflections.

In an earlier analysis,[126] I assumed that Newton used the segment *OGH*, and not *AFO*, as the template, because the former reproduced more accurately the correct orbit of a body in a central field of force. When the segment *AFO* is reflected about the line *OC*, in fact, the farthermost point *A* does not coincide with point *H*, as it should, but instead lies beyond it, as shown in Figure 1.11, so that the reflected segment *OFA* does not coincide with the original segment *OGH*.

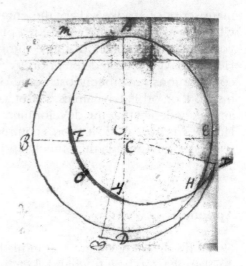

Figure 1.11 Newton's diagram (Figure 1.2) showing only the segment *AFO* of the orbit, the lines *AC* and *BC*, and its mirror reflections with respect to the line *OC*.

The reflection of *A* lies very close to the margin of Newton's letter, which suggests an alternate explanation for the shift of the image of the centre *C* in Newton's diagram. To avoid having to redraw his diagram, Newton may have decided to move the image of *A* away from the margin by shifting the reflected segment *OFA* in such a way that its continuation with the original segment *AFO* produces a smooth curve.

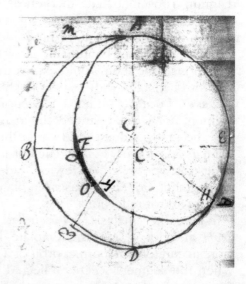

Figure 1.12 Newton's diagram (Figure 1.2) with the reflected images of the segments *AFO*, the arc *AB* and the lines *AC* and *BC*, now shifted so that the reflected point *A* coincides with the original point *H*.

I reproduced this shift, as shown in Figure 1.12, and found that the resulting curve agrees very well with the original segment *AFOGH*, accounting also for the superimposed lines that Newton drew along the segment *FOG* (see Figure 1.2) to cover the overlap of *AFO* with its shifted image. Moreover, as I showed earlier,[127] the closed curve *ABDE* in Newton's diagram is not a circle (although it always has been reproduced as such in the past). Indeed, while the orthogonal axes *CA* and *CB* are of equal length, as are the orthogonal axes *CD* and *CE*, which also are equal to *CH*, but the shift makes *CH* smaller than *CA*, so that the arcs *AB* and *DE* are sections of a circle, while the arcs *BD* and *EA* are sections of an oval – a distortion that is very small owing to their very small eccentricities and hence has not been noticed earlier and is generally neglected in the literature. As a result of shifting the segment *FOH*, Newton also had to modify the next two segments *HIK* and *KL*, which are supposed to be (but only approximately) images of *AFOGH* and *HIK* relative to the lines *CH* and *CK*, respectively.

Therefore, if Newton used the segment *AFO* as a template, then he made a considerable error in calculating this segment. The angle *ACO* in his drawing is 130°, while it should be approximately 104°, first pointed out by Pelseneer.[128] Later, in a Scholium in a draft of his *Principia*,[129] Newton gave this value as 110°, which is close to the value of 107° that I calculated on the basis of Newton's graphical-curvature method for computing orbits.[130] Newton did not publish this Scholium in his *Principia*, however, because by 1686 he had found an analytic expression for this angle for orbits of small eccentricity, which he presented in Book 1, Proposition 43.

The above analysis of Newton's diagram provides further evidence that by the time of his correspondence with Hooke in 1679 Newton had not discovered the origin of Kepler's area law or the conservation of angular momentum. This conservation law would have allowed him to express the velocity of a body along its orbit in terms of its position, as required by his curvature method, and to solve the outstanding problem that he had indicated by his cryptic remark of 1664, 'if its motion [velocity] in that point bee given ...'.[131] Instead, as I have shown,[132] to determine the change in velocity of a body along its orbit, Newton would have had to resort to a further approximation. Apparently, he implemented this approximation poorly, perhaps because he was too much in a hurry to respond to Hooke, who had embarrassed him at a meeting of the Royal Society by exposing an error in his previous letter of 28 November 1679. However, as the cancelled Scholium to his *Principia* reveals, by 1684 Newton had obtained a good approximation to the angle *ACO*, presumably by obtaining the change in velocity of a body along its orbit by applying Kepler's area law – which he had discovered only after expressing in mathematical form the physical principles of orbital dynamics he had assimilated from Hooke's insight of 'compounding the celestiall motions of the planetts of a direct motion by the tangent & an attractive motion towards the centrall body'.[133]

Acknowledgments

I thank Michael Cooper, Malcolm MacGregor, Curtis A. Wilson, and Alan E. Shapiro for helpful comments on a draft of my paper, and Roger H. Stuewer for his thoughtful and careful editorial work on it, which included providing additional references and the biographical notes in the footnotes. I also thank Bernard Cleyet for his help in obtaining the stroboscopic photograph of the trajectory of a ball revolving inside an inverted cone (Figure 1.10).

Chapter 2

Hooke's Programme: Final Thoughts
Ofer Gal

Introduction: One Mystery and Two Questions

> It now remains to know the proprietys of a curve Line (not circular nor concentricall) made by a centrall attractive power which makes the velocitys of Descent from the tangent Line or equall straight motion at all Distances in a Duplicate proportion to the Distances Reciprocally taken. I doubt not but that by your excellent method you will easily find out what that Curve must be, and its proprietys, and suggest physicall Reason of this proportion.[1]

This is Hooke's Programme, and it presents quite a mystery. In this, its final version – which Hooke sent to Newton on 17 January 1680, concluding a short and intense correspondence between the two – the Programme looks extremely familiar. And not only to the uninitiated layman, who may see here, with unchecked hindsight, the now self-evident elements of Newtonian cosmology: inertial motion, curved into an oval by a centripetal force declining with the square of distance. It also appears almost trivial to the trained historian of seventeenth-century science, who recognizes Kepler's motive power, Descartes's motion and Huygens's style investigation of curves. Yet, we well know, this combination of ideas was completely foreign to all these venerable members of the honorary order of the new science, let alone their less innovative contemporaries. So much so, that the designated reader of this paragraph, Isaac Newton, definitely the most skilled person of his time to understand Hooke's Programme and perceive its importance, had to be tutored through it carefully and almost reluctantly. And so much so, that even its author, Robert Hooke, had to be helped with some of its seemingly most trivial aspects.

I attempted in the past to relieve the mystery by details: to follow Hooke's development of the notion of curved celestial motion from his attempt to 'inflect' – gradually bend – light; to trail his construction of a concept of 'power' through his work on spring horology; and to outline Newton's assembly of the mathematical wherewithal to handle Hooke's challenge.[2] There was a point in attending to details: they demonstrated the thoroughly constructed nature of Hooke's Programme, the workmanlike attitude to knowledge best captured in his own words (coloured by undue and probably insincere humility and class propriety):

> As for my part, I have obtained my end, if these my small Labours shall be thought fit to take up some place in the large stock of natural Observations, which so many hands are busie in providing. If I have contributed the meanest foundations whereon others may raise nobler Superstructures, I am abundantly satisfied; and all my ambition is, that I may serve to the great Philosophers of this Age, as the makers and grinders of my Glasses did to me; that I may prepare and furnish them with some Materials, which they may afterwards order and manage with better Skills, and to far greater advantage.[3]

I will attend to some of the details of the intellectual, mechanical and experimental resources Hooke put into the production of his Programme, but my main point here will be a general one. I would like to ask the dangerous but tempting pair of questions: what did Newton learn from Hooke, without which he could not solve the question of planetary motions, and what did Newton manage to do, which was beyond Hooke's grasp – what did Newton have at his disposal which allowed him to complete the formulation of Hooke's Programme so it was ready to be realized?

I think that the answers to these questions will somewhat relieve the mystery, by showing that much of Hooke's and Newton's innovativeness, much of what they had to teach each other, lies in coming to terms with the consequences – indeed trivial in hindsight, but only in hindsight – of the accepted teaching of their predecessors. And I think an important part of the answers lies in what is common to, and what distinguishes between, Hooke's paragraph with which I began and the following one, a scholium which Isaac Newton added to his *De Motu Sphæricorum Corporum in Fluidis* – one of the last entries in the series of *De Motu* papers he submitted to the Royal Society of London between 1684 and 1685 as drafts of his *Principia*:

> The whole space of the planetary heavens either rests (as is commonly believed), or moves uniformly in a straight line, and hence the communal centre of gravity of the planets ... either rests or moves along with it. In both cases ... the relative motions of the planets are the same, and their common centre of gravity rests in relation to the whole of space, and so can certainly be taken for the still centre of the whole planetary system. Hence truly the Copernican system is proved a priori. For if the common centre of gravity is calculated for any position of the planets it either falls in the body of the Sun or will always be very close to it. By reason of this

deviation of the Sun from the centre of gravity the centripetal force does not always tend to that immobile centre, and hence the planets neither move exactly in ellipse nor revolve twice in the same orbit. So that there are as many orbits to a planet as it has revolutions, as in the motion of the Moon, and the orbit of any one planet depends on the combined motion of all the planets, not to mention the action of all these on each other. But to consider simultaneously all these causes of motion and to define these motions by exact laws allowing of convenient calculation exceeds, unless I am mistaken, the force of the entire human intellect. Ignoring those minutiae, the simple orbit and the mean among all errors will be the ellipse of which I have already treated.[4]

Three Stages of Hooke's Programme

But before attending to the two paragraphs, here are the promised details. Hooke published three versions of what we call his Programme, the last and most consequential one, if one is willing to consider a letter from London to Cambridge as a publication, was the one we started with. The most elaborate version was published six years before the correspondence with Newton as a two-page appendix to Hooke's 1674 Cutlerian Lecture *Attempt to Prove the Motion of the Earth*. It was a promise of a soon to be completed 'System of the World ... answering in all things to the common Rules of Mechanics', which

> depends on three Suppositions. First, That all Cœlestial Bodies Whatsoever, have an attraction or gravitating power towards their own Centers, whereby they attract not only their own parts ... but ... also ... all the other Cœlestial Bodies that are within the sphere of their activity; and consequently that not only the Sun and the Moon have an influence upon the body and motion of the Earth, and the Earth upon them, but that [all the planets], by their attractive powers, have a considerable influence upon its motion as in the same manner the corresponding attractive power of the Earth hath a considerable influence upon every one of their motions also. The Second Supposition is this, That all bodies whatsoever that are put into a direct and simple motion, will so continue to move forward in a streight line, till they are by some other effectual powers deflected and bent into a Motion, describing a Circle, Ellipsis, or some other more compound Curve Line. The third supposition is, That these attractive powers are so much the more powerful in operating, by how much the nearer the body wrought upon is to their own Centers.[5]

The *System of the World* remained an unfulfilled promise – knowing Hooke, one almost adds 'of course' – and the would-be abstract in the appendix to the *Motion of the Earth* is the last time Hooke laid down his principles for *physica coelestis* so explicitly. Yet the 17 January 1680 letter to Newton contains one important feature missing from the 1674 version: a law for the decline of the 'gravitating power' with distance. If in 1674 Hooke admits that 'what these several degrees are I have not yet experimentally verified', in 1680 he suggests that they are 'at all Distances in a Duplicate proportion to the Distances Reciprocally taken'. This addition, however – the famous inverse-square law – was not added in that six-year span; it is both much older with Hooke and completely new to Hooke's Programme. These are not contradictory claims, as I will show momentarily, but for the time being suffice it to note that in his first introduction of the Programme to Newton, eight weeks earlier (24 November 1679), the inverse-square law is not mentioned. 'I shall take it as a great favour', he writes in his first letter, 'if you will let me know your thoughts of that [hypothesis of mine] of compounding the celestiall motions of the planetts of a direct motion by the tangent & an attractive motion towards a central body'.[6]

Hooke, to be sure, is so succinct in this first introduction, that he clearly expects Newton to have no difficulties recognizing the essential concepts of the Programme: the planetary orbits are a process of constant change; the effect of an attraction from the sun, which curves the planets' initial inertial rectilinear motion. Yet it is as clear that he does not feel that the ideas that the attraction is universal and that it declines with distance – let alone that this decline follows a particular law – have to be forcefully asserted. Perhaps he assumes that Newton (who, despite his denial, had read the 1674 *System of the World*)[7] does not need to be reminded of them, but he obviously does not see them as the real fundamentals of his Programme. And indeed, heavenly attraction and its properties are exactly the features that are speculated, but left undecided, in Hooke's first ever presentation of his Programme, in an address to the Royal Society on 23 May 1666:

> [A]ll the celestial bodies, being regular solid bodies, and moved in a fluid, and yet moved in circular or elliptical lines, and not straight, must have some other cause, besides the first impressed impulse, that must bend their motion into that curve. And for the performance of this effect I cannot imagine any other likely cause besides these two: The first may be from an unequal density of the medium, thro' which the planetary body is to be moved ... But the second cause of inflecting a direct motion into a curve may be from an attractive property of the body placed in the center; whereby it continually endeavours to attract or draw it to itself.[8]

The real innovation of this paragraph is the very exposition of the planetary trajectories as a riddle.[9] 'I have often wondered', Hooke related to the honourable members, why the planets should move about the sun according to Copernicus's supposition, being not included in any solid orbs ... nor tied to it, as their center, by any visible strings; and neither depart from it by such a degree, nor yet move in a straight line, as all bodies, that have but one single impulse, ought to do.[10]

'New science', indeed, in all its glory: Hooke does not only refer to the planets as 'any solid bodies', but also presents their orbits as a question demanding an answer; as an effect asking for a cause. He is not impressed by the magnificence of the celestial cycles; he is not worried by the need to 'save the phenomena' – to subject apparent irregularities to mathematical rule. He asks his audience to be surprised by the very fact that there is order, because, as they are all supposed to know, 'all bodies, that have but one single impulse, ought [to] move in a straight line'.

Two Possible Progenitors

But here again is the core of the mystery: were they not, indeed, supposed to know this? Why was Hooke so lonely with his Programme? Was it not but a trivial application of the Cartesian credo, 'that all movement is, of itself, along straight lines (Descartes's 'second law of nature'?[11] Trivial it may be for the modern reader, but not for Descartes himself. The person responsible more than anyone else for the concept of rectilinear inertia never suggested that bodies, let alone '[A]ll the celestial bodies, which *are* moved in circular or elliptical lines, and not straight, must have some other cause, besides the first impressed impulse, that must bend their motion into that curve'. Descartes's immediate conclusion from his second law was that 'bodies which are moving in a circle always tend to move away from the centre of the circle which they are describing'.[12] Of course, this tendency away from the centre implies that bodies which remain in orbital motion are somehow forced against their rectilinear tendency, but this turns out to be very different from assuming that the very occurrence of orbital motion is a puzzle to be solved by 'some other cause, besides the first impressed impulse, that must bend their motion into that curve'. Especially it is a far cry from assuming that the 'celestial bodies' require such causal explanation. And indeed, Descartes never attempted such a move, and in particular, in spite of his somewhat extravagant account of the motions of the heavens, never tried to explain away the fact that 'the matter of heaven, in which the planets are situated, unceasingly revolves'.[13] For him it is

God, who 'in the beginning caused [the particles of heavenly matter] to begin to move with equal force, each one separately around its own center ... and also several together around certain other centers ... '.[14]

So here is a beginning of a solution to our mystery: Hooke's Programme's indebtedness to Descartes's *Principia Philosophiæ* does not diminish its originality; Hooke's genius, as it was demonstrated in his mechanical and technical achievements, was not so much in raw ideas but in their unique assembly and audacious application. The Cartesian ingredients of the Programme may have struck his audience as familiar, but their unperturbed application to circular motion, on the one hand, and to the heavens on the other, would have surprised Descartes himself.

And indeed, if we are to search for Hooke's intellectual mentors, it is not Descartes who offers the best lead, but Kepler. Looking at Hooke's concept of heavenly causation, it is not difficult to observe that he structures it after the example set by that enigmatic writer, well known but little understood in Hooke's milieu, whom Hooke himself cites often in various contexts, often misunderstanding the details.[15] In particular, the innovation of Hooke's 23 May 1666 paper read to the Royal Society is very reminiscent of Kepler's surprising move in Chapter 33 of his *Astronomia Nova*:

> It was demonstrated in the previous chapter that the elapsed times of a planet on equal parts of the eccentric circle (or on equal distances in the aethereal air) are in the same ratio ... to the extent that the that a planet is farther from the point which is taken as the centre of the world, it is less strongly urged to move about that point. It is therefore necessary that the cause of this weakening is either in the very body of the planet, in a motive force placed therein, or right at the supposed centre of the world.[16]

Kepler did not assimilate the notion of rectilinear inertia the way Hooke has, so it never occurs to him that circular motion should be explained away. When he does get to discuss the rotation of the planets, he accounts for it by the sun's own rotation 'upon its centre of axis'. But he is completely entitled to brag 'Physicists, prick up your ears! For here is raised a deliberation involving an inroad to be made into your province'.[17]

Yet just as it was a mistake to see the notion of primary rectilinear motion curved into orbit as a trivial application of Cartesian ideas, it would be a mistake to take Hooke's notion of celestial causation to be an easy expansion of Keplerian ones. The best way to perceive the difficulty is to have a quick look at the writings of the prominent English astronomers of the generation before Hooke: Wing, Streete and Ward. All of them refer to Kepler as their great immediate predecessor, but none appears to suspect that there is anything revolutionary hidden in his work.

Three Experiments, One Image and One Neglected Discovery

But what is more interesting and important than the conservatism of Hooke's predecessors, is the fact that Hooke's adoption of Kepler is far from straightforward. In fact, it is mediated through a complex of experiments, devices and speculations. A fine example of this is Hooke's employment of Kepler's ideas concerning light and gravity in his own attempts to develop accurate instruments of optical observation. It begins with Hooke's attempt to solve a problem that worried astronomers since Tycho and Maestlin; atmospheric refraction, about which he might have read in Wing the citation from Kepler 'Magno Astronomiae damno in investigatione motus solis & Æquinoctorioun factum est, ut Refractiones a Veteribus neglectaem'.[18] He approaches the problem by suggesting that the light entering the atmosphere is not refracted but 'inflected': namely, curved gradually by the changing density of the atmosphere. The nexus of light and gravity, physics and astronomy, is already Keplerian in flavour, but Hooke gives clearer evidence that Kepler is his main resource by using an image that Kepler was the one to introduce and develop in the *Astronomia Nova*, viz, that of the optical cone. Hooke uses this image as part of an account of optical behavior, yet does not apply it directly to light, but to the 'inflecting' atmosphere.

This is, in short, how it goes: in order to have his 'inflection' account for observational discrepancies, Hooke needs to demonstrate both that there is, indeed 'multiplicate refraction of ... rays of light within ... a medium, whose parts are unequally dense',[19] and that the atmosphere is such a medium. He does both by experiments, but of somewhat different sort. The existence of inflection is demonstrated by direct illustration: one such illustration is the shadow HPNOM in the salt water tank in 'Fig: 1' (Figure 2.1), purportedly curved by the changing density of the water in the tank (which increases with the salt concentration towards the bottom). Another is the size of the arrow C in 'Fig: 2' (Figure 2.1) which changes continuously as the density of the air in the glass ball B changes with temperature. The claim that the media in the tank and the ball can model the atmosphere, namely, that atmosphere is indeed 'a medium, whose parts are unequally dense', has to be supported in a more circumventing manner; through 'a means ... for the finding by what

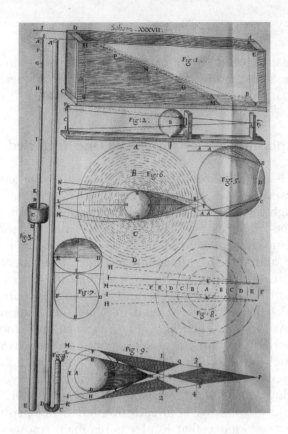

Figure 2.1 'Schem. XXXVII' in *Micrographia*
(Hooke 1665, between pp. 220 and 221)

degrees the air passes from such a degree of density to such a degree of Rarity'.[20]

The 'means' consists of a series of Torricellian experiments, in which Hooke uses mercury to expand and compress a column of air in the tubes on the left-hand side ('Fig: 3' and 'Fig: 4' of Figure 2.1). Their results demonstrate the heterogeneity of the atmosphere; like the mercury in the tubes, Hooke concludes, the air's own weight compresses its lower strata more than its upper ones, 'somewhat [according to] the hypothesis of the reciprocal proportion of the Elaters to the Extensions' or Boyle's pressure law.[21] It is in the calculation by which he draws his atmospheric conclusions from his mercury experiments that Hooke betrays his indebtedness to Kepler. The calculation is based on the assumption of an atmospheric 'Cylinder indefinitely extended upwards', weighing on the mercury tube. But Hooke finds it necessary to add

[I say Cylinder, not a piece of a cone, because, as I may elsewhere shew in the Explication of Gravity, that triplicate proportion of the shels of a Sphere, to their respective diameters, I suppose to be removed by the decrease of the power of Gravity].[22]

The combined image of spherical envelope and conic expansion is taken directly from Kepler's hesitant deliberations about the proper way to apply the analogy he draws between light and virtus motrix in Chapters 35 and 36 of *Astronomia Nova*. Kepler uses light to develop a concept of universal motive power – he has no interest in gravity in this context. Hooke, who perceives Kepler as a great expert on gravity,[23] follows his lead to speculate about optics, shifting seamlessly from Kepler's heavenly motive power to terrestrial gravity, demonstrating the audacity to move between realms that I referred to above. And in the process he makes a tremendous discovery, whose importance he will only understand at the final stages of his correspondence with Newton.

Two Diagrams

But before attending to this discovery, which will help clarify the epistemic relations between Hooke and Newton, we come to the most important difference between Hooke and Kepler – the most important reason why Hooke's Programme is not a trivial extension of the *Astronomia Nova* any more than it is of the *Principia Philosophiæ*. The difference can be illustrated by two diagrams. The first is the one

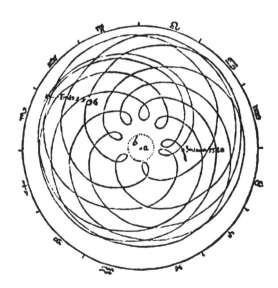

Figure 2.2 Kepler's 'accurate depiction of the motions of the star Mars'. (Kepler, *Astronomia Nova*. Gesammelte Werke, vol. 3 (1937), p. 64)

by which Kepler introduces his fundamental line of thought at the beginning of the *Astronomia Nova*:

> This is the accurate depiction of the motions of the 'star Mars', which it traversed from the year 1580 until 1596, on the assumption that the earth stands still, as Ptolemy and Brahe would have it. These motions, continued farther, would become unintelligibly intricate, for the continuation is boundless, never returning to its previous path.[24]

Kepler does not feel he needs to elaborate much; being 'unintelligibly intricate' should be enough of an argument to convince the reader of the absurdity of such an orbit and of the theories that give rise to it. It is hardly surprising to find such confidence in cosmological order in Kepler. He is, after all, the one to write that 'geometry ... is coeternal with God, and by shining forth in the Divine Mind supplied patterns to God ... for the furnishing of the world, so that it should become best and most beautiful and above all most like to the Creator'.[25] But compare this to Hooke's approach to the following diagram, sent to him by Newton on 13 December 1679:

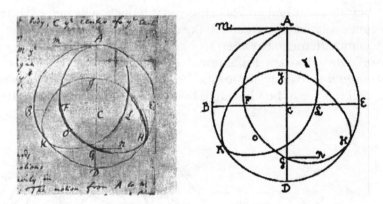

Figure 2.3 Newton's diagram from his 13 December 1679 letter to Hooke. The stone falling through the earth from A along FOG and so on changes its apsides with every orbit.
(Original, on the left, from Lohne 1960, p. 27; transcription, on the right, from Pelseneer 1929, p. 244)

The broad similarity between Newton's free-hand sketch of the imaginary fall of a stone through the earth and Kepler's 'accurate depiction of the motions of the star Mars' is not accidental. When Newton submits this diagram to Hooke, the argument he tries to convey is very similar to Kepler's: your suggestion, he tells Hooke, is *prima facie* absurd; it leads to planetary orbits which do not have a repeating line of apsides – they are unruly, and thus cannot be.

Hooke has an answer for Newton. It is seemingly a wholly Keplerian answer; relying on Kepler's second law (if in the old version of inverse ratio between velocity and distance, which Kepler himself abandoned for the area law) and the Keplerian idea that the attraction from the sun 'always is in subduplicate proportion from the Center Reciprocal'.[26] These combined, Hooke suggests, can create just enough balance between the inertial motion along the tangent and the accelerating motion towards the centre, so as to insure that 'the auges will unite at the same part of the Circle and that the neerest point of accesse to the center will be opposite to the furthest Distant'.[27] But in fact, Hooke's lesson to Newton here is radically anti-Keplerian. It is no coincidence that he writes 'the same *part* of the Circle' and not 'the same point'. A few lines later he adds an even less committed phrase:

> What I mentioned in my last [letter] concerning the Descent within the body of the Earth was But upon the Supposall of such an attraction ['always is in subduplicate proportion from the Center Reciprocal'], not that I believe there really is such an attraction to the very Center of the Earth, but on the Contrary I rather Conceive that the more the body approaches the Center, the lesse will it be Urged by the attraction – possibly somewhat like the Gravitation on a pendulum or a body moved in a Concave Sphaere where the power Continually Decreases the nearer the body inclines to a horizontall motion, which it hath when perpendicular under the point of suspension, or in the Lowest point, and there the auges are *almost* opposite, and the nearest approach to the Center is *about* a quarter of a Revolution.[28]

The model with which they were working – that of a stone falling through the earth – was not completely adequate, concedes Hooke, because within the sphere of the earth the attraction does not proceed all the way to the centre. 'The Gravitation on a pendulum' is a better model, but not because it promises better order – more accurate alignment of the apsides ('auges') than 'the same part of the Circle'. Just the opposite: all Hooke is willing to offer is that 'the auges are *almost* opposite' and 'the Center is *about* a quarter of a Revolution'.

Order and Change

We thus return to answer the first of our original queries. What Newton learned from Hooke, what has never occurred to him before their correspondence and what he could not have learned from

anyone else – definitely not from Descartes or Kepler – is this
unabashed use of 'almost' and 'about' in relation to cosmic order in
general and celestial motions in particular. But this is what Hooke's
Programme entails, over and above those all-important details. To
'compound' closed curve orbits from inertial and accelerating motions
is to succumb to the idea that these orbits are not really closed. And it
is exactly this realization that Newton expresses in that never-to-be-
published scholium cited above:

> the planets neither move exactly in ellipse nor revolve twice in the same
> orbit. So that there are as many orbits to a planet as it has revolutions, as in
> the motion of the Moon, and the orbit of any one planet depends on the
> combined motion of all the planets, not to mention the action of all these
> on each other.[29]

The tone of Newton's queries to Hooke as well as his scholium, and
especially the disappearance of the latter from the published versions
of the *Principia*, reflect some stress; it was probably not easy for the
Cambridge mathematician to come to terms with such unruly universe
(I would even suggest that Newton developed much of the
idiosyncrasies of his religion in response to this tension, but this is a
subject for another paper). For Hooke, however, there was never
much difficulty in assuming a universe of grand changes and massive
displacements. His posthumous 'Discourse of Earthquakes',[30] for
example, is dedicated to the idea that 'the great part of the Surface of
the Earth hath been since the Creation transformed and made of
another Nature'.[31] Delivered from 1668 until shortly before his death,
this *Discourse* is set to explain the finding of 'Bodies resembling the
whole Bodies of Fishes' in locations 'many Hundreds of Fathoms
above the level of the Surface of the next adjoining Sea'. Hooke does
so by surmising that 'the departing of the Waters to another part or
side of the Earth', and 'the eruption of some kind of subterraneous
Fires, or Earthquakes, whereby great quantities of Earth have been
rais'd above the former Level of those Parts'.[32] And he goes as far as to
suggest

> that the Center of Gravity or Method of Attraction of the Globe of the Earth
> may change and shift places, and if so, then certainly all the fluid parts of
> the Earth will conform thereto, and then 'twill follow that one part will be
> cover'd and overflow'd by the sea that was before dry, and another part be
> discover'd and laid dry that was before overwhelm'd.[33]

And if that is not enough, Hooke is willing to admit 'That there have
been many other Species of Creatures in former Ages, of which we

can find none at present; and that 'tis not unlikely also but that there may be divers new kinds now, which have not been from the beginning'.[34]

So if it is change that Newton learned from Hooke, what did Hooke learn from Newton? The clue to this answer lies in that discovery Hooke made while working on his inflection experiments: 'I say Cylinder, not a piece of a cone, becaus … that triplicate proportion of the shels of a Sphere, to their respective diameters, I suppose to be removed by the decrease of the power of Gravity'.[35] Hooke is discovering here the inverse-square law of gravitation. This is a simple calculation: the difference between the '*triplicate* proportion of the shels of a Sphere, to their respective diameters' and the simple proportion in the case of a cylinder is removed by the decline of gravity with the square of distance. This should have been an extremely important discovery for Hooke. After all, from the inception of his Programme he was looking for a way in which to work 'attraction' into it. In his 23 May 1666 paper to the Royal Society he makes sure to point out that he does 'not … suppose that the attraction of the sun to be exactly according to the same degrees, as they are in a pendulum'.[36] In the 1674 sketch of a 'System of the World' he explicates that his hypothesized 'attractive powers are so much the more powerful in operating, by how much the nearer the body wrought upon is to their own Centers', and then adds that 'what these several degrees are I have not yet experimentally verified'.[37] Seemingly, Hooke has a ready answer to the question of 'degrees': gravitation, he knows as early as 1665, declines as the square of distance. Why, then, does he not use it?

Two Different Concepts: Attraction and Gravitation

The answer for this riddle is also the answer of the indebtedness of Hooke's Programme to Newton, and it can be found in a very conspicuous feature of the correspondence between Hooke and Newton, in which, as we said, the Programme received its final formulation. Note, again, Hooke's final formulation of the Programme:

> It now remains to know the proprietys of a curve Line (not circular nor concentricall) made by a centrall attractive power which makes the velocitys of Descent from the tangent Line or equall straight motion at all Distances in a Duplicate proportion to the Distances Reciprocally taken.[38]

It is 'a centrall attractive power' that is 'in a Duplicate proportion to the Distances'; not gravity. Hooke finally makes use of his 15-years-in-the-waiting law, but instead of simply using 'the power of Gravity' to which it was applied in the original, he prefers the supposedly more general but much vaguer 'attractive power'. This is no accident. Indeed, he does not offer his law for the dependence of 'attraction' on distance until Newton specifically suggests that 'Gravity be supposed uniform'. And through their correspondence, it is Newton who tries to introduce gravity into the discussion, while Hooke remains loyal to the 'attractive motion towards a central body' which he employs in his first formulation of the Programme. This is no simple terminological preference; when Hooke wants to answer Newton's challenges directly – as in the case of Newton's suggestion to consider a body falling through the earth – he is not shy of talking about 'gravitation to the … center'. When Hooke returns to his own preferred terminology a couple of lines later, however, it is again a 'Theory of Circular motions compounded by a Direct motion and an *attractive* one to a Center'.[39]

So it is not the case that Hooke simply forgot the inverse-square law for gravity. He ignores it in his Programme because he distinguishes explicitly between 'attraction' and 'gravitation' and rejects the latter for the former. But if not a kind of attraction, what could gravity be? A clue to the answer is to be found in the experiments Hooke used to illustrate the Programme when first introducing it to the Royal Society in 1666. Hooke establishes the feasibility of 'the inflection of a direct motion into a curve by a supervening attractive principle'[40] through a series of demonstrations with conic pendulums – pendulums which circulate horizontally, rather than oscillate vertically. The pendulums exhibit 'that circular motion is compounded of an endevour by a direct motion by the tangent, and another endeavour tending to the center',[41] and display the dependence of the final orbit on the relations between the parameters of the two motions. And when the demonstrations succeed Hooke adds 'another experiment by fastening another pendulous body to the shorter string on the lower part of the wire'.[42] The purpose of this double pendulum experiment is to illustrate a hypothesis 'concerning the ebbing and flowing of the sea', presented to the Society a week earlier by John Wallis,[43] and it is in the terms of this hypothesis that we find Hooke's conception of gravity and gravitation.

Wallis's idea, which Hooke clearly has little difficulty in adopting, is to explain the tides by the motion around the sun of the common centre of gravity of the earth and the moon. Prima facie, Wallis may appear to be suggesting an idea very similar to Hooke's Programme: a mechanical account of complex motion around the sun. Yet a closer look reveals that Wallis's hypothesis is based on static, rather than mechanical intuitions. Unlike Hooke's 'supervening attractive principle', which causes 'the inflection of a direct motion into a curve' Wallis's gravity only provides a 'bond or tie', a kind of a rigid connection, that creates a common centre of gravity. It is, indeed, a connection over distance, as the gentlemen of the Royal Society noted, inquiring 'how two bodies, that have no tie, can have one common center of gravity'.[44] But as their complaint reveals, they, too, perceived Wallis as suggesting that, reaching across space, gravity 'ties' bodies, rather than affects motion.

This, then, is why Hooke's Programme could not be formulated, let alone realized, without Newton's contribution. Hooke's easy expansion of his experiments to include Wallis's Galilean hypothesis indicates that it was Wallis's concept of gravity that he had in mind when he carefully distinguished gravity and attraction. And it was in demolishing this distinction that Newton's co-operation proved essential for Hooke's Programme. If Newton's insistence on using 'gravity' in the correspondence and ignoring Hooke's careful distinction seemed as either careless or arrogant, his use of it in the scholium demonstrates that it is. Newton has, in fact, a very clear idea on how to bridge the distinction:

> The whole space of the planetary heavens either rests (as is commonly believed), or moves uniformly in a straight line, and hence the communal centre of gravity of the planets … either rests or moves along with it. In both cases … the relative motions of the planets are the same, and their common centre of gravity rests in relation to the whole of space, and so can certainly be taken for the still centre of the whole planetary system … By reason of this deviation of the Sun from the centre of gravity the centripetal force does not always tend to that immobile centre, and hence the planets neither move exactly in ellipse nor revolve twice in the same orbit.[45]

The sun, explains Newton, is both the centre of gravitation and the centre of gravity. Gravity is a type of attraction all right, and this attraction creates *both* a 'common center of gravity' *and* a motion about it. This is indeed a development of Hooke's own great intellectual innovation – the idea that change and stability are utterly compatible in cosmology; that planetary orbits, to use a less flowery language, can be an outcome of continuous bending by attraction from a distance and do not need to be perfect in order to be stable. Yet Hooke arrives here at the limits of his own inventiveness. If Descartes could not fully grasp the significance of rectilinear inertia to heavenly motions, Hooke could not complete the celestial merger of 'centre of gravity' and 'centre of attraction'. This move, which allows the use of Galilean terrestrial statics to account for Keplerian celestial mechanics, was left for Newton.

Two Different Difficulties

There is a reason, then, why Hooke's Programme looks so familiar to us when it was so difficult for its contemporaries. From the purely conceptual perspective the Programme requires, indeed, only the application of mechanical concepts easily available to late seventeenth-century savants: rectilinear inertia; accelerative force; the expansion of terrestrial dynamics to *physica cœlestis*. But such general perspective is available only in hindsight. For Hooke's readers, coming to terms with the full consequences of these concepts proved to be exceedingly difficult. Difficult, that is, for the honorable gentlemen of the Royal Society – the chorus behind Hooke and Newton – but also for the two heroes themselves, who arrive, each at his own instance, at a juncture through which he has to be helped by the other, even though the direction to be chosen appears obvious. For Newton, the difficulty presents itself first with the seemingly obvious idea that the effect of centripetal power on an inertially-moving body will be an orbit around the centre of attraction (rather than a spiral ending in that centre). He is then struck by – and finally accepts – the even more difficult realization that a mechanical account of the planetary motions entails an ever-changing vista of the heavens. For Hooke, the hardest notion to swallow is even more surprising in its hindsight simplicity. It is the idea that celestial attraction and terrestrial gravitation are one; that gravity can both 'inflect ... direct [planetary] motion into a curve' *and* 'bond' the 'planetary heavens' into a system that 'either rests ... or moves uniformly in a straight line'. It was in stating the exceedingly difficult obvious that Hooke and his Programme distinguished themselves.

Chapter 3

Robert Hooke as an Astronomer: Hooke's Optical Research and Instruments in their Historical Context

Hideto Nakajima

Introduction

Who was Robert Hooke? He was an experimental philosopher, a City Surveyor and an assistant to Boyle. We may also characterize him as the author of *Micrographia*, discoverer of Hooke's Law, restless genius, English Leonardo in the seventeenth century, the man who knew too much or who spent a curious life.[1] Though not one of the above characteristics seems to be sufficient to cover Hooke's overall activities, all scholars will agree with the fact that Hooke has been evaluated as a relentless but lesser enemy of Sir Isaac Newton. Michael Hunter and Simon Schaffer pointed out that it is a comparison from which Hooke has suffered to an undeserved extent, due not least to the almost God-like reputation accorded to Newton by many commentators.[2] To save Hooke's reputation, they emphasized that we should see his research in its proper context. But in what context? Their discussion remains rather vague here.

In this chapter, the author will argue that we can interpret a considerable part (of course, not all) of Hooke's activities consistently if we see them in the context of observational astronomy. Hooke's commitment to optical instruments, including telescopes, was to improve the level of astronomical observations in his day: observations of celestial bodies in the solar system on the one hand, and precision astronomical measurements on the other. The former tradition was started by Galileo at the beginning of the seventeenth century, and the latter, which we may trace back even before Ptolemy, reached a new stage with the establishment of the Greenwich Observatory in 1675.

Hooke's harsh criticism of Newton's reflector in 1672 was a natural response of an observational astronomer. Hooke invented and improved optical instruments to enhance the ability of astronomical observations, whereas Newton was satisfied simply with an invention of an optical contrivance based on his new theory of colours. Newton did not care much about what new observations would become possible by his telescope.

Hooke's Astronomical Activities at the Royal Society

Hooke was the Curator of Experiments of the Royal Society, and his activities were recorded in its official documents. It is reasonable to suppose that important contributions among them, which were regarded as worth publishing, were printed in the *Philosophical Transactions*. In the journal, we can count 36 articles relating to Hooke. More than half of them seem to be composed by Hooke himself, and most of the rest were reports by the editor on Hooke's research.

As shown in Table 3.1, among the 35 articles by or on Hooke, 12 treat observations of planets (especially Saturn, Jupiter and Mars), the moon and the sun. Another two are on the improvement of telescopic lenses, and another two are on micrometers for telescopes. In total, 16 papers deal with astronomical observations and instrumental improvements for astronomy. Here the author would like to emphasize the fact that the number of papers on observations supersedes those on instrumental improvements. This seems to suggest that astronomical observations had much more importance for Hooke than the

Table 3.1 Topics of articles relating to Hooke's work in *Philosophical Transactions*. Data include articles in *Philosophical Collections* (1679–82), which Hooke edited when *Philosophical Transactions* was suspended.

Topic	No. of publications
Observations of planets, moon and sun	12
Improvement of lenses	2
Micrometer	2
Microscopy and *Micrographia*	3
Barometer	3
Sounding	2
Information on distant places	2
Book Review	2
Others	7

improvement of optical instruments themselves. In Hooke's mind, optical instrumentation had specific targets: better observations of celestial bodies in the solar system and precision astronomical measurements.

Astronomical Observations in the Mid-Seventeenth Century

Why was Hooke interested in the observation of planets, the moon and the sun? It was because the observation of these celestial bodies was an important issue among natural philosophers in the middle of the seventeenth century. The activities of Christiaan Huygens at the Royal Society give us a good clue to make it clearer. In Thomas Birch's *History of the Royal Society*, based on the Society's records from 1660 to 1687, Huygens's name appears on 113 pages.[3] In some cases, plural entries were made on the same page and multiple subjects were discussed under the same entry. Taking this into account, Huygens's name appears a total of 144 times in these pages. Among all entries, 19 are on telescopes and optics, 16 are on astronomical observations, 23 are on the air pump, 22 are on the motion of bodies and 24 are on clocks. Thus about a quarter of all entries relate to astronomy and the improvement of astronomical observations. Principal subjects in entries on astronomical observation are Saturn and Jupiter. It is well known that Huygens discovered a satellite of Saturn with his telescope, and that he showed that the strange shape of Saturn was caused by its circular ring.

Christopher Wren, a good friend of Hooke, was also interested in the ring of Saturn, but he believed that it should be elliptical in shape. It is worth noting that Wren wrote in his *De Corpore Saturni* of 1658 that it did not seem useless or inglorious (because it still remained to be done) to describe the lunar appearance more accurately, or to show the more than lunar fickleness of Saturn in a variety of figures, as the mathematicians improved the theory of dioptrics and craftsmen daily promoted the art of working big lenses.[4] The improvement of optical instruments was an essential element for the advancement of observational astronomy.

Albert van Helden gave us an excellent description of the history of the use of telescope in astronomy.[5] In 1610 Galileo discovered the satellites of Jupiter, curious appearances of Saturn and the phases of Venus. In the next year he first observed sunspots. In spite of these Galilean achievements, the telescope broke into the arsenal of the professional astronomer only gradually. Some uses for it were mapping the moon, observing the satellites of Jupiter to solve the problem of longitude at sea and observing transits of Mercury and Venus to determine astronomical constants. When other astronomers became interested in observational astronomy, it was in areas where there was an obvious problem, such as the appearances of Saturn, or an obvious use for their studies, such as the lunar work by Hevelius and Gassendi. Around 1650, new discoveries started to flow. These included discoveries of the satellites of Saturn and surface markings on Jupiter and Mars which gave evidence of the rotation of these planets. The author will show that Hooke's astronomical and optical research was in line with the history that Helden summarised.

Observation of Celestial Bodies in the Solar System

The first article just after the introduction of the inaugural volume of the *Philosophical Transactions* (1665) was entitled 'an Accompt of the Improvement of Optick Glasses' (pp. 2–3). This is a review of a book on Giuseppe Campani, an able young telescope craftsman, who had recently won a telescope contest (*paragone*) over Eustachio Divini, his predecessor, in Italy. Giovanni Domenico Cassini (Cassini I), who attended the contest, later made many discoveries with Campani telescopes.[6] The review reported that, in the book of Campani, when optical glasses ground with a turning tool (where the lens is made without using a mould) were used for observations of the rings of Saturn and belts of Jupiter, the possibility of the rotation of Jupiter around its own axis was discussed.

Just after the review follows an article entitled 'Spot in one of the belts of Jupiter'. This is a report on Hooke's observation of 9 May 1664. Hooke saw a spot on Jupiter, which moved from east to west in two hours. The spot could be a permanent spot of Jupiter or a shadow of its satellite. If this were a permanent spot, Hooke's observation was evidence of the rotation of Jupiter. More decisive evidence of rotation was given by Cassini. He concluded from the observation of a permanent spot that the time of rotation of Jupiter was 9 hours 56 minutes. Cassini's discovery was reported in the same volume of the *Philosophical Transactions* (vol. 1, pp. 143–5). The editor suggested the possibility of rotation of Mars, Venus and Mercury.

To this forefront of observational astronomy, Hooke made his original contribution. He delivered his observation of Mars at the meeting of the Royal Society on 28 March 1666. It was published in *Philosophical Transactions* under the title 'The particulars of those observations of the planet Mars' (vol. 1, pp. 239–42). Hooke's observation was performed on the spots of Mars in February and

March with a 36-foot telescope. He concluded that Mars did move around its own axis. He said to the Royal Society meeting that 'Mars, as well as Jupiter, the earth, &c. moves about his own axis in about 24 hours'.[7] An article immediately following Hooke's shows that, almost at the same time in Italy, Cassini made a similar observation of dark spots on Mars (ibid, pp. 242-5). Cassini's observations continued from February to June, and his results for Mars were similar to Hooke's. Both Hooke and Cassini's observational data were published in *Philosophical Transactions* (see Figure 3.1).

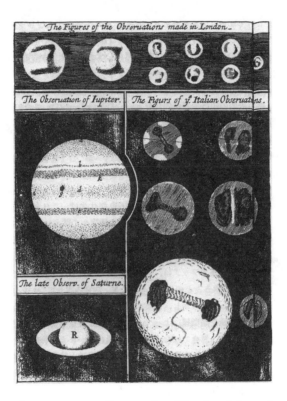

Figure 3.1 Observations of Mars by Hooke (above) and Cassini (right, below).

Usually the discovery of the rotation of Mars is ascribed to Cassini.[8] However, as the present author has shown, Hooke seems also qualified to claim his priority.

Hooke's observations of Jupiter and Mars made a strong impression on Hevelius, a leading astronomer of the time. Hevelius wrote a letter to Oldenburg in October 1666, and wanted to know details of the 60-

foot telescope which Hooke used to observe Jupiter.[9] Hooke sent an answer to Hevelius via Oldenburg, to which Hooke attached a figure of the telescope he used in order to show the way to hoist it up, illustrated as Figure 3.2.[10]

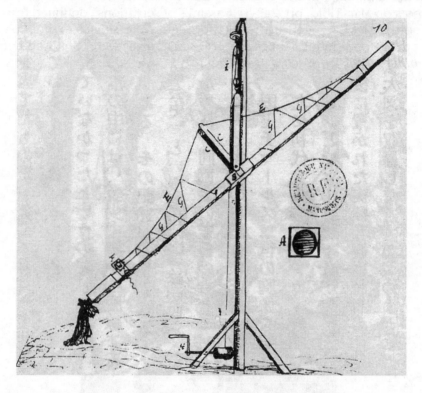

Figure 3.2　　Hooke's illustration of a long telescope for Hevelius.

Hevelius hoped to obtain a similar telescope, and he asked Oldenburg to seek advice from Hooke on the selection of it.[11] The telescope was shipped to him in August 1669. Though the focal length of its lens was 50 feet, shorter that expected, Hevelius praised it as the best telescope he had ever used.[12] A picture of the telescope was published in Hevelius's *Machina Cœlestis, pars prior* (Gdansk 1673), on the page between pages 392 and 393.

Hooke's 60-foot telescope seems to have been regarded as an emblematic instrument of the Royal Society. The picture which Hooke sent to Hevelius was put into the frontispiece of Sprat's *History of the Royal Society* (London, 1667), just behind Boyle's air pump (see Figure 3.3).[13] Boyle's air pump was drawn here because of its emblematic status.[14] Hooke's telescope research had similar importance for the Royal Society. It is reasonable to conclude that Hooke competed and collaborated with first-class astronomers of those days at the forefront of astronomy, and that Hooke was regarded as a leading user of telescopes.

Figure 3.3(a) Frontispiece from Sprat's *The History of the Royal Society of London* (1667).

Figure 3.3(b)   Part of the background (enlarged) of the Frontispiece
from Sprat's *The History of the Royal
Society of London* (1667).

Long Telescopes and Hooke

As Figure 3.3 shows, Hooke used so-called long telescopes.
Traditional history of telescopes tends to focus on explanations of
spherical and chromatic aberration, and references to the theoretical
investigations of Galileo, Kepler, Descartes, Huygens and Newton. As
a result, one is left with the impression that the telescope was an
instrument which turned into the sophisticated instrument by the
science of optics.[15] But astronomers had a much more practical
solution to avoid both spherical and chromatic aberration: long
telescopes with long focal lenses. Hooke, Cassini, Hevelius, Wren and
others made sophisticated observations with long telescopes.

Hooke's commitment to astronomy is seen even in *Micrographia*,
his book of microscopy. Hooke recorded in it observations with long
telescopes. Observation 59 of the book was entitled 'Of multitudes of
small Stars discoverable by the Telescope',[16] and Observation 60, the
final part of *Micrographia*, was entitled 'Of the Moon'.[17] Figures in
Schema 38 of *Micrographia* were related to these Observations:
figures of Pleiades, Orion and craters of the moon, which were
observed by Hooke with a 36-foot telescope.[18]

A lens-grinding machine for long telescopes was discussed in the
Preface of *Micrographia*.[19] This was a two-axis engine (Figure 3.4).

Hooke insisted that, provided great care is taken, 'I see no reason,
but that a Glass of a thousand, nay of ten thousand foot long, may be
as well made as one of ten.'[20] Hooke's machine and his optimism
were, however, criticized by the French natural philosopher Adrien

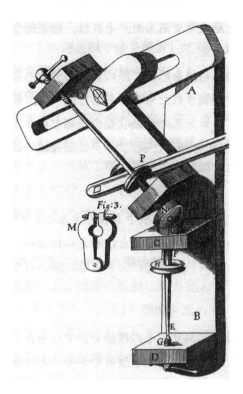

Figure 3.4 Hooke's lens-grinding machine, from *Micrographia.*

Auzout in 1665. Auzout doubted the feasibility of the engine, and claimed that 'his Engine was published upon a meer Theory' (*Philosophical Transactions,* vol. 1, p. 58). Hooke defended his machine in the article following Auzout's. Their exchange was finally published by Auzout under the title of *Réponse de Monsieur Hook aux considerations de M. Auzout* (Paris, 1665).

Instruments for Precise Astronomical Measurement

When professional astronomers started to use telescopes, they were mainly interested in celestial bodies in the solar system. Many important discoveries were made around 1650, and long telescopes were used for them. In the next stage, that is, in the second half of the seventeenth century, the telescope became a fully-fledged research instrument which was used not only for discovery but also for measurement.[21] The revolution in positional astronomy brought about by the combination of pendulum clocks, measuring arcs with

telescopic sights and the micrometer, in the period 1665–80 was
profound.[22] Hooke was at the front line of seventeenth-century
astronomy here again. He strongly advocated the uses of telescopic
sights and eyepiece micrometers.

Eyepiece micrometers became a topic in the Royal Society in the
mid-1660s. In one of the letters which were exchanged between
Hooke and Auzout on the lens-grinding machine, Auzout promised
that he would explain a way to assign the 'Bigness of the Diameter of
all the Planets' (*Philosophical Transactions*, vol. 1, p. 63). When the
way was reported by Oldenburg to a meeting of the Royal Society on
9 January 1667:

> Dr Wren and Mr Hooke, having related to the society several ways, which
> they had known long before, of taking the diameters of the planets to
> seconds, were desir'd briefly to describe them, that so it might be signified
> to the Parisian philosophers, that it was a thing not at all new among the
> English.[23]

Hooke mentioned the instrument as early as 1665. In *Micrographia* he
wrote that long telescopes 'should be fitted with a Rete [reticule], or
divided Scale, placed at such a distance within the Eye-glass, that they
may be distinctly seen, which should be the measures of minutes and
seconds'.[24]

Below the 36-foot telescope in the courtyard of Gresham College
(Figure 3.5), we can see sketches of micrometers with a net (reticule)
and a divided scale.

To Auzout, not only Hooke but also Richard Towneley claimed
English priority. Townley introduced to the Royal Society a knife-edge
micrometer, which was invented by William Gascoigne in about 1640.
In 1667 Hooke gave a description of this device in *Philosophical
Transactions* vol. 2, pp. 541–4. Actually Gascoigne's telescopic
observation with a micrometer was recorded in his letter to Oughtred
of 1640 and 1641.[25]

The priority of Gascoigne in micrometers was claimed again in 1717
by William Derham (in *Philosophical Transactions* vol. 30, pp.
603–10). In the same article, Derham also tried to prove that
Gascoigne was the first to apply telescopic sights to astronomical
instruments. Gascoigne's achievement was not lost by his death. It
was transferred to the members of the Oxford group through
mathematicians and instrument makers.[26]

On the advantage of telescopic sights for precision astronomical
measurement of the angular distances of fixed stars, Hooke started an
exchange with Hevelius in the latter half of the 1660s, just around the

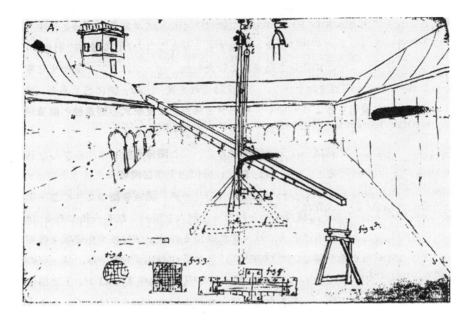

Figure 3.5 Hooke's manuscript showing a long telescope at Gresham College and illustrations of eyepiece micrometers (a net and a divided scale).

(Royal Society Classified Papers 20, fol. 134r. © Royal Society)

time when a 50-foot telescope under Hooke's direction was shipped to Hevelius. In May 1668, Hooke wrote on telescopic sights to Hevelius. However, Hevelius's reply raised objections, and questioned in particular Hooke's claims for the greater accuracy of small instruments having telescopic sights over much larger ones with plain sights.[27] Hevelius appealed to his own observational record as evidence for the ability of open sights. He made a defence of open sights over telescopic sights also in his *Machina Cœlestis* (pp. 293ff.). Against this defence, in 1674 Hooke published his *Animadversions On the first part of the Machina Cœlestis ...*, insisting that open sights can hardly distinguish an angle much smaller than a minute of arc.[28]

This exchange shows that Hooke took a positive attitude to instrumental improvement for precision measurement. Instruments for precision measurement for positional astronomy were just becoming essential tools for professional astronomers in the latter part of the seventeenth century. For example, Flamsteed used a seven-foot sextant equipped with a telescopic sight at Greenwich Observatory. Hooke's mural quadrant with a telescopic sight was mounted at the Observatory in 1676.[29] In the case of the eyepiece micrometer, Hooke used one in an attempt to measure the parallax of a zenith star, which is caused by the revolution of the earth around the sun. In June 1669 he started the observations at his rooms in the Gresham College. He published the results of his observations in 1674.[30]

Newton's Reflector Telescope in its Historical Context

It was at the end of 1671 when Newton sent his reflector telescope to the Royal Society. He wrote a letter to Oldenburg in February 1672 to explain its theoretical background. The letter was published in *Philosophical Transactions* vol. 6, pp. 3075–87 under the title 'New theory about light and colors'. Newton believed that he had proved that different refrangibility of rays of light hindered the improvement of the refracting telescope. Hooke did not admit that, and criticized Newton harshly.[31]

The controversy between Newton and Hooke has been analysed from the viewpoint of the theory of colours. Preceding research mainly focused on Hooke's defence of the modification (or qualification) theory of colours, and on Newton's objection to it. Westfall, one of the best scholars of Newton, believed that modification theory originated in Aristotle.[32] It explained colours as a mixture of darkness and light. But the present author has shown that this was not the case for Hooke, and elucidated that, for Hooke, modification theory simply meant wave (or pulse) theory of light. In this framework, Hooke said 'I do readily assent' to different refrangibility of colours, the heart of Newtonian theory of colours. Hooke attacked Newton because he had detected Newton's hidden belief in the corpuscular theory of light.[33]

To understand their antagonism properly, we need to see another aspect of the controversy: Newton's claim of the superiority of reflectors over refractors. Newton believed that his new theory of colours definitely demonstrated the limit of refractors because it showed the inevitability of chromatic aberration with glass lenses. Though Hooke accepted Newton's discovery of chromatic aberration, he emphasized that chromatic aberration was not insuperable.[34] Hooke was optimistic about the future of refractors.

Why did Hooke believe in the advantage of refractors over reflectors? If we remember the fact that Hooke was a leading user of telescopes, his attitude is easily understood. The problem with chromatic aberration had been *actually* solved by the development of the long telescope. Important discoveries had already been made with it. Astronomers were starting to use it even for precision measurement of the angular distance of fixed stars with the help of telescopic sights and eyepiece micrometers. Of course, long telescopes were not easy to handle, and a contrivance to make them shorter was expected. Hooke proposed some ways for it. In February 1667, he talked of the possibility of folding the path of light by mirrors.[35] Hooke also proposed in *Philosophical Transactions* vol. 1, pp. 202–3 to fill the space between two lenses with water or oil to increase the focal length.

In this context, Newton's reflector was understood as an improvement of telescopes by contracting them when it appeared.[36] The response of the Royal Society to the reflector was not so philosophical, even though Newton stressed its theoretical advantage. And in seeking Royal support for the invention the Society saw a practical or strategic potential, but to realize this potential it had to be demonstrated that the principles and techniques could be extended to larger instruments.[37]

The telescope Newton sent to the Society was simply a prototype. Its observational ability remained at the level of a 3- or 4-foot refractor. Newton could see 'Jupiter distinctly round, and his Satellites, and Venus horned' with it.[38] But they had been observed already by Galileo more than 50 years before. As Huygens wrote to Oldenburg, bigger and practical reflectors must have been made.[39]

Reflectors had, however, two serious defects: weakness of the reflection by the mirror, and its tendency to tarnish. The transmission efficiency of the mirror Newton used was only about 20 per cent.[40] It should be noted that Hooke himself endeavoured to make a larger Newtonian reflector in 1672.[41] But a contemporary gave a pessimistic evaluation of it: John Collins wrote to James Gregory in December 1672 that the Newtonian telescope 'will not obtaine repute in the World, the mettall suddainly tarnishing'.[42] Thus the Newtonian reflector remained little more than a curiosity,[43] and had no importance in the seventeenth century.[44] In Hooke's time, it was reasonable to use refractors. Indeed, the refractor co-exists with the reflector, and they are used for different purposes.

Conclusion

In the seventeenth century, human beings created three important scientific instruments: the air pump, microscope and telescope. They opened a world that was not accessible without them. The air pump gave us the way to see phenomena in a vacuum. The microscope and telescope showed us a world that our naked eye could never see.

Scientific instruments became the decisive means for the development of science. They started to produce the object of scientific research. Advancement of science was now conditioned by instruments.

The author would like to point out the importance of seeing Hooke's commitment to three important instruments in the seventeenth century. He himself made a practical air pump for Boyle, with which Boyle achieved great discoveries. Hooke was almost the first natural philosopher who saw the micro-world with microscopes. It is well known that *Micrographia*, his representative work, made a strong impact, even on the general public. Air pumps and microscopes were for the advancement of natural philosophy. Then, why do we not put his optical instruments in the context of scientific research?

The author has shown in this paper that Hooke's optical instrumentation was not for its own sake, but was intended to improve astronomical observations. He used long telescopes to observe details of planets (surface markings, rings, and so on) and the moon (selenography). He advocated the use of telescopic sights and eyepiece micrometers, which soon became essential tools for professional astronomers. They applied these instruments to positional astronomy of fixed stars. Hooke criticized Newton's reflector because its observational ability did not supersede refractors, even if reflectors had theoretical advantage. We should not see Hooke's instruments and astronomical activities separately. They were united in history, and developed hand-in-hand.

PART 2
INSTRUMENTS FOR NATURAL PHILOSOPHY

Chapter 4

Instruments and Ingenuity

Jim Bennett

The centrality and ubiquity of instruments in Hooke's oeuvre are generally accepted, and in fact are characteristics of his work that have never been doubted. What may have changed in more recent times are the judgements drawn from that consensus. Where former commentators were inclined to see 'limitations' in Hooke's science through comparisons with the more abstract work of Newton, Hooke's concern for the particular and the material, alongside his appreciation of the diversity of the natural world, as well as his talent for devices of investigation and application, are now esteemed on their own terms. Materiality and manipulation are themes that characterize our view of Hooke and, although they are far from giving a complete picture of his work, the source of this characterization can readily be found in his own words. A single example illustrates also the youthful confidence of *Micrographia*: 'The truth is the Science of Nature has been already too long made only a work of the Brain and the Fancy: It is now high time that it should return to the plainness and soundness of Observations on material and obvious things.'[1] Although he often indulged in theoretical explanation and speculation, Hooke seeks to present himself as an innocent observer, a direct and intuitive thinker and a plain speaker. His 'true Philosophical Historian' will avoid, he cautions in a phrase that flouts his own advice, 'all kinds of Rhetorical Flourishes, or Oratorical Garnishes, and all sorts of Periphrases or Circumlocutions'.[2]

Instrumentation is central to Hooke's most complete and lasting contribution to the history of science, his *Micrographia* of 1665. All too often his work seems transient, fragmentary and incomplete, and his programme of endeavour fractured, interrupted and postponed, but in *Micrographia* that very inclination to move on to fresh subjects and new observations shapes a work presented as a series of individual inquiries held together by a single methodology and a common ambition.

The name 'Micrographia', coined for the first time in Hooke's title, was a happy choice but Hooke was good with words. The major influence on practical mathematics had been the 'Geographia' of

Ptolemy, with many editions published through the sixteenth century, a good number of which carried the alternative title 'Cosmographia'. 'Cosmographia' was also used by other mathematicians, for example in the popular work initiated by Peter Apian and carried on in revised editions by Gemma Frisius. The seventeenth century saw many inventive uses of the suffix 'graphia', such as 'Onomatographia' and 'Glossographia', all the way to the 'Historiopolitographia' of Raoul Boutrays. In the area of practical mathematics, we find 'Hydrographia' and 'Topographia' in use in surveying, 'Horologiographia' and 'Sciographia' in dialling, while John Greaves's 'Pyramidographia' would have been familiar to Hooke and his associates. In astronomy, some prominent linguistic inventions came from Hooke's antagonist in instrumentation, Johannes Hevelius, with his 'Selenographia' and 'Cometographia'.

Not only was *Micrographia* a demonstration of what could be achieved through the dedicated application of an instrument, it contains the first sustained attempt to provide an intellectual justification for the use of instruments – a general account of what they were, why they were needed and what they could do. Much had previously been written about mathematical instruments, a category with which Hooke is very familiar and one that he uses in his writing,[3] but that is not the subject he addresses in the preface to *Micrographia*, or in the later 'General Scheme', where he revisits the role of instrumentation. Mathematical instruments were not relevant to natural philosophy and Hooke does not deal with them here. In terms of his subject, there was little to say about them – they comprised a familiar category that had been around for centuries and presented no difficulties in appreciating their role or status. They were for tasks in practical mathematics, such as finding the time, measuring the latitude, performing a calculation, surveying an estate or drawing a map. They were not for making discoveries in nature or for regulating theories or explanations in natural philosophy. Not so the optical instruments – telescopes and microscopes – or the apparatus of experimental philosophy. If they were to claim legitimacy in yielding insights into the natural world, especially where virtue was placed in the plain and unaffected observation of 'material and obvious things', some account was needed of how they fitted into the programme.

Hooke's basic tenet was that mankind was fallen and his senses corrupted – they were both inadequate, so they needed to be augmented and assisted, and unreliable, so they needed regulating. Instruments were 'artificial organs' that went some way towards redressing the effects of man's disobedience in Eden and the subsequent erosion of his faculties through sin. Not only could degenerate sight be repaired, to some extent, but so could hearing, touch, taste and smell, also by artificial means. They could be regulated and disciplined as well as augmented, so that their judgements would be more reliable and consistent.

So to a charge that it must be inconsistent to privilege plain experience while advocating artificial instruments, Hooke's answer would be that his instruments are a means, albeit imperfect, of seeking to recover that natural view of the world God intended for man in his innocence in Eden. In that sense the view in a microscope or telescope is more natural than that of the naked eye, and listening through ear-trumpets ('otocousticons') brings us closer to our true selves.

Instruments, in a broader sense than direct aids to sense, were also useful to the reason in matters of natural philosophy. For Hooke the natural world operated by mechanical action, though the machines of nature could be tiny – well beyond unaided sight, and even beyond the current power of the microscope. A familiarity, however, with instruments, devices and machines in the everyday, macro world tuned and prepared the mind for constructing explanations of the unseen, micro world that lay behind all the phenomena of our experience.

There are many instances of Hooke using this idea in a very explicit way. This example comes, not from *Micrographia*, where there are many, but from 'General Scheme'. Hooke says that two things – mathematics and mechanics – 'most assist the Mind in making, examining, and ratiocinating from Experiments'.[4] Mathematics provides a model for careful reasoning, while mechanics, according to Hooke,

> do bring the Mind more closely to the Business it designs, and shews it a Pattern of Demonstration, in Physical Operations, manifests the possible Ways, how Powers may act in the moving resisting Bodies: Gives a Scheme of the Laws and Rules of Motion, and as it were enters the Mind into a Method of accurate and demonstrative Inquiry and Examination of Physical Operations. For though the Operations of Nature are more secret and abstruse; and hid from our discerning, or discovering them, than those more gross and obvious ones of Engines, yet it seems most probable, by the Effects and Circumstances, that most of them may be as capable of Demonstration and Reduction to a certain Rule, as the Operations of Mechanicks or Art.[5]

This is one of a number of clear, careful and explicit statements in Hooke's writings of the direct engagement between mechanical demonstrations and theorising, and between practical mathematics and natural philosophy, all based on mechanical assumptions about the natural world.

Already, in Hooke's account of instrumentation and its significance, we have seen a strong moral dimension. The agenda for Hooke's programme of experimental philosophy, with its central employment of instruments, included recovery from the effects of the Fall and the achievement of an innocent, trustworthy, uncompromised view of nature. The outcomes of applying this steady and reliable vision to investigating the world would be both moral and spiritual, as he explained in *Micrographia*:

> all the fine dreams of Opinions, and universal metaphysical natures, which the luxury of subtil Brains has devis'd, would quickly vanish, and give place to solid Histories, Experiments and Works. And as at first, mankind fell by tasting of the forbidden Tree of Knowledge, so we, their Posterity, may be in part restor'd by the same way, not only by beholding and contemplating, but by tasting too those fruits of Natural knowledge, that were never yet forbidden.[6]

I hope we can take it as well established, so as not to spend time going over well-trodden ground, that instruments appear throughout Hooke's work, that – broadly understood to include mechanical devices as well as measuring instruments – they were central to his thinking as well as to his experimental and professional practice. We might even agree that he was the most committed advocate and designer of instruments across the broadest range of activity up to his time. What we might do instead is to look more closely at this moral dimension to instrumentation for Hooke, by examining what he and his colleagues meant by 'ingenuity', a term they use frequently in relation to instruments as well as to mechanical devices more generally, and something that clearly was seen as a virtue in the worlds of practical mathematics or mechanics and of the experimental mechanical philosophy. Indeed promoting the ingenious was central to Hooke's understanding of the mission of the Royal Society. He told Oldenburg in May 1665, the year of the publication of *Micrographia*, that publications given the Society's imprimatur '… aim chiefly at this, that ingenious conceptions, and important philosophical matters of Fact may be communicated to the learned and enquiring World'.[7] The career of instruments was dependent on ingenuity: the advance of the two principal examples of artificial organs, the telescope and the microscope, would result from 'the Industry of some of the many Ingenious Men, that are now imploy'd about it'.[8]

One of the best-known attributions of an ingenious achievement to Hooke comes from Samuel Pepys, who bought a copy of *Micrographia* in 1665 and recorded in his Diary: 'Before I went to bed, I sat up till 2 a-clock in my chamber, reading of Mr. Hooke's Microscopicall Observacions, the most ingenious book that ever I read in my life'.[9] Even before publication, work of this kind was identified with ingenuity, when Henry Power wrote in his own book on microscopy, his *Experimental Philosophy* of 1664, 'you may expect shortly from Dr. Wren and Master Hooke, two Ingenious Members of the Royal Society at Gresham, the Cuts and Pictures drawn at large, and to the very life of these and other Microscopical Representations'.[10] Hooke returned the compliment by referring to 'the Ingenious Dr. Power' in the Preface to *Micrographia.*[11]

The adjective 'ingenious' could be used to qualify things or people – there were ingenious devices and ingenious inventors who designed them. Hooke did not restrict its attribution either to relatively humble practitioners such as makers or navigators, or to natural philosophers of note and reputation. In the latter category would be William Gilbert, held in the highest regard by English experimental philosophers of the seventeenth century, whose account of the earth's magnetism was 'very ingenious, and seem'd very rational'.[12] But Hooke also referred to a possible method for longitude by Jupiter's satellites being used by 'a skillful Navigator, or any other ingenious Person',[13] and to his hope that the imperfections in maps and charts would be amended by 'the Industry of ingenious and skillful Artists'.[14] If we think of named contemporaries whom he judged ingenious or capable of ingenuity, they included Christopher Wren[15] and the Savilian Professor of Geometry, John Wallis, whose method for demonstrating the proper 'diagonal' division of a quadrant was 'very ingenious and accurate',[16] but also the clockmaker Thomas Tompion, the inventor Denis Papin and the mechanical entrepreneur Samuel Morland. The person most frequently described as ingenious in *Micrographia* is Descartes.[17]

Tompion and his fellow mechanics are acknowledged when Hooke is describing his alternative to the diagonal division of a quadrant, where a micrometer screw works in a rack along the limb of the instrument. We can return to this quadrant as an exemplar of Hooke's ingenuity. He says that with the help of the figures he provides, making the instrument

> ... will be easie enough to any ingenious Workman; but if any person desire one of them to be made, without troubling himself to direct and oversee a Workman, he may imploy Mr. Tompion, a Watchmaker in Water-Lane near Fleetstreet; this person I recommend, as having imploy'd him to make that which I have, whereby he hath seen and experienced the Difficulties that do occur therein, and finding him to be very careful

and curious to observe and follow Directions, and to compleat and perfect his Work, so as to make it accurate and fit for use.[18]

Tompion appears again in Hooke's unpublished account of what he calls 'Aerostatick Instruments'[19] – instruments, in other words, for that most ridiculed activity in Restoration experimental philosophy, the weighing of air – 'the experimentall searchers after it reproached', as Hooke says, 'with the most Insidious calumnys and Satiricall obloquys'. On the contrary, for Hooke, far from being 'a fruitless and trifling Labour' the study of the atmosphere was very useful and essential to well-being. He has a number of methods of making the variation in barometric height more visible, one of which

> … was tryed at Mr.Thomas Tompions, A person deservedly famous for his excellent Skill in making watches and Clocks, and not Less Curious and dexterous in the constructing and handwork of other nice mechanick Instruments. And it Remained in his workroom near a twelve month till a person [inserted by Hooke, 'Sr Sam. Morland'] well pleased it seems wth the contrivance removed some parts of it to make some further and better improvement vpon that principle which was done by meanes of a beam with a counterpoise instead of the wheel wch. I had made vse of, And varying it also by making the Reciepient to Rise and fall instead of the tube, which was very ingenious and in some cases might be more convenient then the way I had made vse of.

Morland had a more general reputation for ingenuity. Described as 'an ingenious mechanist' as early as 1653,[20] he was eventually given the title 'Master of Mechanicks' by Charles II. His inventions included calculators, the 'signpost' barometer and a speaking trumpet, and he marketed a range of pumps for raising water. One pump was designed as a 'gunpowder engine', a form of internal combustion engine. Papin followed Hooke as Curator of Experiments to the Royal Society and made important contributions to the development of the air-pump, as well as being skilled in hydraulics, and it was in that context that Hooke described him as 'ingenious'.[21] One of his inventions that became well known at the time was his 'steam digester' – a kind of pressure cooker that could soften bones.

What did Hooke and his associates mean by 'ingenuity'? It included, of course, cleverness, originality and dexterity, but it carried other content as well. Through its connection to the adjective 'ingenious', ingenuity could refer to intellectual capacity, talent or 'genius', including a capacity for invention or construction. But through its connection to the adjective 'ingenuous', it could refer to honesty, openness, candour or sincerity. In the seventeenth century, not only could ingenuity refer to sincerity and trustworthiness, 'disingenuity' was used for the opposing vice of deceitfulness or guile.

The two senses of ingenuity could be mingled. A shared attitude in this circle of mechanical philosophy held that a truly ingenious device was not just clever or effective; its design should be clear and evident, and should avoid ostentation and unnecessary show. Elegance, clarity and intelligibility were all part of ingenuity. The concept was thus a vehicle for incorporating a certain morality and a particular aesthetic into mechanics and in turn into natural philosophy.

The confusion or mingling of meanings could even extend to the adjective 'ingenious'. Hooke used 'ingenuous' in the standard sense at least once in a text about instruments (see below) but at one point in the preface to *Micrographia* he says he is confident that 'any ingenious Reader' will understand that his seemingly exaggerated praise of John Wilkins is sincerely meant.[22] From the context, the meaning is clearly closer to sincere, open and sensitive than to clever and inventive.

Both Hooke and Wren had a series of inventions and devices that would be described as ingenious in our usual sense – self-acting and recording weather clocks, self-regulating furnaces, constant oil lamps, and so on – and in a letter, probably dating from the mid-1650s, written to accompany an explanation of his double-writing instrument, Wren, while not actually using the term ingenuity here, presents the aesthetic of mechanical invention as follows:

> the misapprehending World measures the Excellence of things by their Rarity, or Difficulty of Framing, not by the Concinnity and apt Disposal of Parts to attain their End by a right Line as it were & the Simplest way. Any New Invention in Mechanicks perform'd by an Operose way of divers unessential though well compacted Parts, shall be admired together with the Artist, meerly for the Variety of the Motions and the Difficulty of Performance; comes a more judicious Hand and with a far smaller number of Peeces, & those perhaps of more trivial Materials, but compos'd with more Brain & less ostentation, frames the same thing in a little Volume, & such a one I shall call a Master.[23]

I want to use two letters from Wren as points of departure for considering the parallel attitudes of Hooke, his friend and close working associate. The letter I have just cited relates to mechanics and the aesthetic it espouses was also embraced by Hooke. An example of this is the approach he takes in his most confident and outspoken treatise on instrumentation, the *Animadversions On the first part of the Machina Cœlestis of … Johannes Hevelius*, deriving from a lecture given at Gresham College in December 1673 and published the following year. It was an uncompromising critique of the astronomical instruments Hevelius had described in his *Machina Coelestis* of 1673, assaulted by Hooke on a number of individual grounds but generally on account of Hevelius's refusal to apply telescopic sights to his instruments for angular measurement. Hooke maintained that Tycho Brahe had, a century previously, already arrived at a fundamental limit to the accuracy of plain or open-sighted instruments, namely the resolving power of the human eye, and that further improvement would not be possible without assisting the eye with telescopic sights. Hooke refers again to the notion of human decay when he says that 'I judged that whatever mens eyes were in the younger age of the World, ours in this old age of it needed spectacles'.[24]

For all the enormous dedication, effort and expense Hevelius has lavished on his programme of building instruments and making observations, his refusal to recognize and adopt the fundamental advance of the telescopic sight seems to Hooke a perverse and stubborn denial of the evident and inevitable. This denial has diverted Hevelius into a pointless attempt to 'improve' the mechanics and the management of his instruments, thus rendering them more complex and cumbersome, when an advance of principle would have brought an immediate step-improvement in their performance.

Hevelius's work is *not* ingenious, it is 'great and laborious',[25] he has been 'exceedingly circumspect' and 'industrious',[26] and he is commended for his 'care, labour, and diligence'[27] or for his 'infinite tedium, trouble, labour and cost'.[28] His instruments are 'machinations and contrivances',[29] creating 'trouble', 'clutter',[30] and 'all the other cumber'.[31] The theme is carried throughout *Animadversions*, while at the same time the alternative arrangements proposed by Hooke are offered as being plain, straightforward, inexpensive and easy to use.

We have noted already the ingenuity of Wallis in demonstrating the geometrically accurate method of diagonal division of an arc scale. However when Hevelius subdivides the scale on a quadrant by 'diagonals' that are not straight, as Tycho had done, but curved to account for the decreasing radii of the concentric circles that make up the longitudinal lines of the transversal scale, he is 'industrious and careful',[32] and shows 'extraordinary labour and curiosity' and 'infinite trouble and pains'.[33] One alternative Hooke proposes, using a moveable glass template 'the Division of one Degree serving for the whole ninety', would be 'much more certain, exact and plain'.[34] Another, where a supplementary arc carried by the index arm is used for the subdivision of the main arc, is 'altogether as easie, and as Geometrically true … thereby to shew very minute Divisions, very easily and very plainly'.[35] Hevelius does have another method of subdivision and it is 'exceedingly ingenious',[36] but it was not his invention. Hevelius ascribes the technique to Benedictus Hedreus, but Hooke says that Hedreus 'was not so ingenuous as to confess that he received this invention from another' and Hooke traces the invention to an obscure tract by a certain Pierre Vernier.

Enhanced accuracy is combined with reduced complexity, trouble, inconvenience and cost when the inventor follows the path of ingenuity. Hooke finds Hevelius's sextant 'very great and chargeable', compared with his own 'single, plain way without any trouble or perplexity'.[37] Hooke's proposal for making a catalogue of the stars by a mural semicircle '... will be nearly 30 times more accurate, the charge not a quarter, and the labour not near a tenth part so much as in other wayes made use of by Ticho and Hevelius'.[38]

Hooke's design for an equatorial quadrant was an astonishing ensemble of mechanical ingenuity. Nothing of the kind had ever been designed or built. It was driven by a conical pendulum clock, had Hooke's micrometer screw subdivision of the scale, could be used by a single observer by the superimposition of the target images in two telescopic sights, and by diverting the drive through Hooke's universal joint the quadrant could be set in a vertical plane and follow the sky in azimuth. This arrangement whereby 'a small Automaton' relieved the observer of the tedium of keeping the instrument up with the motion of the sky contrasts with Hevelius's method of adjusting a quadrant to the heavens, which required 'his most extraordinary and indefatigable care, pains and industry'.[39]

The second letter I want to cite from Wren carries the proper aesthetic of mechanics into natural philosophy, by way of the assumption of a mechanical nature. In July 1663, responding to the Royal Society's anxiety over preparing an entertainment for an anticipated visit from the king, Wren is troubled by the impossibility of finding a 'contrivance' that would match an almost impossible set of conditions: it should be 'luciferous in philosophy', its 'use and advantage' should be 'obvious without a lecture', it should 'surprise with some unexpected effect' and it should be commendable for its 'ingenuity'. The values of the court seemed incompatible with the virtues of experimental mechanical philosophy:

Experiments for the establishment of natural philosophy are seldom pompous. It is upon billiards and tennis-balls, upon the purling of sticks and tops, upon a vial of water, or a wedge of glass, that the great Des Cartes hath built the most refined accurate theories, that human wit ever reached to; and certainly nature, in the best of her works, is apparent enough by obvious things, were they but curiously observed. The key, that opens treasures is often plain and rusty; but unless it be gilt, the key alone will make no shew at court.[40]

The same morality was adopted by Hooke: nature was evident in the plain and the obvious, and insight came from artless, ingenuous, innocent apprehension. In the preface to *Micrographia* he says that for the reformation of natural philosophy

> ... there is not so much requir'd towards it, any strength of Imagination, or exactness of Method, or depth of Contemplation ... as a sincere Hand, and a faithful Eye, to examine, and to record, the things themselves as they appear.[41]

and he presents himself as '... a man so qualified ... only with resolution, and integrity, and plain intentions of imploying his Senses aright'.[42]

Establishing an opposition between the virtues of true ingenuity on the one hand and the values of the court and the vagaries of fashion and popular esteem on the other was a useful resource for Hooke and others in dealing with difficulties they met with in promoting their experimental philosophy. A morality that was distinct from the transience of popular opinion was a valuable bulwark against ridicule. William Petty, for example, was recognized in mechanics and experimental philosophy for his ingenuity, his inventions including a double-writing instrument, a seed-planting engine and his famous 'double-bottomed ship' or catamaran. Completed versions of his ship were named 'Invention', 'Invention II' and 'Experiment'. However Pepys records Petty being ridiculed at court:

> Thence to White-hall, where in the Dukes chamber the King came and stayed an hour or two, laughing at Sir W. Petty who was there about his boat ... Gresham College he mightily laughed at for spending time only in weighing of ayre, and doing nothing else since they sat.[43]

The ridicule extended to his double-bottomed ship, a design supported by Pepys: 'I believe that he was abused the other day, as he is now, by tongues that I am sure speak before they know anything good or bad of her [the ship]. I am sorry to find his ingenuity discouraged so'.[44]

Hooke, however, was the chief target of what Wren called 'the misapprehending World'. He was mercilessly lampooned in Thomas Shadwell's *Virtuoso*, written by an author who was very well informed on the doings of Hooke, Petty and the Royal Society in general. Hooke was hurt, as we know, immediately and directly when he went to see a performance of Shadwell's play, and there is plenty of evidence of his sensibility in his published work. When writing about discovering the internal motions of plants and animals by the sounds they make, he breaks off by saying that 'I could proceed further, but methinks I can hardly forbear to blush, when I consider how the most part of Men will look upon this'.[45] In his 'General Scheme' Hooke advises that

> Those things which others count Childish and Foolish, he may find Reasons to think them worthy his most attentive, grave and serious Thoughts; and those things which some are pleased to call Swingswangs to please Children, have been found to discover Irregularities even in the Motion of the Sun it self.[46]

It was perhaps mindful of the ridicule he had received for his apparent obsessions with fleas and lice that he asserted that the true philosophical historian 'may perhaps see Cause to account those the most precious and rich, which are generally esteem'd the most vile and sordid'.

An instrument of which he was particularly fond, the hygroscope, came to his mind as an example of a profound outcome from a commonplace circumstance: if 'swingswangs' can discover the motion of the sun, '... from the turning of a Straw, [the philosophical historian] is able to foresee a Change in the great Ocean of the Air'. This straw was the beard of a wild oat, subject to microscopical examination in *Micrographia*, where its extreme sensitivity to moisture is harnessed to the design of an instrument for measuring the humidity of the atmosphere.[47] Here Hooke also sees a clue to the nature of muscular action, whereby a large force is occasioned by a tiny stimulus, and his everyday, unregarded straw is celebrated as 'the very footstep of Sensation, and Animate motion'. So the severe aesthetic that governed a proper approach to inventive mechanics was relevant also to the natural world. Here nature had used a 'contrivance' that was 'the most plain, simple, and obvious', for nature – and nature's Creator – was always ingenious.

The link between the mechanical and the natural is of the utmost importance to Hooke and it is here that we see the value of the work done by the notion of 'ingenuity'. We might say that the virtue of ingenuity performed a role in Hooke's practical mechanics that was equivalent to that played by the virtues of clearness and distinctness in the philosophy of Descartes. Just as clearness and distinctness secured a link with the natural world, guaranteed by God, so ingenuity could secure a link to a natural philosophy that was itself mechanical in the sense employed by Hooke, that is, inspired and informed by a knowledge of gross or macro mechanical action. If the practice of experimental philosophy was to deliver insights into the contrivances designed by the Creator, and to offer fallen man some recovery of the original innocence and knowledge of mankind, the moral dimension we have noted in the concept of ingenuity – linking the ingenious with the ingenuous – was completely appropriate. Both nature and man were ingenious in Eden and, if we are to return to that primitive and profound apprehension of the natural world, we must espouse and practice ingenuity in all its meanings – intellectual, manipulative, aesthetic and moral.

Hooke begins *Micrographia* with a contrast between the imperfect productions of art and the perfect ingenuity of nature, however far it is challenged by the probing vision of microscopy. The point of a needle, a dot on a page of print and the edge of a razor blade quickly reveal their absurd imperfections, whereas the eye of even so sordid a creature as a fly is a contrivance of the greatest exactness and precision. The microscope reveals 'the rudeness and bungling of Art … whereas in the works of Nature, the deepest Discoveries shew us the greatest Excellencies'.[48] Hooke's account 'Of the Water-Insect or Gnat' leads him on to musing on 'the goodness and providence of the infinitely wise Creator in his most excellent contrivances and dispensations' and to cautioning his readers that however natural it may seem to attribute purposefulness to a complex machine or to a living creature, '… there is nothing of intention or ratiocination to be ascrib'd either to the Animal or Engine, but all to the ingeniousness of the contriver'.[49]

Chapter 5

Hooke's Design for a Driven Equatorial Mounting

Allan Mills, John Hennessy and Stephen Watson

In his second Cutlerian lecture, Robert Hooke critically discussed the newly published *Machina Cœlestis* of Johannes Hevelius.[1] When preparing this material for the press he took the opportunity of including illustrations of some astronomical instruments of his own devising.[2] One of these was a quadrant mounted equatorially so as automatically to follow a chosen star as it moved across the celestial sphere. There is no evidence that Hooke ever made a practical version of this paper invention. Instruments mounted in this way and driven by a waterwheel were known in thirteenth-century China,[3] but there is no reason to think reports of them had reached Europe, even though Tycho Brahe did make use of certain instruments rotatable manually on an equatorial frame.[4]

Hooke's well-known design is shown in Figure 5.1, isolated for clarity from a very cluttered original plate. We see a stoutly-braced quadrant, doubtless to be equipped with his recommended telescopic sights,[5] mounted on a shaft set parallel to the Earth's spin axis. At its upper end, this polar axis carries a second shaft at right angles to itself. This declination axis permits, by its initial rotation and clamping, prior setting of the instrument platform to a given declination. Balance is achieved with an adjustable counterweight. The great advantage of this arrangement is that rotation of the polar axis alone, once per sidereal day, is sufficient to keep a chosen star in view for a long period of time. The whole assembly is analogous to the popular 'German' equatorial mounting for an astronomical telescope.[6]

The Conical Pendulum Regulator

Hooke has conceived a clockwork drive to turn the polar axis, but has realized that a conventional oscillating pendulum would result in a visibly jerky motion in an eyepiece of moderate magnification. He

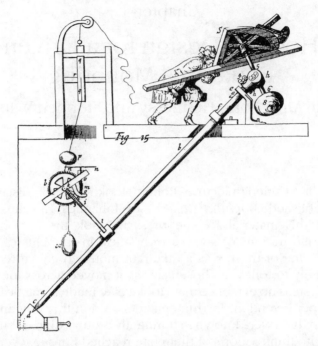

Figure 5.1   Hooke's design for a weight-driven equatorial mounting.

therefore proposed a conical pendulum rotating in a constant direction. This form of pendulum intrigued Hooke for a number of years,[7] as it did Huygens in the same period.[8]

The diagram given in Figure 5.2 represents a conical pendulum. Using the symbols given there, it may be shown[9] that its rotational period T is given by the expression

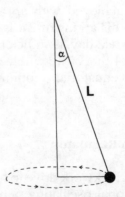

Figure 5.2   The conical pendulum.

$$T = 2\pi \sqrt{\frac{L \cos \alpha}{g}}$$

from which it can be seen that:

a   the period is equivalent to that of a simple pendulum of length equal to the vertical distance of the bob below the point of support; and

b   a simple conical pendulum with a given length will not exhibit a constant period of rotation unless its angle of inclination α remains constant.

Hooke appears to have known that in order to circumvent (b), the centre of gravity of the bob would have to be guided in such a way that it rose or fell upon an imaginary parabolic path, and he even seems to have devised moving templates to be fixed at the apex of the cone to induce such a motion.[10] They would have been analogous to Huygens's cycloidal cheeks for the simple pendulum. These refinements were not formally published or applied in Hooke's time. In his drawing (Figure 5.1) we see only a simple friction clamp clasping the pendulum cord so that the observer could shorten (but not lengthen) the suspension.

Negative Feedback

The centrifugal governors pioneered by James Watt to control the speed of steam and other rotary engines are quite well known, but they are not simple conical pendulums.[11] For one thing they usually spin so fast that the downward force due to gravity becomes negligible by comparison with the radial centrifugal forces. Powerful springs may therefore be used to oppose the latter, giving the advantage that the governors may be used in any orientation. Second, they always incorporate some form of strong negative feedback (such as linkage to a throttle valve in the steam supply) to control the final position taken up by the spinning weights. A clear example is provided by the classic wind-up gramophone motor (Figure 5.3). It has both linear springs and an oil-soaked felt pad that may be set to positively limit the axial sliding motion of a brake disc linked to the rotating weights.

In Hooke's design the bob of the conical pendulum will be accelerated upon increasingly steep paths into orbits of greater radius

Figure 5.3 The 'Garrard' wind-up gramophone motor.

and vertical height above the rest position, being opposed by both air resistance and the natural periodicity of the conical pendulum. The energy required must be supplied by the driving weight and (as in any clock) the mechanical advantage of the intermediate gears means that a comparatively small force will hold back a heavy weight. The energy required to overcome air resistance varies as the square of the velocity, but that required to keep the pendulum moving is a minimum at resonance. A heavy bob will exert greater control. (Hooke does show an oversize bob in his drawing.) An uneasy balance between the pendulum and driving weights is therefore possible, but feedback is weak and true isochronism non-existent. Regulation will therefore be poor. Clocks with conical pendulums do exist,[12] but are collected more for their novelty and decorative value than their timekeeping ability.

The Mechanical Drive

It is the mechanism sketched beneath the floor in Figure 5.1 that has attracted most comment, for when reproduced alone its mode of operation is far from clear. However, elsewhere in Hooke's original plate is the assembly reproduced here as Figure 5.4. He visualizes a sector of a large worm wheel fixed to the polar axis, rotation of a meshing worm then resulting in motion at the sidereal rate. Power to do this is supplied by a heavy weight hanging by a cord from a co-axial drum. The regulating escapement is conceived as another worm wheel driving – at a much-increased speed – a worm bearing a horizontal fork, this last being engaged by a peg protruding below the bob of the conical pendulum described above. The idea is that the fork drives the conical pendulum whilst the latter controls the descent of the weight – just like a conventional pendulum and anchor escapement.

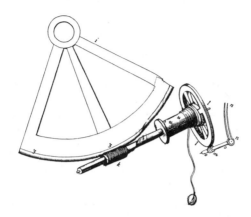

Figure 5.4   Hooke's design of weight-drive and governor.

Can a Wheel Drive a Worm?

This question is the nub of the usual objection to Hooke's proposal, for it is common knowledge that a worm driving a wheel can have a very large reduction ratio, enabling formidable weights to be raised by a simple manual hoist of the type shown in Figure 5.5.

This winch is intrinsically safe since it will not spontaneously run backwards ('overhaul') with the wheel driving the worm. Even if the

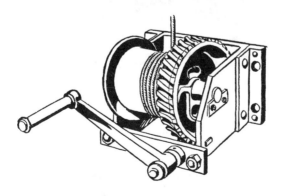

Figure 5.5   A simple worm gear hoist.

operator releases the handle entirely, the load will not descend. In fact it cannot even be pulled down, no matter what extra tension is applied to the cable: it must be wound down by turning the handle in the opposite direction. The belief has therefore grown up that a worm can slowly turn a matching wheel, but the wheel cannot turn (at a higher speed) the mating worm. A few apparently anomalous exceptions to this general rule do exist. Three examples follow.

The Turnspit or 'Jack'

Unlike most of us today, Hooke would have seen examples of the type of weight-driven mechanical turnspit (Figure 5.6) illustrated by Joseph Moxon in his *Mechanick Exercises*.[13] Chosen as an early exercise for apprentice blacksmiths, this machine includes a wheel driving a coarse worm at a ratio of about 1:32. Both wheel and worm were to be made by forging and hand filling. The extended spindle of the worm carries a two-vane 'fly', the air resistance of which balances the driving force when the rotational speed reaches a fairly constant value. So Hooke would have known that, under certain conditions, a wheel *can* drive a mating worm at a higher speed.

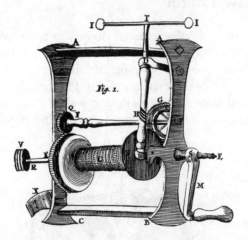

Figure 5.6   The turnspit or 'jack' illustrated by Joseph Moxon in 1678.

The Swiss Musical Box Movement

This very successful design (Figure 5.7) has been in mass production for generations, and is still available at a low price. It currently incorporates a 1:20 step-up gear consisting of a moulded nylon wheel driving a single start worm of highly polished steel. A 'fly' of fixed shape and area mounted on its axis tends to assume a certain speed, just as in the turnspit mechanism.

Figure 5.7 A modern musical-box movement.

The Wind-up Gramophone Motor

The 'Garrard' coiled spring motor (Figure 5.3) that has already been mentioned employed a wheel driving a worm to obtain a 1:18 step-up in speed to its centrifugal governor.

Efficiency of Gears

An explanation of these apparent anomalies is given by the theory of machines. It may be shown that for any machine to 'overhaul' its efficiency must be greater than 50%.[14] Experiments gave the following efficiencies for different gear systems:[15]

Table 5.1   Efficiencies of various gear systems found by experiments

Type	Efficiency (%)
Spur gear 2.25:1 nylon	88–90
Spur gear 3:1 brass	65–91
Worm Gear 57:1	12–16
Worm gear 100:1	2–8

The spur gear systems would (as expected) run in either direction, but the worm gears (like the winch) would not permit the wheel to drive the worm. This is in accord with the 50% efficiency criterion.

Worm Gears of Enhanced Efficiency: The 45° Helix Angle

The 'reversed' worm gears in the musical box and gramophone motor were unsuited to experimental measurement of their efficiency, but did suggest that a worm drive with an efficiency greater than 50% would embody a worm with a coarse thread. This criterion is more precisely stated by the helix (or 'lead-in') angle, which is defined as the instantaneous angle between the crest of a thread and the normal to the axis of the screw. It depends on both pitch and diameter. It can be seen intuitively that ordinary threads, with close pitches and shallow helix angles, will strongly resist being forced to turn by an axial thrust. The standard nut-and-bolt fastening depends on this. In the worm gear we have two shafts at right angles to each other, so one might guess that a helix angle of 45° would be optimal for the combination. Reference works confirm this.[16] Moxon's turnspit mechanism would at best have had smooth (but initially unpolished) mating surfaces on the iron worm and wheel, suggesting that helix angle is a more important parameter than coefficient of friction. It will be noted that the overall ratio of the gear will also depend on the diameter of the matching worm wheel. Compact step-up worm gears will tend to be of low ratio.

A Practical Demonstration

The short helices on the governor shafts of the music box and gramophone motor appear to have been produced on special machines dedicated to this application. The modern computer-controlled general purpose lathe available to us could not generate a screw of coarser lead (the distance a nut advances in one revolution) than 16 mm. A 4-start thread was cut on a shaft 11.5 mm in diameter, giving a helix angle of 54.3° and a pitch (crest-to-crest) of 4 mm.[17] A 30° threading tool was employed. A mating wheel with 120 teeth at 4 mm pitch was produced on a milling machine fitted with a dividing head. The resulting worm gear is shown in Figure 5.8. It has the following characteristics: a brass wheel of 153 mm outside diameter, 6 mm wide with 120 teeth of 4 mm pitch; and a steel worm of 11.5 mm outside diameter with a 4-start thread of 4 mm pitch and 16 mm lead. The helix angle is 54.3° and the ratio is 30:1. A ball-type thrust bearing was fitted to take the axial load.

Figure 5.8 A 'reversible' worm-and-wheel gear.

It proved possible to turn the assembly by hand in either direction, with the worm driving the wheel or, as a step-up gear, with the wheel driving the worm. The efficiency of the combination was measured by securing grooved pulleys of known diameter to the shafts, hanging a known load from a cord wrapped around the 'wheel' pulley, and then finding the torque on the worm required to make the load rise at a slow and uniform rate. The results are presented as the solid line in Figure 5.9. It will be seen that, except at the lower and higher loads, the efficiency of this less-than-ideal design was above 50%. The worm gear is close to the limit for reversibility.

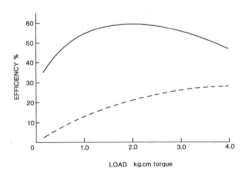

Figure 5.9 Efficiency versus load of the worm gear illustrated in Figure 5.8.

A narrow strip of soft leather looped over the worm shaft and lightly loaded increased the friction sufficiently to prevent the wheel being turned by hand to drive the worm. The permanent braking torque of

0.3 kg cm introduced by the leather band gave rise to the dashed curve in Figure 5.9, which lies below the 50% efficiency level.

A Partial Construction of Hooke's Drive

The 'reversible' worm-and-wheel shown in Figure 5.8 was fitted with a 15 cm long counterbalanced fork on the vertical worm shaft, and then arranged to engage a rod protruding below the bob of a conical pendulum (Figure 5.10). The suspension cord of the latter could be adjusted to maintain a length of 100 cm between a point of suspension vertically above the centre of the worm shaft and the centre of gravity of the bob. The latter was made of discs of steel threaded upon a rod, so that its mass could be varied. A fishing line swivel in the cord minimized spinning. A drum secured to the wheel shaft held a fine cord terminated by stackable weights going up to 500 g, a ratchet and detachable handle facilitating manual rewinding.

Figure 5.10   A partial reconstruction of Hooke's design for a drive mechanism.

The length of the suspension cord was adjusted to give a conical pendulum of length 100 cm after stretching. With an orbital radius of 10 cm this resulted in a nominal orbital period of 2 seconds, so that the wheel of the 1:30 worm gear should make one turn every minute. It was found that the lighter the driving weight the smaller the mass of the pendulum required to control its descent, but the heavier pendulums associated with greater driving weights gave better control. Specifically, a heavy pendulum of weight 2.7 kg held the rotation period of the large wheel at 1^m 0^s ± 1^s when the driving weight was increased from 360 to 440 g (10%).

An adjustable friction brake was fitted to the shaft carrying the wheel to allow simulation of the extra load entailed by a coupled telescope and gearing. Setting this brake enabled 1 kg and 2 kg driving weights to be utilized and controlled, so that the worm wheel continued to make one turn per minute. The excess energy appeared as heat in the brake drum.

Clock-driven Telescopes

Hooke's vision of an equatorially mounted astronomical telescope driven at the sidereal rate via a large worm gear became reality in the nineteenth century, with the development of reflectors and refractors so large as to necessitate the involvement of engineers as well as astronomers and opticians. They were familiar with the Watt governor for steam engines, and realized it could be refined to give close control of a weight-driven gravity drive by the addition of a device that provided a resistance increasing very rapidly once a set speed was exceeded. The principle is clearly demonstrated by the oiled felt pad in the constant speed gramophone motor illustrated in Figure 5.3. Some energy was of course wasted and appeared as heat in the retarding device. This was acceptable, particularly when electric motors either wound-up or entirely replaced the heavy driving weight. Important contributions to the development of 'clock drives' of this nature were made in the nineteenth and twentieth centuries,[18] but none of these acknowledges Hooke's work.

The centrifugal governor designed by Young is shown diagrammatically in Figure 5.11.[19] Besides the friction brake, it incorporated an ingenious linkage that transferred the pivot of each lever arm to a point outside the rotation axis, the relative lengths of the links being so designed that (over a short range) the weights moved along a surface of revolution that approximated the paraboloid required for isochronism.[20] More sophisticated versions permitted adjustment of the set speed by the observer whilst the drive was running – just as Hooke had proposed.

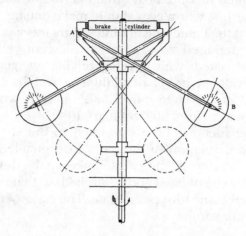

Figure 5.11 Simplified diagram of a nineteenth-century centrifugal governor for large weight-driven astronomical telescopes.

Conclusion

Robert Hooke foresaw all the requirements of the classic clock-driven equatorial mounting for astronomical telescopes in 1679, but two centuries had to pass before the technology existed to put his ideas into practice.

Chapter 6

Assessment of the Scientific Value of Hooke's Work

S. H. Joseph

Varied Opinions

The reputation of Robert Hooke has come a long way since its revival started 50 years ago. According to one writer, 'It needs to be said that the numerous discoveries of Hooke form the basis of modern science'[1] and according to another, 'It is impossible for the unbiased historian to say whether Newton or Hooke made the more significant contribution'.[2] Elsewhere, claims are made for Hooke's achievement that exceed even the most favourable interpretation of the evidence.[3] Mixed views of Hooke survive, though, for example: '*Micrographia* ... presented not a systematic investigation of any one question, but a banquet of observations ...'[4] versus '*Micrographia* ... amply demonstrates how brilliantly eclectic, yet how tightly controlled, a series of physical investigations can be'.[5]

Hooke's work was great in quantity and scope, ranging over many technical and scientific areas, and laying down sound bases for what were to be lasting fields of investigation. The breadth of his work, as well as his inventiveness and his instruments, are regarded as second to none.[6] These very qualities, however, may have been an impediment to Hooke achieving the highest scientific reputation, for which depth, focus and theoretical rigour are supposed to be required.[7] These requirements are essentially technical, so we will look at the technical assessment of Hooke's work, to see if they have been met.

Considerable progress has been made in the technical analysis of Hooke's celestial mechanics.[8] This has demonstrated the key role that Hooke played in the origination of modern dynamics by framing the concepts, the problem and the programme for its solution. Hooke's work on the spring oscillator has also received assessment. The advanced status of his work has been pointed out: his use of the relation between the square of the velocity and the area under the force-displacement curve is the integral form of the second law of motion.[9] His deduction of the invariance of period with amplitude is sound, but his expression for the dependence of time on displacement is not. Another commentary on the work[10] fixes on this error and concludes that the entire work was invalid. But, as Pugliese has pointed out,[11] this was not Hooke's only work on harmonic oscillation: his earlier extensive work on pendulums included the identification of a circular pendulum with two perpendicular linear ones,[12] and he later employed the modern view of harmonic oscillation as a projection of motion around a circle, and stated correctly that time was distance around the arc.[13] The variety of opinion in this case may simply arise from the selection of evidence by the various commentators.

There is, however, another possible cause for differences of opinion on the work of Hooke. This can best be demonstrated by reference to an example: the commentary on 'On Spring' by Moyer.[14] Moyer points out that Hooke's presentation confuses his proportional law of spring with the inverse relation between pressure and volume that is reported for air. He concludes, from this evident lack of basic rigour, that 'Hooke – unlike his contemporary Newton – apparently only had a limited allegiance to the dictates of equation and number'. Let us examine the problem that Moyer describes in more detail.

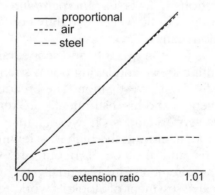

Figure 6.1　Comparison of the proportional law with the extension of air and of steel.

Figure 6.1 illustrates a graph of load versus extension for an ideal cylinder of air, together with the linear relation. The reciprocal relation is approximately proportional for small extensions; this, as Moyer explains, can be quantified using the expansion later developed by Taylor. We should recall that even to depict the problem in the style of

Figure 6.1 requires the concept of general functional dependence, pioneered by Leibniz. Hooke is thus unable to produce a rigorous explanation of the situation. He might in this circumstance have decided to omit reference to air as a spring medium because it was not exactly linear. However, that approach would also have excluded steel. In Figure 6.1 the behaviour of a steel wire is also indicated, showing that it is even less close to proportionality than air. Furthermore, the behaviour of the coil spring that Hooke describes elsewhere in 'On Spring' is not exactly proportional because of geometric factors quite apart from the properties of the material of which it is made; that too would be excluded on the basis of rigour.

Moyer assumes that a demonstration of limited rigour forms a significant conclusion in the understanding of Hooke's work, but it is evident that the rigorous application of elementary equations can describe only a small part of the underlying science and technology. A wider technical view provides many considerations in support of the content of 'On Spring'. Hooke did not deal explicitly with the approximate nature of his law, but the experimental configurations that he described (a long wire, a loosely coiled spring, bending of wood) show that he appreciated that the deformation of the solid material must be kept small. Air is a supreme spring medium, and is now widely used as a medium for the storage of energy, so it has a clear place in 'On Spring'. The art of approximation is central in the development of science: Hooke's approximation is widely made in the present day, often without rigorous statement, often for the reason that progress is impossible without it. Had Hooke been more dictated to by equations, he would have been at a standstill. Recalling Newton's abandonment of celestial mechanics when unable to complete exact calculations, we might revise Moyer's conclusion to read: Hooke – unlike his contemporary Newton – was apparently blessed by a limited allegiance to the dictates of equation and number.

From this we see that a narrow assessment made by reference to textbooks, in which rigour is a simple matter of the application of the correct elementary law, will find aspects of Hooke's work to be simply erroneous. On the other hand, if we apply broader technical considerations, and a more thorough analysis, the issue of rigour takes a proper place among the many other factors in our appreciation of Hooke's contribution.

Technical assessment by the application of elementary laws has been attempted on two other examples of Hooke's work,[15] with the conclusion that Hooke's work contained a mere show of scientific analysis, and that a proper analysis proved that the devices that Hooke proposed would not function. This assessment has been reaffirmed by

Bennett,[16] and referred to by Inwood,[17] who echoes Westfall's view that Hooke's analysis of sails is the nonsensical product of an old man in decline. Unfortunately, as we will see in the following section, Westfall did not even apply the elementary laws correctly: Hooke's analyses were sound, and both the devices he proposed do work.

The present paper attempts a broad technical approach and a thorough analysis. In the following section, five accessible examples of Hooke's published work on mechanics and materials are examined, with a technical commentary that includes theoretical analysis and accounts of experimental demonstrations.

Examples of Hooke's Published Work

On Small Glass Canes

In 'An attempt for the explication …'.[18] and 'On small glass canes'[19] Hooke investigates a readily observable phenomenon: the rise of a column of liquid in a minute tube dipped in water. The occasion for such an enquiry is the remarkable ease of manufacture of glass tubes of less than 0.3 mm diameter, by heating a section of the tube until it is soft, and then drawing it out. Hooke proceeds in a two stage experimental proof that the phenomenon is one of many which share a common cause, which he terms the 'congruity' of materials in contact. In modern terms the phenomena he describes, with care and accuracy, are: immiscibility, drop formation, wetting, mixing, wicking, surface minimisation, sessile drops, intermediate suspension, menisci positive and negative, surface contamination, surface suspension and forces between bodies so suspended. These phenomena do indeed share a common cause, which we now call 'surface energy', and in current undergraduate textbooks just these examples, with the addition of only soap bubbles, are given of its effects.

The experimental proof that Hooke describes and illustrates,[20] (Figure 6.2 here) is dedicated to demonstrating that a pressure is required to push air into a glass tube filled with water. Hooke argues that in the phenomenon of capillary rise, the same pressure acts, and is sufficient explanation of that phenomenon. His argument is easily misunderstood to imply an incorrect assertion, that the pressure of the air in the tube is less than that of the air outside.[21] A more careful reading shows that he actually meant that the pressure of the air in the tube *on the water in the tube* must be less than the pressure of the air outside *on the water outside*, by an amount equal to the pressure required to push the air into the tube filled with water. This

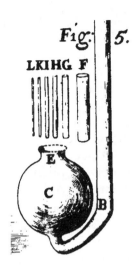

Figure 6.2   The arrangement for
demonstrating the pressure required to push
air into (and water out of) a minute tube.

demonstration was thus theoretically sound; it covered a point in the
exposition of capillary rise which remains difficult today, that
somehow pressure is lost between the air and the bulk of the water in
the tube. This is now explained theoretically by attributing a tension
to the surface of the water, which, given the meniscus of that surface,
will sustain a pressure drop. The surface tension analogy does not
explain all surface phenomena, however, and surface energy, which
exactly corresponds to Hooke's congruity, remains the most
satisfactory approach.

Hooke also attributed a mechanical property to the liquid surface,
that of rigidity, which does provide some of the observed properties
of the surface, but is altogether less satisfactory than the tension
analogy. It is curious that Hooke did not present soap bubbles and
films as exemplars, particularly since we know that he looked at the
colours in them. Their behaviour is rather well described in terms of
surface tension and not in terms of rigidity; the possibility remains that
they were excluded for exactly that reason.

It should be remarked that the pressure observed in the experiment
on the apparatus of Figure 6.2 is not entirely due to the energy
required to push the air into the minute tube: water is also pushed out
of the top end of the tube, which increases the area of water surface
there, which also requires a pressure. This additional pressure is about
the same as the pressure to push the air in, so the observed pressure is
about twice that due to the effect that Hooke was demonstrating.

In an apparatus constructed to replicate that of Figure 6.2, the
pressure was successfully demonstrated as a difference in water level
of about 70 mm. Operation of the apparatus was not easy, because in

some cases the equilibrium was unstable, so that at a critical difference of level the water in the minute tube was suddenly expelled. It is thus difficult to compare the observed pressure difference quantitatively with that required for capillary rise in the same tube. In another experiment it also proved possible, using Hooke's technique for microscopic measurement, to obtain a quantitative relationship between capillary rise and the diameter of the minute tube.

We see in this work strong emphases on bringing together a wide variety of phenomena, and on tackling conceptual difficulties with great care. Although his experimental techniques were adequate to do so, the work did not extend to quantitative measurements. The correct association of all these phenomena with a common cause, and the lack of incorrect associations, is remarkable for the period. It is an example of how Hooke could arrive at the correct conceptual framework for a problem. Many of the phenomena that he described will have been familiar in working with paints and varnishes in his early training. As with his celestial mechanics[22] it is reasonable to assume that this conceptual advance was in part due to Hooke's technical experience outside the laboratory.

Descending Bodies in a Medium

In 'An account of how much descending bodies press upon the medium …'.[23] an experiment is described that contrives a particularly sensitive verification of fundamental fluid mechanics by including the fluid medium in the measurement (see Figure 6.3).

Figure 6.3   The body before its descent in the medium.

A glass cylinder containing water was suspended from the left arm of the balance, and a sinker was hung, also from that arm, suspended by a fine thread so that it hangs just below the water surface. The thread is carefully cut, and the result observed: Hooke reported no movement of the balance arm. This did not agree with his experience that resistance to motion through the fluid increases with speed, and he expressed caution about drawing conclusions. Other arrangements were tried, in which the thread was hung from an independent support arm; in that case, the left arm of the balance descended, as he expected.

The analysis of the experiment of Figure 6.3 is a nice puzzle question in mechanics. Its power lies in the fact that the sinker is first suspended statically and solidly, then moves steadily in a medium that is also suspended. Previous discussions[24] have accepted the lack of movement without comment. However, in the operation of a similar apparatus, with a sinker of submerged weight 50 gm, it is observed that when the thread is severed, the left arm moves up by about 4 mm, which is clearly visible. This movement coincides with the downward motion of the sinker, but happens so quickly that it is hard to observe exactly. The lack of apparent movement in Hooke's apparatus can be explained by his use of a much smaller submerged weight (about 0.4 gm). This was done to make the descent slow enough to observe properly. Unfortunately the movement of the arm is approximately proportional to the submerged weight; with his submerged weight the movement is at most 0.06 mm, and so not observable.

Experiments with a range of submerged weights indicate that the movement increases with submerged weight, and vanishes as the submerged weight is reduced to zero. This is essentially because the motion of the balanced weights, the motion of the sinker and the motion of the water displaced by the sinker sum to zero: and the sum of the latter two (they are opposite in sign) is proportional to the submerged weight. The apparatus is thus an excellent way of demonstrating momentum balance. We might remark that the measurement of motion of solid objects was reported less than a month after the report of the descending bodies experiment, with unsatisfactory results.[25]

Here we have an example of a carefully focused, refined experiment which failed where a cruder, broader approach could have succeeded. It is interesting to speculate that an adaptation of the descending bodies apparatus in which the fluid was absent (and the sinker more robust) could have provided more intelligible results on solid motion. In combination with the above experiments with different submerged weights, a demonstration of the equivalence of fluid and solid motion is also possible. The use of refined apparatus in controlled conditions is characteristic of scientific rather than technological activity; in this case, such characteristics may have militated against a conceptual advance.

Of Glass Drops

In 'Of glass drops'[26] Hooke takes a phenomenon that is striking, complex and commercially significant, and systematically investigates it. This leads, through an experimental and theoretical exposition of the thermal properties of solids and liquids, including the design of thermometers ['... brought to a great certainty and tenderness'], to setting up a sound conceptual framework for the nature of heat and the study of its effects.

The phenomenon of the drops is complex: it involves thermal expansion, differential cooling, stress analysis, elastic energy and fracture mechanisms. Hooke first described analytical experiments on the drops. The sharp end was easily broken off the drop, which then shattered. He carefully ground off the blunt end instead, with the effect that the rest of the drop remained intact. When the drop shattered, the pieces flew in all directions and could not be properly studied. He developed a means to encase the drop in resin and retain the pieces, despite the violence of the explosion. The pattern of fracture was observed under the microscope, and very carefully recorded, as shown in Figure 6.4.[27] Annealing (familiar from the glass works) suppressed the phenomenon.

Elastic energy (spring) is stored in the drop because the outer crust solidifies when the core is still hot and soft and expanded; the core subsequently cools, but its consequent contraction is incompatible with the dimensions of the solid outer crust. In the cooled drop the core is thus held in an expanded state, and the crust in a compressed one, in an opposing equilibrium. When the crust is broken so as to expose part of the core, its tension fractures it, and the equilibrium is lost. The stored energy in each is sufficient to shatter the material. Hooke made seven assertions, which, together with their explanations and analogous experiments that he described, explain this situation completely. By analysing the pattern of fracture he was able to visualize the stresses (distension and flexure) that caused it. The analogous experiments are properly constructed to expose the elements of the explanation and demonstrate their actions.

The form of Hooke's investigation is of particular interest: an obscure and elusive technical phenomenon was studied *in situ*. With

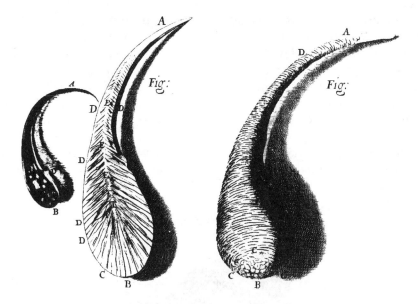

Figure 6.4   The reconstructed glass drops.

high craft, instrumentation and careful observation its mechanism could be discerned. A complete theoretical analysis was impossible (and remains so today), but the mechanism could be analysed into its components. The analysis could be validated by constructing critical experiments to test each component as a theoretical construct. This discourse is an inspiring example of the unity of technical, experimental and theoretical practice. It would form an excellent text for the instruction of students, and of practising technologists, today. It does not correspond exactly to conventional modern scientific method, but the science and technology are inextricably interwoven. A suitable term to describe the discourse would be Hooke's own: 'experimental philosophy', of which it is a paradigm.

Lampas

The Cutlerian lecture *Lampas*[28] deals with flame and, at greater length, the means of keeping it steady. In the study of flame, Hooke again uses in situ experiments, but his analysis of the mechanisms of combustion is tentative, and he does not go on to construct validating experiments as he did with the glass drops. This is to be expected, given the extreme complexity of the nature of flame and the difficulty of experimenting with it. A critique of his experiments is beyond the competence of the present author, but it can be remarked that they show a breadth of vision whose absence is a conspicuous problem in technical practice today. It would have been easy, in a work mainly dedicated to providing better oil feed to a lamp, to assume the response of the flame to the supply of oil. Such assumptions have led to numerous technical failures, where specialist development of one part of a process or product has ignored the response of the other parts.

On initial inspection, the first of the several devices which he proposes for maintaining a constant oil feed seems too ingenious to be true.[29]

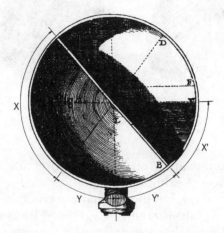

Figure 6.5   The first constant level device of *Lampas*.

A hollow spherical box is divided in equal halves by a diaphragm (seen in section in the figure, running top left to bottom right) and freely pivoted about an axis through its centre (perpendicular to the section). The upper right half is the receptacle for oil, the lower left is a solid counterpoise. To demonstrate the constant level action, we imagine the counterpoise to be made by filling the solid half of the sphere with a substance half as dense as the oil: then, in the figure, the actions of the spaces Y and Y' are evidently equal and opposite, and so too are the actions of X and X', since X has half the density and twice the space of X'. The same arguments apply if the form of the box is any solid of revolution.[30]

Previous commentary on this work stated that 'It consistently used the word *weight* where the word (or the concept) *moment* was needed' and concluded that Hooke could not distinguish these concepts properly.[31] The statement is false, and the conclusion extremely improbable. Hooke uses the verb 'counterpoise'[32] consistently throughout to describe the action of a turning moment, and 'weight' to describe the weight of an equal volume, that is density. His analysis follows the one above, and is quite satisfactory. Westfall further states that the device does not work unless the dry half of the box contains a substance half as dense as the oil, which would be technically unfeasible. This too is untrue: so long as the weight and centre of gravity of the dry half coincides with that of a hemisphere of the specified substance, its action is the same, however it is constructed. As Hooke states, 'Let there be a counterpoise ... fixed somewhere in the Line PO, so that the said upper [solid] Hemisphere shall have half the gravity of the under [liquid filled] Hemisphere upon the Center of motion O'.[33] Westfall takes this to specify the total weights of the hemispheres, and ignores the phrase 'upon the Center of motion'. Hooke not only understands moments about a centre, but employs the concept of centre of gravity, which appears to be beyond Westfall's knowledge of mechanics.

Although it is clear that an idealization of the device is theoretically correct, we cannot conclude that it can be readily constructed or reliable in practice. A device was 'delivered' or 'produced' to the Royal Society,[34] but its performance was not described. There is a technical problem that the oil is in a box that moves, so it is not easily brought to the fixed flame. Hooke proposed to feed it through a tapered gudgeon, which both seals and freely turns, at the axis of rotation. Unfortunately, free rotation implies some leakage of oil, so difficult compromises may have to be made between undesirable leaks and unwanted friction: friction at the pivot would not be constant at the very slow rotational speeds, so the oil level would not be maintained exactly constant.

Lampas is not the earliest record of the constant level lamp: some ten years previously Hooke presented a device to the Royal Society of similar form but in a different arrangement.[35] The oil is placed in a semi-cylindrical stationary container. A float of the same form is fitted within the container, freely rotating on the common diameter. The analysis[36] treats the volumes of the oil and of the float as though their actions balance against each other, and follows the same line of argument as for the first device of *Lampas* above. The action of the oil in the space between the container and the float is ignored, and the figure is drawn so as to make that space vanishingly small. An elaborated embodiment of this second device also appears in *Lampas*:[37]

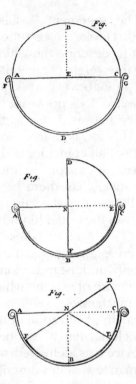

Figure 6.6 The earlier constant level device presented to the Royal Society.

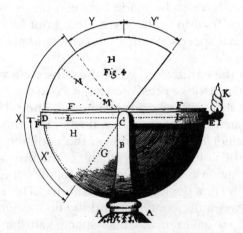

Figure 6.7 The second constant level device of *Lampas*.

The oil container is mounted on gimbals, and the oil fed through a rotating seal. An explicit proviso is made that the clearance between container and float be as small as possible while allowing free movement of the float. The second device is treated more briefly than the first: for a demonstration of its action, Hooke refers only to his explanation of the first device.

In associating the action of the two devices so closely, Hooke has missed a trick. The position of the float in the second device cannot depend on the shape of the container: it is simply determined by the level of the oil relative to the axis of rotation. With this insight, we may analyse the equilibrium of the float by following Archimedes: the action of the oil on the float is equal to the action required to support the volume of oil displaced by the float. Now, in Figure 6.7, the volume of oil displaced is in X′, and so the action of the oil exactly supports the solid in X, which has half the density and twice the space of X′. The theoretical outcome is thus that it does work as claimed. In practical terms, the permission of any form of container is important: the manufacture of two closely conforming shapes is problematic, the hollow shape particularly so, and an exact coaxial arrangement also difficult. In addition, the supposed inexactness of the device, due to the necessary clearance, would mislead attempts to improve an embodiment of it. Furthermore, the technical problem of bringing the oil to the flame through a rotating seal is eliminated in the second device.

Perhaps the most intriguing aspect of these devices is their genesis: how could anyone have thought up such an arrangement? It is plausible to construct a derivation of the first device of *Lampas* from considering the familiar ascent of the arm of a balance when the weight on it is reduced. In the diary entry of 26 September 1675 Hooke notes the invention of a 'candlestick to keep the flame at the same height by a wire helicall and by a poyse in Helico spirall':[38] this presumably worked on a similar principle. Although this entry immediately predates the presentation of *Lampas*, it is made long after the earlier lamp presentations. For an oil lamp, if the oil container is set on a balance, then as the oil is consumed its level will go down but the container will rise. If the two effects can be made equal and opposite, a constant level will be maintained. For small angles of tilt, the desired outcome can be obtained by adjusting the sensitivity of the balance; this is customarily done by adjusting a weight placed vertically below the pivot of the balance. To extend the effect to accommodate large changes in the volume of oil, large angles of tilt must be considered. The only way to keep the geometry of the oil simple is to make the container into a volume of revolution. Once this is done, the balance weight and its centre of gravity can be calculated by considering the half full and part full conditions, but it appears that Hooke did not proceed in this way. Instead, he made the balance weight also a solid of revolution, which makes the existence of a solution immediately evident.

The genesis of the second device of *Lampas* may well have been a derivation from the first device. This conjecture is supported by Hooke's explanations of the second one, in both early and later presentations, being much the same as of the first, and by the fact that the explanation shows limited understanding of the second device. It is also hard to formulate an alternative independent genesis of the second device. It remains to explain the earlier chronology of the second device: a possible reason is that the second device is easier to construct than the first. At the earlier date, although both devices had perhaps been conceived, it may only have been possible to demonstrate the second. The demonstrations at the later date may have taken place to mark the publication of *Lampas*. It is not clear from the record whether these involved the first or the second device; thus the first device may never have been constructed.

A proof of the second device has been obtained by constructing a working model according to the specifications in *Lampas*. Although simple in construction and of low precision, its operation was as claimed. In a test, 130 ml of water was added to a vessel without the device, producing a rise of 13 mm in surface level. With the device fitted, the level remained constant to within ±1 mm.

Strait Sails

Hooke had managed, in *Lampas*, to demonstrate that mechanical analyses of both flame and of hydrostatics were possible without recourse to an element of fire or to a 'hylarchic spirit' of fluids. In 'A Lecture of the preference of strait to Bunting sails' Hooke again tackles a practical problem in applied fluid mechanics, but this time without employing experiments.[39] The problem is to convince sceptical navigators that a tight sail delivers more speed through the water than a bellying one. Hooke first asserts that the power of a fluid is proportionate to its gravity and velocity (that is it has the mechanical properties common to any substance) then goes on to detail how to compare the power of a flow of water with the power of a flow of air, by assuming that their powers are proportional to the density multiplied by the square of the velocity. This assumption is still made in fluid mechanics in the present day; indeed, the calculation of drag on a bluff body is now done using the same formula together with an empirical drag coefficient to deal with bodies of various shapes. The importance of the comparison between air and water becomes evident later in the discourse, where Hooke points out that the motion of a ship through water is determined by a balance between the power of the water (in resisting motion) and the power of the air (in driving it).

Actually, Hooke's demonstration does not require the drag formula to be valid, since he is comparing the effects of different geometries under identical wind conditions. The key to the demonstration is his statement 'The power of the Wind therefore is to be computed acording to the bigness of the Prism of the Air which cometh to dash or strike against the Body that is expos'd to it; and according to the velocity that this prism is mov'd forwards to strike against it.[40]

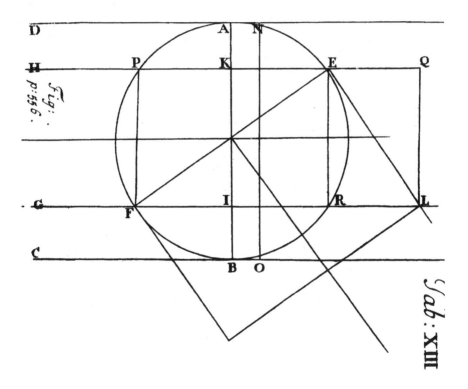

Figure 6.8   The sail set along EF is struck by the prism of air moving from HG.

He first demonstrates that the power of the air will be perpendicular to the sail. From this he is able to make reasonable estimates of the relative powers of the wind, in the case where the way is perpendicular to the sail, for a direct and an oblique wind, using the projected area of the sail and the component of the change in motion of the wind perpendicular to the sail.

The case where the sail is set at an arbitrary angle to the way is considered, but the analysis is referred. The demonstration that a straight sail is superior is obtained by consideration that if there is a preferred angle to the wind then it will hold all over a straight sail, but only over part of a bellying one. His avoidance of the problem of the sail set at an arbitrary angle shows caution: he might well have realized that a best angle should be obtained by a compromise between squareness to the wind and squareness to the way, but the mathematics of an optimisation was out of reach. His analysis of a curved sail omits consideration that the final direction of the wind off it is more advantageous than off the straight, but his conclusion that a straight sail performs better is one shared by yachtspeople today. The forces exerted on the rigging by a straight sail are disproportionately large, however, which was perhaps the technological obstacle to the adoption of his recommendations by the mariners of his day.

Hooke's realization that the speed of the ship through the water is determined by the balance between the power of the wind and the resistance of the water is particularly interesting. By elegantly transforming the frame of reference to that of the ship, he further demonstrates that both these factors are susceptible to the same drag formula, since, relative to the ship there is a counter current of water upon the hull.

Previous technical commentary on this work[41] is a catalogue of errors: Hooke's unessential empirical drag formula is taken to be an essential theoretical conclusion based on the theory of impact; the validity of this assumption, and the completeness of the demonstration that follows it but does not depend on it, are ignored; Hooke's realization that 'the water moves against the Sail' is taken to 'have the unfortunate consequence that the ship must sail right side up and upside down at the same time'.[42] The first error indicates a failure to appreciate the applied nature of the discourse, presumably due to Westfall's focus on fundamental theoretical issues. The second error shows an ignorance of basic fluid mechanics, a subject which has few neat theoretical results and receives little attention in a scientific education. The third error can only indicate a deliberate intention to denigrate Hooke and his work, since even a person without specialist historical knowledge should know the meaning 'a sailing vessel' for the word 'sail', which renders Hooke's elegant insight intelligible.

Discussion

It has been pointed out that Hooke laid the foundations for the modern principle of the conservation of energy in mechanics.[43] The examples of his work considered above show the concept of energy appearing repeatedly, in the form of 'spring' stored in the glass drops, or of 'congruence' of substances in contact, or of the 'power' of fluid motion or the heat from the flame. Hooke's work was broad, but that does not mean it was without a coherent theme. The concept of energy appearing in various interchangeable forms is perhaps the biggest idea in science, crossing disciplines and governing our lives. We have also seen that previous assertions that Hooke's work was not scientific because it lacked rigour were at best inadequate and at worst simply erroneous. It appears that Hooke has the depth, focus and rigour that are supposed to be required for scientists of the highest repute.

We should also remark, having refuted claims that Hooke's work is unscientific, that the thesis supported by these claims[44] that technology cannot have contributed to the 'new science' falls as well. The above examples of Hooke's work portray such a wide variety of technical aspects that they may enable us to develop our ideas about the relationship, often debated, between science and technology. We should first say roughly what we mean by these terms. Technological work is associated with application to short term goals, trial and error experiment, approximate measurement, heuristic analysis and success in controlling a particular configuration, which does not include deep theoretical insights and so cannot be generalized. Scientific work is associated with theoretical goals, planned experiment, precise measurement, rigorous mathematical analysis and the production of fundamental theories. Let us attempt to identify the various aspects of Hooke's work from the above commentaries in these terms, to see if any pattern emerges.

The most obviously scientific investigation was the 'weight descending': a planned experiment in fundamental fluid mechanics, using precise apparatus, producing a measured outcome. The planning and the precision produced narrow experimental conditions, which concealed the underlying mechanics, and led to a conclusion that was not general. Hooke referred to his wider technological experience of the behaviour of fluids to distrust that conclusion. A broader investigation, with a range of simpler experiments, would have also exposed these limitations. In this case we see work of which the method fits the term 'scientific', but the outcome does not.

The rise of liquid in minute tubes is now a classic laboratory experiment, but was then a curiosity arising from a novel technology.

This technology permitted a familiar phenomenon (wicking) to be studied in a controlled way. A very general concept arises in this work, but it came from Hooke's bringing together a diverse range of natural and technical phenomena, drawn from his experience, and only in small part from the experiment. The experiment was not extended to include measurement, but such measurements, although they might have produced a 'law of capillary rise' which would have confirmed the understanding of the mechanics, it would not have deepened it. In the latter part of the presentations Hooke lists seven conjectures consequent on his insights, four of which relate to fundamental science and three to applications. The scientific and technological aspects of this work are intermingled, in motivation, in method and in outcome.

The glass drops were another technical novelty; his investigation shows how, with an elementary understanding of its underlying principles, theory and experiment can be combined to elucidate a mysterious phenomenon. His construction of controlled experiments is scientific, but they are used to explain a technical system in technical terms, not to derive fundamental insights. This explanation is particular to the system, but extends our understanding of some fundamental concepts (stress distribution, thermal expansion). The technical system was, and is, of great practical interest. The motivation and outcome of this work are both technological, and the method is scientific. It corresponds closely to what is now called engineering science.

In 'the preference of strait sails' Hooke uses mechanical insights into a technical system to demonstrate a significant, but controversial, result. The motivation is entirely practical, and the outcome is now a basic part of engineering. Its degree of rigour must be considered in the context that no rigorous treatment has yet been achieved; his heuristic analysis is similar to the current engineering one.

In *Lampas* he employs direct geometrical reasoning to synthesize an elegant and intriguing device. This showed that his philosophical algebra was not just a passive analytical tool. The virtuosity of the performance was an impressive piece of rhetoric, but the engineering analysis was incomplete and the attention to detail was lacking. If the device had been widely produced these defects could easily have been rectified. The defects are not greatly to Hooke's detriment: the design of a successful artifact is an intellectual challenge as great as any other.

The preceding examples show the intimate relationship between science and technology in Hooke's work. Fundamental conceptual advances arose from technological investigations, as they did in his celestial mechanics.[45] Scientific procedures were part of the investigations, which produced particular results, which are of lasting interest. Motivation for the work was a mixture of theoretical development and practical application, and its outcomes were equally mixed. We can identify ways of working that correspond to engineering science and engineering analysis, in which science and technology are combined. We have thus a better picture of how technology and science combined to advance technical knowledge. Technological advances lead to novel processes, devices, techniques and curiosities, as well as improved means for investigating them. If carried out with sufficient profundity, the investigations could reveal new insights into fundamental problems. These were in the form of a 'truth only dimly understood', but that truth preceded the 'truth clearly demonstrated' that we associate with science. Technology opened up the new territory first, and drove discovery forwards. This technological activity incorporated scientific investigations, and constructed explanations with experiments and theories. Technology could be profound and rigorous, just as science could be shallow and trivial.

This role for technology is incompatible with a previously accepted culture which elevated the status of pure research[46] and identified imagination and innovation with theory.[47] This culture has been challenged extensively,[48] but is still firmly entrenched in science textbooks. The accepted culture is found in the textbooks in various forms, both implicit and explicit. The subject is structured as a series of well defined laws to be learned first, and then deployed to solve problems constructed to be exactly soluble in terms of those laws. The history content of the curriculum conveys that the laws of science were conceived in their final form by pure scientists, most of whom were theorists, and that technological advances came from the application of these laws.[49] The culture is thus sustained by appeal to a grand and ancient tradition for which there is only dubious external support. It is, moreover, unpopular with science students, who are baffled and disheartened by the 'laws first' textbook presentations and find it inimical to clear thinking and inspiration.[50] It appears that the content of the textbooks is without conceptual, historical or pedagogical justification.

It is practically impossible to acquire the competence necessary to make a technical assessment without entering into this culture. This may explain, at least in part, the errors and inadequacies we have seen in some previous assessments of Hooke's work. Some pitfalls of technical assessment have been clearly demonstrated in the main section of the present paper, but so have some of the advantages. The work of Hooke can only be assessed properly by a careful reading, a broad technical appreciation and an adequate competence in the subject matter. Technical commentary can be a valuable tool for assessing historical evidence, but only if the training by which it is made possible is also the subject of scrutiny.

PART 3
SPECULATIVE PHILOSOPHY

Chapter 7

Hooke on Memory and the Memory of Hooke

Douwe Draaisma

On Saturday 21 June 1682, his appointed day of duty to the Royal
Society, Robert Hooke presented a lecture on memory to his fellow
members. The text was included in his *Posthumous Works* under the
title 'An Hypothetical Explication of Memory: how the Organs made
use of by the Mind in its Operation may be Mechanically understood'.[1]
In his lecture Hooke maintained that purely material explanations may
be given for all memory processes. It was a strange lecture in more
than one respect. Hooke had never before taken up a psychological
subject, nor did he afterwards; his theory of memory stands
completely separate from his other work, which dealt with physics
and matters mechanical. Second, Hooke's theory of memory was
virtually unanticipated, nor did he have any followers. Historian of
psychology Graham Richards has said that Hooke's theory 'rests in
glorious isolation as a one-off piece of proto-psychological theorizing
of a kind for which the intellectual climate was quite unripe'.[2] Equally
enigmatic was a third aspect. In circles of the Royal Society metaphors
were treated with suspicion or downright hostility. The preferred
'manner of discourse' was plain, simple, literal language. Hooke's
lecture, on the other hand, was a long sequence of metaphors,
analogies, comparisons and similes. Hooke was acutely aware of the
tension between his use of metaphors and the Royal Society's view
that nature would only reflect itself truthfully in literal language. He
therefore had to negotiate his way out with a handful of defensive
remarks on the kind of language suited for the description of memory.
There is no doubt that Hooke spoke to a captivated audience. Some of
the Fellows who had been unable to attend his lecture asked him to
repeat it the following Saturday. And so he did.

With the exception of psychologist Singer and Hooke's biographer
Inwood,[3] recent scholarship has largely neglected Hooke's theory of
memory. It is my intention in this chapter to reconstruct some of its
context, and to do so in a specific way: I will use his metaphors and
analogies as a means to understand more of the man, his theory and

his intellectual surroundings. My purpose is threefold: first, to demonstrate in the pleasure of being able to make sense of a text which would otherwise remain a series of somewhat arcane speculations on the workings of memory; second, to demonstrate that research into metaphors is a particularly helpful aid in contextualization; third, to show that Hooke's lecture may stand strange and isolated within his own work, his time and the reigning literary technologies of his colleagues, but that to the present day historian of psychology his theory of memory fits into a familiar pattern. Or rather, I will argue that Hooke's theory is perhaps the oldest example of a tradition with some remarkable common features: roughly that of 'a physicist doing psychology of memory'.

Phosphorus and Memory

One of the central metaphors in Hooke's lecture on memory was phosphorescence. In Italy, Germany and England a frantic search was underway for chemical processes capable of producing phosphorescent materials. Scientific societies corresponded on experiments and exchanged samples. One evening in 1677, at Boyle's quarters in Pall Mall, Hooke had attended a spectacular demonstration of phosphorescent substances by the German alchemist Johann Crafft.[4] In the darkness, the shutters closed, the candles removed, the Fellows witnessed how Crafft broke a minute part of matter into tiny fragments and scattered them over the carpet. To their delight the crumbs started to glow, twinkling like stars for a good while, without doing any harm, Boyle wrote, 'to the Turky Carpet they lay on'. Next Crafft had asked Boyle to give him his hand. The alchemist gently rubbed some of the matter on the back of Boyle's hand which started to glow intensely. When he blew on it, the light seemed to extinguish, but soon recovered its luminescence. Equally spectacular was Crafft's demonstration of writing in the dark. He took some of the substance on the tip of his finger and started writing on a sheet of paper. After a short while there appeared, in capital letters, across the full width of the paper, the word DOMINI, so bright that one could discern the fingers holding the sheet of paper. It was a fascinating sight, Boyle wrote, 'having in it a mixture of strangeness, beauty and frightfulness'.

Crafft's process was based on the lengthy distillation of large quantities of human urine. Another phosphorescent substance that cropped up regularly in Hooke's reports was the Bologna Stone, a mineral found in the vicinity of Bologna in Italy. Seventeenth-century researchers were fascinated by its ethereal light. Balduin, for instance, wrote to Henry Oldenburg that there resided in his piece of artificial phosphorus an 'innate and invisible philosophical fire, attracting by magical means the visible fire of the sun and emitting and throwing out in the dark its splendour in return'.[5]

The twinkling stars on the Turkish carpet, Boyle's luminous hand, the glowing DOMINI, perhaps even the splendour of a philosophical fire – all this must have continued to glow in Hooke's imagination long after the event, for five years later phosphorescence reappeared in his treatise on human memory. In Hooke's view every sense is linked with a special substance in the brain suited to the retention and reproduction of impressions reaching the brain via that sense. According to this principle, there must also be a substance in the human brain capable of preserving light impressions. In order to lend plausibility to this hypothesis Hooke referred to the Bologna stone. If this substance, he argued, has the capacity to receive the impressions of light, retain them and emit them in the dark, why should one not just as easily find a substance in the brain capable of preserving light stimuli and hence forming the physical residue of our visual memories? The Bologna stone, he reasoned by analogy, may show us 'a Specimen of a certain Qualification not to be found in most other Bodies, which may yet possibly be done much more powerfully and effectually by the Chymistry of Nature in the Digestions and Preparations made in the wonderful Elaboratory of the Animal Body'.

The structure of the argument is clear. If it is possible to produce a substance chemically that can retain light and emit it again, it is also possible for brain matter to absorb and reproduce light impressions in a purely physical way. The light in the Bologna stone pointed to a material property which the human brain – thanks to the 'Chymistry of Nature' – possessed in a perfect form.

At the same time this phosphorus metaphor illuminates the scientific milieu in which Hooke operated. In 1681, a year before his lecture on memory, Hooke received a report *Il Fosforo or a Preparation of the Bolognian Stone, whereby it shines in the dark*, sent by the Academy of Physics and Mathematics in Rome. His knowledge of the latest developments was first hand. Together with Boyle he had conducted experiments with the 'Pneumatick Engine', showing that phosphorus continued to shine even in a vacuum. Demonstrations featuring phosphorus were considered ideally suited for a wider public than just the research community, such as acquaintances, servants, women and children. Semi-public demonstrations like those of Crafft, Hooke and Boyle played a part in creating a public scientific culture. Experiments with phosphorus were emblematic of this new style of scientific research. In using his phosphorus metaphor, for an audience of researchers all of whom had either attended the demonstrations and experiments or read about them in the *Philosophical Transactions*, Hooke was appealing to a shared experience. The reference to the Bologna stone enabled everyone to picture the special properties Hooke was attributing to brain matter. The fact that there was still no clear explanation for phosphorescence could be regarded as a further parallel, for there was as yet no explanation for the visual memory either. What better metaphor could there be for the operation of the visual memory than the substance that still retained an aura of mysticism and refused to surrender its secrets even to the most advanced scientific instruments, which did not reflect light, but was itself luminescent, a substance that was one of chemistry's most glorious products? By his choice of metaphor Hooke linked the elusive powers residing in phosphorus with the sense of awe at the miracle of human memory.

Geometry and Mensuration

Hooke's theory of memory followed an exposition on time and the consciousness of time. Our knowledge of time, he argued, cannot be derived from our senses, since sense impressions are transient in nature. Perception of duration and frequency presupposes the operation of a memory. In Hooke's view the estimated duration of a period is a derivative of the number of remembered events in that period. It was this hypothesis that led him to a discussion of memory. Hooke conceived of memory as a material organ, explicable in purely mechanical terms. That our faculty to recollect has a corporeal nature is demonstrated by the fact that it can be influenced by physical factors like fever or excessive drinking. It may even be completely destroyed by external force, like 'a Fall, or great Blow upon the Head'. Hooke invited his audience to think of memory as a 'Repository' or 'Storehouse' of ideas. Our senses act as 'Collectors or Carriers', delivering impressions to the storehouse. Actual storage, however, requires the simultaneous activity of the soul, which gives the impressions a certain shape and motion before inserting them in the common repository, where they are preserved and retained for future use by the soul.

Hooke did not wish to bother with the question of the exact location of the soul. He simply assumed that the soul was 'somewhere in the Brain of a Man'. From this position the soul could receive impressions and form new ideas. Ideas, Hooke pointed out, are preserved in the order in which they are formed, like the links in a coiled chain. The idea most recently shaped, the psychological present, is the beginning of the chain, the oldest idea corresponds to the last link. Each new idea shifts the chain one position further into the past. Our estimation of duration depends on the number of ideas interposed between the present and some idea at the far end of the chain. Distances in time, then, are marked by the length of the chain of memories. Thus, time came to be conceived of as a spatial quantity. Hooke was particularly proud that he had brought time and memory under what he called 'the Consideration of Geometry and Mensuration'.

Perhaps we should pause here to point out that Hooke introduced a completely new type of question in his theory of memory. In traditional spiritual theories, memory was conceived of as a non-spatial entity, a *quasi*-space at best, and questions like the *rate* at which ideas were formed, their *number* or their *location* in memory, hardly made sense. Hooke, however, energetically addressed the quantification of memory processes. The rate at which the soul forms ideas and inserts them in memory may vary widely from person to person, he declared. For some there may be 'Four of them formed in a second Minute of Time', others possibly form less than one idea in two seconds. He then proceeded to estimate the number of ideas in the memory of a man of normal mental and physical constitution, being 'neither very quick, nor very dull'. This resulted in a truly impressive piece of number crunching. Hooke multiplied the number of ideas with the seconds in a man's life, reaching the spectacular outcome of 'a thousand Millions of distinct Ideas', correcting this figure for 'Infancy, Old Age, Sickness and Inadvertency' and ending up with one million ideas per year. Upon reflection, Hooke considered this outcome, which amounted to 2738 ideas every day, to be probably far too high. He then switched to a manner of computation informed by introspection rather than by calculus. If a man reflects on how many ideas he may have added to his store in the last month, he will probably find that the number will not exceed two or three hundred a day. So a man of 50 may have deposited 1 826 200 distinct ideas in his storehouse. This would seem a realistic figure, Hooke concluded.

Hooke felt that even the initial figure of one hundred million ideas was not a physical impossibility. Very small quantities of matter may contain innumerably many living creatures, each of them with its own shape and with sufficient room to move. As a pioneer in microscopic research Hooke was familiar with small dimensions. A few years earlier he had observed 'animals' in rainwater that were no bigger than a thirtieth part of the breadth of a hair. This would mean that one cubic inch could contain 'eight millions of millions' of these minute creatures.[6] In the human brain, it would appear, there is no such thing as a lack of space for memories.

The Microcosm of Memory

In order to clarify the position and actions of the soul Hooke introduced a second metaphor, more elaborate than the coiled chain of ideas. The soul, he pointed out, 'forms to itself a Microcosm, or Picture of the Macrocosm, in which it radiates, and is sensible of every thing contain'd therein, in the same manner as the Sun in the Macrocosm'. The representation of the human mind as a microcosm of the universe gave Hooke an opportunity to cite all kinds of optical and astronomical laws as analogies for the processes in memory. Forgetting, for example, may be due to the interruption of the sun's rays by other images. Hooke likened this to an eclipse of the moon. Hence an image may be apparently lost and recovered immediately when the obstacle is removed. Images that are closer receive more powerful radiation from the soul, 'in a duplicate proportion to their Distance reciprocal, much the same with that of Light', which is why memories become fainter with time. In this ratio we recognize the inverse-square law. In a letter to Newton two years earlier, Hooke had applied the same ratio to the force of gravity. As a law of memory, though, the ratio has an apparent exception: some events make a particularly deep impression and are then remembered clearly, however long ago the image was formed. Hooke's explanation is that powerful impressions are remembered more often and subsequently constantly recreated, so that they always remain close to the centre.

In his remarks on attention, Hooke uses metaphors which are a faithful reflection of contemporary views on the nature of light and radiation. Those views had been inspired by Descartes's *Dioptrique*, which represented light as a pressure that is displaced instantaneously in a transparent medium or 'plenum'. Descartes clarified this theory with the analogy of a blind man who 'sees' with his stick: when the stick touches an object the blind man can tell the shape of the object by the resistance. In Hooke's microcosm of memory the soul becomes aware of the content of stored ideas by propagating from itself 'a Radiation like the Sun, by which, as by a Stick, it becomes sensible of all those Ideas that are yet unwasted within the Repository, feeling as it were their Form, their Resistance, and their Reactions to its Radiations'. In short, Hooke has quite directly projected Descartes's laws of optics into his theory of memory. His microcosm is a heliocentric Cartesian universe.

Over three centuries later we can see that Hooke's theory of memory anticipates modern theory in a number of interesting ways. Examples include the relationship between the number of memories and estimation of duration, the clear distinction between storage and reproduction and the emphasis on the active role of attention in forging enduring memories. The metaphor of the 'Storehouse' can be recognized in standard theoretical terms like 'long term storage' and 'storage capacity'. That stored material may disappear as a result of 'decay' or because other material makes it inaccessible ('interference'), are still the two main hypotheses on forgetting and both are mentioned by Hooke. In addition, Hooke provided an explanation for the fact that powerful impressions are vividly remembered irrespective of the time that has elapsed, which is identical to the current hypothesis of 'trace consolidation': whenever we remember the event concerned the trace is renewed and reinforced. Anyone tempted to make sarcastic observations on the laborious calculations regarding the number of stored ideas in the warehouse should look at the way in which the number of 'bits' in the human brain is currently calculated. The author of an article giving an overview of the field, Landauer, uses a method essentially identical to Hooke's. He makes as accurate as possible an estimate of the *rate* at which material is added to the memory and multiplies that by the length of life. On the basis of memory tasks after reading tests, Landauer arrives at an 'input rate to long-term memory' of 1.2 bits per second, where Hooke's estimate had been one idea per second. For someone aged 70 that gives a total of 1.8 billion bits. Like Hooke, Landauer deducts one-third for sleep.[7]

Only by Similitude

Given the audience he was addressing on that June day in 1682, Hooke's 'Explication of Memory' contained a potential source of dispute. The founding fathers of the Royal Society had set high standards for the kind of language used to describe experiments and formulate theory. In 1667 Thomas Sprat wrote in his *History of the Royal Society* that members were expected to keep to succinct and simple language, purged of 'the trick of Metaphors'.[8] A year before another member, Samuel Parker, had gone much further. Parker advocated a general ban on the use of figurative language in scientific discourse. He expressed a particular horror of metaphors, whose 'wanton & luxuriant fancies climbing up into the Bed of Reason, do not only defile it by unchast and illegitimate Embraces, but instead of real conceptions and notices of Things, impregnate the mind with nothing but Ayerie and Subventaneous Phantasmes'.[9] Hooke justified himself on two grounds for his departure from the literal style prized by the Royal Society. The first was that processes in the human mind fundamentally elude literal description. The second was that graphic images enable the imagination to grasp the relationships between hypothetical processes. There is more to be said about both these arguments.

In the seventeenth century the philosophical status of memory was linked to the question of human immortality. As a result, reflections on its material substratum acquired religious significance. Hooke wrote his treatise against the background of Cartesian dualism and was careful to represent only memory, not the soul, as a material instrument. This enabled him to describe memory processes in spatial and physical terms similar to those used in describing the material world. But this also created a conceptual problem. Because how does one 'locate' a non-spatial entity like the soul, in relation to a material – and hence spatial – memory? Hooke, as we have seen, did not pronounce on the exact position of the soul ('somewhere in the Brain of a Man'). His other indications of place are always linked to metaphors: at the distribution point of the warehouse, at the start of the chain of memories, in the centre of the microcosm. Writing on the relationship between soul and memory, Hooke states, 'It is not, I conceive, possible to be truly understood or described, but only by Similitude'. The relationship between soul and memory can be described and explained only through comparison, in images. Metaphors are quite simply indispensible.

But Hooke ingeniously made a virtue of this necessity. A full appreciation of the subtleties of his logical dexterity requires a short digression on the mechanistic tradition, as it had emerged in the Royal Society. Following Boyle, a strict distinction was made between facts and theories. *Factual* discourse comprised statements on observable phenomena, or 'matters of fact'. *Theoretical* discourse comprised hypotheses on the explanation of the 'matters of fact'. Shapin and Schaffer have indicated that the epistemological status of the terms in theoretical discourse was uncertain.[10] Generally they were described, without further definition, as 'notions'. For example, in his research with the vacuum pump Boyle had introduced the term 'spring of the air' to explain the elasticity of air. This 'spring' was explained in turn by the hypothesis that air consists of spring-like particles. The compression of these tiny springs was supposed to explain the resilience of the whole, just as a bale of wool can be compressed because of the elasticity of the constituent fibres. Boyle, quite deliberately, did not answer the question as to how the resilience of the particles was to be explained: in his view 'notions' should be linked as directly and graphically as possible with 'matters of fact'. A figurative explanation like the 'spring of the air' met those requirements: a hypothetical explanation of the causal mechanisms underlying the 'spring' did not.

In his papers on physics Hooke followed these ideas on research and theory as well as he could. In one of his articles, Hooke explicitly defines how hypothetical mechanisms can be linked to 'matters of fact'. The good experimenter, writes Hooke, should have some provisional hypotheses prior to the experiment if the experimental outcome is to have real informative value. In order to acquire a sufficiently extensive repertoire of hypotheses, the experimenter would be well advised to compare nature with as many 'mechanical and intelligible ways of working as the mind is furnished with'.[11]

Returning to the treatise on memory, one is struck by the fact that here too Hooke is trying to follow the criteria for physical research. The idea that hypothetical explanations for memory processes are 'notions' which can be understood only through mechanical, graphic analogies, and the recommendation that in formulating hypotheses one should use comparisons with familiar 'mechanical and intelligible ways of working', recur early in the introduction to the 'Explication of Memory', in virtually identical terms. 'Because', Hooke writes,

> nothing is so well understood as when it is represented under some sensible Form, I would, to make my Notion the more conceivable, make a mechanical and sensible Figure and Picture thereof, and from that shew how I conceive all the Actions and Operations of the Soul as Apprehending, Remembring and Reasoning are performed.

Thus, metaphors and graphic images are not only necessary to the understanding of memory processes, they can also have the same heuristic value as in physical research. Analogies like attention-as-radiation, forgetting-as-lunar eclipse or visual memory-as-phosphorescence give the imagination a hold on what would otherwise remain vague 'notions'. Appealing to the need for graphic imagery Hooke included in his theoretical discourse the same metaphors and analogies which had met which such suspicion in the Royal Society.

This already constituted something of a dialectical triumph over his own principles. But Hooke went further still. He claimed to have brought memory within the scope of 'Geometry and Mensuration' – in modern terms, to have quantified memory processes. On closer inspection one can see that Hooke has smuggled in size and number along with the metaphors. By comparing the ordering of ideas with an ever-lengthening chain Hooke was able to take the distance between a given idea and the beginning of the chain as a measure of duration. By placing memories in a quasi-solar system, Hooke could impose his 'inverse-square law' on the relationship between the strength of a memory and its age. Both 'quantifications' only had meaning within a purely imaginary space. Hooke ordered mental processes by acting *as if* they were spatial. Metaphors were the tools he used to create space in a memory that otherwise would have remained closed to the imagination.

A Physicist's Memory

Graham Richards included Hooke in his section of 'forgotten anticipations of psychology'.[12] Considering that the topic of his lecture is memory, this is a sorry paradox. But even a theory which stands isolated in its time may have some representative features in the eye of a historian who can see a longer stretch of tradition. I would argue that Hooke's work is an early example of a style of theorising which over the centuries has constantly associated itself with new technologies. His theory exemplifies a psychology in which state-of-the-art techniques for storing and reproducing information came to provide metaphors for hypothetical processes in memory. A nineteenth-century example would be Francis Galton's use of his own invention of composite photography as an analogy for the way human memory forms prototypical images or generalized ideas. More recent examples are Feigenbaum's use of computer programs as models of memory, the proposal by Van Heerden and Pribram to view holograms as analogies for memory or the theory formulated by the theoretical physicist John Hopfield, specifying that the properties of what is now called a Hopfield network may explain the neurological substratum of human memory.[13] Within the compass of this short chapter I cannot begin to explore what links all these later 'physicists of memory' with Robert Hooke, but a telling resemblance would certainly be the confidence with which they extrapolate the properties of a physical state of affairs – be it a luminescent mineral or something so articulate as a hologram – to the domain of memory. Their explanations are formulated with the help of literary technologies derived from contemporary physics, and more often than not these hypotheses seem to profit from the awe and enthusiasm raised by new inventions.

Hooke, Galton, Feigenbaum, Pribram and Hopfield obviously have widely diverging interpretations of memory. But what they all have in common is that they conceptualized the hidden processes of remembering and forgetting in terms of a metaphor that invoked a series of concrete, comprehensible images. This is precisely what metaphors are designed to do – they are not simply passive instruments of thought. Metaphors lay the tracks for trains of associations, they direct the way we think, name and hypothesize.[14] This is the very reason why metaphors are such a profitable instrument of historical understanding. After all, Hooke's metaphors reflected his social and scientific environment. Without being used with that intention, metaphors capture an intellectual climate. In a sense metaphors *themselves* function as a memory. In metaphors we find preserved what the author saw around him when he was looking for graphic images for hidden processes in mind and memory.

Seventeenth-century still-life and portrait painters sometimes hung a gilded globe somewhere in a corner, which afforded a glimpse of the artist himself, half-hidden behind his easel. The 'Explication of Memory' reflects the personal universe of a researcher with a predilection for quantification and graphic examples. In his theory of memory Hooke seems to have designed a microcosm of what inspired and motivated him.

Chapter 8

Graphic Technologies

Nick Wilding

Of shapes transformde to bodies straunge, I purpose to entreate
(*Metamorphoses*)

When Richard Waller described Hooke's body, he used two images: it was a fast, lightweight machine and a misfunctioning organic system. The arguments were related by Hooke's own account of his self-transforming bodily practices: 'he first grew awry, by frequent practicing, turning with a Turn-Lath, and the like incurvating Exercises'.[1] By disrupting the correct relationship between subject and object, user and tool, the lathe worked the worker's body into both a machine and its product. This machining of the body into a new state, fusing the organic and the mechanical, was only the first instance of a lifetime of self-reflexive moves in natural philosophical practice. Whether living at low pressure in a vacuum chamber or dosing up on coffee and opium, Hooke's own body was a major site of post-Restoration experimentation.

Hooke not only experimented on his body, but also produced a powerful philosophy of body, combining his own technological programme with a rereading of the Fall to offer the possibility of a technologically supplemented cyborg postlapsarian body that would be functionally equivalent to the prelapsarian Adam.[2] In this story, the capabilities of Adam's body are gradually revealed to us only as our own deficiencies become apparent by technological innovation. Adam authorizes both our technologies and our bodies.

The fantasies of lack underpinning the creation of new supplemented bodies are not, however, entirely produced from within a closed discourse of technological improvement. They are also forged in a comparison between the capabilities of humans and animals. Like some composite Marvel figure, Adam is invested with superhuman animal senses – the astronomer's authority in using a telescope rests on the supposition that Adam's eyesight must rival that of a lynx. This zoomorphic fantasy was not purely physiological, but also psychological: in an extraordinary meditation, Hooke wonders whether a fly's life might not seem so brief to the fly itself, if its rate of experiencing the world were to be quantifiably higher than that of a human.[3]

While the body's perceptions could be enhanced by the addition of supplementary technologies, they could also be replicated and refined outside of the body itself. The thermometer, barometer, hygroscope, and so on, all instrumentalized senses found to be too dull in the human. Hooke not only attempted to standardize these instruments' measurements to provide both a community and a history of users, and calibrate the instruments against each other, but also introduced what to us might seem an obvious development, a mechanism enabling automatic self-recording.

A clock-driven paper-feeder was added to the weather-clock, allowing it to record its data automatically. Every fifteen minutes, punches would mark the instrument readings on the unfurling scroll. The paper could then be read off into standard measurements.[4] Whether or not the weather-clock worked or was used, its significance is immense: as the *Philosophical Transactions* remarked, 'All this to be performed by one only motion, driving all the parts of the instrument; which is therefore the more considerable, that itself records its own effects'.[5] The weather-clock relates to bodily organs not just by attempting to combine their labour and establish their inter-relationships, but by introducing a completely new dimension into the instrument, that of objective time. The idea of an instrument that could record measurements against time transforms it into a model of the one organ that had thus far resisted even theoretical mechanical simulation: memory. Hooke regarded memory as an organ; its workings, too, could be replicated and externalized. By instrumentalizing one metaphor of the nature of memory, time itself could be written. Given the subjectivity of time proposed in the relative psychology of the fly, the weather-clock did much more than reduce the labour of meteorological observation: it provided a permanent account of objective time. Its observational rate, four times an hour, makes it a mechanized organ of perception suited to its subject in precisely the same teleological (and partial) way Hooke conceived all bodily organs to be designed for specific functions. By working for a week between windings, it provided an ideal, superhuman observer of slow events. One should remember that the *Diary* itself started off as an attempt to provide standardized meteorological observations, an all too human 'memoranda', before it failed and became a record of Hooke's life.

The weather-clock marked the scroll using punches, presumably piercing or imprinting on the paper without ink. Before discussing the relationship between this instrument and Hooke's proposed model of human memory, I should like to sketch out a description of Hooke's use of the graphic mark.

The 'Observations' of *Micrographia* open with a series of jokes, themselves deployments of the Restoration natural philosopher's most valuable resource, a sharp wit to be used against dull spirits. While it has been argued that the *Micrographia* had no rhetorical model to follow, its obsession with questions of order (epistemological and political) is apparent from the start. The polysemic play on the point of entry to the text is also an act of parodic boundary fixing: the 'point' of the text is that it will replace Euclid's 'semeion', the mathematical part or immaterial sign, with a series of physical points. The disconcerting mise-en-âbyme of the microscopic reading of a full stop is only one of these jokes. The punning point hijacks Euclid, but on the way also parodies the start of *Leviathan*, where axiomatic logic is deployed to fix the foundations of political science. The play of the sign also allows him to present the text as an anti-scholastic zone, as he revisits duncical debates on Aquinas's angels with a joking reference to the needle-point giving 'a hundred armed Mites room enough to be rang'd by each other without endangering the breaking one anothers necks, by being thrust off on either side'.[6] The point of the point, though, is not merely to give a stiletto jab through overinflated discourses, but to question the metaphysical foundations of an abstract, non-materialistic notion of the point. A major enquiry in Hooke's theories of light, perception, memory and reasoning would be where, when and whether the physical point ever becomes immaterial.

Hooke's theory of the nature and workings of memory is mainly contained in his seventh 'Lecture of Light'. It has received attention from historians of psychology for its remarkable materialist model.[7] In arguing that memory should be understood as an organ, he invokes the same logic of supplementary arts that potentially characterize other postlapsarian senses.[8] This argument is important in that it indicates that from the start, Hooke intends not only to provide a model for the organ's function (by way of mechanical explanation), but also offer technical aids for its correct functioning. The two enterprises are intimately linked, and offer a clear escape route from the labyrinth of existing mnemonic techniques: rather than relying on a representational model of manipulable memory images, Hooke's mechanization of the memory as an organ facilitates its use as a tool or instrument.

The instrumental nature of the organ of memory means that it is directly plugged into the other organs of perception. This deontologising move collapses any representational notion for the receiving and storing of sense perceptions. What Hooke posits is an entirely material system, going beyond even a Lucretian model of simulacra. While it is unclear in Hooke's system exactly what happens to the perceived idea as it is received by the soul in order to form the material memory, at no point does he employ writing as a model, at least in its usual sense. As ideas enter the brain (and we must remember that this is a purely physical motion for Hooke, of the tiniest particles imaginable, on the cusp of non-materiality), they are received by the soul in order, and linked one to another. This 'Chain of Ideas' then forms the memory (which is conceived of precisely as this chain). The chain is, of course, a physical object, not a metaphor, located within the brain. Each 'idea' (either a perception or a reasoning) actually bears with it two meanings: its content and its relative position in the chain. The position is nothing other than perceived, subjective time. The ideas are revitalized by the soul, which illuminates them. As they move further from the soul, with the lengthening of the chain as new ideas are formed and time is felt to pass, they become more difficult for the soul to illuminate. Light bouncing from one idea to another, or ideas eclipsing each other, produce the well-known effects of random memories and mental blocks. Ideas also themselves have the power to draw the soul's attention to them, can be directly attached to each other by associative, rather than chronological, chains and can be simultaneously contemplated and compared. The soul has a general overview of its entire memory, but this claim may be purely a move to deflect anti-materialist critiques of the preceeding points. A rudimentary form of this model is apparent in the weather-clock: the instruments replicate the organs of perception; the scroll replicates the production of a chain of ideas. The soul can work on this external memory in just the same way as it does on its own internal memory, interpreting information, drawing patterns, making sense.

What, though, is the meaning of this model? Hooke's use of explanatory images from contemporary natural philosophy (vibration, luminescence and the heliocentric cosmos) has been noted; less attention has been given to more mundane metaphors of memory. The lecture repeatedly refers to the memory as a 'repository', 'store-house' and so on. In its non-representational concern with 'things' not 'words', memory's nature, use and problems are identical to those of an actual repository or museum. These were not abstract problems for Hooke in the late 1670s: issues of the correct selection of objects, organization, access to and use of the Royal Society's Repository were a constant concern in Hooke's efforts to transform it from an aristocratic cabinet of curiosity (producing only more curiosity), to a true representation, or sampling, of nature that might become the proper, privileged place for conducting research into nature. If discussions about Restoration Memory are also discussions about the Royal Society's Repository, then other analogies also fall neatly into place: the memory is reliant on an active soul to make it work; the soul of the Society (the Curator of the Repository) therefore should be acknowledged to be Hooke. Conversely, other social identities and activities that might be expected to provide suitable models to explicate the nature of memory are excluded: the memory is not an archive, especially not an archived Oldenburgian correspondence: in Hooke's model, this would be some other bodily function. But the relationship between the psychological and social models is not merely one of naturalizing a rhetoric of social advancement or consolidation of institutional power: Hooke's professional identity paradoxically naturalizes the organ of memory.

How is this function of memory incorporated into larger (corporeal and social) organic systems for the production of scientific facts? In the Preface to *Micrographia*, Hooke describes the gulf that separates not only fallen bodies from the prelapsarian ideal, but the failures in the workings of the mind. Sense, Memory and Reason are seen as a continual organic system. Their correct integration is fundamental to the production of natural philosophy: 'upon the evidence, the strength, the integrity, and the right correspondence of all these, all the light, by which our actions be guided, is to be renewed, and all our command over things is to be establisht'. While the role of technology might be relatively straightforward for the rectification of deficiencies in Sense, 'the adding of *artificial Organs* to the *natural*' is more problematic for the cases of Memory and Reason. Indeed, the *Micrographia* offers no concrete directives other than 'watchfullness' to discipline these organs into behaving correctly. In answer to the question of the right relationship between the senses, he claims

> The *Understanding* is to *order* all the inferiour services of the lower Faculties; but yet it is to do this only as a *lawful Master*, and not as a *Tyrant*. It must not *incroach* upon their Offices, nor take upon it self the employments which belong to either of them. It must *watch* the irregularities of the Senses, but it must not go before them, or *prevent* their information.[9]

Correct philosophical reasoning is also correct political reasoning: Restoration science must be monarchical, but not absolutist; it respects social hierarchies and the natural division of labour; it is non-interventionist in trade. The network of actors required to bring their accounts and artefacts into the repository should be regulated, but not forced. But how should Reason and Memory be disciplined into the correct use of material the modified Senses have delivered? The existence of such a technique is hinted:

> The next remedies in this universal cure of the Mind are to be applyed to the *Memory*, and they are to consist of such Directions as may inform us, what things are best to be *stor'd up* for our purpose, and which is the best way of so *disposing* them, that they may not only be *kept in safety*, but ready and convenient, to be at any time *produc'd* for use, as occasion shall require.[10]

The 'Discourse' explaining how this should be done, however, exists only in an incomplete form. Richard Waller added the following note to his edition of the work: 'the last and chief Part of this Physical Algebra, or New Organ, viz. The method of ranging the Experiments and Observations in order, so as to frame and raise Axioms from them is wanting (which I believe was never wrote by the Author)'.[11]

The 'General Scheme' is closely related to the Preface to *Micrographia*, in its attempt to secure natural philosophy's right working by disciplinary reform. Its treatment of the failures and correctives for memory and reasoning go far beyond the earlier text. Rather than engaging in a reconstruction of the workings of memory, it pragmatically addresses its shortcomings:

> Man's Memory seems very shallow and infirm, and so is very prone to forget many Circumstances, besides it cannot so well propound all it does remember, to be examin'd at once by the Judgement; but prefers some things first in order, before others, and some things with more Vehemence and greater concern, and accordingly the Understanding is more apt to be sway'd to this or that hand, according as it is more affected or prest by this or that Instance, and is very liable to oversee some considerable Passages, or to neglect them.[12]

Memory, or the repository in which the intellect is to work, is not a neutral system, but has its own tendencies to (mis)order its material, which introduces biases into the judgement of the intellect. Moreover, each subject is endowed by his own character to value some kinds of information over others, so the material that finds its way into the memory is already preselected. While the failures of the senses of perception are relatively easy for Hooke to rectify, Reason and Memory are more problematic. The tool that will mend their breakdowns is not physical, but philosophical: it is what Hooke calls his 'Philosophical Algebra'. The Algebra, however, should be seen not as some enclosed system of thought, but as continually interacting with material technologies, as the peculiarities of unmodified human sense organs produce only a partial reading of the world, which may be modified by the Algebra's own identification and reparation of the misprivileging of supposedly natural experience. The essential reconstruction of Memory is to impose correct order onto its unsorted heap of ideas:

> the Intellect should first like a skilful Architect, understand what it designs to do, and then consider as near as can be, what things are requisite to be provided in order to this Design, then those Materials are to be carefully sought for and collected, and safely laid up in so convenient an Order, that they may not be far to seek when they are wanting, nor hard to come by when they are found.[13]

This disciplining is less a philosophical system than a technique, comparable to trade skills. As a skill, Memory must make do with its supplementary aids, external copies of its own idealized form, and these may most conveniently be stored in the traditional medium of ink and paper.

> The Method of distributing the Matter of Philosophical History, both for making Heads of Inquiry, and consequently also of registring them, need not be very nice or curious, they being in them laid up only in Heaps as it were, as in a Granary or Store-House; from thence afterwards to be transcribed, fitted, ordered and rang'd, and Tabled.[14]

While this might seem like the *nth* reiteration of the Baconian call for a History of Everything, Hooke's notion of proper method is more dynamic, designed to provide a tool for actual use, an expanding resource for the natural philosopher/'Ratiocination' to work with:

> Every thing being here reduced to Regularity, Certainty, Number, Weight, and Measure; for whereas in the common ways of Ratiocination, Examination and Inquiry, all things are trusted to the immediate Powers of the Faculties of the Soul, viz. the bare Senses, Memory and Reason; in this [philosophy] they are none of them left, without their Armour, Engines, and Assistants, the Senses are helped by Instruments, Experiments, and comparative Collections, the Memory by writing and entering all things, ranged in the best and most Natural Order; so as not only to make them material and sensible, but impossible to be lost, forgot, or omitted, the Ratiocination is helped first, by being left alone and undisturbed to it self, having all the Intention of the Mind bent wholly to its Work, without being any other ways at the same time imployed in the Drudgery and Slavery of the Memory, either in calling particular things to Memory, or ranging them in Order, or remembring such things as belonging to another Head, or in transposing, jumbling, ranging, methodizing, and the like; for first all things are set down in their Order, the ultimate End, the intermediate, and

other Ends that are aimed at in order to the great one, the Steps and Ways that lead to each of these, then Engines and Helps are propounded; the Progress, that has been made and the Distance to come, is plainly to be seen for all things are registered in their due Order, as fast as made.[15]

The great advantage of external Memory over internal is that it can employ reason itself, rather than chronology, to order its contents.

This programme is obviously a radical alternative to the weather-clock as a replication of the internal workings of Memory, as described in the seventh 'Lecture on Light': the reliance on writing in 'General Scheme' bypasses the mechanism of Memory and forces its way directly into its contents. By diverting sense perceptions from the memory to the page, they can be correctly reordered and then reread in the correct order. Constant reordering and rereading will eventually produce a correctly ordered Memory, a memory whose chains both embody and enact the work of the understanding itself, a memory whose order resembles that of the world.

The actual form of the Histories thus produced is of particular significance: rather than compiling a closed encyclopaedia of the new philosophy, Hooke's ideal is a combination of expanses of writing, infinitely adaptable. The first consideration, then, is of space: it 'ought to be compris'd ... in as little room as possible, so as to appear and come under View all at once that the Eye may the more quickly pass over it from one Particular to another'.[16] Not only textual form, but the text itself, should be designed to allow the user to view the contents of this externalized and institutionalized Memory. Hooke suggests the use of 'some very good Short-hand or Abbreviation', but also hints that in the (missing) second part of the Algebra (the 'Rules and Methods of proceeding or operating with this so collected and qualify'd Supellex'), the History will be written in 'as few Letters or Characters as it has considerable Circumstances'. Given Hooke's close relationship to John Wilkins, his use of Wilkins's 'Real Character', and his ongoing involvement with the Paschall Circle, it seems likely that he had some development of the character's radical rethinking of the nature of script as the basis for this text.[17] Wilkins's terms famously embody a definition of their objects, through a tabular scheme organising all common experience and knowledge. This seems to be precisely the hierarchical organising structure Hooke regards as desirable for his own tables. Moreover, by the establishment of correct relationships within the tables, the script itself would become a disciplinary tool for correct thinking. The relationship between (natural philosophical) memory and the text could then be inverted, for the text would contain not only correct knowledge, but the correct (and only) way of thinking it. By attacking the representational mode of thought in traditional scripts, the *Essay* would also have provided Hooke's artificial memory with a writing technology closer to his model within the body. Moreover, establishing the true philosophy could happen gradually. Leibniz suggested just such a productive relationship between a universal script and philosophy in a note to a letter from Descartes to Mersenne; Hooke shows how it might be practically accomplished, appropriating the technology of common-place books and art collections of rearranging the relationships between textual fragments by continual cutting and pasting, until the true philosophy fell into place. The missing Algebra claimed to provide a sure way of identifying gaps in knowledge and providing the correct method to fill them. It seems that these gaps would be rendered visible as blank space in the correctly organized book.

The copy-book of knowledge is a unique manuscript, a work in progress that cannot be replicated until it is finished. It therefore occupies and creates a privileged physical and social space proper to its compilation and consultation. Its authority relies both on the successful centralization of knowledge and restricted access to those permitted to reorder its contents. Its correct editing (which is also an editing of the self) necessarily produces a non-replicable social function, in order that the text ultimately produced might be replicable.

The dynamic role writing was to play in the production of natural philosophy goes far beyond that of disseminating experimental narratives: it is a central part of experimentation itself. In Hooke's brief 'Method of making Experiments', the writing up of experiments forms the final part of the process, but feeds back in a loop to its start and is also important in the central demonstration.[18]

The almost juridical authority invoked by Hooke in the collection of signatures proving the veracity of the experimental result might make us wonder what Hooke thought the proper status and use of such documents might be. His 'Proposalls for the Good of the Royal Society',[19] the various notes on reforming the Society, or setting up an alternative, and his charges against Oldenburg of improper conduct in the archive all reveal a deep tension between the need to publicize the group's activities and restrict access to work in progress. Questions of propriety and property, of individual and institutional identity and the writing and rewriting of the archive occupied him continually, especially in his attempts to make sense of disputes with Huygens, Newton and Flamsteed.[20] Bennett has remarked that a historio-graphical bias towards Hooke's controversies has distorted our view of his mechanical philosophy;[21] one might add that this attention has tended to try to resolve the disputes posthumously, rather than analyse their condition of existence. Hooke's solution to the problem of the written records might be a good starting point. In his 'Proposalls', he recommended that the curators' quarterly discourses should be transcribed *verbatim* into a register book, 'there to be perused by any member of the society at any seasonable time & by none els whatever. and the Discouse to be putt up in a cell proper for it to be kept'.[22] His notion of publishing was similarly restricted: the monthly gazette for absent Members had to be kept secret from non-members for one year after its publication. While his poor track record with the *Philosophical Collections* and general failure as Secretary reveal his inability to gain institutional support to implement this more restricted economy of scientific exchange, its existence does imply a profound dissatisfaction with Oldenburg's running of the system. The offer of a private, unmediated correspondence with Newton was one way to avoid the pitfalls of the institutional claim to his productions; refusing to write or make knowledge public was another. But, as Shapin has recently argued with respect to technological innovation, the problem was both peculiarly Hooke's own and that of the Royal Society in general: whereas the Académie des Sciences was expected to fulfill the role of patent office, the Royal Society was never granted this privilege.[23] Its knowledge was therefore always self-authenticating, at best, and not woven into the state apparatus until Newton appropriated the authority of the Mint to render the Society the proper place for the evaluation of technological schemes.[24] Hooke had to search for proof of his demonstrations within the Society's own archives; what he found was often more proof of biased archiving.[25] If the register books were supposed to provide an institutional memory, they also needed an institutional soul. The mutual destruction of credit between Oldenburg, Hooke and Newton both produces and is produced by conflicting models of the correct mode of proceeding in the exchange, use and archiving of documentation.

This conflict plays out on a larger scale, too. What kind of knowledge was proper to the Royal Society? From whom should it be received, and in exchange for what? What was the proper use of such knowledge? Hooke's projected 'Histories' might at first sight be seen as part of a long-term Baconian plot to appropriate guild knowledge by the state apparatus. The failure of the pro-technological agenda championed by Sprat to become incorporated into the larger Leviathan of the state may well have pushed the first generation further towards an ideology of experimentation, but it left its own technological claims in a strange status. This was recognized even by Shadwell, whose final charge against Gimcrack is both that he is useless and that he has produced improper (because too successful) technology. The rioting ribbon-makers seeking the death of the virtuosi were not figments of his imagination: in 1661, Thomas Powell had published his *Humane Industry: or, a History of most Manual Arts*, which described a protest against technological innovation in Gdansk at the end of the sixteenth century. This account was first published by Secondo Lancellotti, as related to him by the son of the German painter Anton Möller.[26] Marx then got hold of this account via Beckmann, misindexing and misdating it on the way.[27] Starting life as a curious anecdote exemplifying past and present vice, the story becomes an Enlightenment warning of the ignorance of the masses. Only with Marx are the voices of the ribbon weavers finally heard. The section on the history of machine-breaking concludes, 'History discloses no tragedy more horrible than the gradual extinction of the English hand-loom weavers.'

The problem, fundamentally one of the correct place of knowledge in the early modern world, was already weakly addressed by Sprat in *History of the Royal Society of London*:

[Tradesmen] are generally infected with the narrowness that is natural to *Corporations*, which are wont to resist all *new comers*, as profess'd Enemies to their *Privileges*: And by these interested [sic] men it may be objected, that the growth of *new Inventions* and *new Artificers*, will infallibly reduce all the old ones to poverty and decay.[28]

The attempted appropriation of guild-knowledge by natural philosophers and their new institutions could be seen as precisely the social dynamic embodied by Hooke. The compilation of a complete 'History of Trades' had as its ultimate aim not the neutral archiving of knowledge as such, but the production of technological remedies to reduce labour. Gimcrack's plea, 'I never invented anything of use in my life' is not applicable to Hooke, but the Society's failure to provide a safe repository for the knowledge he gained on his peripatetic apprenticeships, and its inability to negotiate an official position within the State bureaucracy for receiving, evaluating and keeping patents made it curiously incapable of running itself to the satisfaction of its curator. As Rob Iliffe has persuasively argued, Hooke's experience in the watch dispute with Huygens convinced him that the Royal Society was 'not competent to judge matters which were the proper business of tradesmen and craftsmen'.[29] Hooke may have been the most important matrix through which information passed between the two worlds, but he resisted the drive to judge, appropriate and profit from trade knowledge. While Hooke's reconstructions of the organ of memory might prepare us for an institutional model designed to perform just such a task, his own perception of archival betrayal, institutional mistreatment and trade culture blocked the transferral of such information into the archive. When Hooke delivered his lecture on the nature of memory, there were objections that the soul had been rendered material. Hooke's example shows just how locally circumscribed the soul's interest might be.

Chapter 9

Hooke's Ideas of the Terraqueous Globe and a Theory of Evolution

Ellen Tan Drake

Introduction

Hooke's system of the Earth, as expressed in his 'Discourses of Earthquakes' published posthumously in 1705, embodies some fundamental concepts about the Earth that are startlingly on target and markedly different from other theories of the Earth expressed by his contemporaries. His *Posthumous Works* include these lectures on 'earthquakes' given for more than a 30-year period from about 1664 to 1699.[1] His most perceptive ideas about geology were expressed in the series of lectures that ended on 15 September 1668, and in the series between 28 May 1684 and toward the end of 1687. He contributed significantly to many basic concepts concerning his 'terraqueous' globe; some of these were: the organic origin and significance of fossils; cyclicity of the processes of sedimentation, consolidation, uplift, erosion and denudation; various processes of petrifaction; subterraneous eruptions and earthquakes; biologic evolution; oblate spheroid shape of the Earth; polar wandering; and universal gravitation.

In this paper I will present some of Hooke's ideas of the terraqueous globe, especially those having to do with cyclical processes of sedimentation, erosion and uplift, and his insightful conclusions about the significance of the occurrence of fossils. I will relate how ingrained prejudices of the received opinion, representing the prevailing thought, delayed the emergence of a revolutionary scientific idea – that of Biologic Evolution.

Hooke's Terraqueous Globe and Cyclicity of Terrestrial Processes

Formulating theories of the Earth was a popular activity among many intelligentsia of the seventeenth century. The underlying motivation for such theories was to show that natural laws are God's laws and therefore must synchronize with the processes recorded in Scripture. The sentiments of the physician and naturalist John Woodward perhaps typified the age. He wrote: 'the terraqueous Globe is to this day nearly in the same condition that the Universal Deluge left it: being also like to continue so till the time of its final ruin and dissolution'.[2] Further, there was no sea before the Deluge. Most of Hooke's contemporaries thought that 'figured stones', their name for fossils and minerals alike, were formed by some magical or astrological influence and were a *lusus naturæ*, a trick of nature, formed as a result of the Earth's latent 'plastick virtue' generating these animal-like shapes as well as the pretty, faceted crystals and stones. Some of the intelligentsia did recognize fossils as organic in origin but they were thought to be relics of Noah's Flood. The age of the Earth was less than 6000 years, the date of 4004 BC for the beginning of the world having been firmly established by Bishop Ussher (1581–1656).

Hooke's system of the Earth was very different from those of his contemporaries because he based his ideas on his own observations of terrestrial processes that constantly demonstrated to him their ability to change the surface features of the Earth. These include erosion and deposition, volcanism and earthquakes, which, along with the effect of wandering poles on an oblate spheroid Earth, produce repeated exchanges of land and sea areas. I have already discussed polar wandering and the shape of the Earth.[3] In the history and development of ideas, Hooke's 'Discourses of Earthquakes', in my opinion, laid the foundation of the science of geology.

He derived his conclusions about geologic processes from his examination of the cliff shores of the Isle of Wight, his birthplace. Hooke often climbed these cliffs, not just as a boy but later also when he returned to his home town, Freshwater, during the lifetime of his mother. As an adult he carried a walking stick, collected specimens and examined the sediments and fossils under the microscope he designed and built. He also drew the specimens he saw with skill and accuracy (Figure 9.1).

He noted the types of sediments deposited and their provenance and scrutinized with great care their imbedded fossil organisms. He thus repeatedly witnessed the cyclic dynamic processes taking place – the erosion of the cliffs and re-deposition of the eroded materials into 'layers' in the sea. He marveled at a layer chock-full of fossils of marine animals some 60 feet above the surface of the sea. The semi-consolidated or solid layers, he concluded, were made of loose materials washed down into the sea from the cliff shores 'by degrees'. These layers were then compacted and consolidated into stone,

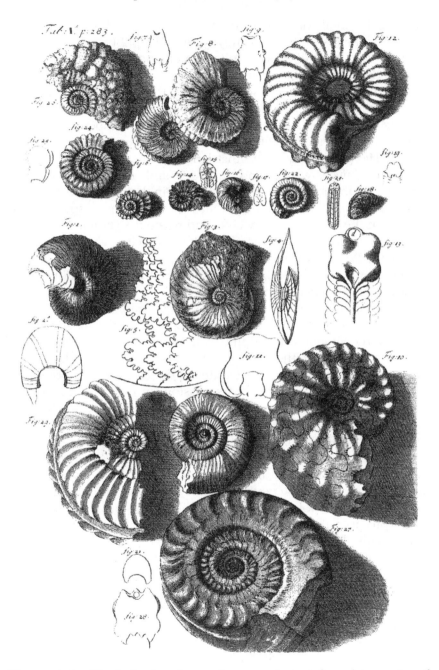

Figure 9.1 Hooke's drawings of ammonites, referred to as 'snail-stones' or 'snake-stones'.
(Hooke 1705)

trapping the shells of animals, then raised up out of the sea through earth movements, either violently or imperceptibly 'by degrees' to begin another cycle of erosion and sedimentation.

Much discussion in his lectures is devoted to the processes by which loose sediment beomes consolidated, and through petrifaction, turns into hardened rock. He noted that the tops of very high mountains like the Alps are made of layers that have marine fossils embedded in them, proving that even the tops of high mountains had been at the bottom of the sea. He was keenly aware that land is constantly subject to such erosional agents as water, wind, snow ice, and currents. Just as floods from rivers carry away all things that stand in their way and cover the land with mud, 'levelling Ridges and filling Ditches', so tides and currents in the sea wash away cliffs and waste the shores. As the Nile delta is enlarged by sediments, the Gulf of Venice is 'choak'd with the Sand of the Po', and the mouth of the Thames grows shallow from sand brought down with the stream, so 'Cliffs that Wall this Island do Yearly founder and tumble into the Sea'.[4]

Hooke's comprehension of the slow cycles taking place, changing 'by degrees', indicates that his use of the word 'earthquake' was not limited to the violent, catastrophic earth movements of seismicity and volcanic eruptions. Rather, the term can also mean other diastrophic forces that change the surface features of the Earth and embody such processes of earth movements as erosion and deposition or slow sinking or raising of the land. The word 'earthquakes' in the title and text of his series of lectures, however, has prompted some later writers, such as the distinguished Newton biographer Richard Westfall to call him 'the first Catastrophist'.[5] But throughout his lectures it is evident that Hooke was also concerned with the 'very slow and almost imperceptible' actions of sand, water, wind and ice. These processes are less violent but constant and persistent, and in time they 'much promote the levelling and smoothing of the Surface of the Earth'. This leveled surface referred to by later geologists as peneplanation would then again be subject to being raised either by violent motions such as faulting leading to earthquakes or by gradual earth movements and the whole process of erosion, deposition and petrifaction begins anew. Implicit in this process is the geological concept of the unconformity, very important to the understanding of the depositional history of a series of rocks. Hooke therefore was clearly putting forth a cyclic theory, discussed by Drake[6] and by Ito who recognizes that some of Hooke's ideas were not wholly unacceptable to his contemporaries.[7] To Hooke all things in nature 'almost circulate and have their Vicissitudes'. In expressing this cycle his writing becomes almost poetic:

Generation creates and Death destroys;
Winter reduces what Summer produces;
The Night refreshes what the Day has scorcht,
And the Day cherishes what the Night benumb'd.[8]

He clearly realized that the present is indeed the key to the past so that in these respects he was also a Uniformitarian. But he was not such in the strict sense of repeated closed cycles as exemplified in the ideas of the famous English geologist and friend of Darwin, Charles Lyell, hence Hooke's use of the modifier 'almost' for the verb 'circulate'. He thus described a system that repeats and cycles but is not closed and static, so the cycles may change eventually into some other geologic environment and activity as a result of changing conditions in climate, rainfall or topography. In addition to these slower, cyclic processes Hooke certainly believed that great earthquakes and volcanic eruptions also made significant changes to the surface features of the Earth. Large sections of his 'Discourse' describe reports of these events around the world and the devastation they caused, indicating that he was extremely well read and kept up to date with events around the world. If Hooke could have entered the later debate among geologists between Uniformitarianism and Catastrophism, therefore, he might have been totally mystified, as he would have seen no reason why one had to be on the side of one or the other.

From the start he questioned the validity of the narration in *Genesis* and asserted that Noah's Flood was nothing special, not because Hooke was a disbeliever but because he distrusted the truthfulness and accuracy of the biblical account, written by men about things that happened before the invention of writing. He wrote:

> The great transactions of the Alterations, Formations, or Dispositions of the Superficial Parts of the Earth into that Constitution and Shape which we now find them to have, preceded the Invention of Writing, and what was preserved till the times of that Invention were more dark and confused, that they seem to be altogether Romantick, Fabulous, and Fictious, and cannot be much relied on or heeded, and at best will only afford us occasions of Conjecture.[9]

Hooke's understanding of the sediments depositing into 'layers' indicates that he was fully cognizant of geologists' Law of Superposition, but I think he would have considered it self-evident. This 'Law' states what Hooke would have thought obvious and common-sensical: that the bottom layer of a series of rocks, when it was being laid down in its watery grave, had no other layer of sediment on top of it so that the bottom layer of any series, unless all the layers are overturned, must be considered the oldest. This simple rule was expressed by Hooke's contemporary, the much-admired Dane, Nicolaus Stenonius, better known as Steno, writing in Italy.

Steno was among a few of that age who also thought fossils to be of organic origin, but he believed they were relics of Noah's Flood. Hooke rejected the exclusivity of the Flood as the sole cause of all the features of the Earth and the occurrence of fossils, asserting that there have been many great floods in the past; he further objected to all explanations that invoked 'Astrological and magical Fancy' for the occurrence of fossils. He insisted that fossils were petrified organic remains having nothing to do with the Flood nor were they formed from 'any kind of Plastick virtue inherent in the earth'. He also asserted that crystals and minerals were inorganic in origin. The latter, he explained in association with his various ways of sediments hardening into rock, were formed either from precipitating from solutions as in rock fissures and caves forming what we now refer to as stalactites and stalagmites, or were formed deep in the Earth from molten rock and later exposed by uplift and erosion. He wrote, the aqueous solutions 'by degrees produced several conical pendulous Bodies of Stone, shap'd and hanging like Icicles from the Roof of the Vault; and dropping on the bottom, it raises up also conical Spires, which, by degrees, endeavour to meet the former pendulous Stiriæ'.[10] These solutions can cement loose sediments into rock. His understanding of the processes that change sands and muds into rock and shape terrestrial features was in several ways more profound than that of Steno,[11] as was his understanding of the formation of crystals.[12] Ironically and true to Hooke's usual bad luck and fate, Steno, rather than Hooke, is widely hailed by geologists today as the founder of geology. Gordon Davies wrote, 'the neglected Hooke had an understanding of Earth-history which is in some respects superior to that of the much lauded Steno'.[13]

Hooke's Theory of Evolution and its Reception

Hooke, therefore, was alone in his age to argue that fossils were not the relics of Noah's Flood. More significant than Hooke's insistence on the organic origin of fossils were his ideas of biological evolution and the fact that some species have clearly disappeared and are no more. The concept of extinction to Hooke was a logical conclusion; he wrote in 1667: 'There have been many other Species of Creatures in former Ages of which we can find none at present, and ... there may be divers new kinds now, which have not been from the beginning'.[14] With a leap of imagination he thus recognized both the extinction of species and the generation of new ones. He believed environmental changes to be 'the reason why we now find the shells of divers Fishes Petrify'd in Stone, of which we have now none of the same kind', because we find fauna and flora peculiar to certain places, and not to be found elsewhere. If some disaster or change happens to that place and it becomes unsuitable for the fauna and/or flora, then they would be destroyed or changed to adapt. By the same token, new varieties of the same species could be generated if we alter the soil, climate or nourishment. In contrast to most of his contemporaries who were not only ignorant of the true meaning and significance of fossils, he also realized perceptively the usefulness of fossils as records of the past. Interested in reconstructing the past he wrote:

> There is no Coin can so well inform any Antiquary that there has been such or such a place subject to such a Prince, as these will certify a Natural Antiquary, that such and such places have been under the water, that there have been such kind of Animals, that there have been such and such preceding Alterations and Changes of the Superficial Parts of the Earth.[15]

Extinction, however, was a particularly difficult concept for his contemporary audience to accept. Their passionately expressed objections were paraphrased and succinctly summarized by Hooke himself in his lectures: his contemporaries believed that extinction 'would argue an imperfection of the first Creation, which should produce any one Species more than what was absolutely necessary to its present future state, and so would be a great derogation from the Wisdom and Power of the Omnipotent Creator'. To these men, it would be sacrilegious to suggest that a creation of God could be so imperfect as to need to change or evolve. Hooke's arguments to counteract this sentiment were persuasive because he understood his audience well. He reasoned that certain species may be of a certain size now but were much bigger in a former age and further, some forms have changed so much that they cannot now be identified as the same species. Also, mixtures of creatures can produce forms different from their ancestors. He pointed to variations as a result of breeding among domestic animals as examples that people might understand, as such practice was already known by then. Darwin also used similar observations to support his ideas on evolution, referring to such changes in domestic animals as 'artificial selection'. Hooke asked, why could such changes not be achieved also in natural conditions? Why should these changes offend God? To Hooke, God designed the model and the conditions allowing the world with all its creatures to evolve; while God might have been the ultimate cause (which he referred to as 'That extraordinary Earthquake'), the immediate causes are always natural ones.

More startling than his general statement on the usefulness of fossils to reveal the history of a region was this famous quote expressed by Hooke more than 100 years before the great stratigrapher William 'Strata' Smith:

> And tho' it must be granted, that it is very difficult to read them, and to raise a *Chronology* [Hooke's own italics] out of them, and to state the intervalls of the Times wherein such, or such Catastrophies and Mutations have happened; yet 'tis not impossible, but that, by the help of those joined to other means and assistances of Information, much may be done even in that part of Information also.[16]

Hooke was unfortunately ahead of his time. Charles Lyell was clearly impressed by Hooke's intellect, as he quoted this passage in his famous *Principles of Geology*, but he stopped after the words 'yet 'tis not impossible', and placed a period there.[17] This bit of creative editing has upset later writers who, instead of recognizing Hooke's original and almost clairvoyant thinking, warned readers not to read too much into this statement, thereby diminishing Hooke's originality. Hooke was clearly not a stratigrapher. The discipline of stratigraphy was a later development. The science of the chronological ordering of sedimentary layers according to their fossil assemblages and correlating them over great distances was developed by the painstaking work of the late eighteenth-/early nineteenth-century engineer and canal builder William 'Strata' Smith. But credit should be given Hooke for recognizing the *potential* usefulness of fossils in this seminal but fruitful thought.

Besides the pure abhorrence of the concept of extinction labeled by Hooke's critics of his time as 'absurd and extravagant', some others expressed another argument: just because we do not find some animals alive now does not necessarily mean that they do not exist somewhere in the world yet to be discovered. This was the respected churchman John Ray's argument against extinction, and on this issue Ray's theory of the Earth, similar to Hooke's, departs from Hooke's, but there is some evidence that Ray plagiarized Hooke.[18] Hooke's response to this line of rhetoric was: granted, we are not familiar with all the vast varieties of animal and plant life in the world, so we will not insist that they are not existing somewhere. But for now, we will simply assume that the animals represented by their fossils are no more – that is, extinct. He wrote, 'we will, for the present, take this Supposition to be real and true, that there have been in former times of the World, divers *Species* of Creatures that are now quite lost, and no more of them surviving upon any part of the Earth'. But he went on to say

> And yet I do not see how this doth in the least derogate from the Power, Wisdom and Providence of God, as is alledged, or that it doth any ways contradict any part of the Scripture, or any Conclusion of the most eminent Philosophers, or any rational Argument that may be drawn from the Phænomena of Nature; nay, I think the quite contrary Inferences may, nay, must, and ought to be made.[19]

This was clearly an impassioned plea for the rationality of his hypothesis. Hooke's attitude toward God and the Bible is both rational and practical, without denying the existence of one or denigrating the importance of the other. To him the concept of evolution was inescapable, given the fossil evidence.

But the strong prevailing feelings bolstered by the ever-present influence of religion, as we have seen even today, have kept these ideas from being developed in the seventeenth century. It is enough, I suppose, that they were aired at all. A copy of Hooke's *Micrographia* was found in Darwin's library. Although Hooke's ideas on evolution were not specifically expressed in *Micrographia*, some of Hooke's insightful ideas about the organic world in that book as well as his ideas on biologic evolution in his *Posthumous Works* could well have passed through the mind of Darwin. Certainly Lyell was impressed. Hooke, therefore, along with his many other accomplishments should be considered an early evolutionist, a precursor of Charles Darwin. The Russian scientist A. P. Pavlow, speaking in French on Robert Hooke as an evolutionist at the 7 March 1925 meeting of the Society of Naturalists of Moscow and of the Congress of Russian Zoologists, said:

> It seems strange to speak of an evolutionist, having lived at an age when neither comparative anatomy nor paleontology yet existed, at an age when Scheuchzer, describing the skeleton of a giant fossil salamander, took it for the skeleton of an antediluvian man; when the fossil teeth of shark were taken for the petrified tongues of birds (glossopetræ); when Aldovandri, in his famous and voluminous Zoology, described and reproduced a number of dragons, all imaginary, as having really existed and depicted alongside of each example, the plant or species of grass that the animal ate.[20]

Pavlow's statement expresses an appreciation of the brilliant mind of the remarkable Robert Hooke that has been all too rare in the literature.

Hooke's Concept of Time

While his contemporaries assigned the cause of all the uneven surfaces of the Earth to the Flood which left the fossils where they are found, Hooke relied on his own observations of the dynamics taking place at the coastal cliffs of the Isle of Wight. He said that the quantity and thickness of the sediments in which the fossils are mixed argue that there must be a 'much longer time of the Seas Residence above the same, than so short a space [of time] can afford'. He knew from the biblical account that the duration of Noah's Flood was stated to be only about 200 days. He appears, therefore, to be openly questioning the traditional European chronology, which, of course, was the Scriptural chronology. Hooke, therefore, was alone in his age to argue that fossils were not the relicts of Noah's Flood, an event that 'lasted but a little while'. His own knowledge of the hundreds of feet of sediments exposed in the cliffs of the Isle of Wight enclosing marine fossils was more convincing than the words from Scripture. Some of these fossils were giant specimens, like the giant ammonites, that he correctly assumed did not exist any more.

All through his lectures Hooke showed that he desperately needed the Earth to be older than a few thousand years in order to accommodate his cyclicity of processes, his polar wandering and his theory of evolution – all needing great lengths of time to accomplish. Being a mathematically-minded man, it would have been inconceivable that he did not try to estimate and calculate the duration of time it took for the repeated processes of erosion and deposition that he witnessed. His writings show that his early lectures on earth science ignored Scriptural constraints of time as totally irrelevant. It was only later when religious considerations became so prevalent and he encountered so many accusations of the 'derogation of God' that he felt the need to corroborate some of his ideas by searching through the classics. He then found it necessary to mollify his audience if he mentioned a time element he knew to be offensive to them because it exceeded the biblical chronology. For example, he said that if such and such duration seems too long for you to accept, think that perhaps a day at the beginning of the world might have been shorter than now.[21] He repeatedly referred to Egyptian and Chinese histories that told of events of 'many thousand Years more than ever we in Europe heard of by our Writings', but to placate his listeners, he quickly added, 'if their Chronology may be granted, which indeed there is great reason to question'.[22] It is evident, however, that Hooke was an admirer of Chinese history and culture, as he not only cited events in the reign of various emperors, he even tried to learn the Chinese language.[23]

His repeated reassurances to his audience to disregard the element of time because it was contrary to Scripture served some of his present-day critics to say that he too was steeped in religious dogma. Nothing can be further from the truth. My interpretation is that he needed and wanted the Earth to be much older than the 6000 years allowed by the bible. But Bishop Ussher's edict for the beginning of the Earth, at 9:00 a.m. on the 26 October 4004 BC, was hardly open for debate. Also, Hooke knew he had to be politic: if he thought the Earth was at least millions of years old, he was quiet about it. He stated that the Chinese 'do make the World 88,640,000 years old'. Some of the men for whom he had the greatest respect were churchmen like his old sponsor John Wilkins, Bishop of Chester. The conferment of his own doctoral degree at Oxford in 1691 was 'warranted' by the Archbishop of Canterbury, John Tillotson. Being a loyal friend and protégé he could not have flaunted an idea that would have offended practically everyone in the seventeenth century.

There is no evidence, however, that he could have conceived of the billions of years we know now for the age of the Earth. Nevertheless, Hooke forged ahead with his creative and fruitful ideas that laid the foundation for the science of Geology. Moreover, there is convincing evidence that James Hutton, widely recognized as the father of modern geology, was familiar with Hooke's ideas, adopting those with which he agreed and arguing passionately against those with which he disapproved.[24] Among the latter was Hooke's polar wandering or 'axial displacement' idea that, although fully vindicated today, had, by Hutton's time, been rejected from the day he introduced it. It was unnecessary, therefore, for Hutton to attack it so strenuously, which he did in both his *Abstract* and his *Theory*, unless he was quite familiar with Hooke's writings and this idea of polar wander troubled him deeply.

While Hooke could not conceive of an Earth of an unfathomable age of billions of years, Hutton put forth an earth 'with no vestige of a beginning and no prospect of an end'.[25] Hutton's very quotable and poetic dictum was wrong, of course, the lifetime of our Sun and Earth being finite, but it freed geology from the constraint of biblical chronology. Hooke's persistent questioning of the Scriptural time scale and all his geological contributions, however, laid the foundation of geology, and geologists and historians alike should recognize this fact.

Hooke's Undeserved Obscurity

I am puzzled why Hooke's name is so relatively obscure today. Part of the reason certainly must be that modern lives have become so complex that few people have the time to read all that Hooke wrote and learn about all his achievements and contributions to science. A glance at the contents of this book reveals the extent of Hooke's interests and expertise. On the other hand, Steno's short pamphlet, the *Prodromus*, though written in Latin, can be easily read from translations and digested.[26] But it must be said also that scholars have been burdened by erroneous and prejudicial information passed down through the ages. Some Newton scholars and admirers are still prone to denigrating Hooke. While Hooke was honored and respected during his lifetime, somehow since his death, through the last three centuries, he has suffered from a bad press. Richard Waller, the editor of his *Posthumous Works*, who knew Hooke as an old man, described him in 1705 as having a mistrustful and jealous personality. Others more recently, sometimes on the basis of Hooke's spontaneous feelings of the moment expressed in the privacy of his diary, have labeled his character and personality in derogatory terms, criticizing him for being jealous and claiming more credit than he deserved. In actuality, credit has been accorded to others for work done by him and whose priority was clearly his. An unsuspecting researcher could end up not liking Hooke's character and thus be negatively swayed in his judgment of the true importance of Hooke's science, not to mention the sheer volume of all that he contributed to many other facets of human endeavor. We forgive Newton's character defects, which were plentiful and often injurious to others, because of the magnificent *Principia*. Newton is pictured as a godlike heroic figure in the literature, even in poetry and especially in children's books, perpetuated by such powerful and magical legends as the apple legend. Hooke is usually represented by later writers with all his warts and human foibles and is hardly mentioned in children's books. Yet Hooke was highly respected in his day, a fact that would seem to be contradicted by his extraordinarily bad luck and almost consistently 'bad press' that plagued him for too long. This pejorative press on top of his bad luck contributed to Hooke's undeserved obscurity during the past three centuries. Yet of all the great luminaries of the seventeenth century, including the immortal Newton, Hooke was the least hampered by Medievalism and probably contributed the most to science and technology. While recent scholarship has corrected many misconceptions of Hooke, it has not had time to seep into the general perception of the educated public so that Hooke's obscurity and misconceptions of him still seem to be the norm.

His bad luck is shown in numerous ways.[27] A few examples follow. He was the first to prove the Power and Towneley hypothesis by experimentation now known as Boyle's Law. He was the first to invent a pocket watch using a spring-balance wheel, but Christiaan Huygens is generally credited with the invention, and the date-inscribed pocket-watch he presented to Charles II in 1675 to prove his priority is now lost. He was the first to track a comet in 1665 and propose that it was the same that came in 1618 and predicted that it would come again in another interim of the same duration. But the discovery of the periodicity of some comets is attributed to Edmond Halley who was nine years old at that time. Hooke was the first to express clearly and concisely a theory of combustion based on experimentation but John Mayow has been given the credit. He anticipated Newton in some of the fundamental ideas underlying the Universal Law of Gravitation, notably the concept of centripetal force, necessary for the full comprehension of the gravitational problem, and communicated his ideas to Newton but never received credit. He was the first to describe the iridescent interference colours seen when light falls on a layer of air between two thin glass plates but, ironically, these are known as 'Newton's Rings'. He designed both the great dome of St Paul's Cathedral and the Monument to the fire of 1666, but both are generally attributed to Christopher Wren. Finally, as has been shown in this paper, he was the true founder of the science of geology, but Steno is generally praised for this role. While this list of his accomplishments contains necessarily simplified versions of more complicated issues, it is clear that the importance of his contributions to each activity has been unrecognized until recently, and then only by scholars working in those fields.

He was unlucky in other ways too. He had poor health throughout his life, suffering from headaches, indigestion, colds, dizziness and insomnia; how he could have accomplished as much as he did having such a constant array of debilitating symptoms is remarkable indeed. His position as Curator of Experiments at the Royal Society supposedly paid a salary of £80 per annum, but he hardly ever received it, especially in the early years. When the miserly 'philanthropist' John Cutler offered him £50 per annum to give a series of lectures, the Royal Society promptly reduced his ephemeral £80 to £30 per annum. Hooke gave his lectures, but Cutler never paid up during his lifetime; Hooke had to sue Cutler's estate and won when he was himself an old man and by then not needing the money. When Hooke died he was buried with due respect at St Helen's Church in Bishopsgate with his colleagues at the Royal Society (except Newton) in attendance. In the late nineteenth century his remains, mingled with those of hundreds of his fellow Parishioners, were disinterred and re-buried in a mass grave at Wanstead.[28] A commemorative stained glass window in St Helen's Church featuring Hooke as one of the 'London Worthies' was destroyed during the Irish Republican Army bombing of the City of London in April 1992. So far neither the church nor any other group has been sufficiently interested to contribute to its replacement, so, as of this writing, there is just a plain glass there. None of the thousands of instruments and models he constructed or the fossil specimens he collected survived Newton's presidency of the Royal Society and the move from Gresham College. His portrait which certainly existed at one time and should have been in the possession of the Royal Society and displayed along with other prominent members and officers of the Society is missing. It is as if Fate, in collaboration with his detractors in the literature, also wished to erase his memory.

Conclusion

In spite of the negative depictions of Hooke's character, as mistrustful, suspicious, irascible, and so on, the image one receives from reading Hooke's own writings, or those of his friends like John Aubrey, is that of a scientist for all ages: curious, ingenuous, indefatigable and filled with wonder.[29] While examining some fossils, for example, he broke a rock into two 'with a smart stroke of a Hammer' and delighted in discovering two small 'Snake-stones', or ammonites, within it. What present-day geologist has not wielded that 'smart stroke of a hammer' and found a fossil or two in the broken stone and was as pleased as if he or she had found gold? When he discovered, with the aid of his microscope, a perfectly formed foraminifera shell, no bigger than the point of a pin, his description of it in his famous book *Micrographia* makes the reader almost feel the excitement that he felt.[30] And indeed, in *Micrographia* he was the first person to document the existence of microorganisms. The image of the seventeenth-century Hooke looking down his microscope is not much different from a micropaleontologist today bent over his or her microscope. The difference is that the latter does not have to design and construct the microscope first.

Moreover, in contrast to what has been written about him, Hooke's writings reveal him to be meticulously honest, giving credit where due; he never seemed to fail to mention the slightest person's name who presented him with a fossil specimen or otherwise gave him information. He was very open about his ideas; discussed them with friends in coffee houses and gave them in lectures; he was sociable, gregarious and loyal to his friends. If he seemed paranoid later in life, it was because some people *did* seem to borrow freely, and without acknowledgment, from his intellectual property that was so generously shared with his world.

Hooke's contributions to science and technology were not only prolific but they were of fundamental importance to the state of knowledge and development of science in our own day. The world owes a great debt to Robert Hooke. He was the first evolutionist, and has been recognized by Rossiter as the first English geologist.[31] Geologists in general however should recognize Hooke as the true founder of their science.

PART 4
ARCHITECTURE AND CONSTRUCTION

Chapter 10

Hooke and Bedlam

Jacques Heyman

Summary

Hooke's diaries record his employment in 1674–76 as architect for the new Bethlehem Hospital at Moorfields. The entries are brief, but a clear picture emerges of Hooke's role as designer and, more generally, of the way the building industry operated after the Great Fire of 1666. The volume of work was so great that traditional arrangements were no longer possible; the Gothic master builder was replaced by the Renaissance architect and the contractor, and the Wren 'practice', of which Hooke was a 'partner', evolved a recognizably modern industrial structure for carrying out the vast programme of new building.

Introduction

The diaries of Robert Hooke[1] are summary in recording everyday events, and single words suffice for the character assassination of his colleagues; they are rather fuller when describing new and exciting scientific matters, whether astronomical, physical, chemical or biological; detailed when recording his finds and purchases in second-hand bookshops; and obsessive when noting the state of his health – his appetite, his hours of sleep, his experimentation with new medicines, his consumption of chocolate. Laconic though they are, Hooke's notes on the effects of quack cures are in the nature of laboratory records of experiments on his own body, these notes then being available for future consultation.[2] His day-to-day business, however, varied as it was, was constantly before him, and seemingly needed no elaboration – there are almost daily references such as 'with Sir Ch:Wren', sometimes with a place specified ('at coffee house', 'at Pauls'), but often with no clue as to a reason for the meeting. (Hooke usually refers to Wren as Sir Ch:Wren, but to others, however eminent, often by surname alone.)

The very frequent meetings of Hooke and Wren (apart from attendance at the Royal Society[3]) were concerned with their building activities, in which Wren was of course the senior partner. Indeed, their relationship is in some sense implied in their appointments for the rebuilding of St Paul's: Wren was Surveyor and Hooke the Assistant Surveyor. However, Hooke was in his own right Surveyor for the City, and responsible for the approval of all reconstruction after the Great Fire of 1666. Included in this rebuilding were, of course, Wren's 51 churches,[4] and in practice many of the drawings for new buildings in the City were approved by both Hooke and Wren. It is now certain that two 'Wren' churches, St Edmund the King and St Benet Paul's Wharf, were designed by Hooke alone, and that he made major contributions to at least three others (St Margaret Lothbury, St Martin Ludgate and St Peter upon Cornhill).[5] Hooke was, in fact, and in a final sense justly, totally overshadowed as an architect by Wren; and, in the same way, and equally justly, he was overshadowed as a scientist by Newton. The fact remains that Newton had learned about colours in thin films from Hooke,[6] but the coloured rings in the famous experiment are called Newton's Rings – in the same way the Monument, the pillar in Fish Hill commemorating the Great Fire, and confidently attributed to Wren, was designed by Hooke.

It is unfortunate that almost all of Hooke's undisputed work as an architect in London (apart from the Monument and the two 'Wren' churches) has been destroyed, whether by fire or by demolition and reconstruction. One of his major buildings in the period 1674–76 was a totally new hospital for the insane, Bethlehem (or Bethlem, Bedlam). In that period the diaries record nearly 100 visits to Bedlam – every three or four days he was 'with Mr Hoskins at Bedlam', 'at Bridewell about Bedlam', 'at Bethlem with Committee', or simply 'Bedlam'. Despite their terseness, these references piece together to give a clear picture of how building operations were carried out in the late seventeenth century, and of how the architect stood in relation to his client and to his contractors.

Bedlam

The Priory of St Mary of Bethlehem was founded at Bishopsgate in 1247, just outside the city walls; the site is now occupied by Liverpool Street Station. It was first described as a hospital in 1329, and in 1403 it was noted that the hospital cared for men deprived of reason. The religious order was dissolved by Henry VIII, and the government of the hospital of Bethlem was transferred to the City of London in 1557. Ten years later Bethlem was united with Bridewell (the House of Correction) under a single management.[7]

Bethlem Hospital could care for only 25 patients, and, besides being too small, the buildings were decaying. In 1673 the managing committee decided that Bedlam should have a new building, and Hooke's design, for 120 patients, was built on the adjacent site of Moorfields, again just outside the City walls (and today just north of London Wall). This building, Hooke's building, was found in turn, after over a century, to be too small and in a bad state of repair; it was pulled down and a third hospital was opened in 1815 at St George's Fields, Southwark. The replacement followed closely Hooke's arrangements for Moorfields – the building consisted of an imposing central block, with two long wings housing the patients (now increased to 200 in number).

By 1930 there were about 100 hospitals in Great Britain catering for the mentally disordered, and these were, in general, established in rural areas. By contrast, urban London had now encroached on the third Bethlem in Southwark – a fourth hospital was established in Beckenham, and 700th-anniversary celebrations were held there in 1947. The wings of the Southwark hospital were demolished, and the central mansion is now the Imperial War Museum.

In the mean time the Maudsley hospital had been established in 1923 at Camberwell, as a small institution with strong research interests. The Maudsley and Bethlem were amalgamated to form a postgraduate teaching hospital in 1948, under the newly formed National Health Service. This medical school was taken over by London University just before the amalgamation, and renamed the Institute of Psychiatry; 20 years later, in 1967, the Institute of Psychiatry moved to a new building adjacent to the Maudsley in Camberwell. The Maudsley took over the management of the District catchment area service for the mentally ill in 1991, and Bethlem Royal and Maudsley Hospitals became an NHS Trust in 1994. Finally, another NHS reorganization in 1999 resulted in the Bethlem and Maudsley forming part of a large mental health trust: South London and Maudsley NHS Trust. Although the Bethlem Hospital in Beckenham just manages to hold on to its ancient name, this is not detectable on the hospital's letterhead, which bears the dismal new acronym SLAM.

Moorfields

On Tuesday 14 April 1674, Hooke records in his diary:

> At Belinsgate, Mr. Hawes. With Dr. Allen at Bedlam. Viewd Morefields for
> new Bedlam. Drew up report for him. At Sir W. Turner. Undertook new

Designe of it. DH. Met Esq. Warder at the Wardrob and designed staires, windows, doors &c. Bought next the Blew Anchor in Duck Lane, *Clusis rariorum plantarum historia* 6s., and *ejusdem exoticorum libri* 10s., *cum observationibus* P. Belloni 4s., Cardanus *de proportionibus* and Algebra 2s. Paid him by Harry. At Garaways. Drank Tea which drove away all sleep and much disturbed me. Slept distemperd, sweat much. I paid Harry. Bette Orchard first came. At Garaways, Colwall, Wild, Aubery, Collins, &c. Collins his life, &c.

This is the complete entry, and records one kind of typical day for Hooke – other days record scientific activities. Garaways was a notable coffee-house in Change Alley, Cornhill – Hooke sometimes repeats himself, and it is likely that he paid only one visit to Garaways on 14 April, where he met friends. He bought books – the sums are considerable, and he carefully notes the costs. (On other days he may well note 'not paid'.) The word 'design' covers a range of activities, and he probably made sketches of stairs and so on for the Esquire Warder. The 'new Designe' of Bedlam, however, represents an undertaking to act as architect for the new hospital. DH = dined home. Betty Orchard was a new maidservant, who broke a glass on 22 July but came to Hooke's bed on 26 July (Hooke records the matter with his shorthand for a sexual event – the zodiacal sign for Pisces); by 15 August 'Betty turned out intollerably carelesse', and she was discharged on 30 September.

Sir William Turner had been Lord Mayor of London (1668–69), and from 1669 to his death in 1693 was President (of the Governors) of Bridewell and Bethlem. Dr Thomas Allen was the non-resident physician of Bethlem from 1667 to 1684. Hooke was evidently commissioned, on or before 14 April 1674, to design the new hospital in Moorfields. He was already working at Bridewell, which had been partly destroyed by the Great Fire, and on 25 June 1674 Hooke 'shewd Sir W. Turner Designe of Bridewell' for some proposed reconstruction. On 3 July he was 'at Bridewell about Bedlam', and on 10 July he was 'at Davys about Bedlam module'. 'Module' can mean a physical model, or a drawing showing the intended building, or simply a specification – in any case, on the next day, 11 July, Hooke 'at Bridewell agreed the module for Bedlam'.

The specification was thus approved, and on 28 September Hooke 'set out Morefield for Bethlehem with Sir W. Turner, Sir Th: Player, &c'. (Sir Thomas Player was Chamberlain of London.) On 12 October it was 'agreed about Bethlem Hospitall', and a week later Hooke was 'at Bedlam governors'. Building work started at the end of the month; on 29 October, Hooke was 'with Mr. Fitch at Morefields … set out Bethlem wall'; the next day he was again 'with Mr. Fitch at Morefields';

on 2 November he was 'at Mr Mosier with Mr. Fitch at Morefeilds'; on 3 November he was 'at Bethlem'; and on 6 November he was 'at Morefeilds with Scarborough'.

John Scarborough became Clerk of the Works at the Greenwich Palace in 1681, and later filled other equally important posts; he was a member of Wren's office, used by both Wren and Hooke as a measuring clerk – that is, as a quantity surveyor. John and Thomas Fitch, brothers, were master bricklayers in the full medieval sense; they were skilled craftsmen who were also capable of acting as architects for building projects. In 1674 Thomas Fitch had just completed the work of cutting and wharfing the Fleet Ditch (Hooke was concerned with the design); Thomas was knighted in 1679, and created a baronet in 1688. Hooke had known the brothers for several years, and in October/November 1674 John Fitch contracted to build the wall for the new Bethlem – presumably a boundary wall. In November/December Hooke records meetings with Fitch and visits to Moorfields.

On 6 January 1675 Hooke discussed with Sir Thomas Player and the Treasurer of Bethlem (Ducane – or Du Cane, Du Quesne) the layout of the grounds for the new hospital. Hooke had several meetings during the month with the Treasurer and the Committee, and by 25 January he had arrived at a final design: 'Deliverd in propositions about building Bethlehem'; on 28 January he was 'at Treasurer Ducanes. Presented Designe, liked well'. Formal approval was given, and on 3 February 'Fitch took Bethlem work'. On 5 February Hooke 'set out Bedlam in Morefields'.

Thus John Fitch was appointed 'general contractor' for the project, presumably with specialist responsibility for brickwork (and masonry generally). Financial estimates could now be prepared, and on 15 February Hooke 'finished estimate of Bedlam. Deliverd it to Treasurer'. In the mean time, five days earlier, Hooke had been 'at Bethlem with Committee. Agreed about directions for carpenters and for piling yellow firbanks of 12 and 14 inch square for 35 sh. per load'. On 2 March 'Fitch began the planking ... of the foundation'.

The site of the new Bethlem was the original ditch just outside the old City wall, and it would have been essential to provide firm foundations in such made ground of poor quality. The word 'pile', however, is ambiguous. Straightforwardly, it implies vertical stakes ('12 inches square') driven to such a depth as to provide sufficient support to the footings of the building. Alternatively, it could mean simply a mass of material – certainly, a common way to provide a good base for walls was to lay baulks of timber horizontally, to fill interstices with rubble masonry and to plank over to form a level surface for the brickwork. One hundred and twenty-five years later, in 1800, an architect's report to the governors found the building to be dangerously insecure (and this led to demolition and the move to Southwark in 1815). The report stated that the walls had not been laid on (vertical) piles, and that the brickwork had been simply set down on the surface of the soil, a few inches below the floor.

During the next 18 months, from March 1675 to October 1676, Hooke paid at least weekly visits to Moorfields to see Sir William Turner or the Treasurer Ducane, and to meet the Committee. With the planking of the foundations under way, on 5 March 1675 'at Bethlem hospitall. Masons proposalls received', and on 8 March 'to Ducanes. Committee agreed with Waters, Hutchinson and Cartwright āā ⅓'. These were individual masons – Cartwright, for example, was a leading contractor mason who was often employed by Wren – apparently taking one third each of the work under direct contract from the Committee. On 18 March Hooke was 'at Morefields. Directed Cartwright and Fitch'.

Detailed design proceeded in step with the work: 9 April 'At the Bedlam Committee who after some bickering left the matter of the stairs to me. Promised me Gratuity'. (This is the first mention of the question of Hooke's remuneration as architect for the hospital.) On 9 June 'agreed about the sewer, the window under gallery, oak door cases, etc', and on 1 July 'we agreed about slating'. Further contractors were engaged on 12 July: 'Bedlam Committee agreed with Ain and Gee for Slating Bedlam with Slates of Plinmouth Nayled on Lathes with 4d nayles 2 in every slat bigger than 5 inches and to 3 double that is 2 coverd at 26 sh. 6d. per square'.

An all-stone facing to the front of the brickwork was ordered by the Committee on 19 July, and on 7 September 'they agreed Lucarnes 12 Carved Cantilevers, Lanthornes & flats', and 12 dormer windows were indeed constructed in the pitched roofs of the hospital. On 20 October agreements were reached with the glaziers, with the quality and size of glass specified together with the weight of lead. Building continued through the winter, with decisions being made about chimneys, straw houses, a turret and so on. The work seems to have been substantially complete by April/May 1676, and visits by Scarborough (the measurer) are recorded. The building committee continued to meet during the summer, and the contractors' bills were scrutinized on at least eight occasions during October. On 2 October, Hooke 'lookd over masons bills of Bedlam', and four days later he was 'with the Treasurer valuing carpenters bills'; finally, on 24–28 October there were 'severall committees at Bedlam about auditing bills where things went according to my prices'.

At the end of the year Hooke counted his moneys, and on 31 December he records the extraordinary sum of £1300 as owing to him, mainly for professional fees and unpaid salary; in this total is included £200 'due from Hospital for Bedlam building and Surveying'. On 11 January 1677 'Scarborow here. To Bedlam, Mr Chase, Whistler, Pilkington, Crisp, Spires, Goald, Stanly, Chadwick and Ducane, 2 presbiterian dogs, Botteler, (Haines absent), Mr Fitch. Upon arguing my busnesse. They voted I should have either £300 or £250 and soe Reported it'. The new building had attracted great public interest, and on 18 January Hooke 'promisd Stevenson should paint Bedlam and Loggan Grave it'. On 23 February Hooke 'received by Scarborough order for £200 for Bedlam', but on 6 March 'to Ducanes. He put me off for the £200'. Again, on 23 March, 'spake to treasurer for money. Putt off'. At last, on 1 June, 'to Mr. Ducanes, Bridewells treasurer, and gave him receipt for £50 which I Receivd 20 sh. of it in grates, 1 guinney, the rest in money, gave his man 2s.6d., being part of £200 orderd by Hospitall'. On 3 August 'at Ducanes Received £50 upon Bedlam warrant, which with the former £50 made £100, remaining due £100', and on 4 September 'at treasurer Ducane, he Denyd me money still with putt offs'. A third instalment of £50 was received by Hooke on 22 December, and on 22 February 1678 he 'dunnd Ducane who promisd March next to pay me £50'. The final payment was in fact received on 4 May.

Hooke's fee of £200 as architect and surveyor – designer and site supervisor, with attendance at site meetings – compares with a total expenditure of some £17000 on the new hospital. During the same period he was acting in the same way in respect of a new house for Lord Montagu (on the site now occupied by the British Museum); his agreed fee was £250 for a house costing £2300.

Building in London after the Great Fire

The character of the building trade changed completely, and permanently, within 50 years in the seventeenth century.[8] The new way was foreshadowed by Inigo Jones with his Banqueting House for Whitehall Palace, 1619–22, built by Nicholas Stone, master mason; and by his remodelling of parts of Old St Paul's, including the west portico 1633–42, where he employed the master mason Edmund Kinsman. Inigo Jones was not himself a builder – he had not pursued the arduous career of apprentice and journeyman to master, learning on the way the hidden secrets of his craft. To be sure, the stonemason's skill, although difficult and not to be achieved without the long training of the masons' lodge, was not complex – the mastery of form attained by this apprenticeship could be grasped by a gentleman without getting his hands dirty. Inigo Jones had himself had some craft training, as a joiner, before emerging as an artist, a theatrical designer and architect. It is Wren, however, and Hooke and the designers in Wren's practice who are the real first British architects, willing and able to design buildings without themselves having had hands-on experience.

Until about 1620 the building trade in England was medieval,[9] with individual masters entering into design/build contracts with their clients. For example the Strong family, owners of freestone quarries in Gloucestershire and Oxfordshire, were able to act as both designers and builders (and suppliers of stone). Canterbury Quadrangle at St John's College, Oxford was built under this arrangement about 1634 by Timothy Strong and his son Valentine; later Valentine's sons Thomas and Edward carried on the family business. Both were working masons who were also well schooled in the architectural treatment of stone. Thomas opened a shop in London immediately after the Great Fire to sell his own complete services, and to supply any other builder with stone from his Cotswold quarries. The abilities of the Strongs were appreciated by the Wren office, and they became trusted and important contractors for St Paul's and several of the Wren churches – on their side, the Strongs were perfectly willing to execute designs which were not their own.

The consultant architect was not in fact unknown in medieval times. William Hurley, King's Carpenter, designed the unique and completely novel timber lantern for Ely Cathedral in 1334; the lantern was constructed by the local master carpenter, Geoffrey de Middylton. Later in the century, in 1394, the King's Master Mason, Henry Yeveley, was in charge of the remodelling of Westminster Hall (whose hammerbeam roof was designed by another King's Carpenter, Hugh Herland). And a century later, the designer and builder of the fan vaults of King's College Chapel in Cambridge, John Wastell, received advice from the Vertue brothers, who had built similar vaults at Bath and at Westminster Abbey. However, in all these instances the consultant architects were master builders; master was instructing master.

It was in this medieval, Gothic climate in which the seventeenth-century building trade operated, but now in a climate which reeked of the smoke of the Great Fire. The rebuilding programme was so vast that the existing structure of the trade could not deliver the number of buildings needed. A master mason, with his own men and his own quarry and with a limited amount of capital, could, with design/build contracts, make only a small contribution to (say) the 51 churches rebuilt after the Fire. It is the scale of the work on the churches, at St Paul's and on private houses that jackbooted the building industry into its modern form.

This scale may be appreciated by a modern comparison – it is difficult, in the restoration of say a Gothic cathedral, to spend more than £2m per annum. Such a sum implies a large number of workmen, a steady supply of building materials, constant supervision and checking by the architect, the production of new drawings to solve unforeseen problems, and so on – the organization of the work has to be controlled very tightly. The expenditure at Bedlam in 1675/76 was £17 000 over the two years, and the tightness of control is explicit in Hooke's entries in his Diary. At St Paul's alone the expenditure averaged £20 000 per annum over 35 years, which at once gives a measure of the intensity of the operation – it was not unusual to have nearly 200 men on site, journeymen and labourers.[10]

Wren's office had evolved ways of handling such enterprises which are close to modern practice. Wren himself notes the three main ways of placing work with contractors. First was the traditional fixed-price contract – the builder undertakes to complete the work to a given specification for an agreed sum of money. The method was open to abuse, but was appropriate for specialized subcontracts, such as providing lead to a timber roof. Second was an unsatisfactory arrangement of payment by valuation – the completed work was valued by an independent referee, and the contractor paid accordingly. Finally, the method used in general by Wren for his major contractors, and used in general today, was work by measure; the work was specified technically (the construction of a wall, for example) and a unit rate agreed with the builder (so much for each completed square foot); the finished work was then assessed by the 'measurer' – the quantity surveyor. These practices can be detected in Hooke's notes for Bedlam – he agrees a unit rate for piling the foundations, and again with the subcontractors for roofing.

With these arrangements individual builders could be paid as work proceeded. Substantial capital would still be needed, and Fitch was evidently able himself to take on the £17 000 contract at Bedlam. At St Paul's, however, the Building Fund provided the capital, and Wren could dispense this to best advantage. He started with two main contractors on site simultaneously, and sometimes had three or four working on different parts of the Cathedral. The first share of the big masonry contracts went to Joshua Marshall, Master Mason to the Crown in the Office of Works, and the second to Thomas Strong from the Cotswolds. The Strongs were at St Paul's from start to finish.

All these contractors, at St Paul's and at the individual sites of the churches (25 were already being built when the work started on the Cathedral), were controlled from the Wren office by one or more of the partners in the architectural practice – Wren and Hooke, Woodroof and later Hawksmoor. The quantity surveyor – Scarborough the measurer – could report on all the buildings, and he could if necessary be sent to Ducane to try and collect Hooke's professional fee for the design of Bedlam. It is clear that, as a partner, Hooke was using Wren's practice to process all the work involved at Bedlam.

The problem of cash flow no longer bore directly on the builders involved in a major contract, but the problem was still there for the client. The Building Fund at St Paul's received voluntary contributions (approaching £10000 per annum in the early years), and an Act of Parliament of 1670 allocated 'coal dues' to the Building Fund at the rate of 4½d per chaldron or tun of coal landed at the Port of London – this brought in £4000 or £5000 per annum. As time went on the work benefited from substantial donations, but after 20 years (and various severe fluctuations in income) the Building Fund was deeply in debt. The debts were, in the main, to the principal contractors, and in 1694 these contractors made an extraordinary proposal – that the debts should be considered as loans from the contractors to the Building Fund. Work could then proceed with the loans attracting 6 per cent interest; over £24000 was transferred in the books from debt to loan. Strong, for example, was recorded as being owed the huge sum of £2500 – the contractors had become rich men. But not disproportionately rich; £24000 on an expenditure of say £½m is about 5 per cent, and the contractors' profits were perfectly reasonable. Thus work could continue, and a new Act in 1697 gave at least some measure of financial security. The contractors were eventually repaid, and more generous provision was made in 1708 to cover the final years.

These kinds of financial arrangement have hardly changed over 300 years, with a building fund (for, nowadays, the major repair of a cathedral) established with half the contributions coming from Government and half from public subscriptions and donation. And then, as now, there was the obvious temptation to charge routine expenditure – furnishing for the Dean's Vestry, new hassocks, rebound copies of the Bible – to the Building Fund.

Hooke as Engineer

Three of the four or more professionals found on a modern building site are already evident at Bethlem, namely the architect (Hooke), the quantity surveyor (Scarborough) and the contractor(s) (Fitch and others). Another professional may nowadays be represented by several personages – the structural engineer, the geotechnical expert, the heating engineer, the mechanical and electrical engineer, and so on. The last two had not of course emerged in the seventeenth century, and Hooke, as architect, was his own structural and geotechnical engineer, insofar as an engineer was needed at all. The problems encountered at Moorfields were not novel, but of a kind well known to the contractors, although, from the history of the building, it seems that the 'traditional' design of the foundations was not in fact entirely adequate for the poor ground.

In general, Hooke would have relied on the experience of his chosen contractors to provide adequate 'engineering' input for a particular construction. A project that may have caused Hooke some concern was the Monument – certainly he paid many visits during the building of the 'Pillar on Fish Hill'. The Monument is some 60m high, and Hooke must have had confidence in the contractor, Joshua Marshall, the King's Master Mason; it was built nearly ten years after the Fire, and the Wren office had by that time gained a full understanding of the capabilities of the available builders. Joshua Marshall was taken on by Wren at St Paul's as the Monument was nearing completion.

Again, Wren and Hooke had been concerned with the design and execution of the Fleet River Ditch, and no doubt relied heavily on the expertise of Thomas Fitch in the cutting and lining of channels. At the same time that Bedlam was being built, John Fitch worked on at least two other buildings for Hooke – Montagu House was built between 1675 and 1680, and the new building for the Royal College of Physicians in Warwick Lane was completed in the 1670s.

As for Bedlam, Montagu House at Bloomsbury was built on made ground, not good for providing firm foundations, and this provides a first instance of an engineering contribution to the design. Both Wren and Hooke were familiar with Alberti's *On the Art of Building*, published two centuries earlier, in which he advocated the use of inverted arches buried in the soil to carry the weight of construction.[11] Such inverted arches distribute the loads more evenly to the ground, and Hooke used brick arches of this form at Montagu House. The idea was picked up by Wren almost simultaneously for the foundations of the new library at Trinity College, Cambridge, again built on very poor ground.[12]

A second example of 'engineering' outside the vocabulary of the traditional builder concerns the dome of St Paul's Cathedral. On 5 June 1675 Hooke records in his diary: 'At Sir Chr. Wren ... He promised Fitch at Paulls. He was making up my principle about arches and altered his module by it'. Hooke's 'principle' was that the shape of a perfect arch carrying specified loads should be that of a hanging flexible chain carrying the same loads, but inverted. The shape for a uniform loading is that of a catenary – it could be obtained experimentally, but Hooke (and other contemporaries in the Royal Society) were unable at the time to obtain the shape mathematically. Hooke had in fact stated his principle at a meeting of the Royal Society in 1670, and in 1671, at a further meeting, he extended the principle from the two-dimensional arch to the dome. He stated, incorrectly, that the perfect shape was that of a cubico-parabolical conoid – but the difference between that surface and the exact mathematical surface is very small indeed.[13]

The essential point of Hooke's 'principle' is that a hanging chain, and the three-dimensional equivalent, can never become vertical at the abutments, so that the drum supporting a dome should slope inwards rather than be vertical. Wren built the dome in this way, and disguised the slope by adding a vertical colonnade externally – Hooke's dome for St Paul's has survived, apparently uniquely for masonry domes, without experiencing the usual heavy meridional cracking.

Both of these problems in structural engineering, the inverted foundation arch and the perfect dome, would have been illuminated by mathematical modelling, but they actually needed no mathematics for their solution. They did indeed require a deep insight into mechanics, that is, into an appreciation of the way forces might act in a masonry structure – and the idea of the inverted chain gives just such an insight. In general, however, other structural problems faced by Hooke could hardly be called engineering; they were problems of craft technology whose solutions were readily available, and which in earlier times might have been found in the secret books of the masonic lodges.

Chapter 11

Robert Hooke's Montagu House: London Architecture with Continental Flair

Alison Stoesser

Introduction

For Robert Hooke the year 1674 was an unusually significant one architecturally speaking. It was then that he began work on two of his most prestigious commissions, namely, on Bethlem Hospital, or Bedlam, as it was popularly known, and on Montagu House. Work was also in progress on the Royal College of Physicians, begun in 1670, and on the 'Fish Street Piller', or The Monument, begun in 1671.[1] The design for the latter was worked out with Sir Christopher Wren, with whom Hooke also collaborated on designs for the City churches to replace those destroyed in the Great Fire of 1666.[2] Sadly only the Monument and the churches remain today as a tantalizing reminder of his architectural achievements. Montagu House, one of the outstanding town mansions of the time and the subject of discussion of this paper, reveals the characteristic eclectic nature of Robert Hooke's architecture and stands as a good example of his use of European architectural treatises, handbooks and prints,[3] in combination with a readiness for practical innovation and adaptation of ideas from contemporary buildings. His close friendship with Sir Christopher Wren undoubtedly also contributed rich dividends to Hooke's ideas on architecture.[4]

The Patron

Ralph Montagu, the Master of the Great Wardrobe to Charles II, a member of the Privy Council,[5] and erstwhile Ambassador Extraordinary to France, had married Elizabeth Wriothesley, daughter of Thomas Wriothesley, Earl of Southampton, by his second marriage, and widow of the Earl of Northumberland, in 1673. Elizabeth was one of the wealthiest women in England with an income of £6000 a year and, through her and her family connections, Montagu was able to commission a large representational residence on one of the most sought-after sites in London.[6] After being accorded the highest rank of reception by Louis XIV of France on presenting his papers as Charles II's Ambassador to France in 1669, Montagu had become an ardent Francophile and had developed a taste for extravagant living.[7] At first sight his appointment of Robert Hooke as architect for his London house does not, therefore, seem an obvious choice, as Hooke was very much a pragmatic man, adapting whatever style seemed appropriate to the project-in-hand. Sir Christopher Wren would have seemed the more likely candidate, as his enthusiasm for French models in architecture was well known,[8] but, given his heavy duties as Surveyor of the Royal Works, Director of the City Churches rebuilding programme and architect of St Paul's Cathedral, even if Montagu had approached him, he would have been unlikely to have had time to devote to a private residential commission and, in addition, reluctant to take on an awkward client.[9] Montagu, moreover, could have been drawn to Hooke through personal acquaintance, since his attendance at Westminster School had overlapped with that of Hooke.[10]

The Commission

Hooke first mentions the commission for Montagu House in his *Diary* on 31 July 1674,[11] when he had apparently been told of it by John Flamsteed, the future Astronomer Royal.[12] Unfortunately Hooke gives no details of how he was appointed as architect. His next diary entry regarding the commission is for 2 September, where Hooke simply mentions that he went to view the plot selected for the house in Southampton Fields with 'Mr. Montacue'.[13] For the next eight years Hooke's *Diary* will be peppered with references to Ralph Montagu and Montagu House,[14] in which it is evident that Hooke also had responsibility for overseeing the interior decoration, as well as designing the garden.[15] The grandness of the design became apparent early on in the project, as Hooke already mentions the planned 'great Ro[o]me' on 10 December 1674.[16] On the other hand, no detail was too slight for Hooke's attention, as his mention of the need to follow up on the use of 'bad morter' and faulty 'stock bricks' indicates.[17]

Although Montagu was a demanding client, if one is to judge by his frequent discussions with Hooke on every stage of the project, the Diary entries show that Hooke maintained a good relationship with him, being invited to dinner by him, asking him to bring books back from France and often being shown works from Montagu's large painting collection.[18] Montagu also asked Hooke to accompany him on a trip to France and introduced Hooke to potential clients in London, such as the Earl of Oxford.[19] He was evidently so pleased with the design that he wanted to show it to the Portuguese Ambassador.[20]

Despite Montagu's grandiose ambitions, there were restrictions on the plan of the house, any additional buildings, its exact position on the plot and its height. The first two mentioned were dictated by the deed of sale on 19 June 1675 of the land,[21] which was until that time owned by Rachel Russell, wife of William Russell, second son of the Earl of Bedford, and also a daughter of Thomas Wriosthesley but by his first marriage, and thus half-sister to Montagu's wife. The deed of sale stated that the house should be suitable for a gentleman, with appropriate offices and stables, a forecourt with a brick wall and gardens behind the house.[22] It was also implicit that it should not outrank the house on the adjacent land, Southampton House, the home of Russell himself, and should be positioned on the same building line as Southampton House.[23] That Russell took a close personal interest in the staking out of the ground is evident from his presence at the plot on two occasions and a subsequent visit by Hooke to Southampton House.[24] This explains why, although the plot was large, the house was situated relatively close to the front of the plot. On his visit to Montagu House on 10 October 1683 John Evelyn considered this a fault:

> The Court at Entrie, & Wings for Offices seeme too neere the streete, & that so very narrow, & meanely built, that the *Corridore* [is] not proportionable to the rest, to hide the Court from being overlook'd by neighbours, all which might have ben prevented, had they plac'd the house farther into the ground, of which there was enough to spare.[25]

The fourth restriction, that on height, had come into force with the Rebuilding Act of 8 February 1667, which was passed to improve housing standards after the Great Fire in 1666. This stated that a mansion house could have no more than four storeys.[26]

The Design of the House

Hooke mentions in his *Diary* that he made several different designs and models before Montagu approved the final version in February

1675.[27] Three months before this, Hooke had bought two books, namely Philips Vingboons's *Afbeeldsels der Voornaemste Gebovwen uyt alle die Philips Vingboons Geordineert Heeft (Illustrations of the Finest Buildings Designed by Philips Vingboons)* and Le Muet's *Manière de Bien Bastir Pour Toutes Sortes de Personnes,* both of which undoubtedly influenced his design. Also useful for plans and elevations of Parisian hôtels de ville were Jean Marot's *L'Architecture Française,* or *Le Grand Marot,* and *Recueil des Plans, Profils etc.* or *Le Petit Marot.*[28] The idea of a main block with wings, a forecourt, a monumental street screen and entrance was derived from contemporary Parisian town house models. However, the façade depicted (Figure 11.1) in William Morgan's map[29] – the only source for its appearance before the house was gutted on 19/20 January 1686 – comes from Dutch models, specifically Philips Vingboons's unexecuted design for the Amsterdam Town Hall of c.1647 (Figure 11.2).

Since Morgan also accurately depicts the street screen, known to have survived the fire,[30] we can be sure that the façade shown is a reliable portrayal. It consists of a main block of nine bays with a

Figure 11.1 Façade of first Montagu House.
(Detail from Morgan 1682)

Figure 11.2 Philips Vingboons's design for Amsterdam Town Hall.
(Ottenheym 1989, p. 226, fig. 61) Photo: Utrecht University.

frontispiece of three bays springing forward and pavilions with two
bays each, 13 bays in all. The frontispiece is crowned by a triangular
pediment, which has a carved decoration within it, and a rectangular
balustrade behind. The hipped roof of the main block is detached
from the cupolas which adorn the pavilions. Hooke has simplified
Vingboons's façade by removing the Corinthian pilasters from the
façade and changing the number of bays in the main block in relation
to the pavilions. The articulation is, therefore, somewhat different but
the basic design strongly resembles that of Vingboons. The large
window with a balcony on the first floor of the frontispiece, also
present in Vingboons's design, has been retained by Hooke. In
addition Hooke has used an ornamental device favoured by Andrea
Palladio and Sebastiano Serlio in the sixteenth century[31] and, in his
own time, at Clarendon House, Piccadilly, built by Sir Roger Pratt in
1664–1667, namely, that of alternating triangular and segmental
pediments over the windows on the uppermost floor. The interplay

with the large central pediment is an extension of this alternation and was drawn from Vingboons's designs, such as that for Michael Pauw's house, Herengracht, Amsterdam.[32] It also appears that Hooke has used smooth rustication on the whole of the façade apart from the main entrance and the stairs leading to it. This idea could have been derived from other designs by Vingboons,[33] although it was also used on French town houses of the period.

The general plainness of the design, however, has more in common with Dutch models than with French, where frequently the windows are decorated with elaborate sculpture or details on the surrounds. The only decoration on Hooke's façade appears to be the use of string courses and rustication to add interest. The simplicity of the façade is continued on the wings running from the main house pavilions to those of the street screen. The wing façades are broken by ornamental gateways with monumental archways, narrower versions of the main entrance to Great Russell Street. Bearing in mind the presence of powerful neighbours, Hooke may have opted for a plain façade on the main block to harmonize with the undecorated appearance of Southampton House, from which he certainly copied the main door with its segmental pediment (Figure 11.9). He must have been persuaded by Montagu to devise the grand street entrance despite this.[34]

What the house showed in simplicity, the main entrance made up for in its deliberate magnificence. In this respect Hooke's design trumped Southampton House, which, as Morgan's map of London of 1682 shows, had much more modest entrance gates. Unfortunately, however, the entrance lost some of its impact, as unlike Southampton House, there was no open approach to Montagu House across a square. Even as early as 1674 there were buildings on the other side of Great Russell Street, which prevented an open aspect.[35] The entrance was arched, flanked by double pilasters with Scamozzian Ionic capitals garlanded after Vignola (Figure 11.3), and is remarkably similar in conception to Jean Marot's illustration of Monsieur Iabba's town house entrance (Figure 11.4), although Marot illustrates Doric pilasters instead.

Hooke was also to design an almost identical entrance gate for the Royal College of Physicians, on which he was working at this time. The Montagu House wings had similar entrances but with only single pilasters flanking the doors. The configuration of the pavilions with pointed roofs, street screen and cupola above the entrance shows a strong similarity with the entrance to the Palais d'Orleans, illustrated by Marot (Figure 11.5).

The screen wall facing to the street, with its rectangular brick panels, could also come from this design. The balustrade with urns on

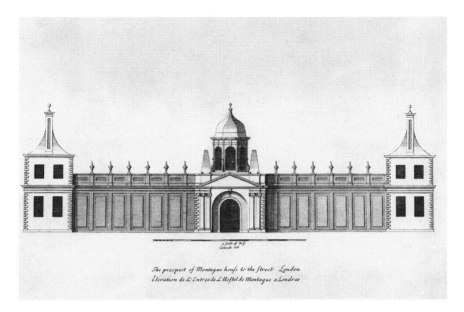

Figure 11.3 Montagu House screen and entrance.
(Campbell 1715, vol. 1, plate 35) Photo: Geremy Butler.

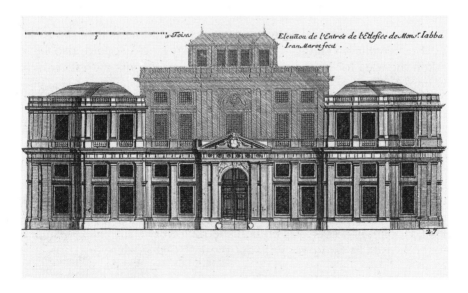

Figure 11.4 Monsieur Iabba's town house.
(Marot c. 1660–70, plate 27) Photo: Utrecht University.

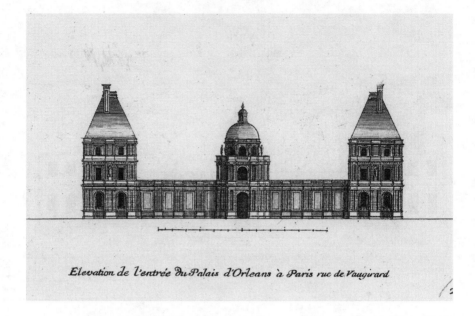

Elevation de l'entrée du Palais d'Orleans à Paris rue de Vaugirard

Figure 11.5 Palais d'Orleans.
(Marot c. 1600–70, plate 2) Photo: Utrecht University.

top appeared in several Marot engravings, including that of the Hôtel
de Bretonvilliers (Figure 11.6), from which Hooke could also have
taken the idea for his inward springing pointed roofs with their high
chimneys.

On the inside of the street screen Hooke added a colonnade with
Ionic pillars. Colonnades of this type for residential purposes were
ultimately derived from examples in Palladio's *I Quattro Libri*, such as
Villa Repeta.[36] The basic shape of the cupola lantern above the main
entrance is remarkably similar to that of Jacob van Campen's
Amsterdam Town Hall, built between 1647 and 1665, with its
octangular form and round-headed windows,[37] while the bell-shape
of the cupola itself is derived from Vingboons's designs for the Town
Hall. Hooke, however, has embellished it further with volutes, similar
to those used by Sir Roger Pratt at Coleshill, Oxfordshire (c.1650).

The Distribution of the House

We have no visual evidence for the distribution of the rooms in the
house and can only rely on contemporary or near contemporary

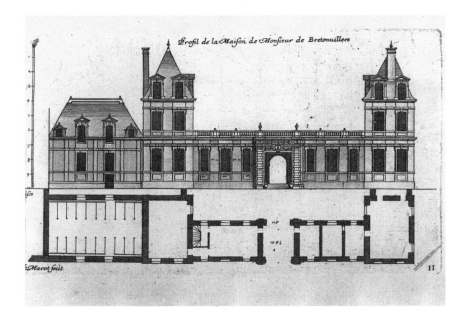

Figure 11.6 Hôtel de Bretonvilliers.
(Marot c. 1660–70, plate 11) Photo: Utrecht University.

accounts for information. Hooke, himself, does not comment on his ground plan but it appears that the distribution of the first house was similar to the second house, which replaced it in 1687 after the first house burnt down. This knowledge derives from a statement in Montagu's memoirs, published around the time of his death in 1709. The statement relates to the lawsuit that ensued between the Earl of Devonshire, who was residing in the first house at the time of the fire, and Montagu, who was claiming damages from Devonshire. Montagu was 'obliged to bear the loss, and Rebuild his house himself; in doing which, it was observable, that the *first Model was so exquisitely Perfect; that no Alteration could be made to Advantage: But the House was exactly Built, in the Figure it had before...*' [my italics].[38] Slight changes were in fact made to the second house in its appearance and it was enlarged so that the wings were attached directly to the house. However, the distribution seems to have been substantially the same, as John Evelyn mentions that the *salon* was on the first floor in the first house,[39] which was the case with the second house (Figure 11.7) as well.

It seems likely that this would have been flanked on both sides by apartments with a withdrawing-chamber, bedchamber and closet, as

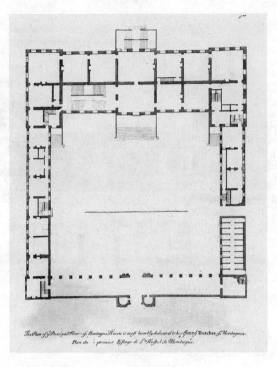

The Plan of y Principal Floor of Montagu House is most humbly dedicated to her Grace y Dutches of Montague.
Plan du premier Estage de L'Hostel de Montague.

Figure 11.7   Plan of second Montagu House.
(Campbell 1715, vol. 1, plate 34) Photo: Geremy Butler.

was common in France at this period, the closest plan being that of
Vaux le Vicomte (1657-1661) (Figure 11.8), although François Mansart
placed this sequence of rooms on the ground floor.[40]

Evelyn describes Montagu House as being 'built after the French
pavilion way'.[41] The plan for the second house, depicted by Colen
Campbell in *Vitruvius Britannicus* in 1715, shows that the principal
rooms were linked to each other in an *enfilade*, which Palladio had
used to spectacular effect in his design for Daniele Barbaro's Villa
Maser, built c.1550–58. Hooke, however, ignored the Palladian
concept of the internal distribution being reflected in the façade, as
Evelyn notes that 'the fronts of the house [are] not answerable to the
inside'.[42]

Structure and Technology

However, Hooke did make use of Italian Renaissance architects for a
structural feature of Montagu House. To distribute the weight of the

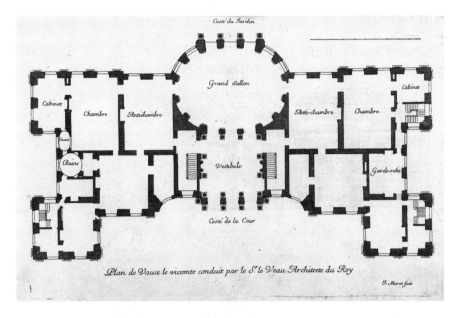

Figure 11.8 Plan of Vaux le Vicomte.
(Marot c. 1670, no plate number) Photo: Utrecht University.

colonnade evenly, Hooke employed Leon Battista Alberti's principle of inverted arches. A diagram of it appeared in Louis Savot's book *L'Architecture Française des Bastimens Particuliers*, which Hooke owned.[43] This idea was also applied by Sir Christopher Wren at Trinity College, built between 1675 and 1684, and this method may well have been discussed by the two friends.[44] It was used where the ground was unstable, which was the case of the site at Montagu House, and, as the name implies, meant that the columns were supported on brick arches placed under the ground in an inverted U-bend.[45] Joseph Moxon, whom Hooke had encouraged to publish his *Mechanick Exercises* in 1678, mentions Hooke's application.[46] Hooke also turned to modern technology and Montagu House shows one of the earliest uses of sash-windows in Britain.[47] Hooke was clearly fascinated by this new invention, as he also used sash-windows at the Royal College of Physicians and Bedlam. The evident benefit of additional light inside and the influence on the proportions of a building externally cannot be underestimated.[48]

The Garden

The only visual evidence for the design of the garden is again the depiction in Morgan's map of London (Figure 11.9).

Figure 11.9 Montagu House with garden and Southampton House. (Detail from Morgan 1682) Photo: Geremy Butler.

It shows regular geometrical beds in the French manner.[49] These may have been given grass parterres in the English tradition or ornamental flower patterns in the French mode.[50] Unfortunately Morgan depicts no real detail of the garden design. Hooke, however, does give a little more information in his *Diary*, mentioning a semi-circular terrace with semi-circular steps, fountains and sunken beds.[51] The most famous semi-circular steps were those designed c.1505 by Bramante for the Belvedere Court in the Vatican and later illustrated by Serlio but they were also used in French mansion gardens.[52] Sunken beds were also popular in France.[53] It is likely that Hooke, in designing the garden, would have used the prolific prints produced by Israel Silvestre and Adam and Gabriel Perelle. The garden must have been attractive, if exposed, as John Evelyn mentions it in his Diary as 'a fine, but too much exposed Garden' and as being 'large, & in good aire'.[54] Montagu evidently enjoyed walking in it, as Hooke mentions spending time with him there three times in his *Diary*.[55]

Internal Decoration

The decoration of the 'Great Roome' and stair-case was evidently splendid, if Evelyn's description is to be believed:

> *Signor Virios* fresca Paintings, especialy the funeral Pile of Dido, on the Stayre Case & Labours of *Hercules*, fight with the *Centaures*, *Effeminacy* with *Dejanira*, & *Apotheosis* or reception amongst the Gods, on the walls & roofe of the Greate roome above, I think exceedes any thing he has yet don, both for designe, Colouring, & exuberance of Invention, comparable certainly to the greatest of the old Masters, or what they so celebrate at Rome.[56]

Montagu had brought the painter Antonio Verrio over from France to decorate the house. Hooke refers to him as the 'Italian', but Hooke visited Montagu House a number of times with Verrio, indicating co-operation in the decorational programme. Unfortunately none of this decoration survived the fire but Verrio also worked at Burghley House and this gives some indication of the type of style he would have used.[57] It is very much in the mode of Italian Baroque painting with the mythological themes popular in Italy throughout the seventeenth century and the accompanying strong illusionistic architectural elements.[58] Hooke paid a great deal of attention to details in the house, such as the carpentry of the doors, stair-cases, the chimney-pieces and outside the railings of the stairs to the main entrance, as well as the chimneys.[59]

The Second House

Much has been made of Evelyn's comment that on 19 January 1686 'This night was burnt to the Ground my Lord Montagues Palace in Bloomsbery …'. and Horace Walpole's remark almost a century later that Pierre Puget designed the second house.[60] There is no doubt that the foundations of the old house were used and quite possibly walls still standing. The house is more likely to have been gutted, than completely destroyed.[61] The wings and the street screen must have survived, as they are indicated on Morgan's map and appear again in

Colen Campbell's illustration of the street screen and Sutton Nicholls's engraving of the second house (Figure 11.10) showing the wings now directly attached to the house.

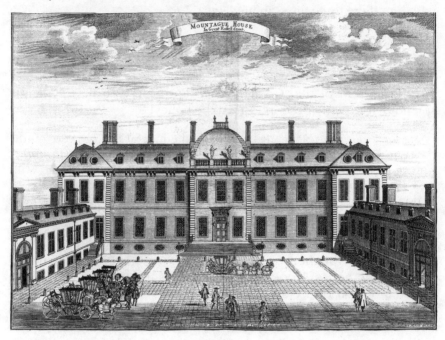

Figure 11.10 Façade of second Montagu House with wings from the first house.

(Engraving by Sutton Nicholls c.1750) Photo: Geremy Butler.

Despite the fact that the old house was used, there were changes: the main block was enlarged by two bays and the pavilions by one each. It is quite possible that Hooke was originally involved in the second design, as the drawing in the British Library seems to substantiate.[62] Although the final appearance of the house had a few more French touches, such as the mansarded roofs on the pavilions and a four-sided cupola over the salon, the likelihood that Puget designed it seems remote, since his elaborate Baroque style was quite different from the second design. There is also no evidence that he spent time in London during this period.[63] Instead of a full four storeys, the fourth floor was now integrated into the roof with dormer windows. Hooke's drawing shows a grandiose loggia facing the garden but this was not executed. The reasons why Hooke may not have been so directly involved were two-fold. His distress at the death of his niece Grace in

1687 and the blow to his pride of the publication of Sir Isaac Newton's *Principia* in the same year, without acknowledgement of his research,[64] undoubtedly contributed to his possible reluctance then to be involved in demanding architectural projects. This was precisely the year when construction of the second house was initiated.[65] Since no diary exists for this year, this can only be mooted as a possibility. The other reason was almost certainly financial. Montagu had made huge losses to the tune of £46 000 due to the fire and his attempts to recoup damages from his tenant, the Earl of Devonshire, were unsuccessful, so he therefore looked for other funding, for which he turned to France.[66]

Conclusion

Montagu House was an impressive example of Hooke's talent in weaving together elements from different architectural styles from a wide variety of sources, including Dutch, French and Italian treatises, prints, his own practical experience and experimentation with old and new techniques and the rich interchange of ideas with his close friend and collaborator, Sir Christopher Wren. It also reveals his ability to satisfy a demanding client. The remnants of the first house in the form of the street screen and wings and the second house attracted the eye of artists until they were torn down in the 1840s to make way for the completion of the British Museum and their impressions can only give us a tiny glimpse of the magnificence and grandeur of one of the most admired London mansions of the seventeenth century.

Acknowledgements

My deepest thanks to Michael Cooper and Michael Hunter for their interest in this subject, to Lisa Jardine for her encouragement and advice, to Marjorie Caygill, Christopher Date, Tony Spence and Gary Thorne for their helpful discussions and making archival material available from the British Museum, and to His Grace the Duke of Buccleuch for giving me permission to visit Boughton House.

Chapter 12

The 'Mechanick Artist' in Late Seventeenth-Century English and French Architecture: The Work of Robert Hooke, Christopher Wren and Claude Perrault Compared as Products of an Interactive Science/ Architecture Relationship

Hentie Louw

The comparative approach adopted in this paper for assessing the scientist-cum-architect, Robert Hooke's contribution to architectural history might seem unnecessarily oblique, particularly at a meeting dedicated to a celebration of the achievements of the man. But there are good reasons for this. In the first place, it is very difficult to write a conventional architectural historical account of Hooke's work, linking a narrative to a notion of demonstrable stylistic progression. This is not simply the result of incomplete information; enough material exists, the problem seems to lie with the object of study itself. Hooke is not the only English architect of the period with a fragmentary profile of this kind – for most of the seventeenth century, architectural design in this country remained essentially an ad-hoc amateur activity dictated by opportunity rather than full-time commitment within an organizational framework – but his case seems to suggest deeper causes. The second reason for adopting this approach is that it offers an opportunity to investigate the emergence of a new class of 'professional' in the field, the scientist-architect. It is a phenomenon unique to the late seventeenth century in pre-modern architectural history, and there were only ever a handful of individuals whose careers fit this description. It therefore seems sensible to look at three of the principal figures together as the basis for setting criteria for judging the defining characteristics of the development.

Claude Perrault (1613–88), Christopher Wren (1632–1723) and Robert Hooke (1635–1703) all came to architecture in the 1660s without any previous connection with the building industry and made their major contributions to the field after having established reputations for themselves as scientific men of special talent. Perrault, who was the oldest, was a medical practitioner and professor in various medical sciences at the University of Paris before becoming a member of the Royal Academy of Sciences upon its foundation in 1666. His scientific research focused mainly on anatomy and botany, but his interests in natural philosophy were wide-ranging and his facility for mechanical invention found an outlet in the Academy's ambitious project to record all the machinery used in France, the so-called *Traité de Mécanique*, that began in 1675. In the course of his career he designed several machines and systems for constructional application. As a practising architect he is chiefly remembered for the Paris Observatory (1667–83), and for his role in the design of the famous East Front of the Louvre (begun 1667), but his principal contribution to the field probably lies in his theoretical work. This includes a translation of Vitruvius into French (1673 and 1684) and a major treatise on the classical orders and architectural proportion, *Ordonnance des cinq espèces de colonne selon la méthode des anciens* (1683).

The careers of Wren and Hooke are, of course, familiar but need to be outlined briefly, for the sake of parity. Christopher Wren – who ended up as the only 'professional' architect of the three – had a special interest in physics, mathematics and astronomy and began his career as a professor of astronomy, first at Gresham College, London, then at Oxford University until 1673. He was a founder member and eventual President of the Royal Society. Wren's first building dates from 1663 and he became centrally involved with the reconstruction of the City of London after the Great Fire, but only began to devote himself seriously to architectural practice following several official appointments; first as Surveyor General of the King's Works (1669–1718), then as architect in charge of the rebuilding programme of the City churches destroyed in the fire (from 1670), including the construction of the new St Paul's Cathedral (1675–1710). Although Wren's position as a courtier with administrative responsibility for a succession of large-scale civic projects curtailed his scientific research, he continued to find opportunities for demonstrating his exceptional flair for research-based technical invention in the various architectural projects with which he became involved, either in an operative or an advisory capacity. Under his leadership the Royal Office of Works and the St Paul's Cathedral site became the national centre for architectural and constructional development.

Robert Hooke shared most of his lifelong friend Christopher Wren's scientific as well as architectural interests. However, unlike the latter and despite a significant involvement with architectural and surveying practice from 1666 onwards, his main focus remained scientific research, which he conducted from his position as Professor of Geometry at Gresham College and Curator of Experiments at the Royal Society. He pioneered several branches of scientific enquiry, and played an important role as a link between the London industrial and scientific communities. Hooke's architectural practice covers a wide spectrum reflecting his many diverse connections, but he is known mainly for three London projects, The College of Physicians (1672–78), Bethlehem Hospital (1675–76) and Montagu House (1675–79).

Context

The techno-cultural background in which Hooke, Wren and Perrault operated was conditioned by the rise of a new intellectual movement, 'experimental philosophy'. This school of thought rejected the Aristotelian conception of science, which ascribed a low status to technology and, instead, came to regard the mechanical arts as a model for experimental enquiry aimed at gaining a deeper understanding of physical phenomena and finding useful applications for natural forces. The movement's progressive utilitarian stance comes primarily from the writings of the English philosopher Francis Bacon (1561–1626), whose argument for a systematic study of the work of technicians in order to develop an empirical culture for the new science links up, as Rossi and others have shown, with a theme consistently explored in technological writings from the fifteenth century onwards and inspired the subsequent 'trades' history' programmes of both the English and French scientific communities during the latter half of the seventeenth century.[1] In the Baconian scheme architecture, along with other arts of manufacture, carpentry, weaving, clock-making, and so on, were deemed a field of study of lesser importance to the natural philosopher than those arts directed towards the management of natural materials and forces, agriculture, cookery, chemistry,[2] and the subject cannot be said ever to have occupied a central place in the work of the major English co-operative venture for the promotion of scientific research, the Royal Society of London (established 1660). Its Parisian counterpart, the Royal Academy of Sciences (established 1666), for a variety of reasons, assigned architecture an important place in the scientific movement.

Yet, despite the apparent lack of consistent evidence confirming a significant contribution to architectural development coming from this quarter, the subject's intellectual roots in mathematics and its total dependence on technology in practice ensured it remaining, throughout the period, a potential beneficiary of, and an important reference base for, scientific research aimed at utilitarian application. Moreover, everything we know about the architectural careers of Hooke, Wren and Perrault suggest that coming to architecture with the mindset and skill-base of the natural philosopher gave them a different perspective on the subject from those of fellow architects without this background. It is to signify this special quality, combining technical ingenuity and artistic creativity within the framework of natural philosophy, that a descriptive title, sometimes used by contemporaries for Robert Hooke, namely 'Mechanick Artist', was adopted here for this new type of architectural figure. The term is also suggestive of a progression, indicating a potential resolution of the dualistic concept of artist-engineer usually applied to earlier personalities whose careers straddled the science/art domain: Brunelleschi, Leonardo da Vinci, Galileo and Simon Stevin.

Considering the specific advantages that science could offer the building world at this moment in history, two contextual factors stand out as being particularly relevant: in the first place the industrial landscape of Northern Europe in the seventeeth century was marked by the progressive breakdown of the medieval guild structure in the face of a rising mercantilism. This process did not run its course until the late eighteenth/early nineteenth century, but the new order was sufficiently securely established by the third quarter of the seventeenth century to turn its attention to the systematic formation of an alternative knowledge-base that could sustain future industrial development, hence the interest in the potential contribution of the natural philosophers to this campaign. In France the codification of industrial knowledge that formerly rested with the trade and craft guilds came to feature in the official policy of Colbert from 1675 onwards when the science academy was charged with this responsibility.[3] One of the noteworthy architecture-related outcomes of this development was the publication by the secretary of the institute, André Félibien's, *Des Principes de l'Architecture, de la Sculpture, de la Peinture, et des autres arts qui en dependent* (1676) and, although the campaign had lost its momentum by the early eighteenth century, the idea eventually bore magnificent fruit in Diderot's comprehensive *Encyclopédie* later in the century.

In England, where the state played no significant role in the scientific movement, the 'History of Trades' project was driven largely by the Royal Society's awareness of the need to demonstrate the potential utilitarian value of its work in order to retain public support, but it ran out of steam well before the end of the century. Joseph Moxon's *Mechanick Exercises, or the Doctrine of Handyworks* (1703), the closest English equivalent to Félibien's work, was one of its few tangible products. However, although less systematic than the French campaign the legacy of the project in this country is evident in the stream of architectural trade manuals and dictionaries subsequently produced, and which became increasingly sophisticated and 'scientific' as the eighteenth century progressed. These ensured that the building revolution sparked by the reconstruction of post-Fire London, and which compensated to an extent for the lack of state sponsorship, had long term benefits for the whole country.

The second factor conditioning the late seventeenth-century architectural scene in England and France was the rise of the Baroque. Its emphasis on grandiose architectural statements, complex spatial arrangements, combined with a taste for abundant decorative expression, placed unusually severe logistical and technical demands on a building industry still emerging from a constricted medieval industrial world. Louis XIV's extravagant building campaign, brilliantly managed by Jean-Baptiste Colbert, set the pace, scale and standards to which other European countries aspired. Progressive architecture of this kind therefore would have provided a special challenge to a new science keen to explore its mechanical potential and seeking a suitable arena to demonstrate the superiority of its rational method in the vacuum being left by decline of the traditional craft institutions. Again the French took the lead with the founding in 1671 of the Academy of Architecture by Colbert, with a mandate for rationalizing all architectural production in service of the state. The Baroque also embodied the concept of a 'Gesamtkunstwerk', that is the idea of a work of art/architecture being the product of various disciplines working harmoniously together towards a common goal, which resonated with the new science's emphasis on collaborative working rather than individualistic enterprise.

Defining Criteria

Having looked at the context within which they worked it remains to be seen to what extent the scientists Hooke, Wren and Perrault, functioning in the architectural domain, demonstrated the qualities associated with the new science and its practitioners and, following on from that, determine what impact this predisposition had on their architecture. But, how would one define these new-found 'scientific' characteristics? Without laying claim to being comprehensive it is proposed that the list below covers the relevant aspects. Such a person could be expected to:

be as curious about technological achievements as natural phenomena;
be egalitarian in outlook and able to collaborate with others;
be attentive to detail;
be rational and objective in approaching tasks;
be experimental and progressive;
have good problem-solving skills;
have superior powers of analysis;
have a capacity for theoretical explanation and speculation;
have a tendency to reason empirically;
have a propensity for technical invention; and
have good organizational skills.

Many of these qualities would, of course, also have been present, singly or in combination, for a number of other seventeenth-century architects who were not natural philosophers. It would, for example, be difficult to argue that any of the above 'mechanick artists' could match Louis XIV's chief architect, Jules Hardouin Mansart (1646–1708) as an organizer; or, François Mansart (1598–1666) for attention to architectural detail as a controlling mechanism in design. It is in the range and depth that these elements were present in the work of Hooke, Wren and Perrault that they stand apart from their fellow architects. Not that this aspect was necessarily beneficial to their architecture. Sir John Summerson has argued, with respect to Christopher Wren, that the latter's essentially 'unpoetical' approach to the subject undermined his creative potential; that he never managed satisfactorily to resolve the antithesis between intellect and imagination in his work and therefore could never achieve true greatness in the art form.[4]

This criticism, as far as stylistic issues are concerned, would also seem to hold true for the architecture of Robert Hooke, which displays, to an even greater extent, the basic arbitrariness and lack of emotion that Summerson sees as the outcome of a primarily empirical design method. To Hooke, as the rare statements by him on the essential qualifications required by an architect testify, the emphasis seems to have fallen mainly on matters related to surveying, material knowledge and quality control. Admittedly these comments were made in the context of wide-ranging lectures on natural philosophical topics, and reflect the contemporary trend in using architectonic metaphor in philosophical debates.[5] But nowhere in Hooke's writings is reference made to the aesthetics of architecture and, as M. I. Batten has pointed out, in over 20 years of architectural practice there was virtually no stylistic development in his work.[6] In this respect, as shall be seen later, Wren's and Claude Perrault's approach to architecture was very different.

The careers (architectural and otherwise) of all three men demonstrate to an unusual degree the capacity to organize, to collaborate and to solve problems of a practical nature. It is indicative of what Summerson has called a 'Royal Society type of mind',[7] that is, a bureaucratic mind-set which was ideally suited to civil service, and which was equally dominant in the circles in which Perrault moved. In the eighteenth century these qualities would come to be associated more with the engineer than the architect, in other words, the 'architect-bureaucrats' who, especially in France, would trace their origin to the same late seventeenth-century scientific institutions.[8] It was Wren's outstanding ability as a rational, efficient organizer of men and materials as much as his design and technical skills that turned the Office of Works and the St Paul's building team into the engines of progress that transformed the London building industry and set the standards of workmanship for the rest of the country. Under his enlightened rule English architectural craftsmanship reached a high point and it was this skilled workforce that sustained the development of the English Baroque.

Robert Hooke was an integral part of this world, which, by the standards of the time, showed a rare spirit of progressive co-operation among the various tradesmen and professionals involved. Master craftsmen, at least as far as England is concerned, enjoyed considerable creative self-sufficiency and the relationship between them, the architects and the scientists was evidently based on mutual respect. It was a perfect arena for someone as multi-talented and unorthodox as Hooke to show off his many skills. Unhindered by the bonds of an administrative employment or class prejudice he acted as consultant, agent and entrepreneur, switching at will between his scientific and architectural interests – a veritable 'Mr. Fixit' whose exact contribution as a catalyst, acting within these domains is perhaps still not fully understood.[9] Unlike Wren, whose position as Surveyor-General inevitably formalized his relationship with artisans, and Perrault, who was constrained by the rigid hierarchy of Colbert's 'dictatorship of labour', Hooke could mix freely across social and professional boundaries. His career therefore explores like no other the limits of the 'ingenious artisan v. mechanical philosopher' conundrum underlying the trade history project of the natural philosophers, from an architectural as well as scientific perspective.

Hooke's most unequivocal statement on this issue came in 1683, during a critical phase of his dispute with Sir John Cutler about the payment of arrears of his annuity as Cutlerian Lecturer. In response to the claim that he had failed to honour the terms of the original agreement of 1664, that stipulated the propagation of the cause of technology by lecturing on craft practices and industrial processes as part of the Society's History of Trades programme, Hooke defended his position, arguing:

1   that, in his view, the Society and country will be more advanced through teaching 'perpetuall & universal knowledge', than 'mechanic' knowledge, which is focused on the here and now and which is not part of natural history;

2   that, as every tradesman knows, the operative part of a trade cannot be taught by words alone, whereas the 'speculative and rationall part' may;

3   that, since nothing could be taught without first explaining the 'reason and cause', which then also 'give light, rules, & hints for further inventions', it made sense to lecture from first principles, using trade practice as a basis for experiment and to illustrate theoretical points;

4   that the vindication of a philosophical introduction to trade practices would prevent jealousy and prejudice between the tradesmen and gentlemen harming the promotion of 'naturall science' and the work of the Royal Society;

5   that he did not think he should be encumbered with the compilation of mechanical knowledge already familiar to him when he is engaged with 'unheard of discoveries & demonstrations in physicks'; and

6   that the 'first and continued understanding' of the project in his mind was 'to explaine nature first, then art'. He added that the pleasure he got from this freedom to follow his 'fancy' was what kept him on the scheme rather than following more lucrative employment elsewhere.[10]

This clearly demonstrates that, while Robert Hooke might have thought of himself as a 'mechanic', this did not mean that he felt much empathy with the traditional craft culture and its secret ways, or that he identified with craftsmen as such – a position which accords with the Albertian tradition in architecture.[11] Once the particularized knowledge-base of a craft/trade was understood Hooke seems to have lost interest in its pursuit. Likewise, the physical skill aspects linked to the various crafts/trades that he cultivated during his career: he always functioned in a directive role in relation to craftsmen, working with them not alongside them, even though he seems to have been highly skilled in several crafts. The history of trades and manufactures project was therefore to him a means to an end – the acquisition of mechanical knowledge towards a higher objective, the study of nature. Already at the start of the venture, in 1664, he had reservations about his part in it, calling it a, 'very hard, difficult and tedious task',[12] and he seems to have stuck with that view. This position was in accordance with the Baconian perspective – which gave priority to the study of technology for the sake of scientific development over its study for the sake of utilitarian application. In the *Parasceve* added to *Novum Organum* (1620 – Hooke owned a copy of the 1650 edition) Bacon emphasized this point: 'For I care little about the mechanical arts themselves: only about those things which they contribute to the equipment of philosophy'.[13]

As we have seen, architecture and the building crafts were placed in the lesser utilitarian category by Bacon, which may help explain the apparent lack of interest on Hooke's part in theoretical speculation in the field. More so than either Wren or Perrault, he seems to have regarded architecture as a problem-solving rather than an autonomous creative concern, and the subject never quite caught his imagination to the extent that scientific research did. It is even possible that Robert Hooke may have had personal reservations about his place in architecture on epistemological grounds. In the second of his 'discourses' on earthquakes – apparently written in late 1686, when he was anticipating the publication of the full version of Newton's *Principia* – Hooke resorted to an architectonic analogy to explain their different approaches to natural philosophy. The Newtonian method, he claims, was 'analytick', proceeding from the causes to the effects, like an architect who – according to the Albertian model – has the whole concept of the design in mind at the onset, and therefore acts with premeditation. His own approach, on the other hand, was 'synthetick', that is proceeding from the effects to the causes, and was more akin to a 'Husbandman or Gardener' – slower to bring things to fruition, but more 'natural' and, ultimately, more likely to produce 'true and certain' results.[14]

This is not to say that Hooke did not take architecture seriously, or that he could not produce work of a very high standard, only that, as with the crafts, he did not himself consider it as his true métier and, despite a notorious tendency towards boastfulness, never personally laid claim to high achievement in any field other than science – what he, in the Preface to *Micrographia* (1665) called, the 'real, the mechanical, the experimental philosophy'. Just how closely integrated Hooke's conception of the mechanics of the natural world and artificial invention actually was, is illustrated by a comment in one of the Cutler lectures of the 1670s: 'I design always to make them [that is, 'Observations of Nature' and 'Artificial Improvements'] follow each other by turns, and as 'twere to interweave them, being apart but like the Warp or Woof before contexture, unfit either to Cloth, or adorn the Body of Philosophy'.[15] For architecture to have occupied a special place within the Hookean scheme for experimental mechanical philosophy it had to have scope for exploring both sides of the equation – the inventive application of mechanical knowledge to solve particular constructional and industrial problems from first principles, rather than relying on conventional craft knowledge, as well as serving as a vehicle for expanding the theoretical boundaries of the new science. Here then we have the main challenges facing the late seventeenth-century scientist-architect or mechanic artist, and the criteria by which to get the measure of Robert Hooke's achievement in the field.

The Appliance of Science

The first of these concepts is straightforward and reasonably well researched. All three architects engaged in technical invention directly related to the construction industry and developed new machines, building components and structural systems as well as improving existing ones. Usually, this occurred in response to practical problems that presented special challenges. On the face of it, Claude Perrault's achievement in this category of work seems less impressive than that of either Hooke or Wren, but is not without interest. He is perhaps best known for the reconstructions of ancient machinery, published in his translation of Vitruvius (1673 and 1684), but this work also contained contemporary inventions, including Perrault's improved version of the machine designed by the master carpenter Poncelet Cliquin in 1674 for lifting the enormous pediment stones of the East Front of the Louvre into position. Perrault designed other weight-lifting machines that were never put into practice as well as an adventurous structural timber bridge system for a single span of nearly 200 feet.[16] Perrault is also reputed to have experimented with a counter-balancing system for windows,[17] possibly in connection with the Observatoire in Paris during the 1670s, and is credited with being the driving force behind the unusually innovative construction team responsible for building the East façade of the Louvre from 1667 onwards.[18] Whether or not he had played a significant role in the development of the revolutionary reinforced masonry system employed in the famous colonnade is still an open question.

However, as its most likely designer, Claude Perrault was obviously involved with the development from the very beginning, and it has been argued that it was his theories on muscular action within the human body, developed through his anatomical research, that served as the initial source of inspiration for the design concept.[19]

As the only full-time architect of the three, and with a portfolio of work that included most of the major contemporary monumental building projects in England, Christopher Wren had the advantage of being able regularly to experiment with novel structural solutions in situ. This he did throughout his architectural career, often drawing on suggestions from, or theories developed by, others. The best known cases are: John Wallis's 'geometrick flat floor' concept[20] from which he developed the trussed ceiling of the Sheldonian Theatre, Oxford (1664); Alberti's inverted arch foundation – a technique which was also introduced into France at the time[21] – was employed at St Paul's Cathedral (1675), Trinity College Cambridge, Library (1676) and Tom Tower, Christchurch, Oxford (1681); and Robert Hooke's cubico-parabolical conoid principle, employed in the building of St Paul's dome (1675 onwards).[22] In every case Wren was able to introduce significant adjustments that made the application of these principles feasible in practice – the articulation of the design problem and identifying the requirements for its solution count amongst his strongest points as an architect. He was also particularly adept at exploiting the opportunities offered to architectural design by chance encounters and overlapping fields of enquiry. One telling moment of the kind – recounted by Wren's friend Roger North – occurred during the building of the Queen's Apartment, Whitehall Palace (1688–93). North asked Wren why, in the gallery adjacent to the Thames, he omitted the additional row of square windows close to the ceiling, customarily used in England to ensure good interior light in Italianate designs. Wren's reply was that the reflection of the sky on the water would provide sufficient light for the ceilings. North noted that it was 'an Ingenious thought and fully satisfied me'.[23]

Another instance of a related kind is provided by the method of obtaining indirect lighting through the layered dome structure of St Paul's Cathedral; Robert Hooke's microscope designs are thought to have provided the inspiration for this.[24] Many of the innovations that emerged from Wren's architectural practice were one-off opportunistic solutions that did not add up to a structural theory, but in one area, structural carpentry, his experimental method seems to have had a lasting influence.[25] And there were probably collateral benefits for other industries from his progressive attitude to technology, a notable example being the brick cone glass-house, an innovation that had a significant impact on the development of the English glass industry. The first of these, the Falcon Glass House, was erected in 1688, in Christ Church, Surrey, directly across the river from St Paul's Cathedral.[26] No specific evidence have yet been found to link either Wren or Hooke with this development, but their pioneering work of the 1670s on the stability of arches laid the groundwork for this development, and, as Mr. Robert Crayford pointed out to the author, Wren's use of a brick cone to support the lantern over the main entrance vestibule at Chelsea Hospital in 1687 could be regarded as a likely precedent for the Falcon cone.

It would seem as if Wren and Hooke did their most original experimental work in the field of building technology in close collaboration through Wren's early architectural practice, combining the latter's strategic thinking and mathematical knowledge with Hooke's flair for mechanical research. One of the most enduring legacies of this brilliant partnership was the counterbalanced vertically sliding window, commonly known as the 'sash-window'. The first of this type, a modification of the French unbalanced mullioned sliding window, appeared in Whitehall Palace shortly after Wren's appointment as Surveyor-General of the King's Works in March 1669, and over the next three decades the technology for the new window type was perfected at the Royal Office of Works under Wren's supervision. It would, however, appear as if the critical step that underpinned the development of the characteristic two-sash format of the English sash-window for the next two centuries, namely, the omission of the central mullion and the concomitant re-adaptation of the counterbalancing system to fit the new pattern, was first taken by Robert Hooke at the College of Physicians at the end of 1674, before being refined at the royal palaces during the 1680s and 1690s.[27]

The difficulty of disentangling the experimental work of Wren and Hooke during the crucial early phases of their architectural careers makes an analysis of the sum total of Hooke's contribution to the field problematic, since his own architectural commissions did not offer the same opportunities for exploring new inventions and constructional ideas. Still, there is some evidence: for example, it is known that he also employed the Albertian inverted arch system for the foundations of Montagu House in the mid-1670s,[28] and in his *Diary* he recorded that on 15 August 1675 he was, 'at At Sir J. Mores contrived about window with canvas and rowlers', which suggests a roller blind of some kind.[29] Other instances of this kind may yet emerge. However, because he was essentially a research scientist – albeit one with an unusual interest in craft practices and industrial processes – it is perhaps through this work that his influence was most felt during his lifetime.

In the 'Catalogue of Particular Histories' attached to his *Novum Organum*, apart from 'architecture generally', Francis Bacon had listed several topics related to architecture that were worthy of the attention of the natural philosopher: painting, sculpture, modelling, stone cutting, the working of iron, woodworking, lead working, brick and tile making, cements and glass making.[30] Hooke seems to have tried them all, and more: he tested different types of stone and wood for strength, experimented with different mixes of cement, devised a mechanized system for the manufacture of bricks, researched glazing techniques for earthenware, and so on, but glass was the material that fascinated him most. The late seventeenth century was a revolutionary period in glass making in England and London was spearheading a campaign that would transform all aspects of the industry and turn England into one of the leading producers, rivaling the Venetians and the French. Throughout his career Hooke engaged with the glass industry at several levels: as an experimental scientist he required glass vessels (he had one made for a vacuum pump big enough to hold a man); as an astronomer and micro-biologist he required lenses for optical instruments; as an architect he required better quality window glass.

There is ample evidence of him working with glass grinders to perfect techniques for producing better lenses (he often made his own), and Hooke's ambitious schemes for the utilization of glass, as well as his exacting standards, must have been a constant challenge for manufacturers to produce better quality materials. It is known that he visited glass houses. Three such visits are recorded: one with Wren in 1673 to the Savoy glass house where George Ravenscroft and partners introduced the manufacture of the flint or crystal glass to England, and on his own, in 1674 and 1677, to the glass house of a certain 'Mr Reine' where he studied the former's techniques for joining glass plates invisibly together. From Hooke's comments in *Animadversions On the first part of the Machina Cœlestis of … Johannes Hevelius* (1674) it is clear that by then he already had a good understanding of the glass making process,[31] and in one of his Cutler Lectures, given in February 1687 on the curvature of the earth,[32] he uses an example from the glass blower's craft to illustrate a point that suggests a familiarity with the 'crown' or spun glass process re-introduced into the country only a few years earlier, c.1684.[33] But the business of glass making was a highly specialized and secretive one, not easily penetrated by outsiders as Hooke found when he tried to discover the secrets of the mysterious 'ruby red glass' produced by a glass-painter from York in 1689–90.

It has been suggested that it was this quest that led him to become involved with a commercial glass making scheme in 1691.[34] The claim is based on a ten-year patent, granted in May 1691 to a certain 'Robert Hooke Esq. and Christopher Dodsworth, merchants' for making 'glass for windows of more lustre and beauty than heretofore made in England'.[35] This included the red crystal glass mentioned before and also the casting of plate glass, a process developed in France during the late 1680s. Robert Hooke's diaries, which might have clinched the matter, are missing for a critical two-year period (October 1690 to December 1692). The affair eventually led to the attempted formation of a joint stock company incorporating most of the leading window glass manufacturers in London. However, a search of the genealogical records established that the person in question was not Robert Hooke the scientist, but a near-contemporary namesake (c.1639–99), who was related through marriage to the Herne family of merchants.

Architecture as Natural Philosophy

The two obvious routes by which contemporaries could develop architecture as a branch of natural philosophy were through its roots in the classical tradition (Bacon included architectural history as a viable research topic for the natural philosopher), and by exploring its potential as a scientific 'instrument'. Regarding the first, in terms of the consistency with which his entire oeuvre is imbued with scientific reasoning, it is Claude Perrault who stands out as the leading figure of the three. His considerable reputation as an architectural theorist rests essentially on his translation of Vitruvius and his treatise on classical proportion, as embodied in the Orders of Architecture. Both works are sophisticated critiques of the classical tradition and place him firmly in the camp of the 'moderns' in the famous literary-philosophical quarrel of the period. Perrault's architectural writings, in the words of Alberto Perez-Gomez,[36] 'questioned the most sacred premises of traditional theory, especially the idea that architecture was something irrefutable, given beforehand'.

Rather than rejecting ancient authority outright as unsustainable, and therefore redundant according to the progressive philosophy of the new science, Perrault sought to systematize classical practice, rooting it in scientific rationality with abstract mathematical rules instead of mythical discourse as its operating principle. In his scheme, blind deference to precedent would give way to relativistic reasoning with the prospect of continuous improvement through the application of the rules of mathematical probability. In effect, as Perez-Gomez noted,[37] 'by turning theory into methodology or applied science, he propelled architecture into the modern world'. The political context in which Claude Perrault's work was produced should however not be forgotten; the scientific rules and standards which he expounded equally served the nationalistic aims of the centralized state created by Colbert and Louis XIV.

Robert Hooke did not produce anything serious in the field of architectural theory. He came late to the subject and never attempted to construct a coherent architectural theory or history of his own. It is, however, conceivable that, since he and Wren were in constant communication on all aspects of architecture, Hooke's views are to some extent reflected in Christopher Wren's writings. As Lydia Soo noted in her recent study of these,[38] the outstanding characteristic of Wren's work is its analytical quality, being essentially concerned with uncovering the principles inherent to past and present architecture. In his natural philosophy related to the subject there is, as J. A. Bennett has demonstrated,[39] nothing of the inconsistency and dualism which architectural historians like Summerson have criticized his buildings for, suggesting that the problem (which seems to be real for his architectural language) may well stem as much from the conflicting practical demands of particular projects as from some unresolvable inner conflict.

Having been brought up as a classical scholar Wren did not question the essential validity of the classical tradition as the touchstone for excellence in architecture, nor its affinity with scientific rationality.[40] As a natural philosopher, however, he was bound to subject its material results to sceptical scrutiny, comparing classical buildings with those produced by other known civilizations according to, so he believed, customary (societal) as well as natural (scientific) rules. He was constantly searching for the 'real order' under the outer appearance of things, relying on geometrical configuration – in contrast to Perrault, who used algebraic formulae as a point of departure. And unlike Perrault he did not conclude that the only route to a progressive architecture based on scientific principles was through the application of universal mathematical laws. Instead his relativistic schema allowed considerable scope for individualistic creativity on the part of the designer within the empirical framework of natural philosophy. According to Soo the idea of historical precedent therefore is 'consistent with Wren's concept of "inventions". Existing architectural models are modified based on the architect's imagination, but also his judgment, which regulates any innovations according to the fundamental principles of beauty, structure and function'.[41] It interesting to note that contrary to the custom for architect–writers of the era (Perrault included) Wren did not use examples of his own work to illustrate theoretical arguments –

signalling perhaps a detached scientific rather than artistic ego at work, or was it simply modesty?

Finally: the notion of the instrument or machine as a route to science for late seventeenth-century architecture. It is a distinguishing feature of the mechanistic approach of the era that a large percentage of those in the forefront of the scientific movement were competent instrument makers and/or designers. This is true to some extent even of the more mathematically oriented scientists like Christiaan Huygens and Isaac Newton. For someone like Hooke – as his famous quarrel with the astronomer Hevelius demonstrated[42] – instrumental enquiry was the only true path to nature's secrets, which stems from his essentially mechanical view of nature.[43] It can be assumed, therefore, that for him the analogy would have extended to architecture as well, and that other scientist-architects like Wren and Perrault would also have made the connection, either consciously or sub-consciously. (I am not here referring to the opportunistic use of buildings for scientific purposes, of which there were many instances, but to structures purpose-built to accommodate a particular activity in such a way that there is a symbiotic relationship between the form, the function and the cultural agenda of the brief.)

Considering the many interpretations that the science/architecture axis has seen over time,[44] there are clearly limits to the case that can be made for a building typology that is essentially founded on mechanistic principles, and subject to scientific rationality, but it would seem possible to identify some projects executed by the three architects in question that could potentially have been conceived of in this way: for Christopher Wren, The Royal Observatory, Greenwich (1675–76) and The Library, Trinity College, Cambridge (1676–84); for Robert Hooke, The Anatomy Theatre, Royal College of Physicians, London (1672–78) and Bethlehem Hospital, Moorfields, London (1675–76); for Hooke and Wren together, The Monument, Fish Street, London (1671–79); and for Perrault, The Royal Observatory, Paris (1667–86).

Of these, the Paris Observatory was the most explicit statement of this kind. The building – which was originally intended to be the home base for the French Academy of Sciences, as well as a working observatory – was one of the very first buildings ever erected exclusively for a scientific function. Working to a brief drawn up by leading contemporary French astronomers, Claude Perrault clearly strove to create a unique monument with a dual purpose: to serve, quite literally, as an instrument for observing the heavens and to honour the patronage of the Sun King, Louis XIV.[45] The plan of the building was geometrically aligned to the movement pattern of the sun as defined by the solstices, equinoxes and the meridian, and incorporated a zenith telescope that cut vertically through the entire edifice; the building was stripped down to the bare minimum of classical ornamentation, relying for architectural effect instead on the quality of the stonework, the solidity and daring of its structural forms, the beauty of the geometric proportioning and the atmospheric effects of light on the interior. In its overt response to the forces of nature the Paris Observatory foreshadowed the mechanistic approach of late eighteenth-century French architects like Antoine Petit and Bernard Poyet. While Perrault's commitment to the one unavoidable condition for the design of any machine, namely functional efficiency, is called somewhat into question by his bitter dispute about the practical shortcomings of the design with the first Royal Astronomer in residence, Giovanni Domenico Cassini (1625–1712) – appointed in 1669 – it is nevertheless under his supervision that the desired changes were subsequently made to the fabric of the building in order to keep up with advances in astronomical methodology.[46] And this process, in itself, mirrors contemporary practice in scientific instrument design.

Compared with the Parisian Observatory project the London Observatory was a much less ambitious affair, but it had some advantages. With a specific scientific brief (to create an 'instrument' for determining longitude through astronomical observation) and three of the country's leading astronomers in charge of the project (Wren as architect, Robert Hooke as his site manager with additional responsibility for designing specialist observational equipment, and John Flamsteed as Astronomer Royal) it seems to have been an ideal opportunity for exploring the relationship between contemporary science and architecture at several levels. In the event, the resultant building was essentially a pragmatic solution – one which served its functional purpose well, but with no apparent attempt made at addressing some of the broader cultural and theoretical issues inherent to the project. It is certainly true that economic and time constraints, combined with insecure and conservative patronage, allowed Wren little scope for grandiose symbolic gestures, but even so he does not appear to have been inclined that way, giving up even the basic option of aligning the walls with the zero meridian (as urged by Flamsteed) for the expediency of building on existing foundations. His reason, it later emerged, was that the building itself was deemed to be essentially for housing the astronomer and storing the instruments, allowing 'a little for pompe'; the real astronomical observations were to be conducted outside in the garden and on the terrace.[47]

Wren and Hooke's somewhat earlier joint project for a new headquarters for the Royal Society (1668–69) provides a further example of their measured pragmatism when faced with the task of designing an appropriate architectural setting for the new science.[48] A programmatically more coherent 'scientific instrument' emerged, as Lisa Jardine has shown,[49] from the Wren/Hooke partnership on the Fish Street Monument project, which was designed to function as a zenith telescope as well as a monument.

There is only one project where Christopher Wren, on his own, came close to achieving the kind of synergy between the functional programme and the mechanism serving it that one associates with the mechanical instruments of the period, namely, Trinity College Library, Cambridge. Here Wren's capacity for the rational analysis of architectural problems, his inventive flair, structural knowledge and classical scholarship combined to arrive at an ingenious solution to a challenging brief. Working from first principles rather than historic precedent he abandoned the traditional design concept of maintaining a direct relationship between internal volume and its external expression, thereby creating a shell that conformed to classical proportional rules while containing an interior space high enough to accommodate both the need for tall bookcases and large overhead windows. Technology is used to maximum effect in order to facilitate the required architectural accommodation: an innovative trussed-girder flooring system combined with suspension iron tie rods was devised to support the heavy loading of the bookcases after the original design proved inadequate, while the large span of the roof structure is accomplished through complex kingpost trusses that were also a further development of earlier systems devised by him. The foundations of the building were strengthened with the Albertian inverted arch type of construction.[50]

Robert Hooke achieved nothing technically quite as adventurous and coherent as this in his independent commissions. His strengths seem to have lain in his knack for commodious and compact planning that demonstrates both his powers for rational analysis of the brief and for spatial arrangement. Unfortunately the two building projects of his that best display these qualities, The College of Physicians and Bethlehem Hospital, no longer survive, and are inadequately recorded. Of these, the College's Cutler Theatre, a top-lit, domed octagonal space, purpose-built for medical lectures and demonstrations, benefited from Hooke's own experience as an experimental scientist and lecturer and it is, not surprisingly, the closest he came to designing an architectural 'instrument'. It was renowned for its good light, acoustics and sight-lines.[51] Bethlehem Hospital for the insane is generally regarded as Hooke's architectural masterpiece. Scientific knowledge in the treatment for this condition was non-existent at the time, but Hooke succeeded in developing an innovative plan that complied with current theories and exploited to the full the conditions of the rural site in order to achieve a lightsome, well-ventilated building. Under Hooke's supervision the contract was completed in record time and the building remained a model for hospital design in England until the nineteenth century.

To conclude: it has been argued throughout the paper that the architectural performance of the three men in question was conditioned by their background in natural philosophy and, hopefully, that thesis has been substantiated as far as the evidence permits. In the final analysis, that influence appears to be less obvious, less profound in Robert Hooke's architectural work than in that of either Wren or Perrault. The reason for this seems to lie not so much in a lack of opportunity, or even talent (although the latter could possibly be a qualitative factor); lack of interest in and/or intellectual commitment to the subject seems the more likely cause, and in this respect it is perhaps significant that there is almost no evidence of theoretical speculation on Hooke's part regarding architectural issues. Does that then make him any less of a 'mechanick artist' than the other two? Only in so far as architecture as a specialist activity is concerned. Contemporaries sometimes criticized Hooke for being too 'commercial' in his approach to his work. From what we have seen there may be some truth to that allegation with respect to his architectural activity and that failing might have hampered his ability to engage with the subject at a higher level. Judging by his own definition, his architecture is less convincing as a vehicle for expanding the boundaries of natural philosophy than that of Christopher Wren and Claude Perrault who, surely, must rank with Guarino Guarini (1624–1683) and Johann Fischer von Erlach (1656–1723) as the Baroque architects who came closest to the ideal of achieving in their architectural work the seamless transition between rational analysis, technical ingenuity and artistic creativity, that the term 'mechanick artist' implies.

Acknowledgements

Thanks to Christine Stevenson, Antoine Picon and Robert Crayford, who read an earlier version of this paper and made useful comments. Also, James Campbell for letting me read the chapter on the relation between architecture and science at the Royal Society, in his unpublished doctoral dissertation, Cambridge University, 1999.

PART 5
LIFE AND REPUTATION

Chapter 13

Robert Hooke: Gentleman of Science

Mordechai Feingold

Posterity has not been kind to Robert Hooke. In 1987, on these very premises (The Royal Society of London), the first-ever conference devoted to Robert Hooke took place. Scheduled to coincide (more or less) with the tercentenary of the publication of the *Principia*, the organizers of the conference set themselves the task to deliver Hooke from the 'invidious comparison with Newton which had bedevilled his reputation ever since his own time'.[1] It is ironic, therefore, that the very conference that was intended to rehabilitate Hooke actually inaugurated another insidious comparison, this time with Robert Boyle, which has proved far more pernicious to Hooke's reputation. Both comparisons were informed by the same agenda, conscious or otherwise: to aggrandize Newton or Boyle at the expense of Hooke. But whereas it was possible to acknowledge Hooke's genius and stature while still denying him a position equal to Newton, the comparison with Boyle precipitated a denuding of not only Hooke's professional identity, but his personal integrity as well. It boggles the mind to comprehend the willingness of so many historians of science to be duped into embracing such a merciless – not to say spurious – representation, grounded on misinterpretation of the evidence and on gross misunderstanding of the nature of seventeenth-century science and its cultural milieu. Perhaps a future historian of our profession will manage to explain this. For my part, I intend to revisit the formative period in Hooke's life and offer a more credible portrait of his character and standing in the scientific community.

As I have just hinted, the driving force behind the unflattering depiction of Hooke in the past two decades was the determination to establish Boyle as the figure on whose image and likeness the English scientific tradition came to be modeled. 'Boyle's presentation of [him]self as a Christian virtuoso', it has been argued, 'was central both to his public identity and to the utility of that identity for the program of experimental knowledge-making'.[2] Hooke could not be accorded his rightful share in that tradition simply because his inclusion would have rendered untenable the entire edifice constructed on the supposition that the science exemplified by Boyle and the Royal

Society followed the contours of genteel society. However, since it was impossible to cast aside the centrality of Hooke's labours to the survival of that community, it became necessary instead to strip him of each and every attribute that constituted Boyle's alleged identity as Christian virtuoso – and, conversely, to argue that whatever attributes Hooke did possess further distanced him from any entitlement to the Boylean ideal. The verity of Boyle's representation is not part of my brief now, though I shall have occasion to point out certain flaws in that interpretation.[3] My intention is rather to ascertain that while contemporaries were undoubtedly aware of the social distinctions between Hooke and Boyle, they had little difficulty in considering them both as gentlemen of science and as 'major claimant[s] to the title of experimental philosopher'.[4]

The evidence marshaled in support of the claim that Hooke was excluded from the rank of philosophers was invariably based on language games and on curious misrepresentation of the historical record. More sinisterly, such evidence was coded with the portrayal of Hooke as a sordid character, recognized by his peers and superiors as such, and treated accordingly. The necessity to depict Hooke in such an odious fashion seemed to have become an inescapable corollary to the portrayal of Boyle as a paragon of virtue. In other words, Boyle's saintly identity became contingent on the representation of Hooke as his moral, temperamental and social antithesis. Consequently, great efforts were devoted to putting an unsavory spin on Hooke's habits and practices in order to enshrine his unattractive identity. First we encounter the tautological argument that since his contemporaries 'did not call him an experimental philosopher', and since Hooke himself did not 'systematically refer to himself as a philosopher', he obviously was not one – notwithstanding the fact that 'he occupied social and cultural terrain staked out by those who did so identify themselves'.[5] Never mind the tautology. On such semantic grounds virtually the entire membership of the Royal Society would be excluded from among the ranks of experimental philosophers for they, too, just like Hooke, were invariably referred to by their title and official capacities and not as philosophers.

Second, so the argument goes, whereas chastity was one 'of the notable marks of Boyle's Christian piety', Hooke, though unmarried, was 'notably unchaste'. Boyle 'publicly advertized his chastity and sensual disengagement, and he did so as signs of his personal integrity and as guarantees of an authentically Christian philosophy'. Indeed, 'Boyle's life *was* widely recognized as a holy one, spreading a holy aura over his practice of philosophy'.[6] In contrast, 'whether Hooke was perceived by his contemporaries as a moral paragon is highly doubtful'. In the classic way of smear tactics, Hooke's sexual predilections were insinuated while it was argued that they were not going to be discussed, leading to the conclusion that 'it is hard to believe that the nature of Hooke's relations with his various housekeepers and his young niece was unknown to those like Boyle who kept such an anxious eye on standards of public morality'.[7] That no evidence exists to substantiate such knowledge is beside the point. More important is the unasked question whether Hooke's contemporaries would have been scandalized *had* they known. After all, most of them were greater philanderers than Hooke had been and, besides, their perception of such peccadilloes undoubtedly differed from today's moral and legal standards. Certainly, the deification of Sir Francis Bacon was hardly affected by the known fact that he had been a pederast. More to the point, historians *can* debase Hooke simply because he happened to record his deeds in a diary. Boyle did not leave a diary but his life may not have been quite as chaste as historians take for granted. What was the precise nature of his relations with his widowed sister Lady Ranelagh, with whom he lived for over two decades? Was it like the 'great love' that Sir Philip Sidney had for his sister Mary Herbert, rumoured to have 'begot' Philip, first Earl of Pembroke? And are we really sure that Newton's relations with his niece Katherine Barton were that different from Hooke's relations with his niece Grace?[8]

Obviously all this is highly speculative. My point is simply that we should not single Hooke out simply because he alone left a diary behind. Indeed, without this diary, Hooke, too, could have been construed by historians as a paragon of virtue. Yet its existence makes it possible to contrast the details of Hooke's daily life and habits with those that are purported to have been Boyle's, with the explicit or covert insinuation that Hooke lacked the credentials necessary for the makings of a philosopher. One claim against him is that his life was provincial to an extreme. He 'worked where he lived' and his life 'overwhelmingly centred on Bishopsgate Street and its immediate environs'. Unlike Boyle, he never traveled abroad and 'the range of his acquaintance in the Republic of Letters' was quite narrow compared with that of Boyle and Oldenburg. Hooke cohabited with apprentices and instrument-makers, and relatively few 'philosophers' – let alone gentlemen – ever visited him. Boyle's laboratory, in contrast, was a Mecca for English and foreign visitors, a crucial fact, we are told, in an era when the 'pattern of movement was understood ... to be a visible sign of the relative standings of the persons involved'. Hence the conclusion that 'Hooke and the philosophical world came to Boyle; Boyle and the philosophical world did not come to Hooke'.[9]

The reason for such a state of affairs is attributed to the combination of Hooke's depravity and the fact that his temperament 'was not one which suited him to a life of conventional sociability'. This last assertion is based on Hooke's portrayal by his biographer Richard Waller as 'Melancholy, Mistrustful and Jealous'.[10] But not only was Waller describing the old Hooke; the entire pattern of Hooke's life in and out of the London coffee-houses belies such a representation. He was arguably the most sociable scientific practitioner in Restoration London, a man who delighted in company and conversation, even if his culinary needs were quite modest.[11] Hooke's heightened sociability was shared by the generality of the active membership of the Royal Society, if not necessarily by Boyle, and the ease with which Hooke moved between professional and polite society is actually a testimony to his considerable social standing. And Hooke had been a welcome guest in polite society ever since his arrival to London. When John Evelyn visited London on 3 March 1664, for instance, he arranged a small dinner party for such a select company as the King's 'greate favorite' John Maitland, second Earl of Lauderdale, John Hay, second Earl of Tweeddale, Viscount Brouncker, Sir Robert Moray, John Wilkins and Robert Hooke.[12] So why did Hooke hardly ever entertain his colleagues? Simply because, unlike them, Hooke did not have a house. He was resident of a college who lacked the space and facilities necessary for entertainment. In fact, in contrast to Oxbridge dons, Hooke did not even enjoy the benefits of high-table to which visitors could be invited, as the communal life of the Gresham Professors – envisaged by the founder – was long gone. Contemporaries were fully cognizant of the fact that there existed no such thing as 'Hooke's table', but did not consider him any less for it. They simply took it for granted that sociability involving Hooke was a matter for the coffee-house or their house.

But it is necessary to return to the issue of Hooke's living where he worked. He was obviously hardly unique in that, as most contemporary natural philosophers, Boyle included, did likewise. Nor was Hooke exceptional in cohabiting with his technicians, instrument-makers and servants. So did Boyle. What set Hooke apart, we are told, was the fact that *socially*, little differentiated him from his support staff, and in practice he dealt with them in a manner altogether different from the one adopted by Boyle vis-à-vis his staff. Boyle's numerous technicians were 'largely invisible'. They did the work but Boyle 'evidently saw no reason so to acknowledge their presence and role in that work'. (Not, mind you, that Hooke referred to *his* technicians in his published works. But this 'minor' difficulty is resolved by charging that Hooke's 'pervasive use of the first person singular accurately reflects, as it does not in Boyle's practice, the extent to which Hooke acted as his own technician'. So, too, he was mightily concerned – unlike Boyle we are invited to infer – with 'the establishment of his innovative priority'.[13]) Furthermore, it is claimed, Hooke '*was* vitally concerned' with the apprenticeship of his technicians. 'They were not his equals, but they were youths who might become, ideally should become, his equals'. Boyle, in contrast, 'was in no way concerned to train his technicians to do what he did; in a sense they could not do what he did because they could not be who Boyle was'.[14] In order to make such a claim it is necessary to dismiss as 'careless' an explicit statement by John Aubrey that Boyle kept at his sister's house 'a noble laboratory, and severall servants (prentices to him) to looke to it',[15] as well as to ignore an equally explicit statement by Boyle himself regarding an 'industrious young man, that, whilst he was my Domestick, I bred up to Chymistry, (of which he now teaches Courses)' in Oxford. Boyle referred to Christopher White who actually was just one in a long line of young individuals whom Boyle helped train to do, for all intents and purposes, what he did. Others included John Mayow, Friedrich Slare, Ambrose Godfrey Hanckowitz and Hooke himself.[16]

Most pernicious is the concentrated effort to drum up these and other alleged facts concerning Hooke's life into a pattern designed to cast him a mere servant:

> Hooke was recognized as a person dependent upon others, a person of at best compromised freedom of action, of ambiguous autonomy, and of doubtful integrity. That is to say, his contemporaries might not generally recognize Hooke as a gentleman. At most, his entitlement to the status and attributes of a gentleman was recognized as problematic.

The implications of such imprinting a mark of Cain on Hooke's activities and relations with other members of the Royal Society will be addressed presently. First, however, it is necessary to scrutinize the claim that Hooke's deference and relationship of servitude that supposedly characterized his mature career were cemented early on in his career. Hooke, it is argued, 'publicly accepted the identity of philosophers' assistant', not the least because he 'had been accustomed to a deferential relationship with gentlemen-philosophers since his student days at Oxford'.[17] Once again, however, the historical record fails to support the claim concerning Hooke's impoverished and servile existence while a student at Oxford.

Hooke was a son of an Anglican minister who died when Hooke was 13 years old.[18] As was the case with many promising Royalist youth, a powerful network of support was mobilized to assist his advancement. Hooke was sent to Westminster where he was warmly received by the Head Master Richard Busby, who not only waived all tuition fees but 'lodged and dieted' him in his house, thereby allowing Hooke to keep his not inconsiderable inheritance of £100 intact. Busby further advanced Hooke's career by recommending him to such powerful patrons as John Wilkins, who encouraged the teenager's studies by presenting him with a copy of his *Mathematicall Magick*.[19] Hence, Hooke arrived at Oxford in 1653 not only well recommended but also comfortably well off. He indeed matriculated a sizar, but not because his poverty mandated that he menially serve others in return for room and board, but – as was to be the case with Newton several years later – in order to avoid paying higher admission fees. In fact, just as Newton entered servitor to a family friend, Humphrey Babington, which almost certainly meant that he was assigned few, if any, menial duties,[20] so did Hooke enter as servitor to Cardell Goodman, a family friend (and administrator of his father's will), which obviously made Hooke's life far more comfortable than that of other sizars.[21] Furthermore, Busby and/or Goodman were also instrumental in securing for Hooke a sinecure at Christ Church in the form of a chorister's studentship, which, we are informed by Aubrey, was actually 'a pretty good maintenance'.[22]

Within two years at the latest, Hooke was drawn into the activities of the Oxford Philosophical Club. Given his academic rank, Hooke was obviously not of equal standing initially but, just like Christopher Wren earlier, he was certainly not considered a servant.[23] In addition to developing a close relationship with Wilkins – who remained a close friend and a staunch supporter of Hooke until his death in 1672 – Hooke studied astronomy with Seth Ward and chemistry (and probably anatomy as well) with Thomas Willis. No evidence exists, however, that Hooke's association with Willis was remunerative in nature. Nor was he in need of such employment. In 1656 Robert Boyle arrived at Oxford and soon Willis (and undoubtedly Wilkins as well) recommended Hooke to him. However, Hooke was not transferred from one master to another as a salaried assistant. Though he was partly recommended to Boyle 'to be usefull to him in his chymicall operations', Hooke's immediate task was actually to serve as Boyle's tutor in mathematics and natural philosophy. As Aubrey put it, Hooke 'read to him … Euclid's Elements, and made him understand Des Cartes' Philosophy'.[24]

Equally clear is that the relations that quickly developed between the two men were not those of master and servant. Hooke became a member of Boyle's household – such as it was in Oxford – living with him, and whatever remuneration he subsequently received was evidently proffered in the form of an annuity rather than wages. Hooke, in other words, stood to Boyle in the same relationship that Thomas Harriot stood to Sir Walter Ralegh, or Thomas Hobbes's to the earls of Devonshire.[25] The close relationship is made clear in Boyle's address of his first published scientific book, *New Experiments Physico-Mechanicall, Touching the Spring of the Air* (1660), to his nephew, Charles Boyle, Viscount Dungarvon. There he not only acknowledged Hooke's construction of the air pump but his contribution to the formation of Boyle's ideas as well.[26] Boyle further attests to Hooke's position as a colleague when calling attention to his acquaintance with Dungarvon, 'who hath also the Honor to be known to your Lordship, and was with me when I had these things under consideration'.[27] Furthermore, in 1661 Hooke published under his own name a sequel to the *New Experiments* as *An Attempt for the Explication of the Phœnomena* and, in the following year, Boyle invited him to contribute his 'ingenious Conjectures' regarding the rarefaction of air to Boyle's *Defence Against Linus*. Such a unique form of collaboration can further be substantiated from the chance survival of Hooke's comments and corrections in the mid-1670s to a draft of Boyle's *A Disquisition about the Final Causes of Natural Things*. As far as we know, no other experimental philosopher – let alone technician – was ever entrusted with such a task.[28] Finally, we may go further in elucidating the intimate relationship between the two from the warm tenor of their surviving correspondence during the 1660s – wholly absent from the Oldenburg-Boyle exchange – and from the fact that throughout much of the period that preceded Hooke's appointment as Gresham Professor, he resided with Lady Ranelagh at Pall Mall.

If my reading of the historical record is correct, then, nothing in Hooke's Oxford career suggests a relationship of servility. Hooke had been a person with modest, but sufficient, means, who easily earned the respect and friendship of more senior members of the Oxford Philosophical Club, including Boyle's. However, the fruitful (and comfortable) companionship with Boyle could not last indefinitely, for Hooke needed to launch his own career. At this juncture the needs of the Royal Society and Hooke's own aspirations intersected. Since the summer of 1662, key members of the Society sought to professionalize the institution's research program, and Hooke's friends were quick to recommend him as the obvious candidate for the task. On 5 November 1662 Sir Robert Moray announced that Hooke was 'willing to be employed as a curator by the society', offering to furnish each of their meetings 'with three or four considerable experiments, and expecting no recompence till the society should get a stock enabling them to give it'. The following week Moray officially proposed Hooke as Curator of Experiments

> who being unanimously accepted of, it was ordered, that Mr. Boyle should have the thanks of the society for dispensing with him for their use; and that Mr. Hooke should come and sit among them, and both bring in every day of the meeting three or four experiments of his own, and take care of such others, as should be mentioned to him by the society.

I may add parenthetically, that the language of the resolution – 'that Mr. Boyle should have the thanks of the society for dispensing with him for their use' – need not be interpreted as denoting servitude. Simply put, the Society's grandees were fully cognizant of Hooke's indispensability to Boyle's researches and they truly appreciated the latter's willingness to part with his friend and collaborator for the benefit of the budding Society.[29]

But Hooke's benefactors were not content to merely appoint him as Curator of Experiments. From the start it was clear that Hooke was groomed for one of the Gresham professorships. Wilkins played a central role in such maneuvers, as he was not only Hooke's patron but also that of his half-brother, Walter Pope, Gresham Professor of astronomy, and Isaac Barrow, Gresham Professor of Geometry. At this stage, Pope appears to have been waiting for a more lucrative position, while Barrow, who commuted to Cambridge on a weekly basis in order to fulfill his duties as regius professor of Greek, could also be expected to resign soon. Then, in April 1663 Pope was appointed travel companion to John Evelyn's nephew, soon leaving for two years – with Barrow substituting for him; later the same year Barrow himself was elected Lucasian professor of mathematics and his resignation became a certainty.

There existed one obstacle: Hooke's scientific ardour made him abandon early his Oxford course of studies and he never bothered to graduate. That was an impediment for a Gresham Professorship and it became necessary to quickly intercede with the Earl of Clarendon – the Oxford Chancellor and Royal Society benefactor – to arrange for the conferral by mandate of an MA degree on Hooke, which was granted in September 1663. It is for this reason, and not because of his inferior status, that Hooke is the only one without a title on the May 1663 list of the Society's members.[30] For his part, Barrow almost certainly refrained from officially resigning his professorship until 20 May 1664 in order to ensure Hooke's succession. However, the plan nearly backfired as machinations among certain of the electors resulted in the election, by the narrowest margin, of Arthur Dacres instead. The Royal Society immediately challenged the election, an action that ultimately forced Dacres to resign ten months later in favour of Hooke – by which time Hooke had already replaced Barrow as deputy for Pope.[31]

No sooner did Hooke fail to obtain the Gresham professorship in May 1664 than John Graunt and William Petty approached Sir John Cutler and urged him to endow a new lectureship for Hooke. Cutler agreed, though it seems that his ideas for the subject matter of the lectures differed from that of Hooke. In the following months, the Society finally moved to elect Hooke as 'curator by office' with a salary of £80 per annum, which, in the first instance, was to be raised by a special contribution of certain members. Once Cutler officially committed himself to endow the lectureship, the Society reduced its contribution, with Hooke's acquiescence, to £30. All in all, it is clear that the annual salary envisaged for Hooke was £130 – as the Society remained confident that Hooke would ultimately obtain the Gresham professorship as well. It is also clear that the Society's grandees were determined to ensure Hooke's status as well by securing for him a proper academic position in addition to the curatorship.[32]

The significance attached to the office of curator cannot be overstated. The Society was founded primarily for the purpose of 'advancing natural knowledge by experiment'. Consequently, the Curator of Experiments was considered, at least initially, as more vital to the Society's mission than any other officer, the president and secretary included. The statutes of the Society, which were in the process of being drafted when Hooke was asked to serve as curator in the autumn of 1662, are quite explicit on this matter, judging by the meticulous care in spelling out the election process and duties of the curator, compared with the rather perfunctory treatment of the other officers. Further to attest to the importance attached to the position of curator is his envisaged salary, upwards of £200 per annum – a remuneration considerably more generous than that enjoyed by either the Savilian or Lucasian professors.[33] Hence it would be wrong to conclude that the detailed statutes were intended to regulate the behavior of individuals of 'uncertain social standing'.[34] In fact, the office of the curator was seen by the Society's architects as analogous to an Oxbridge scientific professorship, and the statutes pertaining to the office of curator were actually modeled in part on the Savilian statutes. Thus, just as the Oxford professors were to be drawn 'from among men of good character and reputable lives', so the Society's curators were expected to be individuals of good credit. Analogous to the electors that monitored the qualification and reputation of the Savilian professors were members of the Society's Council to whom candidates for the curatorship were to present themselves. Nor was there anything particularly demeaning in the stipulations concerning negligence and ejections. The Savilian statutes – just like the statutes of any other professorship – were explicit in specifying the grounds for forfeiture of salary or expulsion from office. Finally, the stipulation that a curator was prohibited from seeking other positions was not an indication that he 'was not free to dispose of his own time', but that, like the Savilian professors, it was expected that the generous remuneration attached to the office would allow the incumbent to devote himself wholly to his duties 'without seeking for or engaging in any other employment'.[35]

Only ignorance of the fundamental principles that informed the architects of the Royal Society can account for the misguided notion that of the Society's chief officers, the curator alone was not expected to be a gentleman. Indeed, it has been exclaimed, 'What Fellow other than Hooke occupied a social rank which would have permitted him to "be summoned to attend the next meeting of the council, to receive their rebuke for the neglect of his office"?'[36] In 1670, when such an incident occurred, Hooke was indeed slacking in his duties – not least because of his other employments. But this mild rebuke was hardly different from the one received by Christopher Wren several years earlier, because of a similar dereliction in his duties as Savilian professor of astronomy;[37] neither case had anything to do with social status.

The primacy of the curatorship was forcefully reiterated in Thomas Sprat's *The History of the Royal Society*. 'Whatever *Revenew* they shall rais', he wrote, 'by this or any other means, they intend thereby to make an Establishment for their *Curators*. To this Office they have already admitted some of their *Fellows*, whom they will employ according to their *Studies* and *sufficience*.'[38] Such privileging of the curatorship may also explain why it was not felt necessary to remunerate Secretary Oldenburg when Hooke was appointed curator. Indeed, the significance we attach today to Oldenburg's correspondence was not necessarily shared by his colleagues in the early 1660s. To some, in fact, it proved a distraction, for the reading of letters took time away from the more important task of performing experiments.[39]

As for Hooke, he instantly proved himself indispensable, not least because the zeal of other members to perform experiments – which was dangerously on the wane even before Hooke had been elected – reached such an ebb that Oldenburg feared the imminent demise of the Society.[40] Conversely, Wren undoubtedly articulated the opinion of many Fellows when he wrote that he knew Hooke to be 'full of imployment for the Society which [he] all-most wholly preserve together by [his] own constant paines'.[41] Hardly surprising, then, that Hooke's incredible versatility and phenomenal success in just about everything he touched – compounded by the increasing reluctance of other Fellows to perform – made his colleagues occasionally impatient, even demanding. Yet the rare occasion when this happened hardly warrant the conclusion that Hooke's 'daily work was largely subject to the will of others', who manifested 'their entitlement to set the terms of Hooke's scientific work and to chastise him when he failed to give satisfaction'. Sir Robert Moray's good-natured reaction to hearing that Hooke required more observations in order to complete his theory of comets is a case in point. 'I would hee had any thing hee desires that hee may have no longer excuses for his slackness in making out his Hypothesis' he wrote to Oldenburg. The constructing of a theory was not a task set on Hooke by the Society, and he was not about to be rushed simply to satisfy the propagandist needs of the Society, a point of view accepted by Moray. A couple of weeks later, when Moray complained that Hooke was learning a hundred trades rather than complete 'taskes lyet upon him', he was hardly disapproving of Hooke's idling his time away; only that he was eager for Hooke to complete his work on a coach for which the Society had taken out a patent.[42]

Problematic in this regard is the affinity forged between privileged economic and social circumstance and a whole set of values – such as integrity, freedom of action and disinterestedness – that its possessors (notably Boyle) uniquely enjoyed. More troublesome still is the claim that wealthy members of the gentry were accorded distinctive and privileged prerogatives in the realm of knowledge, while those divested of such means and status necessarily fell into a condition of dependence, with its contingent forfeiture of free action, integrity and, potentially, credibility. Again, Boyle alone is invoked as 'master of credibility' whose reports were allegedly hardly ever put through a 'process of deliberative assessment', let alone negated:

> A remarkable feature of his relations with the Royal Society, and with the philosophical community in general, was the easy passage enjoyed by his factual testimony from personal claim to collective assent. With some qualifications ... one might even say that his factual testimony was *never* negated by the Royal Society or by those whom it recognized as competent practitioners.

The exceptions that actually prove the rule were the challenges raised by Thomas Hobbes, Benedict Spinoza, Christiaan Huygens, Henry More, Adrien Auzout and Henry Stubbe. Ultimately, however, these individuals do not really count because, 'it is not absolutely clear that any of these episodes *do* involve direct negations of Boyle's factual testimony' and, besides, 'none of these episodes clearly originated from critics who were in dense social interaction with Boyle and his friends'. They either 'tended towards the margins of Boyle's circle' or 'assuredly placed themselves beyond expectation of ever belonging'.[43] In point of fact, however, neither Boyle's social standing nor the respect for his scientific work was expected to shield his experimental results from the process of verification and replication, even among the rank and file of the Royal Society. As Sir Robert Moray informed Christiaan Huygens in July 1661, apropos discussing Sir Kenelm Digby's forthcoming discourse on vegetation, 'in due course, the Society will examine the truth that he claims for his experiments, and will put everything to the test, as they do with all the pieces of Mr. Boyle and others'. Boyle himself attested, on various occasions, to his testimony being challenged, and his need to repeat his experiments in order to persuade critics. Writing to Oldenburg on 29 October 1663, for example, Boyle states that in order 'to be able to satisfy others rather then my selfe about a considerable Particular relating to the Suspension of the Mercury I bethought myselfe of one tryall' that should satisfy skeptics. Nineteen months later Boyle informed Oldenburg that he and Richard Lower had 'been repeating an Exp[erimen]t, to satisfie others rather then ourselves of the Truth of what I was relating at Gresham College when I was saying That I had observd that if the Thorax were sufficiently layd open the Lungs though unhurt would not play'. In an unpublished note Boyle also recalled that in order 'to satisfie some scrupulous Inquirers', he was forced to repeat an experiment to substantiate his claim 'that the white powder or Calx [he made] out of refin'd Gold by disolving it in the menstruum … need not be as it might be suspected to be anything of antimoniall latitant in the menstruum'.[44]

On the other end of the spectrum of credibility – so the argument goes – we find Robert Hooke, whose remunerative and menial status denuded him of integrity and *potentially* compromised his credibility. And though he might not have been routinely distrusted, 'even Hooke's experimental testimony might have conditions laid upon it, and … the authority to do so flowed from his standing as (ambiguous) servant'.[45] While the validity of drawing a one-to-one correlation between the integrity, or lack thereof, of domestic servants, and the scientific expertise of Fellows of the Royal Society, cannot be evaluated here, the evidence derived from the Society's register, ostensibly proving that even Hooke's experimental results and interpretations could be challenged 'costlessly and consequentially', is in need of scrutiny.

Consider the following typical illustrations of such purported mistrust or incredulity: 'Early in 1663, the Royal Society's *Journal-Book* recorded that Hooke, as remunerated Curator of Experiments, "made the experiment of condensing air by the pressure of water; but the trial agreeing not with the hypothesis, it was ordered to be repeated at the next meeting" ' Then, in 1672, when Hooke attempted to establish 'whether air was generated or consumed by burning', his 'colleagues reserved the right to define whether or not his experimental work counted as success or failure;' hence the minutes 'referred guardedly to the experiment "he said, he had made", and members of the society were delegated to act as direct witnesses to a repetition'. The first case is a red herring not only because Hooke was not a remunerated curator yet but, given the subject matter of the experiment, because it may well have been Hooke's own hypothesis that was at odds with the experimental result – and, in any case, requests to repeat an experiment did not imply scepticism in the performance of a member, but were an integral part of the investigative method established by the Society. Nor do the minutes of the Society condone the gloss made on the 1672 case. They do not refer 'guardedly' to the success of the experiment but as a matter of fact – the phrase 'he said, he had made', was a formulaic figure of speech that carried no innuendos. Nor was there a delegation of members to supervise Hooke. Rather, accepting the verity of the experiment, Hooke 'was desired to prosecute these experiments, and to give the Society an account of them from time to time, and to bespeak some members of the Society to assist at them'.[46]

In reality, then, little differentiated the public reception of Boyle's and Hooke's experimental results. Only that by virtue of his position as curator Hooke performed infinitely more experiments than had Boyle – not to mention that Hooke's trials were invariably communal events, and also included experiments at the behest of other Fellows. Consequently, the prospects of failure or controversy were significantly higher in his case, a point that is lost on those who simply mine the documents in order to cull apt phrases in support of preconceived conclusions concerning status and credibility.

Indeed, the myopic culling of phrases has been everywhere prevalent. One of the most important features of Boyle's identity as the Christian virtuoso is said to have been his public modesty. Naturally, by virtue of who he was, such a quality was conspicuously absent from Hooke's very mentality. So what does one do with the following personal statement of Hooke in the *Micrographia*?

I have obtained my end, if these my small Labours shall be thought fit to take up some place in the large stock of Natural Observations, which so many hands are busie in providing. If I have contributed the meanest foundations whereon others may raise nobler Superstructures, I am abundantly satisfied; and all my ambition is, that I may serve to the great Philosophers of this Age, as the makers and grinders of my Glasses did to me; that I may prepare and furnish them with some Materials, which they may afterwards order and manage with better skill, and to far greater advantage.[47]

Obviously, the passage could not be interpreted as testimony of Hooke's embodying the Boylean ideal. Instead it has been used as grist to the mill, as incontrovertible proof of Hooke's self-identification as 'a master of technicians and a technician of masters'.[48] The passage certainly does not warrant such an interpretation. In fact, the public expression of modesty Hooke had articulated there may well have inspired John Locke's similar self-deprecation in the preface to *An Essay Concerning Human Understanding*:

The Commonwealth of Learning, is not at this time without Master-Builders, whose mighty Designs, in advancing the Sciences, will leave lasting Monuments to the Admiration of Posterity; But every one must not hope to be a BOYLE, or a SYDENHAM; and in an Age that produces such Masters, as the Great HUYGENIUS; and the incomparable MR. NEWTON ... 'tis Ambition enough to be employed as an Under-Labourer in clearing Ground a little, and removing some of the Rubbish, that lies in the way to Knowledge.[49]

So who was Robert Hooke? In 1680 John Aubrey described him as 'the greatest Mechanick this day in the world'.[50] This was an expression of admiration that implied neither lowly status and compromised integrity nor his exclusion from amongst the community of experimental philosophers. In Restoration England, truly great 'mechanics' were considered a notch above ordinary philosophers. Small wonder that Hooke thought it the ultimate compliment to extol Christopher Wren in print in the following terms: 'since the time of *Archimedes*, there scarce ever met in one man, in so great a perfection, such a *Mechanical Hand*, and so *Philosophical* a *Mind*'. Three years later Thomas Sprat generalized that very compliment when prophesizing that philosophy will 'attain to perfection, when either the *Mechanic Laborers* shall have *Philosophical heads*; or the *Philosophers* shall have *Mechanical hands*'.[51] After 1687 contemporaries were certain that, thanks to the efforts of another great mechanic, philosophy had indeed attained perfection. Newton himself articulated a distinction between 'true' and 'Vulgar Mechanick' in a 1694 letter:

whilst Mechanicks consists in the Doctrine of force and motion, and Geometry in that of magniude and figure; he that can't reason about force and motion, is as far from being a true Mechanick, as he that can't reason about magnitude and figure from being a Geometer ... there is the same difference between a mere practical Mechanick and a rational one, as between a mere practical Surveyor or Gauger and a good Geometer, or between an Empirick in Physick and a learned and rational Physitian.[52]

Newton, the founder of rational mechanics, obviously prided himself in being a 'true Mechanick' and contemporaries never worried about Newton's identity. I hope that even this brief essay has been sufficient to suggest that they did not worry about Hooke's identity either. He was the greatest mechanic of the age, who *could* 'play the part of the Christian Virtuoso', but who opted instead, along with all other active members of the Royal Society, to pursue experimental philosophy as a gentleman of science.[53]

Chapter 14

Hooke and Westminster

Edward Smith

In the library of Westminster School is a first edition of the *History of the Royal Society*.[1] The copy epitomizes the vitality and the central position of the institution that was Westminster in the latter part of the seventeenth century. The author was the Dean of Westminster and Bishop of Rochester, Thomas Sprat; he was also *ex officio* the chairman of the Governing Body of the School. The book had been a gift of William Lord Brereton to his friend, the mathematician John Pell, who is the author of the marginal corrections. John Pell in turn left the book and a large part of his library to his close friend Richard Busby, the Head Master of Westminster School (and a Prebendary of the Abbey after the Restoration), of whom he was a constant visitor and regular correspondent. On p. 232 is *An Account of a Dog dissected* by the Old Westminster, Robert Hooke, whose circle of friends and colleagues encompassed Pell and Busby and a large part of educated London society. The only one of those named above who was not a Fellow of the Royal Society, Richard Busby, was to play a very significant rôle in education in the second half of the seventeenth century.

Around 1650 Robert Hooke had the good fortune to join Westminster School; the influence upon him of the School and, in particular, of its Head Master was profound. It is my intention in what follows to throw a little light on this largely unexplored part of Hooke's story. I hope to demonstrate that during his time at the School he had the best education that was available and, importantly, that he was encouraged to develop his scientific skills so that when he arrived at Christ Church, perhaps in 1655, his potential was already recognized, his talents developed and he was aware of the profound changes overtaking the world of experimental philosophy. As a result he was able very quickly to gain acceptance in that world, which was to be pivotal in his life. But his relationship with his old headmaster did not end when he left Westminster School. I shall review some of Dr Busby's building projects in which he was helped by Hooke.

It is necessary first to explore the significance of Busby and Westminster School at this time, so that specific academic details can

Figure 14.1   Dr Richard Busby,
Head Master, Westminster School
1639–95.

be set in context. Busby was Head Master for over 55 years. The
stability that his longevity afforded would alone have established his
importance. His remarkable abilities, both in teaching and in
encouraging independence of mind in his pupils, inspired two
generations. Despite the pressures and pitfalls around him, he never
allowed the responsibility of his office nor his personal beliefs to be
compromised. That Busby held uncompromisingly to his principles
was to inspire and bind his pupils to him so strongly that they seldom
wished to break away completely.

Though there was turmoil on its doorstep, through the latter part of
the seventeenth century the School produced a huge range of talented
men.[2] During this time of political and religious foment, on the one
hand Matthew Wren had sent his son to Busby because he perceived
his Royalist allegiance, and on the other, though the Dryden
household had the celebrated Puritan preacher Dod as a member, it
did not feel uncomfortable about the son's education at Westminster.
During the Commonwealth, an Ordinance of the Lords and Commons
abolished the roles of the Dean and Chapter of 'The College of St
Peter in Westminster' and invited Puritan divines to conduct series of
sermons in the Abbey; nevertheless the Arminian tendencies of
Richard Busby were tolerated in the shadow of the same church.
Indeed the Lord Protector himself can hardly have been unaware of
the high church Anglicanism[3] of Dr Busby on which he never
compromised, to the point of being entered as 'sickly'[4] when he
should have been taking the Covenant. The very special qualities that
Busby had were too important to be lost to the nation. The early

eighteenth-century essayist Sir Richard Steele was to say 'I must confess that I am of the opinion Busby's Genius for education had as great an Effect upon the age he lived in, as that of any ancient Philosopher, without excepting one, had on his Contemporaries'.[5] His intolerance of indolence may well have been considered excessive even then,[6] but he also encouraged individual talent and freedom of debate at every opportunity. The biographer of the Nonconformist divine and diarist Philip Henry writes: 'I have heard him tell how much he surprised the Doctor, the first time he waited upon him after he was turn'd out by the Act of Uniformity: For when the Doctor asked him, Pr'ythee (Child) what made thee a Nonconformist? Truly Sir, saith Mr Henry, you made me one; for you taught me those things that hindered me from conforming'.[7] The divine, Robert South, in the sermon that he wrote to preach to Old Westminsters, but which was never delivered because of the king's death, and in which he says that the School publicly prayed for King Charles I not two hours before his execution, gives advice to teachers based on his own experience at Westminster: 'Where they find a youth of spirit, let them endeavour to govern that spirit, without extinguishing it'.[8]

How broad was the curriculum that Robert Hooke followed is hard to discover. Indeed there are few sources to give us a clear overview of what was taught in schools in the mid-seventeenth century, and it is often suggested that many subjects would be taught by private tutors, with the only formal teaching being in classics. For Westminster there is no single document of the right period that explores the full range of subjects. There are three well-known manuscripts (the Laudian, Frowick's and the Shaftesbury),[9] but these give us insight almost exclusively into the classical curriculum that was taught 'up School'. That latter phrase needs further explanation: in Westminster's private language it means 'in the main School Hall', where all the formal class instruction took place until 1884. So Aubrey's statement concerning Hooke, 'I have heard Sir Richard Knight [who was Hooke's school-fellow] say that he seldome sawe him in the schoole', could be interpreted to mean that, rather than *up School*, Hooke studied either in Dr Busby's house, where he boarded, or possibly in the Museum (Library), under the direction, but not necessarily close supervision, of a tutor.

The few mentions in the manuscripts referred to above of books and subjects other than the classics, are to Hunter's *Rudimenta Cosmographica* and to Aratus's *Φαινομενα*. John Locke had purchased George Abbot's *A Briefe Description of the Whole World. Wherein is Particularly Described all the Monarchies, Empires and*

Kingdomes of the Same, etc. in 1649[10] which indicates that the study of geography begun at Westminster under Head Master Osbaldeston had continued under Busby. Aratus's work is largely based on Eudoxus. It was probably studied for the verse rather than the astronomy, but that astronomy was studied is very evident from the number of works on the subject in the Busby Library, which the School still maintains.[11] In the library there are multiple copies of Sacrobosco (John Hollywood), *Sphaera Emendata*, which suggests that it might have been a standard pupil text.

The mathematical texts that are to be found in the Library are all that one might expect. They include William Oughtred (for example, *Circle of Proportions*, 1632) of course and perhaps 20 different editions of Euclid. A number of the latter are octavo (for example, Isaac Barrow's edition) and are perhaps school-boy pocket-size. A detailed breakdown of the mathematical works in Busby's collection during Hooke's time awaits a recataloguing that takes account of the large gift of John Pell's works to the Library later in the century. We can confirm from Pell's correspondence that at least a few years after Hooke, mathematics was enthusiastically studied by Busby and his pupils: Pell assisted Thomas Brancker in the translation of Rahn's *Introduction to Algebra*, which was avidly read by Head Master and pupils.[12] The central position of mathematics in the curriculum is confirmed by the 1688 edition of the Latin grammar which becomes *Rudimentum Anglo-Latinum Grammaticae Literalis & Numeralis* with the addition of 93 pages of arithmetic.

Of oriental languages that are mentioned by Waller[13] we can only speculate. However the Elizabethan Statutes of the School required that Latin, Greek and Hebrew were taught. The Greek and Latin grammars that Busby used were produced from his own teaching, under his own supervision, and seemingly rewritten by each new generation of pupils. Similarly he produced for his pupils a Hebrew grammar.[14] It remained unprinted until after his death, but was regularly transcribed and updated by the pupils. That Hebrew was well established is clear from John Locke's letter to his father about his oration for election to Christ Church.[15] A little later we have confirmation from Evelyn that Arabic too was taught:

> I heard and saw such exercises at the election of scholars at Westminster School to be sent to the University in Latin, Greek, Hebrew, and Arabic, in themes and extemporary verses, as wonderfully astonished me in such youths, with such readiness and wit, some of them not above twelve, or thirteen years of age.[16]

It is difficult to judge exactly when Busby began to teach Arabic at the School. It seems likely that he began teaching it as soon as he felt he was capable of it. On the evidence of his pupils' university careers it seems unlikely that his studies pre-date the publication of the Polyglot Bible[17] early in the 1650's; however very soon after he was involved with the *Lexicon Heptaglotton* of Castell, Henry Stubbe (the physician and pamphleteer who incidentally had been introduced to Sir Henry Vane by Busby and benefited from his charity as a result) and George Hooper (the Bishop of Bath and Wells of whom Busby said 'He was the best scholar, the finest gentleman, and will make the completest bishop that ever was educated at Westminster School') made their way to Oxford in the 1650s to pursue interests in Arabic, which is likely to have begun at the School. In the sale catalogue of Robert Hooke's library[18] sold after his death there are no examples of Hebrew or Arabic: it would appear that he, like so many of his contemporaries at Westminster, chose not to pursue the subjects further.[19] However his interest in language continued, as for many of his friends, with the idea of a universal language and, much later, perhaps through his friendship with Captain Knox, in Far Eastern languages.[20] Perhaps Evelyn was thinking of him when he wrote of the study of Arabic at Westminster: 'Pity it is, that what they attain here so ripely, they either do not retain, or do not improve more considerably when they come to be men'.[21] It should be mentioned that, radically, Dr Busby did introduce the teaching of English grammar. Again the text was written and updated by pupils, but it was finally published by William Walker[22] with a dedication to Dr Busby. Walker was an Usher at Westminster but then moved on to be Headmaster of Grantham Grammar School, where incidentally he just missed teaching Isaac Newton, but in later life was on intimate terms with him.

Music, too, was important in Dr Busby's life: in Thomas Vincent's diary there are several instances of musical evenings, singing, playing the organ or percussion instruments.[23] In the inventory of effects at Busby's death is listed a pair of organs, doubtless including the one upon which Hooke learned his 20 lessons.[24]

That visitors to Westminster, eminent in their fields, should interest themselves in the boys' education would be de rigueur to Dr Busby. For example Henry Aldrich, later to become Dean of Christ Church, a scholar and divine, a musician and an architect, was in 1656 a near contemporary of Hooke; his early skill in mathematics attracted the 83-year-old William Oughtred, who encouraged him with an inscribed copy of his *Trigonometria*, 1657.[25] Similarly Aubrey's report of John Wilkins's gift of *Mathematicall Magick* to Hooke shows an inspirational act at a seminal point in Hooke's career of a text that places the study of applied mathematics in an intellectual context; there were other applied mathematics treatises available to Hooke too in Busby's well stocked Library.[26] The craft and technical skills of Hooke's earlier childhood begin to have an intellectual basis in these works.

It is interesting to speculate when Hooke first employed his practical proficiency in scientific or engineering experiments. He may well have had access to the skills of the artisans working around Westminster Abbey (still surviving even without Dean and Chapter, through the Commonwealth), and possibly had begun to develop the stoop that Aubrey describes as the product of hours spent at the lathe.[27] There is some basis for believing that during his brief school career at Westminster, Christopher Wren had had such opportunity: we know of no recorded interest from him in things mechanical before November 1645, when he was just over 13 and dedicated his 'Panorganum Astronomicum'[28] to his father, presumably during his time at the School. This is an instrument whose purpose appears unexplained and whose description is lost. At about the same time he invented 'a Pneumatick Engine' and 'a peculiar instrument for use in Gnomonicks',[29] presumably his own sundial. Leaving aside Sir Christopher's son's tendency to embroider in *Parentalia*, the letters amply confirm that some sort of opportunity to develop mechanical skills was open to the pupils. It is clear from the inventory of effects in Dr Busby's house in Little Cloister at his death in April 1695 that at some stage he had developed an interest in some of those instruments that also interested Hooke. The effects include:

> a Bambo stick with a Perspective in it; a large long Perspective Glasse 7ft long; a brass Quadrant 12 inches same diameter by Sutton; a Plumbred Quadrant 11 inches same diameter Gunters projection; an Astralobe [sic] 18 inches Diameter; a brass horizontal Dyall 6 inches Diameter; two burning Glasses one of them 8 the other 4 inches Diameter'.[30]

Even if these effects were not in place at the start of Hooke's career, they show a mind open to matters of scientific interest and the practical use of scientific instruments.

In considering Hooke's interest in solutions to practical problems it is tempting to begin by considering his obsession with flying. It were disingenuous of any reader not to admit to at least five 'several ways' of making paper aeroplanes. Beyond that the contemporary boy's mind might quite easily turn to a precursor of hot air balloons: a paper dart thrown across the open central fire in College Hall would very soon demonstrate the lift that hot air would give. Equally he may have had the opportunity to explore kite-flying in nearby Tothill Fields.[31] But, further, how could Hooke explore the mechanical process of man-powered flight at School? It appears to be an idée fixe of the era of course, not just for Hooke, as mentioned by Aubrey and throughout the diary, but also Wren, and other contemporaries.[32] Perhaps Hooke's interest was in part inspired by Busby's copy of Wilkins's *The Discovery of a New World* (1640).

It is clear that Hooke benefited from an institution at the cutting edge of school education. But Busby's importance should be explored in a broader educational context. Henry Stubbe's diatribe, against the University of Oxford in general and Christ Church in particular,[33] may well be written with deep irony, but for the satire to work there must have some marginally believable substance. Busby would have been amused to hear the suggestion: 'Let the Honourable the Governours of Westminster School be entrusted with supreme power of the Colledge [Christ Church] … Let the foundation be supplyed from Westminster School.' Dr Busby believed in widening the availability of education. This led him to an interest in the wider social context. He was engaged in charitable work in a School at Lutton in Lincolnshire and in the Green Coat Hospital (Figure 14.4) in nearby Tothill Fields (the latter with Hooke's professional assistance) and also in further education, which led him to founding readerships in Hebrew and in Mathematics at Christ Church (from which all that appears to remain is the Common Room!).[34] Richard Busby cannot have been less charitable at Westminster School than he clearly was elsewhere. There is some evidence that he used the lesser scholarships of Bishop Williams's foundation for exactly this purpose.[35] Recent evidence[36] suggests that Hooke came to London with only £50; some simple calculations suggest that this would not in the usual course of events have lasted even two years at Westminster. We must assume that despite the diarist Pepys's claim that Busby was 'devilish covetous',[37] he was able to extend charity to Hooke's education.

Robert Hooke acknowledged the debt that he owed to Busby, who became both his employer and his friend. In the formal setting of an affidavit to prove a codicil of Busby's Will, following his death in 1695, Hooke notes his long co-operation with his friend over many projects and years since his school days:

Robert Hooke of Gresham Colledge London Reader of Geometry there and Doctor of Phisick aged Sixty two Yeares or thereabouts being Educed as a Witnesse on the parte of the complainants in this Cause was on the 12th day of July in the year of Our Lord 1697 shewed in person at the Seat of Mr Norton who is the Clerk that deales for the Defendants in the Cause

... being sworne &c deposeth and saith To the first Interrogation That he did know Richard Busby Dr in Divinity late deceased & hath been acquainted with him for the space of forty yeares now last past & upwards this Deponent being Schollar to the said Dr Busby ... that this Deponent assisted him the said Dr Busby in the beautyfieing of the School & Colledge at Westm where in the said Dr Busby laid out about the Sume of Two Thousand Pounds & this Deponent having been so formerly consulted with by the said Doctor Busby in such works & benefactons as aforesaid.[38]

Other than the affidavit there is only one further direct reference to Hooke as a pupil at Westminster. This second one takes us back to the early years of Hooke and Busby's relationship. It is a contemporary list of pupils, perhaps of tutees, by an usher; it is not in Dr Busby's nor the Under Master, Thomas Vincent's, hand. The internal evidence leads to the conclusion that it was written in 1654 or, possibly, 1655, though I incline to the former.[39] Others that I am able to identify from the list who were of Hooke's age appear to go to Christ Church or Trinity in the following year. I believe that though the earliest date we can put on Hooke's arrival at Christ Church is 1654, it is much more likely to be 1655 or later. From the direct evidence of School lists and with nothing primary to conflict with this, we can safely say that Waller is wrong by one or two years.[40] However there is a further curious point that Hooke's age is listed as 16, whereas we know it to have been at least 18. The range of ages at which Westminsters left to go to the universities was broad at that time; indeed it was not unknown that a pupil entered Westminster aged 20! But is this list possibly a sleight of hand from Busby? Could it be that the relatively unschooled Hooke, whose talent was obvious to Busby, had to work at his formal education in forms lower than his age would suggest and that this was a device to save embarrassment?

It is well known that Westminster School nurtured a large number of literary figures, but Westminster also brought together a cross-section of the scientific world. Busby was in regular contact with many Old Westminsters and others, as is noted in both Vincent's and Hooke's diaries, and was abundantly aware of the world around him and of academic developments. Busby was the conduit through which several collections of books and papers passed (Harriot's, Warner's and Pell's, for example). Indeed, if Gunther's reference to 'JG' as John Gee (Busby's manservant/secretary) is correct, even letters from Isaac Newton may well have passed through Busby's hands en route to Hooke.[41] In 1667 the Old Westminster anatomist Walter Needham, close friend of Boyle, Lower and Millington (the latter both Old Westminsters), finally published his paper *De Formato Foetu*, but in the 1664 edition of *De Vitelli in Intestina Pulli Transitu Epistola*, Stensen refers to a rediscovery (of avian outgrowth from intestine to yolk), and says that Needham has ten years priority. There is a series of letters of 1654–55 from Walter Needham to his old Head Master, Dr Busby.[42] It is possible that the letter of 2 May 1655 is referring to this paper. It is certainly the case that these letters are no mere letters of duty or of flattery. In particular that of 4 February 1654, which Busby would have received while Hooke was still at School, is a fascinating statement of the emerging philosophy of the experimentalists: it is a rejection of Descartes, Gassendus and the Rationalists, and a complete acceptance of Baconian views with an insistence that Aristotle should be reviewed in this new light.[43] At the very time that Hooke was his pupil Busby was very clearly part of this important debate: it is unthinkable that he would not have engaged the pupils in this discussion.

When Robert Hooke arrived at Christ Church he would have been intellectually equipped for the next stage of his education. Through Westminster he would have had entrée into the circle that was to foster and encourage his scientific education. All the indications are that Busby would have maintained his contact with him through this part of his career, offering advice and possibly financial assistance.

Robert Hooke's later interest in education will have been influenced by Busby's example and by contemporary debate. John Locke was a lifelong friend of Hooke and a near contemporary at Westminster; I do not doubt that they exchanged views on education generally and from their own experience. John Locke's less literary and almost utilitarian philosophy of education was far from Dr Busby's ideals. It is interesting to note that his belief in firm discipline meant he would consider Dr Busby's corrective pragmatically, if his own system were to break down:

> … A French man it must bee that he may not loose the French tongue or else I might advise you to Westminster or some other very severe schoole, where if he were whipd soundly whilst you were looking out for another fit Tutor for him he would perhaps be the more pliant and willing to learne at home afterwards.[44]

Throughout his life Hooke was actively interested in the education of the young. He encouraged pupils at the Mathematical School at Christ's Hospital where he was a Governor[45] to come to his lectures in Gresham College.[46] It is likely that in his many visits to Busby[47] he met and discussed his projects with the pupils of Westminster; he may well have encouraged them to visit him in Gresham.[48] On at least one occasion Hooke visited his friend and near contemporary in their schooldays Thomas Gale, who composed the inscription for the Monument,[49] at his home in St Paul's School where he was headmaster; here too Hooke would surely have engaged with the pupils. His interest in his old school continued even after his old Head Master's death: he is noted as attending the oath-taking of the new Head Master, Thomas Knipe.[50]

On 5 July 1660, after the Restoration, Richard Busby received the reward of his loyalty and was 'sworne and installed' a Prebendary of Westminster and, four days later, Treasurer.[51] His new status within the community, backed by his considerable income, now allowed him to influence or to initiate several building projects. It was not until 1672 that we are certain from Hooke's diary that he and Busby were once more in regular contact. Though it is not possible to trace through masons' bills the full extent of work that Hooke carried out for Busby in School and Abbey, there are various bills which add some minor detail to Hooke's notes in his diary. Other details are listed following several squabbles over payments and claims of fraud against the Clerk of the Works Thomas Plucknett.[52] In 1670 Busby was given a house in Little Cloister, but it was clearly not in a fit state to be occupied. It was very late in his life that Busby finally moved into this house that Hooke had designed for him, remodelling the original, adding a floor and digging a cellar. There is a photograph (Figure 14.2) of the fine ceiling in the house that shows the date of completion, 1687.[53]

Alas Busby's house was destroyed during the Second World War and not rebuilt, unlike his Library, also executed largely under Hooke's supervision[54] and also bombed, whose ceiling and bookcases are scarcely different from the originals of the seventeenth century. It still houses many of the books that Hooke would have used. The only lasting reminders of this co-operation at Westminster are the marble pavement in the Quire in the Abbey (Figure 14.3)[55] and the Portico into School.[56]

Hooke had also worked on the Solomon's Porch;[57] it remained problematic for some time and, though Hooke oversaw the reglazing of the Rose Window (his glazier, Gregory, calls it the Marigold Window),[58] it was thoroughly reworked finally by Dickinson in 1719–22.[59]

Hooke was rewarded for his service to the Abbey by his appointment as Surveyor with an annuity of £20 on 14 January 1691. By this time his friend Busby was ageing; his servant John Gee endeavoured to keep relations between him and the various workmen and friends on an even keel. There is an interesting letter to Hooke from Gee[60] gently sorting out payment to John Angier for work on the Green Coat Hospital (Figure 14.4).

Figure 14.2 Little Cloister prebendal ceiling, Westminster, 1687.

Busby had paid for a boarding house to be built at the Hospital (a charity school) in Tothill Fields. There is a detailed prescription and estimate of the materials for its building, and Hooke was appointed to survey it. The final bill was in excess of the original estimate and needed Hooke's approval. The building work was carried out by John Angier,[61] who was a governor of the Hospital. It is surely likely that the plan for the Hospital was the result of consultation between Angier and Hooke, they may well have previously co-operated on the speculative house-building in St James's Square where they were both at work in 1677.[62] Later Busby leased a small plot of land from the Chapter[63] and at his own expense built a wall around it to attach it to the Hospital. The wall was also built under Hooke's supervision.[64] It is for another to explore the details of the building and provision of St Mary Magdalene at Willen, but that is perhaps the outstanding testimony to their friendship.

In 1693 Busby determined to beautify St Nicholas's Church in Lutton, the village of his birth. He was very firm that he was not going to repair fabric, that was for the parish; he wanted to embellish. He obtained a licence to do that from Bishop Tenison of Lincoln, who

Figure 14.3   The Quire of Westminster Abbey.

Figure 14.4   Green Coat Hospital, Tothill Fields, Westminster. The building on the right was paid for by Richard Busby.

sought the advice of the village: they whole-heartedly accepted the offer. Hooke instructed the carpenter Noell Ansell to survey the church; he was prepared to offer advice, but he did not want to get too involved, getting wary of the increasingly cantankerous Busby. Indeed by this time Hooke either was ageing himself or using his age as a way of gradually withdrawing from his work at Westminster. An entry in the Chapter Minutes for 1693 reads: 'It was ordered that Dr Hooke with respect to his Age & infirmities, being not able to attend the occasions about the Colledge of Westr be ... discharged from giving himselfe any further trouble in surveying the workes about the Colledge'.[65] At this point it is clear that he did retire; his salary was to be paid up to the next Quarter Day. By Busby's death in 1695 Ansell had produced, to Hooke's design, a communion table and rails for Lutton; Hooke had asked to see the quality of his work before giving him the full commission. Those rails still stand, very similar to those at Willen, the communion table is also there, but in a very sorry state and removed from the central position. The font and pavement are as Hooke had specified, but the characteristic black and white marble floor of the presbytery was swept away by meddling Victorians and replaced by tiles. The pulpit and type have been restored. The former bears Richard Busby's initials and the date of completion, 1703. The type has been returned to its place, albeit at an odd angle in order to reveal the inlay, after having done service for some time in a nearby church vestry as a table used for making sandwiches! It is curious that Hooke's affidavit, from which I have quoted, was needed at all, to prove the jottings of Receiver-General John Needham to be a codicil to Busby's will.[66] The testimony of the Bishop's licence together with the work already completed for the church, but lying in the house in Little Cloister, should surely have been enough.

At Busby's death on 5 April 1695, there ended a long friendship from which Robert Hooke and Richard Busby had gained so much. It was fitting that Busby should be laid to rest under the marble pavement that he had paid for, and that his pupil had executed for him, in the church which had given employment to both.

Bibliographic Note

For a general History of Westminster School the publication with the fullest account of Busby's time is Sargeaunt (1898). An invaluable further guide is Barker (1895), though now somewhat dated. The works on Westminster Abbey are too numerous to mention, but Wren

Society (1924-43) vol. 11 and Royal Commission on Historical Monuments (1924) have perhaps the fullest accounts of the work during Busby's time.

Chapter 15

After the *Principia*: Hooke's Declining Years, 1687–1703

Robert D. Purrington

If one has more than a scholarly interest in Hooke, that is if one has been touched, if only slightly, by his fate at the hands of the mistress we all serve, then one may find his being in fashion today somewhat poignant. Be that as it may, the result is that we surely know more about Robert Hooke than ever before, despite the fact that the general acknowledgement of his importance in the scientific revolution and especially in the formative years of the Royal Society, the result of a battle first waged by those great antagonists, Gunther and Andrade, is quite recent. And now Hooke is fashionable, of all things! Though still, for most people, 2003 is the 300th anniversary of Pepys's death, not Hooke's.

The last two decades have seen an explosion in Hooke studies, and by the end of 2005 there will have been five books published on Hooke in just the last three years. But from much of this writing one could easily conclude that Hooke had died in 1684, or perhaps 1687, for despite the recent attention being given to him, very little note has been taken of the last 15 or even 20 years of his life. There are reasons for this, of course, not the least of which was the publication of the *Principia* in 1687. But that is far from the whole story and it may be useful to trace his steps, as best we can, in those 15 years following the *Principia*. After the *Principia* there is little room for Hooke or, for that matter, anyone else. Newton, the giant, is striding the stage, revolutionizing natural philosophy, shaping the scientific revolution, eventually ruling the Society with an iron hand, or at least that is how the situation is often portrayed today. But it is remarkable that the deliberations of the Royal Society during the decade of the 1690s hardly reflect the existence of the *Principia*.[1]

A second reason why little attention has been given to Hooke's last decade or so is that as he passed the age of 50 his own energies, physical and intellectual, were beginning to wane. In 1687 he had suffered the dual blows of the publication of the *Principia* and the death of his beloved niece and mistress Grace Hooke. Although only

52 in 1687, his health, which had never been robust, would begin a rapid deterioration in the next decade, and his eyesight became worse. By the late 1690s, certainly by the end of the century, Hooke was clearly suffering from the disease which would kill him, variously speculated to be diabetes or congestive heart failure. He was depressed, or at least melancholy, as he repeatedly reports (cries out?) in the very private writings of the later diary.[2] All of this foreshadowed the end of his active intellectual life. Except for some papers in *Philosophical Transactions of the Royal Society*, which appeared erratically during this period, Hooke published very little in the last two decades of his life. His published works, other than *Transactions*, all date from 1680 or before, and few if any of the unpublished lectures collected by Waller in *Posthumous Works* date from after that year. There are a number of Hooke manuscripts, letters and other fragments scattered in various collections, at the Royal Society, in Oxford, at Trinity College, Cambridge, and so on. But of potentially the greatest interest are approximately 100 unpublished fragments, drawings and completed manuscripts in The Royal Society's *Classified Papers*, vol. 20. Many of these fascinating manuscripts, in Hooke's unfortunately crabbed hand, consist of the texts of lectures delivered before the Society and only briefly referred to in the Society's *Journal Books*. These papers, which cover the whole of Hooke's career with the Society, including many relevant to the period under discussion here, await the attention of scholars.[3]

Superficially, however, Hooke's life went on much as before. He rarely missed a meeting of the Society and almost always had something to contribute. He served on the council almost every year in the 1690s and in his final decade he was shown growing deference by the members. He was still seeing Wren on a regular basis, though not as frequently as before, meeting with him not more than a few times a month. This contrasts sharply with the period of the first diary, when they met almost daily, but both were now nearing 60 and their architectural partnership was over, even though Wren was still very busy with St Paul's and other projects, leaving him little time for Society affairs. Wren was still vigorous and moving in elevated circles (he had been knighted 20 years before) while Hooke was increasingly tired, melancholy and lonely. When Hooke and Wren did meet, it was often at a building site, but Man's coffee-house was another favorite spot. He regularly saw Boyle, but less frequently still, for Boyle's health, often problematic, was by now in serious decline (and of course he would die in 1691). He would see his old mentor Dr Busby weekly, often dining with him, and he also met with Pepys fairly regularly either in his own rooms or at Pepys's home. His regular haunt was Jonathan's in Exchange Alley, where he drank coffee with his friends or transacted business, more often than not twice daily (except Sundays). If he did have insomnia, as was certainly the case in the years of the early diary, it is hardly surprising, given the presumed consumption of caffeine. He was seeing his friend and, dare I say, protégé, Halley, at least weekly, always at Jonathan's, and following a meeting, he would invariably repair there with Halley and Hoskins and anyone else who would come along. Jeremy's – formerly Garraway's or rather still Garraway's, but 'Jeremys' to Hooke after Jeremy Stoakes took it over – was also a frequent meeting place, and sometimes Hooke would join the more privileged members of the Society there, as on 21 November 14, when he rode there with Henshaw and met Wren, Sir Joseph Williamson and Lord Carbery, who was then President of the Society.[4] The week before, on 15 November, recounting a session at Jonathan's with Paggin, Houghton, Ashby, Copley, Spence and Currer, Hooke wrote a cryptic 'The last remain'.[5] Likely a comment on human mortality, but perhaps we read too much into it.

It is interesting that what we see in retrospect as an event of monumental proportions, the publication by Halley for the Society of the *Principia*, had little effect on the day-to-day business of the Royal Society or its inner dissensions. Attendance was so poor that the annual elections of November 1688 were postponed to April for lack of a quorum, and then put off again. But the Society limped on.

1687–1703

Thanks to his earlier diary, now in London's Guildhall Library, we can form a fairly good picture of Robert Hooke from his late 30s into his mid-40s. But while it briefly touches on the 1679–80 exchange with Newton,[6] there is nothing on the crucial years of the 1680s. In the later diary we again have a window on Hooke's daily activities during his mid-50s, commencing in 1688 and ending in 1693. There is relatively little of scientific interest, and as much as anything it merely whets our appetite for more information. The existence of these two extensive diary pieces, as well as the other fragments, does suggest that Hooke might have kept something like a continuous diary. Are there other diary fragments lying in an attic somewhere? The chances are slim.

What we know of Hooke's last 15 years comes mostly from the later diary, augmented by the accounts of his life by Waller and Aubrey, plus the archives of the Royal Society, principally the *Journal Books*, since Council minutes are so laconic. Pepys had stopped writing his diary long before due to failing eyesight, and while Evelyn takes notice of Hooke, the diary entries are unrevealing. The later diary spans 16 months starting in November 1688, and then resumes for another eight months in December 1692, giving us only two years of the final 15, the last portion ending less than a month after Hooke's 58th birthday.[7] The later diary is indispensable but sadly incomplete. It is also nearly as laconic as the earlier one, offering, if anything, less insight into Hooke's inner life, though there are some unguarded moments. In particular, it is notable that there are relatively few references to his health in the diary – especially when compared with the earlier one.[8] One could imagine that Hooke's health was good and only began to decline after 1693, but that seems unlikely; he may merely have tired of noting his daily complaints, nostrums, purgings, and so on. Aside from a cold here and there, and fairly frequent 'headakes', Hooke's most persistent health problem involved his eyesight, which was clearly deteriorating. He occasionally mutters irritatedly about someone such as Flamsteed ('vaporing'), or Hoskins ('belged me'), but there is very little of that. At at the very least his spirits were low from time to time, and one suspects that if he took the trouble to write 'Melancholy' in his diary, as he did three times in January, February and March of 1690, he must have been very low.[9]

As we have noted, it was in 1687 that Grace died. As Waller described it: 'In the beginning of the Year 1687. his Brothers Daughter, Mrs. Grace Hooke dy'd, who had liv'd with him several Years, the concern for whose Death he hardly ever wore off, being observ'd from that time to grow less active, more Melancholly and Cynical.'[10] He was lonely, Newton had triumphed and his health slowly worsened. On the positive side of the ledger, however, he could look with satisfaction on the important structures he had created, such as Bedlam Hospital, the College of Physicians and the Monument, as well as the many parish churches he had designed or helped design with Wren. He continued to be involved in establishing codes and practices, resolving disputes, overseeing construction projects, still doing some architecture. He was seemingly as busy as ever.

One somewhat remarkable change in Hooke's habits, a not unfamiliar one in the face of personal mortality, was that he became a regular Sunday morning churchgoer, quite a departure from past indifference. In the earlier diary he was usually 'home all day' on Sundays. His new habits are already in place as the second part (the last eight months) of the later diary opens, so that we cannot know precisely when, or perhaps why, they began.

Hooke never relinquished what it is fair to call the fantasy that the *Principia* had been stolen from him, and that he had been grievously injured by Newton. We do know, however, how crucial was the insight he provided Newton in 1679 when he carelessly asked him 'if you will let me know your thoughts of that of compounding the celestiall motions of the planets of a direct motion by the tangent & an attractive motion towards the centrall body'.[11] Further, we know of Hooke's belated, but serious, attempts to demonstrate that elliptical orbits followed from an inverse-square gravitational force, or at least a central force.[12] How much support these efforts provide for his claim that he had, at least as early as 1684, 'solved' the problem of planetary motion, is in vigorous dispute, and they may simply have been his response to *De Motu*, but what is clear is that he had neither the leisure, the focus nor the mathematical skills to have done what Newton did. Two years after the publication of the *Principia* John Aubrey tried to make the case to Anthony Wood that Newton had failed to acknowledge Hooke's contributions, which was of course the case. He concluded, in this familiar passage: 'This is the greatest discovery in nature that ever was since the world's creation. It never was so much as hinted by any man before. I know you will do him right.'[13] What he then added is probably echoed by any who have tried to decipher Hooke's cramped handwriting: 'I hope you may read his hand. I wish he had writt plainer, and afforded a little more paper.'

The publication of the *Principia* must have struck Hooke like a bombshell. Although we know he had a copy in his library, we cannot be sure that he read it in detail. Still, a quick look would have told Hooke that whatever he had accomplished, the contents of the *Principia* were for ever beyond him. But we do not learn of Hooke's reaction from his own hand, for there is no diary for those utterly crucial years, 1680–88, and the 24 months of the later diary tell us nothing about his evaluation, as a scientist, of Newton's work. We have his charges of plagiarism, which no doubt were sincerely felt, but nowhere is there a even a brief review of the *Principia* of the sort he routinely gave during his tenure as the strongest intellectual force in the Society. It is hardly surprising that Hooke's claims angered Newton and, given what we know of him, incited feelings of retribution. That Newton was less than generous in the matter is obvious, but this was hardly unusual for Newton.

Two years after the publication of the *Principia*, Hooke was in no mood to concede the magnitude of Newton's achievement or its originality, and at a meeting on 26 February 1690 he defended his contributions to natural philosophy, arguing that [his] '... Discovery of the Cause of the Celestiall motions to which neither Mr. Newton nor any other has any right to Lay Clayme ...' ought to be sufficient to silence his critics.[14] His continuing interest in these problems is revealed in his later diary; for example, on 16 September 1689 he notes that he has 'demonstrated equall motion in parabola', Hooke's attempt at the brachistochrone/catenary problem. Nine days later he says 'calculated velocity of falling bodies', which mystifies us a bit, and in November he announces that he has 'perfected Theory of gravitation'. Again, we have no idea what he had in mind, but he may have been still working on the proof sketched out in the 1685 'On Circular Motion' manuscript. Alternatively, he may have been studying the cause of gravity, as he had earlier. But there are few comments of this kind in the later diary. In particular, if he is attempting to wade through the *Principia* at this point, he does not reveal that fact in the diary.

As noted earlier, Hooke hardly missed a meeting of the Royal Society (they were of course still being held at Gresham College), almost always contributing something worthy of finding its way into the *Journal Book*. Except for the years 1691–92 when for some reason his attendance dropped off, Hooke attended between 20 and 30 meetings a year, all the way through 1701.

Echoing the larger problems of the Royal Society, the *Transactions* went through hard times in the late 1680s and early 1690s, with only five numbers being published between December 1687 and October 1692, an average of one per year. And almost as though the *Principia* left everyone speechless, none was published in the years 1688–90. At Jonathan's following a meeting in early January 1689, Hooke offered to resume publication of his *Philosophical Lectures and Collections* if the Royal Society would pick up 60 copies. Nearly a year later, according to the council minutes for 27 November 1689 Hooke formally offered 'to print Treatises in the Nature of Philosophical Transactions' and it was agreed that the Royal Society would purchase 50 copies if he did.[15] Several months later little progress had been made when the council ordered that

'... Mr. Hook have the postage of all Letters of Philosophical Correspondence allowed him on condition that he publish Transactions or Collections as formerly, and that in Consideraton thereof, the Society will take off Sixty Books according to the Order of Council November 27th 1689.[16]

Correspondence with other parts of the British Isles and with the Continent continued to flag, and in April 1691 it was ordered that 'Dr Gale, Dr Aglionby, Mr Waller & Mr Halley be a Committee to Consider of the means of reestablishing the Societys Correspondence'.[17] As late as 25 January 1693, Hooke reported of a meeting that there was 'much talk of transactions to little purpose'. Despite his good intentions, little happened, and the situation only changed in February 1693, when Waller announced he would be handling the Society's correspondence and the *Transactions* as well, and publication resumed, at the rate of about one per month.[18]

Throughout the later diary, which ends on 8 August 1693, three weeks after his 58th birthday, we see continuing evidence that Hooke had not given up his architectural and construction activity. He is almost daily settling accounts with tradesmen, working at Westminster on the Abbey and the school for Busby,[19] on Aske's Hospital in Hoxton, working for Southwell, and so on. These non-scientific duties, from which Hooke derived by far the greater part of his income: surveying, supervising construction and working as an architect, were beginning to wind down, but he was apparently still vigorous, and if the absence of complaints is any indication, his health was still fairly good.

As was true when he was in his 40s, we learn from the later diary what his social life was like, which books he was buying or borrowing, the tradesmen with whom he might have been dealing, a good bit about his household, his troubles with his housekeeper Martha and, especially in the later diary, a great deal about his interest in affairs of the day. This is particularly true in 1688 when the Revolution was going on. But of his scientific thought, we learn little. For that, we have to consult the Royal Society's *Journal Books*.

There we find, beginning as early as 1688 when Hooke was in his mid-50s, Halley gradually beginning to replace him as the life-blood of the Society. Hooke's offerings to the Society from then on are often recapitulation and rehashing of things he had said before. For example, the *Journal Book* records that on 15 May 1689 'Mr Hook read a farther Discourse about his Hypothesis of the changes that have happened in the Earth's Surface, being chiefly a recapitulation of what he had formerly produced on that subject ...'. An editorial comment by the Secretary perhaps, but Hooke's interest in earthquakes and how they must have changed the face of the earth was a continuing one, which he explored in a number of directions. In January 1686 he had discoursed on the matter of fossils, how they came to be petrified deep in the earth and found high above the sea, and he concluded in 1688 that earthquakes occurred every eight years, were related to plague outbursts and were possibly caused by comets. In July 1690 he was interested in an earthquake which had occurred in the Leeward Islands, and a week later he discussed the cooling of the earth and speculated that it was decaying and less productive. He was also interested in the effect of earthquakes at sea and in the relation between very high tides and earthquakes (January 1691). He discussed fossils on several occasions, including 16 November 1691 when he talked of a fossil 'sea horse or Hippopotomus' and he discussed the interstices in nautiloids. Beginning in May 1693, he attempted to understand fables and myths from antiquity in terms of real catastrophes which might have occurred in the earth. Examples were the fables of Phaeton and of Python and Ovid's 'The Rape of Prosperpine'. In July 1694 the *Journal Book* records that 'Doctor Hook read a Discourse tending to prove that there is an annuall alteration in the Poles of the Earth ... ', he discussed Whiston's *New Theory of the Earth*, and in 1701 he discussed earthquakes and petrified trees. Not even Steno could be said to have spoken as clearly and presciently on the question of changes wrought in the earth by its internal heat. This was perhaps the one issue that Hooke pursued continuously and creatively in his declining years, and it would not be a stretch to call Hooke the first geologist in the modern sense.[20]

On other matters, Hooke talked about the zodiacal light, 'subtle parts of the atmosphere left behind', the aurora, Chinese characters, using gunpowder to raise weights, how water bugs stay on the surface of the water, penetration of salt or oil of vitriol into the pores of water, the figure of the earth under the action of 'vis centrifuga', the antiquity of natural philosophy, on the shape and orientation of sails and measuring speed made good, climate, the cooling of the earth, bird migration, the 'petrifying' quality of water as it washes over stones, illumination of a microscope field, the velocity of water flowing from a vessel, sounding the ocean, measuring salt concentration in the ocean, on the tower of Babel, his air barometer for use at sea, range-finding devices, his idea to have a 29-hour day, magnetism, the presence of seas on the moon, equal time descent of water along an 'inverted parabola', and so on. Altogether a remarkable diversity of interests, though, as was typical of Hooke, few of these ideas were fundamental. But that is presentism; who in the late seventeenth century could say what was fundamental and what was not?

Hooke's frequent returns to ideas or inventions from the past included a discourse on 19 February 1690 'tending to vindicate his notion of Light published in his *Micrographia*, in answer to that Theory therof lately published by Mr. Hugens... '.[21] *Micrographia*, had been, of course, published 45 years earlier. He continued at the next meeting, when he also commented on Huygens's notions about the cause of gravity.

Hooke was still occasionally offering an experiment, or describing one he had recently performed. One of a very few examples was the measurement of the speed of sound in July 1689, using the travel time from the Tower of London to Gresham College, though his result of 143 yards per second was out by more than a factor of two.[22] He also described new ideas or inventions, including a sextant-like device equipped with a plumb line for use at sea when a horizon was not visible. Between 1690 and 1695 he proposed an ingenious sea barometer which employed both an alcohol and an air thermometer, devices to measure speed through the water, as well as leeway, and another 'to tell Exactly the distance saild upon every Tack ...' as well as instruments to be carried to the East Indies for measuring the strength of gravity. His fertile mind was still active.

In 1691 Hooke spoke of his discoveries with telescopes and microscopes and in July 1693 he read a letter from Wallis to Molyneux in Dublin containing a proposal for observing parallax due to the earth's annual motion, which, as we know, Hooke believed he had detected almost a quarter-century earlier. The Journal Book records that 'Dr Hook asserted the way propounded by Doctor Wallis to be Inferior to the way that he himself had made use of for that purpose ... and therefore wondered what should be the Doctor's reason for now publishing this way, after 40 years of Concealment of it as he pretends'.[23] In November he read a discourse 'about the Improvements to be made in Naturall Philosophy by Microscopes ...' and followed that in December by again speaking of the use of telescopes in observing parallax. He returned to the latter subject one more time on 26 July 1699 when he read a discourse 'of his Observation [of] Parallax and variation of the fixt stars &c to vindicate his works' and two weeks later read a further discourse 'in Vindication of his Astronomical works'. Nothing was new in all of this, as Hooke strove to protect his priority, though we know that while he may have detected an entirely different phenomenon, he had not observed stellar parallax.

Tantalizingly, Huygens was present at the meeting of 12 June 1689, when Hooke spoke of the cause of gravity and of bi-refringence. Also present was Isaac Newton, in one of his rare appearances (no doubt because Huygens was present), who offered his own ideas on double refraction. Both Hooke and Halley held forth on the 'atoms' of salt, so we know that at this meeting, in the early summer of 1689, all four were in the Reading Room at Gresham College, not far from Hooke's private rooms. Hooke's laconic diary is again of no help to us on this remarkable event. He casually writes:

Royal Society met, shewed Expt of making branched Mochus: Hugens, Newton, Fazio [Fatio de Duillier]: there with Pif and Wall [Pitfield and Waller] at Jon. then wth Sr J. Hosk[ins] one houre solus ... Mr Henshaw well pleasd with my Experiment of Mochus ... Hally arguing against change of Polarity.[24]

Newton is known also to have been present at a meeting on 19 April 1699, by which time he had been living in London for three years. It is not clear that Hooke was also there; perhaps he was ill and Newton came knowing there would not be a confrontation with Hooke.

To those who cling to the idea that Hooke not only never passed up a chance to point out his priority in an idea or invention, but habitually laid claim to the ideas of others, we offer the following modest counter-example. In December 1691, after considering whether condensing air might turn it into water, Hooke spoke of an object-glass Huygens had given to the Society, but 'forbore to Describe the manner of using it, as reserved til Mr. Hugens himself should be present'. As others have noted, Hooke could almost always point to an entry in the *Journal Books* to support his claim of priority. Of course there were times when a claim of priority, based on a simple observation or conjecture, some real but limited insight, as in the case of Newton and the *Principia*, lacked real foundation. Some have argued, not entirely without justice, that Hooke regarded any idea he ever had as permanently his own, whether he pursued it or not. But a decade after the episode of the object-glass, in July 1701, he gave a rave review of Huygens's *Cosmotheoros*; the *Journal Book* recorded 'Dr Hook read a lecture wherein he gave a great Character of Huygen's late book called *Cosmotheoros* but differed from him in his opinion that the moon was not inhabited'.

Neither Boyle nor Wren attended meetings in this period (if silence is any indication) though in December and January of 1688–89 Boyle 'sent his man' to show experiments. Boyle was in poor health and his eyesight, failing for a long time, was worse, and he would be dead in less than three years. Wren, we know, was consumed by the work on St Paul's, Hampton Court, Whitehall and Windsor, and when he spoke at the meeting of 24 January 1700 and again two years later on 18 February 1702, it was the first clear evidence of attendance in a decade.[25] But he continued to be active in Royal Society affairs, as when he served on a committee in an attempt to have Bishop Stillingfleet's library given to the Society, and was frequently on the Council in the decade before Hooke's death in 1703.

It was in the early 1690s that Halley, increasingly, became the intellectual center of the Society. But it was also about this time that he proposed to go to sea on an expedition to measure magnetic variation and to determine longitudes, so that from 1694 or 1695 until he departed in October 1698 his attendance at meetings was sporadic. An appearance in March 1697 was unusual. He was gone much of the next three years (including the famous aborted first voyage) exploring the South Atlantic, eventually returning in August 1700. Back at meetings in the autumn of that year, he was now addressed as Captain Halley, as opposed to the generic 'Halley' that had been used for nearly 25 years, just as Hooke had always been 'Hook'.[26]

Hooke became 'Mr Hook' in the minutes in 1689 and then 'Dr Hook' in late 1691, when he was awarded a Doctor of Physick degree[27] by Archbishop Tillotson. He was elected to the Council in 1686, was off in 1687 and there were no elections (as far as I know) in 1688. He was elected in 1689, and was on the Council in at least eight of the next 11 years. He continued to lecture to the Society and his last *Transaction* was in No. 269 in 1702.[28] But by November of that year, when the anniversary elections were held, there were no votes for the failing Hooke, who had just over three months to live.

During much of this long period, as the Society suffered through a series of aristocratic presidents who rarely attended meetings, Sir John Hoskins was almost always in the Chair.[29] Other regulars in the early 1690s, besides Hooke, were Southwell, Evelyn, Sloane, often Henshaw and Hunt and, of course, Halley. Later Hill, Houghton and others attended, but meetings seem to have been very intimate.[30] As was very much the case in these early years of the Royal Society, even at this time after 30 years of existence, the substance of meetings was often very slim, mostly consisting of anecdotes, hearsay and speculation, an example being Henshaw's venturing in May 1689 that 'the eyes of a flye do contain almost all the Brains thereof'. But more often than not Hooke could be counted upon to address an issue of importance, as when, on 9 January 1689, he discoursed about scriptural wisdom: 'therein shewing, that the Design of the scriptures being not so much to teach Natural Philosophy, as to shew the wisdom and power of God in making the world as it is … .' But there was very little physical science or mathematics, and even less when Halley was at sea.

One of the most remarkable passages in the later diary is one in which we find Hooke describing a meeting at the premises of the instrument maker Thomas Tompion after which he wrote in his entry for 30 March 1693 that he 'Met Mr Zulich[em (Huygens)] at Tompions, but knew him not'.[31] It takes the breath away. Hooke had not seen Huygens for four years, and his eyesight was not what it once was, but on the other hand, it is possible that Hooke declined to know him, given what had passed between them.

The last 15 years of Robert Hooke's life were not happy ones, only partly because of his eclipse by Newton and the slow decline in his reputation abroad, yet he enjoyed the experience of finally coming to be an honored member of the Royal Society which had so often treated him as little better than a hired help. A meeting rarely passed without his holding forth on some topic – which is, of course, how we know he was present, since, unlike the Council meetings, no attendance was taken. Only rarely do we find from Hooke's diary that he was at a meeting, despite there being no evidence from the *Journal Book* that he contributed to the day's discussion.

Though still nominally Curator, Hooke rarely offered a new experiment, and more and more that role was assumed by Halley. Hooke's discourses were increasingly retrospective, recounting earlier demonstrations or inventions, and Waller admits that '… the later part of his Life was nothing near so fruitful of Inventions as the former …' (of how many of us could the same be said?) and that though Hooke intended to 'perfect the Description of all the Instruments he had at any time contriv'd … by reason of his increasing Weakness and a general Decay, he was absolutely unable to perform it …'.[32]

Waller described the decline in Hooke's health during his last five years, in words that are familiar, and which I will not repeat, except for this:

> About September [1697, at the age of 62][33] he thought himself (as indeed all others did that saw him) that he could not last out a month. About which time his Legs swell'd more and more, and not long after broke, and for want of due care Mortify'd a little before his Death. From this time he grew blinder and blinder, that at last he could neither see to Read nor Write …Thus he liv'd a dying Life for a considerable time, being more than a Year very infirm, and such as might be call'd Bed-rid for the greatest part ….[34]

Although there is no reason to doubt this account by Waller, who saw him nearly every week, it is nevertheless true that 1696 and 1697 were very active years for Hooke, at least measured by his participation in the Royal Society, and the same can be said of 1699. If indeed he was seriously ill in September 1697, he made some sort of recovery before the Society resumed meeting in late October, after its late summer recess, missing only one meeting the rest of the year. Indeed, he attended more meetings in 1697 at age 62 than in any other year in this post-*Principia* period, but by that time he probably had few other diversions and may not have been going out much. The next year may not have been a good one, based on his attendance and the nature of his comments at meetings, but, again, he participated vigorously in both 1699 and 1700. Of course Hooke did not have far to go, since the Society met near his rooms in Gresham College, and one can imagine him struggling to the weekly meeting, despite his infirmities, with the aid of Harry Hunt or some member such as Waller. But that he was intellectually active until the end is quite clear. Although the last meeting he attended may have been one on 24 June 1702, in February 1703 we find 'The V.P. desiring Dr Hook to restore the Glasses which the Society had of Mr Huygens; the Dr returned them ...', and two weeks later 'Dr Hook desired the Society to lend him the book lately presented by Dr. Cheyney. It was accordingly lent him for a week'. Exactly a week later, he died:

> ... at last his Distempers of shortness of Breath, Swelling, partly of his Body, but mostly of his Legs, increasing, and at last Mortifying, as was observ'd after his Death by their looking very black, being emaciated to the utmost, his Strength wholly worn out, he dy'd on the third of March 1702/3, being 67 years, 7 months, and 13 days old.[35]

But death would not be the final indignity. The combined forces of Newton's ire[36] and the success of his method consigned Hooke to obscurity for over 200 years, even including the loss of the Royal Society's painting of him. His major buildings were all torn down – though it now appears that the first home of the British Museum may well have been a surviving Hooke building, at least a Hooke facade.[37] The Monument that he built with Wren displays no acknowledgement of Hooke's important involvement. Though buried under the south aisle of St Helen's Bishopgate, his bones were evidently disinterred with others and dumped in a mass grave in north London. And finally, the IRA finished the job of eliminating any hint of a memorial to him by destroying the lancet window in St. Helen's that had been erected in his honour.

And yet, if one looks carefully at the 'Wren' churches in the northeast part of the City, which was Hooke's area of responsibility after the Great Fire, we can clearly see the Hooke style in such churches as St Peter Cornhill, St Edmund the King and St Benet Paul's Wharf to mention but three.[38] It is there and in the Monument itself that we must look for his tribute.[39]

It is fair to say that Hooke did not go serenely to the grave. His health deteriorated rapidly and Waller describes his temper in these last days as 'melancholy, mistrustful, and jealous'. Hooke's intention to settle his large estate upon the Royal Society never came to pass, probably through the misery of these last days, and he died intestate. But as Waller said in his life of Hooke:

> ... all his Errors and Blemishes were more than made amends for, by the Greatness and Extent of his natural and acquired Parts, and more than common, if not wonderful Sagacity, in diving into the most hidden Secrets

of Nature, and in contriving proper Methods of forcing her to confess the
Truth ...

After listing Hooke's inventions, theories and discoveries, Waller
concluded by writing 'For these, his happy Qualifications, he was
much respected by the most learned Philosophers both at home and
abroad: And as with all his Failures, he may be reckon'd among the
great Men of the last Age ...'.[40] Hooke was no Newton, but then
Newton was no Hooke either.

Chapter 16

Robert Hooke: A Reputation Restored

Lisa Jardine

It would be too long, I say, here to insert the discursive progress by which
I inquir'd after the properties of the motion of Light.
(Hooke, outlining his theory of colour in *Micrographia*, 1665)

Since the tercentenary of his death in 2003 Hooke has finally regained
his stature as a multi-talented intellectual, scientist, engineer and
inventor – a towering polymath whose discoveries and inventions are
acknowledged to be of lasting interest and importance.

The question I address is this: if Hooke's achievements and
reputation were as considerable and sustained as we have learned as
a result of the serious attention that has at last been given to them,
what was the process by which that reputation and that
acknowledgement of his considerable achievements were eroded and
lost?

I am going to propose that his position began to be undermined
extraordinarily early, while his career was still at its height, and that
the damage to his reputation came about as the result of bad luck and
a combination of deliberate manipulation and some incompetence (or
at least naivety) on the part of others. I shall argue that the man largely
responsible was indeed the very person Hooke always believed to be
his 'enemy' at the Royal Society, its first Secretary, Henry Oldenburg,
but that in all likelihood the harm he caused was unintentional. The
other culprits were that indefatigable fixer and letter-writer Sir Robert
Moray (as Hooke also always suspected) and Christiaan Huygens. In
Moray's case it is clearer that the harm he caused (amounting to
serious breaches of scientific confidentiality) was not deliberate, and
indeed, that on the whole Moray was keen to defend Hooke's
reputation on behalf of the Royal Society. Huygens is a character who
deserves further investigation, and I will not deal here with his
possible motives.

The lasting association of Hooke's name with exaggerated claims,
arrogance and imprecision began, I shall argue, with exchanges
surrounding a specific contested piece of scientific activity, and was
caused by an exuberant exploitation of the scientific periodical as a

new printed form and the promiscuous exchange and circulation of letters and information between virtuosi in England, France and Holland.

Although Hooke's reputation as an experimentalist and instrument-maker was already considerable at home in England in the early 1660s, he sprang to prominence as a figure of note in the community beyond Royal Society circles with the publication of *Micrographia* in January 1665. *Micrographia* established his international reputation virtually overnight.[1] Immediately it appeared, virtuosi across Europe began exchanging remarks on the book – and above all its magnificent illustrations – in their correspondence.[2]

Christiaan Huygens was an early admirer. Sir Robert Moray mentioned the book to him with pride – and the fact that it included information on lens-making (a topic Christiaan was particularly interested in) – in January, and promised to send him a copy shortly thereafter. He confessed, however, that he had not had time to do more than glance at it himself.[3] On 26 February Moray dispatched a copy of *Micrographia* to The Hague with a covering letter, entrusting it to Sir William Davidson to deliver.[4] Because Huygens somehow missed Davidson, however, the book and letter did not reach him until 25 March. On 26 March Huygens wrote an enthusiastic letter to Moray telling him that he had had no idea the book was of such consequence, and particularly praising the quality of the illustrations and engraving.

The non-arrival of the copy dispatched by Moray was a beginning to Hooke's bad luck. Between the dispatch and arrival of Christiaan Huygens's copy he had formed some superficial opinions on the work based on selected extracts from the text (but none of the illustrations) sent to him by his father Sir Constantijn Huygens, who was in Paris in February 1665 and had swiftly obtained a copy.[5] Sir Constantijn was full of praise for *Micrographia*; based on the extracts he saw, Christiaan expressed surprise at the 'rashness' of some of the conjectures based on limited experimentation. Once he received his own copy he conceded that these were of less consequence than he had thought, because the impact of the microscopical observations as a whole was so considerable. But by this time he had communicated his reservations to his father.

Sir Constantijn Huygens did not keep Christiaan's doubts about *Micrographia* to himself. Among the French virtuosi who seized eagerly upon *Micrographia* was Adrien Auzout – a talented observational astronomer and instrument-maker, whose name is associated with the development of the eye-piece micrometer for long telescopes. As soon as he had heard of it, he had arranged to borrow

Sir Contantijn Huygens's copy.[6] Shortly after Sir Constantijn had returned to Holland, Auzout wrote from Paris to Christiaan Huygens in The Hague: 'A few days ago I received a letter from Monsieur de Zulichem [Sir Constantijn], who told me that you, like myself, had found a quantity of interesting things in Hooke's book.'[7] It was Auzout's interest in *Micrographia* and its author which began the chain of events which impacted directly on Hooke's long-term reputation, largely without Hooke himself participating in events as they unfolded. And it is important to note that Auzout had seen Christiaan's letter to his father expressing reservations about some of Hooke's claims.

Among the 'quantity of interesting things' which had caught Auzout's attention in *Micrographia* were those parts of the text dealing with Hooke's own innovations in microscope manufacture (rather than the extraordinary minute details of natural phenomena seen under the microscope, and reproduced in the plates). A description of a machine for grinding accurate lenses, interpolated into the Preface, particularly intrigued Auzout, since he was already involved in a critique of a similar machine advertised as under development by Giuseppe Campani in Italy, and was himself proposing one to the circle of astronomers lobbying for the setting up of the new Royal Observatory in Paris.[8]

Hooke makes his remarks on telescopes in passing in the Preface to *Micrographia*, but is then drawn into describing an instrument for mass-producing high-quality lenses which he claims to be in the process of testing:

> As for Telescopes, the only improvement they seem capable of, is the increasing of their length; for the Object being remote, there is no thought of giving it a greater light then it has; and therefore to augment the Aperture, the Glass must be ground of a very large sphere, for by that means, the longer the Glass be, the bigger aperture will it bear, if the Glasses be of an equal goodness in their kind. ... I have experimentally observ'd in one of [60-foot focal] length made by Mr. Richard Reives here at London, which will bear an Aperture above three inches over, and yet make the Objects proportionably big and distinct; whereas there are very few thirty foot Glasses that will indure an Aperture of more then two inches over.

The way of achieving this, Hooke went on, is to invent a 'ready way' [a machine] for making telescope object glasses. He was, he claimed, in the process of refining such an 'engine':

> So that for Telescopes, supposing we had a very ready way of making their Object Glasses of exactly spherical Surfaces, we might, by increasing

the length of the Glass, magnifie the Object to any assignable bigness. And for performing both these, I cannot imagine any way more easie, and more exact, then by this following Engine, by means of which, any Glasses, of what length soever, may be speedily made.[9]

In an elaboration of these remarks, marked off from the main body of the text by its distinctive typography, Hooke sets down the technical details of his machine, illustrating his remarks with an engraving on the first plate of the volume alongside the well-known images of Reeves's microscope and Hooke's own scotoscope.[10]

Auzout read the Preface to *Micrographia* in February, and swiftly inserted a critical response into a long letter he had composed the previous year concerning Campani's improved telescopes, which he was currently preparing for publication.[11] The expanded version of his *Letter to the Abbé Charles* appeared in print in Paris in April or May 1665, and Auzout immediately sent a copy of the pamphlet to Oldenburg, with whom he was already in correspondence concerning Campani's observations of the 1664 comet.[12] Oldenburg produced a summary in English, including the criticisms of Hooke at length, and passed it to Hooke. Hooke responded with a letter to Oldenburg rebutting all Auzout's criticisms, and this letter – preceded by Oldenburg's English summary of Auzout's published letter – was published in *Philosophical Transactions* of 5 June 1665 as 'Mr Hooke's Answer to Monsieur Auzout's Considerations, in a Letter to the Publisher of these Transactions'.[13]

The accusation which most exercised Hooke at this stage was that he had not conducted proper trials of his lens-grinding machine, and that to have published an account of such an untried instrument (thereby claiming its priority) was unworthy of the Royal Society, given the Society's commitment to experimental accuracy. As official Curator of Experiments (his appointment recently confirmed in the context of a benefaction from Sir John Cutler to fund his activities) and Fellow of a year's standing, Hooke was extremely anxious to clarify his position vis-à-vis the Royal Society. As he was quick to point out, there was a clear disclaimer placed prominently at the beginning of *Micrographia*, entirely dissociating the Royal Society from any 'Conjectures and Quaeries' of his own. Perhaps, he suggested, Auzot's English had not been good enough for him to follow Hooke's argument:

And therefore I cannot but make this interpretation of what Monsieur Auzout saith in this particular, that either he had not so much of the Language wherein I have written, as to understand all what was said by me, or, that he had not read my Dedication to the Royal Society, which if he had done, he would have found, how careful I was, that the Illustrious Society should not be prejudiced by my Errors, that could be so little advantaged by my Actions.[14]

As it turned out, Hooke's suspicion was entirely correct. Auzout responded – at equal length to Hooke – in a letter to Oldenburg of 22 June. Auzout admitted that his English was indeed poor and that, besides, he had only had *Micrographia* in his possession for two days. Inevitably he had not read it all, particularly since the illustrations were so captivating, and drew his attention away from the text:[15]

> Perhaps if I had read the Epistle [of Dedication to the Royal Society] which [Hooke] addressed to them I could have better understood the design of your learned Society in granting permission for publication. But Mr. Hooke will surely forgive my poor understanding of your language and when he learns that I had his book in my hands for only two days and that I stopped after perusing what concerned his machine and his other fine inventions and after looking at the illustrations and trying to understand whatever seemed new, he will not find it difficult to believe that I did not read all his book.[16]

On 1 July Auzout wrote again, expressing the hope that this letter was with Oldenburg, and announcing his eager anticipation to meet Wren, who was expected in Paris at any moment.[17]

As far as the issue of whether Hooke had conducted proper trials of his machine before announcing it was concerned, there is firm evidence that he had undertaken trials and was continuing to do so. On 3 November 1664 Oldenburg told Boyle: 'Mr Hooke is now making his new instrument for grinding Glasses, the successe whereof you will shortly heare off'.[18] By the end of November Moray was giving detailed descriptions of Hooke's machine and the trials being conducted with it to Huygens, and by September Huygens was reporting to Auzout that there were problems with the operation of the iron circle. In October 1665 Moray (in Oxford) reported to Huygens that Oldenburg had informed him (by letter) that trials were revealing further problems:

> All I can tell you is that [his method] is ingenious, and based on real experiments. ... Mr Oldenburg has communicated to me what you have told him concerning the efforts you are engaged in with telescopes using an invention similar to that of Mr Hooke, for which you have high hopes. I must tell you that if you had explained yourself more clearly perhaps I could have warned you of a difficulty that Mr Hooke has encountered in the fabrication of the machine he has made which has held him up considerably.[19]

As throughout Hooke's career, however, Moray admitted to Huygens that the demands the Royal Society were making on his time were impeding his ability to complete projects undertaken:

> We keep Mr Hooke so fully occupied with a thousand little things that he has not yet given me the description he promised me of his machine for measuring the refraction of light in water [a machine undertaken at the same time as the lens-grinding machine, and also announced and illustrated in *Micrographia*]. As soon as he does so I will forward it to you.[20]

In fact, Auzout knew far more about Hooke's lens-grinding machine than he was letting on in his letters to Oldenburg, even before the publication of *Micrographia*. Throughout the latter half of 1664 he had been receiving copies (at least in part) of letters being exchanged about it, between Christiaan Huygens and Robert Moray.[21]

Huygens and Moray (who had been corresponding in terms of intense affectionate friendship since meeting during Huygens's first visit to London in 1661, sometimes exchanging letters daily)[22] had begun corresponding about lens-making machines in summer 1664. Huygens reported to Moray Campani's claim to have 'a new way of making lenses using a lathe or turning device, and without using any kind of a mould'. Moray responded with the news that Hooke had shown such a machine to the Royal Society 'five or six months earlier', although it had yet to be demonstrated in action.[23] Two months later he gave Huygens a much fuller account of the lens-grinding machine – presumably because by November he had had sight of the diagram and description given in *Micrographia* (licensed by the Society that month):

> I think I told you earlier that a few months ago Mr Hooke proposed a sort of lathe for making the lenses for telescopes without using any form or mould. His invention is, to place the lens on the end of a rod which turns on two pivots, then to have a circle of iron attached to the end of another rod which turns in the same fashion, in such a way that the edge of the circle covers the centre of the lens, then applying pressure with the circle upon the lens so that the two rods make whatever angle is desired; according to how big or small the angle between the rods is, the surface of the lens has the section of a large or small sphere.[24]

In December Moray enlarged on this description in response to a further inquiry from Huygens. By now Hooke had built a prototype, which he had shown to the Royal Society:

Mr. Hooke's machine is set up and I will keep you informed as to the success of this invention, and of all the details of its structure, if it warrants the effort of describing it to you. Concerning moulds or forms, he claims not to use any. But if it turns out to be necessary to use moulds to give initial shape, and then to polish them, as you suggest, on the [iron] circle, be assured that I will keep you informed. But it looks as if the circles will shape the lenses much more quickly than moulds could do, and so moulds are unnecessary, and as you told me, Campani does not use them at all.[25]

Huygens copied at least one of these letters to Auzout, keeping him abreast of the discussion, in connection with Auzout's interest in Campani's machine.[26] He also made a note to himself that the use of the iron circle was an exceptionally good idea, and one that he would consider incorporating into an equivalent machine himself – which in typical Huygens fashion he subsequently did.[27] At the end of December he devoted a whole letter to Auzout to 'explaining the iron circle for working lenses'.[28] A minute for another letter to Auzout, written on 15 January 1665, shows that they were still discussing refinements to the circle.[29] From his further correspondence with Moray it is clear that by now Huygens had built his own prototype machine, and was experimenting with Hooke's 'iron circle'.[30]

Hooke was largely unaware of this correspondence.[31] He knew nothing of this swift transmission to Holland and Paris of material he was presenting to the Royal Society in its official capacity as its recently appointed Curator of Experiments.[32] In Moray's eagerness to be seen by Huygens to be fully au fait with new scientific developments in England, he freely communicated construction details of Hooke's lens-grinding machine, which an expert instrument-designer like Huygens could readily seize upon and adapt. So Moray was transmitting troubling levels of detail concerning a patentable machine, in whose development there was already significant European competition, to his friend Huygens, who in turn discussed technical details with Auzout.

Oldenburg replied to Auzout's letter of 22 June on 23 July, detailing Hooke's further rebuttals of Auzout's continuing scepticism about the practicality of the lens-grinding machine. In view of Auzout's lack of knowledge of English, and Hooke's of French, he offered himself as epistolary intermediary:

Mr Hooke salutes you, and affirms that he is particularly obliged to you for your conduct towards him, in the letter you addressed to me. Surely, Sir, it is indeed the right way to manage a correspondence between two worthy men and fine minds, when each expresses to the other his thoughts and discoveries in a frank and polite way, without offence given or taken. ... If you wish, I will be the go-between, since you do not know enough English to write to him nor he enough French to reply.[33]

All was not, however, quite as it seemed, so far as this letter of Oldenburg's was concerned, and it is now that problems entirely of others' making began to arise for Hooke. For by 15 July Hooke had left London for Epsom, together with John Wilkins and William Petty, to continue Royal Society experiments safely away from risk of the Plague.[34] Even if Oldenburg had shown Hooke Auzout's second letter before he left, there is no indication that Hooke wrote either notes or a full answer. There is, on the other hand, evidence in both the Oldenburg and Boyle collected correspondences that, particularly during the early months of the Plague, exchange of letters between London and the rest of England was hampered by anxieties over infection. On 15 August Hooke wrote to Boyle that he had not been in contact with Oldenburg, and at the end of the same letter he advised Boyle: 'If you have any further commands, you may send it … by the post, I suppose, if not to be left for me at Gresham college from whence I receive letters usually once a week.' When Hooke did hear from Oldenburg, it appears to have been via letters sent to Wilkins. At the end of September Hooke went to the Isle of Wight for several weeks or more, to attend to family business. He returned briefly to London at the end of December, before returning to Epsom.[35] From this point on, then, it looks as if, in the Auzout–Hooke 'controversy', Hooke is being ventriloquized by Oldenburg.

On 13 August Auzout wrote once again to Oldenburg, again responding to Hooke point by point. Oldenburg's translation of this letter into English survives. It is apparently intended for Hooke's use, since it carries marginal annotations goading Hooke to respond to supposed 'slights' by Auzout in the text (which Oldenburg has made rather more provocative than the original): 'What say you to this?'; 'A handsome sting again will be necessary'; 'Me thinks, here you may toss railleries with him'; 'To this I say, He will needs make you say, what you say not'; 'Non sequitur. You must rally with him again'.[36] Perhaps Oldenburg hoped to have Hooke respond to Auzout himself when he returned to London. Perhaps he intended to act once more as intermediary and to write another letter to Auzout, incorporating remarks of Hooke's provoked by his own deliberately antagonistic annotations and prompts. Neither thing happened, because Auzout now acted pre-emptively. In July or August 1665 he republished his original *Letter to the Abbé Charles*, together with the entire correspondence to date between himself and Hooke (via Oldenburg) in French in Paris.

Oldenburg reacted indignantly, claiming he had never intended his last letter for publication. Auzout replied in some puzzlement – surely the correspondence had always been intended as part of a public epistolary controversy:

> I am devastated [tres marri] that you are not happy that I have, at the request of my friends, published the letter that you were gracious enough to write to me to explain Mr Hooke's feelings [concerning my continuing criticisms]. I did not consider this letter to be something belonging entirely to you, but rather as the reply of Mr Hooke, and because we had already both of us begun to print material on that topic, I saw no harm in supplying the rest, since our friends wanted so much to have sight of the continuation of the dispute.[37]

It seems clear from this that Oldenburg had indeed composed the detailed arguments attributed to Hooke in the letter to Auzout of 23 July himself, and now found himself embarrassed by their being made public, thereby bringing the fact to Hooke's attention. Fortunately, as we know, Hooke's French was limited. In what was probably an act of damage limitation, Oldenburg summarized the arguments of Auzout's new book in English, abbreviating and omitting parts he preferred not to have broadcast, and published his synopsis in *Philosophical Transactions*.

Meanwhile Moray, Huygens and Auzout were corresponding vigorously about the controversy, often passing each other's letters on as enclosures, and including copies of the *Journal des sçavans* and *Philosophical Transactions* where appropriate. In early June, Auzout told Huygens that he was eagerly awaiting the arrival of *Philosophical Transactions* which he gathered would contain the first instalment of his exchanges with Hooke: 'I am told from England that Mr Hooke has taken up my objections against his machine in the first book of Philosophical Transactions which I hope will arrive on Sunday. We shall see what he says.'

On 23 July Moray added a postscript to a letter to Oldenburg, written from Hampton Court (whence he was about to accompany the King to Salisbury):

> I had almost forgot to desire you to send to Mr Hugens either the whole former Transaction [June issue], or so much of it as containes Hooks answer to Auzout & withall to let him know what Hook is doing as to his glasses [lenses and telescopes]. I have told him I would give you that task. L. Brounker will let you have hugens's letter.[38]

Oldenburg complied, writing to Huygens four days later:

Sir Robert Moray wishing me to send you Mr. Hooke's reply to Mr Auzout about the machine for turning lenses, I was anxious not to fail him. ... Mr. Hooke is in the country, along with most of the rest of our Society, the plague having widely scattered our mutual friends.

And in a postscript:

My most humble respects to Monsieur your father if he is in Holland. Fearing that the packet would be too bulky, if I sent you the whole issue of the Journal, from which I send you the section containing Mr. Hooke's reply, I have had to truncate it, as you see.[39]

The exchanges amongst this group shaped received opinion concerning the possibility of machine manufacture of precision lenses and has continued to be treated as the authoritative account of the episode ever since.[40] Yet this was an extended conversation in which Hooke had no direct voice, in spite of his playing a starring role. And although Hooke's close friend Wren was in Paris throughout this period, he apparently did nothing to clarify the nature of Hooke's machine, nor the fact that he was now absent from Royal Society circles either in London or Oxford. He was certainly consulted. In April 1666 Auzout reported to Oldenburg that he had spoken to Wren shortly before he returned to England concerning Hooke's method for increasing the focal length of lenses by filling the space between two lenses with liquid (a topic associated with the lens-grinding machine debate).[41]

To understand the circulation of news, gossip and sensitive technical material here, we really need a diagram and a flow chart. By the end of July the Royal Society members had dispersed because of the Plague. Hooke, Wilkins and Petty were at Epsom, together with a substantial amount of experimental equipment and assistant operators. Boyle was briefly with them, then retired to Oxford. Moray was with the King, first at Hampton Court, then at Oxford. For much of the time Brouncker was on a ship off Greenwich seeing to navy business. Huygens was in The Hague throughout this period, corresponding energetically with Oldenburg, Moray and Auzout (his father, however, was in Paris for three months in early 1665).

Wren went to Paris on 28 July 1665. There we know he was frequently in the company of Auzout.[42] From then on he provided a direct epistolary route for information from Auzout and his circle in Paris to both Oldenburg and Boyle.[43]

So we have an epistolary circuit of transmission, detailed explication, claim, counter-claim, assertion, surmise and response, which by mid-1665 has effectively developed a life of its own. The participating correspondents and the readers of the published versions are actually aware of only a small part of the network of exchanges which constitute the 'controversy', and the complex webs of meaning these create.

Auzout and Oldenburg's investment in all of this is pretty clear. From the *Journal des sçavans* in Paris and *Philosophical Transactions* in London was emerging an entirely new form of intellectual debate – one which reached beyond the bounds of coterie and nation into what was apparently a genuine Republic of [Scientific] Letters. Both Auzout and Oldenburg had a stake in such an intellectual organ to enhance their own reputations – and both were remarkably successful at doing so. Hooke was more or less caught in the cross-fire. As a result of Oldenburg's letter-writing, translating and publications he acquired a reputation for boastful claims he could not sustain. Controversy also became associated with his name on the continent, at just the moment when *Micrographia* ought to have established him as a formidable scientific presence.

The story of the simultaneous attempts in London, Paris and The Hague to develop a machine for manufacturing optical lenses is a minor one for the history of science. But we should bear in mind that this very same correspondence, circulating vigorously in Hooke's absence and without his knowledge, contains the 'insider' remarks about his balance-spring watch which were later to cause him such personal grief and anger.

Hooke and Auzout, by the way, remained on cordial terms throughout this sequence of events and orchestrated controversies, despite Oldenburg's promptings to the contrary. Throughout the exchanges, Auzout continued to refer to Hooke in the most respectful of terms, and Oldenburg consistently deleted these from his racy English versions. On 18 December 1666, for instance, writing to Oldenburg to communicate an important astronomical observation, Auzout wrote: 'I think that Mr Hook whom I salute wholeheartedly, as well as Mr Wren, will be very interested.' Oldenburg omitted the phrase 'whom I salute wholeheartedly' from the translation he published in *Philosophical Transactions*.[44] By contrast with Oldenburg's tendency to present Hooke's work as controversial, the issue of the *Journal des sçavans* published on 20 December 1666 contained a review of *Micrographia*, praising it unreservedly in extravagant terms. The review is far longer than any other up to that date and, uniquely for the *Journal* up to that date, reproduces two reduced-size plates (the louse and blue mould).[45]

The controversy conducted in the pages of the *Philosophical Transactions* and of the *Journal des sçavans*, and in Auzout's pamphlet publications issued in the course of 1665, achieved what Auzout wanted – to bring his astronomical expertise to the attention of Colbert and the King of France and secure himself a royal appointment. Oldenburg was more than content that the *Philosophical Transactions* should have become essential reading among virtuosi across Europe, as soon as he began publishing them – by the fourth issue (the one containing the first adversarial exchange of letters between Auzout and Hooke) there was an absolute scramble to get hold of copies immediately they appeared. The élite virtuosi Moray and Huygens cemented their intimate friendship by exchanging sought-after information, and keeping each other 'in the know'. Only Hooke stood to gain nothing from the episode, and, indeed, was kept largely 'out of the know' while it was going on.

Here, then, is a sad story of Hooke's reputation being tarnished – whether deliberately or inadvertently – by others with agendas of their own, just as he imagined with some justification that he had arrived on the international intellectual scene. He always believed he had been wronged – that he deserved better from his colleagues and a more distinguished reputation than he ever achieved. As I hope I have shown, no single individual was responsible (though some blame should surely be laid at the door of Oldenburg). Yet all conspired to cheat Hooke out of his renown, and posterity out of a full understanding of his remarkable abilities.

Now at last, though, the story has a happy ending. Thanks to these conference papers, a further important step has been taken in restoring Hooke's reputation.

Bibliography

This bibliography is made up of the following components.

1 All items included in the bibliography to Hunter, Michael and Schaffer, Simon (eds) (1989), *Robert Hooke: New Studies*, Woodbridge: Boydell (pp. 295–304) have been repeated here, so this listing wholly supersedes that one.
2 All publications relating to Hooke that have appeared since *Robert Hooke: New Studies* have been included.
3 In addition, primary sources and ancillary studies cited by the authors of the various contributions to this book have been included. This means that all references in the notes allude to bibliography entries by giving author and date only.

Aarsleff, Hans (1980), 'Wilkins, John', in (q.v.) Gillispie (ed.) (1970–80), vol. 14, pp. 361–81.
Abercrombie, Patrick (1923), 'Wren's plan for London after the Great Fire', *Town Planning Review* **10**, 71–8 and 6 plates.
Ackroyd, Peter (2000), *London, the Biography*, London: Chatto and Windus.
Adamson, Ian (1978), 'The Royal Society and Gresham College', *Notes and Records of the Royal Society of London* **33**, 1–21.
Agassi, Joseph (1977), 'Who discovered Boyle's Law?', *Studies in History and Philosophy of Science* **8**, 189–250.
Ainsworth, G. C. (1976), *Introduction to the History of Mycology*, Cambridge: Cambridge University Press.
Aked, C. K. (1968–70), 'William Derham and the Artificial Clockmaker Part 2', *Antiquarian Horology* **6**, 416–27.
Alberti, Leon Battista (1988), *On the Art of Building*, trans. Joseph Rykwert et al, Cambridge, Massachusetts: MIT Press.
Albritton, C. C. (1980), *The Abyss of Time: Changing Conceptions of the Earth's Antiquity after the Sixteenth Century*, San Francisco: Freeman, Cooper & Co.
Ames-Lewis, Francis (ed.) (1999), *Sir Thomas Gresham and Gresham College*, Aldershot: Ashgate.
Andrade, E. N. da C. (1935), 'Robert Hooke and his contemporaries', *Nature* **136**, 358–61.

——— (1936), 'Hooke and his editors', *Nature* **137**, 378–81.

——— (1950), 'Wilkins Lecture: Robert Hooke', *Proceedings of the Royal Society, Series A* **201**, 439–73 (also printed in *Series B* **137**, pp. 153–87).

——— (1951), 'Robert Hooke, inventive genius', *The Listener*, 8 February 1951, 215–6.

——— (1953), 'Robert Hooke, 1635–1703', *Nature* **171**, 365–7.

——— (1954), 'Robert Hooke', *Scientific American* **191**, 94–8.

——— (1960), 'Robert Hooke, F.R.S.', *Notes and Records of the Royal Society of London* **15,** 137–45. Reprinted in (q.v.) Hartley (1960).

Andrews, Jonathan et al (1997), *The History of Bethlem*, London: Routledge.

Andrews, W. J. H. (1996), *The Quest for Longitude*, Cambridge, Massachusetts: Harvard University Press.

Anon (1842), 'Gallery of Illustrious Irishmen, No. XIII, Sir Thomas Molyneux, Bart. M.D., F.R.S.', *Dublin University Magazine* **18**, 305–27, 470–90, 604–19, 744–64.

Anstey, Peter (2002), 'Locke, Bacon and natural history', *Early Science and Medicine* **7**, 65–92.

Ariotti, P. E. (1971–72), 'Aspects of the conception and development of the pendulum in the seventeenth century', *Archive for the History of Exact Sciences* **8**, 329–410.

——— (1947), 'The deviation of falling bodies', *Annals of Science* **5**, 342–51.

Armitage, Angus (1950), 'Borell's hypothesis and the rise of celestial mechanics', *Annals of Science* **6**, 268–82.

Arnol'd, V. I. (1990), *Huygens and Barrow, Newton and Hooke, Pioneers in Mathematical Analysis*, trans. E. J. F. Primrose, Basel and Boston: Birkhäuser, originally 1989 Moscow: Nauka F. L. M.

Arons, Arnold B. (1990), *A Guide to Introductory Physics Teaching*, New York and Chichester: Wiley.

Aubrey, John (1898), *Brief Lives, Chiefly of Contemporaries*, 2 vols, ed. Andrew Clark, Oxford: Clarendon Press.

——— (1949a), *Brief Lives and Other Selected Writings*, ed. Anthony Powell, London: Cressett Press, and New York: Scribners.

——— (1949b), *Brief Lives*, ed. Oliver Lawson-Dick, London: Secker and Warburg.

——— (1957), *Brief Lives*, ed. Oliver Lawson-Dick, reprinted, Ann Arbor: University of Michigan Press.

——— (1992), *Brief Lives*, ed. Oliver Lawson Dick, reprinted, London: Mandarin.

——— (2000), *Brief Lives*, ed. John Buchanan-Brown, London: Penguin.

Ayres, F. H. (1951), 'Robert Hooke, 1635–1703. A Bibliography', unpublished thesis submitted for Part III of the University of London Diploma of Librarianship.

Bacon, Francis (2000), *The New Organon*, eds Lisa Jardine and Michael Silverthorne, Cambridge: Cambridge University Press.

Badcock, A. W. (1962), 'Physical optics at the Royal Society, 1660–1800', *The British Journal for the History of Science* **1**, 99–116.

Baillie, G. H. (1951), *Clocks and Watches: an Historical Bibliography*, vol. 1, London: N. A. G. Press.

Baker, T. M. M. (2000), *London. Rebuilding the City After the Great Fire*, Chichester: Phillimore.

Barbour, J. B. (1989), *Absolute or Relative Motion?*, vol. 1, 'The discovery of dynamics', Cambridge: Cambridge University Press.

Barker, G. F. R. (1895), *Memoir of Richard Busby D.D. (1606–1695)*, London: Lawrence & Bullen.

Barth, M. (1995), 'Huygens at work: annotations in his rediscovered personal copy of Hooke's *Micrographia*', *Annals of Science* **52**, 601–13.

Batten, M. I. (1935), ' Partner with Wren', *The Times*, 14 January, pp. 13–14 & 16.

———— (1936–37), 'The architecture of Dr Robert Hooke, FRS', *Journal of the Walpole Society* **25**, 83–113 and plates 35–40.

Baumann, R. (1917), 'Wissenschaft, Geschäftgeist und Hookesches Gesetz', *Zeitschrift Zereines Deutscher Ingenieure* **61**, 117–24.

Beaven, A. B. (1913), *The Aldermen of the City of London*, 2 vols, London: The Corporation of London.

Bechler, Zev (1974), 'Newton's 1672 optical controversies: a study in the grammar of scientific dissent', in Yehuda Elkana (ed.) (1974), *The Interaction between Science and Philosophy*, Atlantic Highlands, New Jersey: Humanities Press, pp. 115–42.

Beckmann, Johann (1782), *Beiträge zur Geschichte der Erfindungen*, Leipzig: Gotthelf Rummer.

Bedford, John (1967), *London's Burning*, London: Abelard Schuman.

Beier, A. L. and Finlay, R. (eds) (1986), *The Making of the Metropolis: London 1500–1700*, London: Longmans.

Beier, L. M. (1989), 'Experience and experiment: Robert Hooke, illness and medicine', in (q.v.) Hunter and Schaffer (eds) (1989), pp. 235–52.

Bekhterev, P. (1925), *Anaytische Untersuchung des Verallgemeinerten Hookeschen Gesetzes*, Leningrad.

Bell, W. G. (1923), *The Great Fire in London in 1666*, London: The Bodley Head.

————— (1924), *The Great Plague in London in 1665*, London: The Bodley Head.

Bendall, Sarah (1997), *Dictionary of Land Surveyors and Local Map-Makers of Great Britain and Ireland 1530–1850*, 2 vols, London: The British Library.

Bendry, R. (1995), 'The Falcon Brick Cone Glass House : the other revolution of 1688', *The Glass Circle Journal* **8**, 55–69.

Bennett, J. A. (1972), 'Christopher Wren: the natural causes of beauty', *Architectural History* **15**, 5–22.

————— (1973), 'A study of *Parentalia*, with two unpublished letters of Sir Christopher Wren', *Annals of Science* **30**, 129–47.

————— (1975), 'Hooke and Wren and the system of the world: some points towards an historical account', *The British Journal for the History of Science* **8**, 32–61.

————— (1980), 'Robert Hooke as mechanic and natural philosopher', *Notes and Records of The Royal Society of London* **35**, 33–48.

————— (1981), 'Cosmology and the magnetic philosophy, 1640–1680', *Journal of the History of Astronomy* **12**, 165–77.

————— (1982), *The Mathematical Science of Christopher Wren*, Cambridge: Cambridge University Press.

————— (1986), 'The mechanics' philosophy and the mechanical philosophy', *History of Science* **24**, 1–28.

————— (1987), *The Divided Circle, a History of Instruments for Astronomy, Navigation and Surveying*, Oxford: Phaidon-Christie's.

————— (1989), 'Hooke's instruments for astronomy and navigation', in (q.v.) Hunter and Schaffer (eds) (1989), pp. 21–61.

————— (1991), 'Geometry and surveying in early seventeenth-century England', *Annals of Science* **48**, 345–54.

————— (1997), 'Flamsteed's career in astronomy: nobility, morality and public utility', in Willmoth, Frances (ed.) (1997), *Flamsteed's Stars: New Perspectives on the Life and Work of the First Astronomer Royal (1646–1719)*, Woodbridge: Boydell Press, 17–30.

Bennett, Jim, Michael Cooper, Michael Hunter and Lisa Jardine (2003), *London's Leonardo, the Life and Work of Robert Hooke*, Oxford: Oxford University Press.

Berger, R. B. with Mainstone, R. J. (1993), 'Chapter 6: materials and structure', in R. B. Berger (1993), *The Palace of the Sun: The Louvre of Louis XIV*, University Park Pennsylvania: The Pennsylvania State University Press, pp. 65–74.

Berlinski, David (2001), *Newton's Gift*, London: Duckworth.

Birch, Thomas (1756–57), *The History of the Royal Society of London*, 4 vols, London: A Millar. Reprinted 1968, New York and London: Johnson Reprint Corporation.

Birch, W. de G. (1887), *The Historical Charters and Constitutional Documents of the City of London*, revised edn, London: Whiting.

Birkett, Kirsten and Oldroyd, David (1991), 'Robert Hooke, physico-mythology, knowledge of the world of the ancients and knowledge of the ancient world', in Stephen Gaukroger (ed.) (1991), *The Uses of Antiquity*, Dordrecht: Kluwer, pp. 145–70.

Birrell, T. A. (1963), *The Cultural Background of Two Scientific Revolutions: Robert Hooke's London and James Logan's Philadelphia*, Utrecht: Dekker & Van de Vegt.

Biswas, Asit K. (1967), 'The automatic rain-gauge of Sir Christopher Wren, F. R. S.', *Notes and Records of the Royal Society of London* **22**, 94–104.

Blay, Michel (1981), 'Un exemple d'explication mécaniste au dix-septieme siècle: l'unité des theories Hookiennes de la couleur', *Revue de l'Histoire des Sciences* **34**, 97–121.

Blondel, François (1675–83), *Cours d'Architecture*, Paris: Lambert Roulland.

Blunt, Anthony (1993), *Art and Architecture in France 1500 to 1700*, 4th edn, New Haven and London: Yale University Press.

Bonelli, M. L. Righini and Helden, Albert van (1981), 'Divini & Campani', *Annali dell'Instituto e Museo di Storia della Scienza di Firenze* **6**, 2–176.

Boston Medical Library (1935), 'Robert Hooke, 1635–1703', *New England Journal of Medicine* **213**, 1040–2.

Bouillin, D. J. (1994), 'Engravings of some of Tycho Brahé's instruments', *Bulletin of the Scientific Instrument Society* **40**, 31–2.

Boyceau, Jacques (1638), *Traité du Jardinage Selon les Raisons de la Nature et de l'Art*, Paris: M. Vanlochom.

Boyle, Robert (1999–2000), *Works*, 14 vols, eds Michael Hunter and E. B. Davis, London: Pickering & Chatto.

——— (2001), *Correspondence*, 6 vols, eds Michael Hunter, Antonio Clericuzio and L. M. Principe, London: Pickering & Chatto.

Brackenridge, J. B. (1995), *The Key to Newton's Dynamics; the Kepler Problem and The 'Principia'*, Berkeley: University of California Press.

Brackenridge, J. B. and Nauenberg, Michael (2002) 'Curvature in Newton's dynamics', in (q.v.) Cohen and Smith (eds) (2002), pp. 231–60.

Bradbury, Savile (1967), *The Evolution of the Microscope*, Oxford: Pergamon.

——— (1968), *The Microscope: Past and Present*, Oxford: Pergamon.

Brahe, Tycho (1946), *Astronomia Instaurata Mechanica*, trans. H.

Raeder, E. Strömgren and B. Strömgren (eds), Copenhagen: Munksgaard.

Brennan, James (1998), 'As-Burnt Surveys', unpublished MSc dissertation, Department of Geomatic Engineering, University College London.

Bronowski, Jacob (1951), *The Common Sense of Science*, London: Heinemann Educational.

Brown, T. M. (1971), 'Introduction', in reprint of (q.v.) Hooke (1705), London: Frank Cass.

Brush, S. G. (1983), *Statistical Physics and the Atomic Theory of Matter from Boyle and Newton to Landau and Onsager*, New Jersey: Princeton University Press.

Bryden, D. J. (1992), 'Evidence from advertising for mathematical instrument making in London 1556–1714', *Annals of Science* **49**, 301–36.

Buchdahl, Gerd (1957), 'Robert Hooke' [review of 'Espinasse 1956], *Scripta Mathematica* **23**, 77.

Buchwald, J. Z. and Cohen, I. B. (eds) (2001), *Isaac Newton's Natural Philosophy*, Cambridge, Massachusetts and London: MIT Press.

Bud, Robert and Warner, D. J. (eds) (1998), *Instruments of Science*, London: Science Museum, and New York: National Museum of American History.

Burke, John G. (ed.) (1983), *The Uses of Science in the Age of Newton*, Berkeley: University of California Press.

Campbell, Colen (1715, 1717 and 1725), *Vitruvius Britannicus*, 3 vols, London. Reprinted 1967, New York: Blom.

Campbell, J. W. P. (1999), 'Sir Christopher Wren, the Royal Society and the Development of Structural Carpentry 1660–1710', unpublished PhD dissertation, Cambridge University.

—— (2002), 'Wren and the development of structural carpentry 1660–1710', *Architectural Research Quarterly* **6**, 49–66.

Campen, Jacob van (1661), *Afbeelding van 't Stadthuys van Amsterdam* [*Depiction of the Amsterdam Town Hall*], Amsterdam: Dancker Danckerts.

Carderelli, François (1999), *Scientific Unit Conversion*, 2nd edn, London: Springer.

Carleton, John (1938; rev. ed. 1965), *Westminster School: a History*, London: Rupert Hart-Davis.

Carozzi, A. V. (1970), 'Robert Hooke, Rudolf Erich Raspe and the concept of earthquakes', *Isis* **61**, 86–91.

Caygill, Marjorie and Date, Christopher (1999), *The History of the British Museum*, London: British Museum Press.

Centore, F. F. (1968), 'Copernicus, Hooke and simplicity', *Philosophical Studies* **17**, 185–96.

——— (1970), *Robert Hooke's Contributions to Mechanics, a Study in Seventeenth-Century Mechanics*, The Hague: Martinus Nijhoff.

Champion, J. A. I. (1995), *London's Dreaded Visitation, the Social Geography of the Great Plague in 1665*, London: Historical Geography Research Series 31.

Chancel, Jean-Marc (1997), *Pierre Puget, Architecte*, Marseilles: Éditions Parenthèse.

Chandrasekhar, S. (1995), *Newton's 'Principia' for the Common Reader*, Oxford: Clarendon Press.

Chapman, Allan (1995), *Dividing the Circle, the Development of Critical Angular Measurement in Astronomy 1500–1850*, 2nd edn, Chichester: Wiley.

——— (1996), 'England's Leonardo: Robert Hooke (1635–1703) and the art of experiment in Restoration England', *Proceedings of the Royal Institution of Great Britain* **67**, 239–75.

——— (2005), *England's Leonardo; Robert Hooke and the Seventeenth-Century Scientific Revolution*, Bristol: Institute of Physics Publishing.

Chartres, Richard and Vermont, David (1998), *A Brief History of Gresham College 1597–1997*, London: Gresham College.

Chilton, D. (1958), 'Land Measurement in the sixteenth century', *Transactions of the Newcomen Society* **31**, 111–29 and 4 plates.

Clark, G. N. (1949), *Science and Social Welfare in the Age of Newton*, 2nd edn, Oxford: Oxford University Press [first published 1935; reissued with additions 1970].

——— (1964), *A History of the Royal College of Physicians*, vol. 1, Oxford: Clarendon Press.

Clay, R. S. and Court, T. H. (1932), *The History of the Microscope*, London: Charles Griffin & Co.

Cobb, Gerald (1942–43), *The Old Churches of London*, 2nd edn, London: Batsford.

Cohen, I. B. (1964), 'Newton, Hooke and 'Boyle's Law' (discovered by Power and Towneley)', *Nature* **204**, 618–21.

Cohen, I. B. (1971), *Introduction to Newton's 'Principia'*, Cambridge, Massachusetts: Harvard University Press.

——— (ed.) (1978), *Isaac Newton's Papers & Letters on Natural Philosophy*, 2nd edn, Cambridge, Massachusetts: Harvard University Press.

——— (1980), *The Newtonian Revolution, With Illustrations of the Transformation of Scientific Ideas*, Cambridge: Cambridge University Press.

———— (1981), 'Newton's discovery of gravity', *Scientific American* **244**, 166–79.

———— (1985), *The Birth of a New Physics*, revised and updated edn, New York and London: Norton.

Cohen, I. B. and Smith, G. E. (eds) (2002), *The Cambridge Companion to Newton*, Cambridge and New York: Cambridge University Press.

Cokayne, George E. (ed.) (1910–59), *The Complete Peerage of England, Scotland, Ireland, Great Britain and the United Kingdom extant or dormant*, 14 vols, London: St Catherine Press.

Colvin, Sir Howard (1995), *A Biographical Dictionary of British Architects 1600–1840*, 3rd edn, New Haven and London: Yale University Press.

———— (1996), *The Panorama as an Architectural and Topographical Record*, London: The London Topographical Society.

Colvin, H. M. and Newman, J. (eds) (1981), *'Of Building': Roger North's Writings on Architecture*, Oxford: Oxford University Press.

Conant, J. B. and Nash, L. K. (eds) (1964a), *Harvard Case Histories in Experimental Science*, vol. 1, Cambridge, Massachusetts: Harvard University Press.

———— (1964b), 'Robert Boyle's experiments in pneumatics', in (q.v.) Conant and Nash (eds) (1964a), pp. 1–64.

Cooke, A. H. (1965), 'The absolute determination of the acceleration due to gravity', *Metrologia* **1**, 84–114.

Cooke, Sir Alan (1999), *Edmund Halley, Charting the Heavens and the Seas*, Oxford: Clarendon Press.

Cooper, Carolyn (1991), 'Making inventions patent', *Technology and Culture* **32**, 837–45.

Cooper, M. A. R. (1982), *Modern Theodolites and Levels*, Oxford: Granada.

———— (1986), 'Robert Hooke (1635–1703) proto-photogrammetrist', *Photogrammetric Record* **15**, 403–17.

———— (1997, 1998a and b), 'Robert Hooke's work as Surveyor for the City of London in the aftermath of the Great Fire', *Notes and Records of the Royal Society of London* **51**, 161–74; **52**, 25–38, 205–220.

———— (1999), 'Robert Hooke, City Surveyor', unpublished PhD thesis, City University, London.

———— (2003a), 'Hooke's career', in (q.v.) Bennett, Jim et al (2003), pp. 1–61.

———— (2003b), *A More Beautiful City, Robert Hooke and the Rebuilding of London After the Great Fire of 1666*, Stroud: Sutton Publishing.

————— (2004), 'Robert Hooke (1635–1703), professional scientist, engineer and surveyor', *Ingenia* **19**, 48–54.

————— (2005), 'The civic virtue of Robert Hooke', in (q.v.) Kent and Chapman (eds) (2005), pp. 161–86.

Cornforth, John (1992), 'Boughton: impressions and people', in Tessa Murdoch (ed.) (1992), *Boughton House: the English Versailles*, London: Faber and Faber/Christies, pp. 12–31.

Corporation of London (1994), *The Official Guide to the Monument*, London: Corporation of London.

————— (2001), *The Livery Companies of the City of London*, 2nd edn, London: Corporation of London.

Cranston, Maurice (1957), *John Locke, a Biography*, London: Longmans.

Crombie, A. C. (1967), 'The mechanistic hypothesis and the scientific study of vision', in G. L. E. Turner and S. Bradbury (eds) (1967), *Historical Aspects of Microscopy*, Cambridge: Heffer for the Royal Microscopical Society, pp. 3–12.

Crowther, J. G. (1960), *Founders of British Science: John Wilkins, Robert Boyle, John Ray, Christopher Wren, Robert Hooke, Isaac Newton*, London: Cresset Press.

Cruz, J. Y., Harrison, J. C., Speake, C. C., Niebauer, T. M., McHugh, M. P., Keyser, P. T., Mäkinen, Jaako and Beruff, R. B. (1991), 'A test of Newton's inverse-square law of gravitation using the 300-m tower at Erie, Colorado', *Journal of Geophysical Research* **96 (B12)**, 20, 73–92.

Dalitz, Richard H. and Nauenberg, Michael (eds) (2000), *The Foundations of Newtonian Scholarship*, Singapore: World Scientific.

Davies, Gordon L. (1964), 'Robert Hooke and his conception of Earth-history', *Proceedings of the Geologists' Associations* **75**, 493–8.

————— (1969), *The Earth in Decay: a History of British Geomorphology 1578–1878*, London: Macdonald & Co.

Davis, Edward B. (1994), '"Parcere nominibus": Boyle, Hooke and the rhetorical interpretation of Descartes', in (q.v.) Hunter, Michael (ed.) (1994b), pp. 157–75.

Deacon, Margaret (1965), 'Founders of marine science in Britain: the work of the early Fellows of the Royal Society', *Notes and Records of the Royal Society of London* **20**, 28–50.

————— (1971), *Scientists and the Sea*, London: Academic Press.

Dear, Peter (1985), 'Totius in Verba: Rhetoric and authority in the early Royal Society', *Isis* **76**, 145–61. Reprinted in Dear, Peter (ed.) (1997), *The Scientific Enterprise in Early Modern Europe*, Chicago: University of Chicago Press, pp. 255–72.

————— (2001), *Revolutionizing the Sciences: European Knowledge and its Ambitions, 1500–1700*, Basingstoke: Palgrave.

De Gant, François (1995), *Force and Geometry in Newton's 'Principia'*, trans. Curtis Wilson, Princeton: Princeton University Press.

De Milt, Clara (1939), 'Robert Hooke, chemist', *Journal of Chemical Education* **16**, 503–10.

De Morgan, Augustus (1885), *Newton: His Friend, and His Niece*, London: E Stock.

Dennis, M. A. (1989), 'Graphic understanding: instruments and interpretation in Robert Hooke's *Micrographia*', *Science in Context* **3**, 309–64.

Descartes, René (1983), *Principles of Philosophy*, translation of *Principia Philosophiæ* (1644) by Valentine R. Miller and Reese P. Miller, Dordrecht, Boston, and London: D. Reidel.

Dickinson, H. W. (1970), *Sir Samuel Morland, Diplomat and Inventor 1625–1695*, Cambridge: Heffer and Sons for The Newcomen Society.

Dictionary of National Biography (*DNB*), 63 vols, (1885–1903), Leslie Stephen, Sydney Lee et al (eds), London: Smith Elder and Co.

Dilworth, C. (1986), 'Boyle, Hooke and Newton: Some aspects of scientific collaboration', *Memorie di Scienze Fisiche e Naturali* **103**, 329–31.

Dilworth, C, and Sciuto, M. (1984), 'Hooke, Grimaldi and the Diffraction of Light', in Pasquale Tucci (ed.), *Atti dell 4 Congresso Nazionale di Storia della Fisica*, Milan: CLUED, pp. 31–7.

Dobson, K., Grace, D. and Lovett, D. (1997), *Physics*, London: Collins.

Dostrovsky, S. (1974–75), 'Early vibration theory: physics and music in the seventeenth century', *Archive for History of Exact Sciences* **14**, 169–218.

Downes, Kerry (1966), *English Baroque Architecture*, London: Zwemmer.

————— (1971), *Christopher Wren*, London: Allen Lane, The Penguin Press.

————— (1988), *Christopher Wren, the Design of St Paul's Cathedral*, London: Trefoil.

Draaisma, D. (2000), *Metaphors of Memory. A History of Ideas about the Mind*, Cambridge: Cambridge University Press.

————— (2001), 'The tracks of thought', *Nature* **414**, 8 November, 153.

Drake, Ellen Tan (1981), 'The Hooke imprint on the Huttonian Theory', *American Journal of Science* **281**, 963–73.

————— (1996), *Restless Genius. Robert Hooke and his Earthly Thoughts*, New York: Oxford University Press.

———— (2005), 'Hooke's concepts of the earth in space', in (q.v.) Kent and Chapman (eds) (2005), pp. 75–94.

Drake, Ellen Tan and Komar, P. D. (1981), 'A comparison of geological contributions of Nicholas Steno and Robert Hooke', *Journal of Geological Education* **29**, 127–34.

Drake, Stillman (1990), *Galileo: Pioneer Scientist*, Toronto: University of Toronto Press.

Dugas, René (1955), *A History of Mechanics*, trans. J.R. Maddox, Neuchâtel: Éditions du Griffon and New York: Central Book Company.

———— (1958), *Mechanics in the Seventeenth Century (From the Scholastic Antecedents to Classical Thought)*, trans. Freda Jacquot, Neuchâtel: Éditions du Griffon and New York: Central Book Company.

Dussieux, Louis E. (1876), *Les Artistes Français à l'Étranger: Recherches sur Leurs Travaux et sur Leur Influence en Europe*, Paris: Gide et Beaudry.

Earle, Peter (1989), *The Making of the English Middle Class*, London: Methuen.

Edwards, W. N. (1936), 'Robert Hooke as geologist and evolutionist', *Nature* **137**, 96–7.

———— (1967), *The Early History of Palaeontology*, London: British Museum (Natural History). Originally published 1931 as *Guide to an Exhibition illustrating the Early History of Palaeontology*, Special Guide No. 8, London: British Museum.

Eerde, Katherine S. van (1976), *John Ogilby and the Taste of His Times*, Folkestone: Dawson.

Ehrlich, Mark E. (1995), 'Mechanism and activity in the Scientific Revolution: the case of Robert Hooke', *Annals of Science* **52**, 127–51.

Ehrlichson, Herman (1992), 'Newton and Hooke on centripetal force motion', *Centaurus* **35**, 46–63.

Ellen, R. G. (1972), *A London Steeplechase*, London: City Press.

Elliott, James (1987), *The City in Maps, Urban Mapping to 1900*, London: The British Library.

Ellis, George W. A. (1829), *The Ellis Correspondence. Letters Written During the Years 1686, 1687, 1688, and Addressed to John Ellis Esq.*, 2 vols, London: Henry Colburn.

Emerton, N. E. (1984), *The Scientific Interpretation of Form*, Ithaca, N.Y.: Cornell University Press.

'Espinasse, Margaret (1937) [as Margaret Wattie], 'Robert Hooke on his literary contemporaries', *Review of English Studies* **13**, 212–16.

────── (1956), *Robert Hooke*, London: Heinemann. Reprinted 1962, Berkeley and Los Angeles: University of California Press.

Evelyn, John (1850–52), *Diary and Correspondence of John Evelyn FRS*, 4 vols, ed. William Bray, London: Henry Colburn.

────── (1955), *Diary*, 6 vols, ed. E. S. de Beer, Oxford: Clarendon Press.

Ezell, M. J. E. (1984), 'Richard Waller, S.R.S.: "In pursuit of nature"', *Notes and Records of the Royal Society of London* **38**, 215–33.

Featherstone, Ernest (1952), *Sir Thomas Gresham and his Trusts*, London: The Mercers' Company.

Feingold, Mordechai (1984), *The Mathematicians' Apprenticeship. Science, Universities and Society in England 1560–1640*, Cambridge: Cambridge University Press.

────── (1994). 'Patrons and professors: the origins and motives for the endowment of new university professorships in seventeenth-century England', in G. A. Russell (ed.) (1994), *The 'Arabic' Interest of the Natural Philosophers in Seventeenth-Century England*, Leiden: Brill, pp. 109–27.

────── (1996). 'When facts matter', *Isis* **87**, 131–9.

────── (2000), 'Mathematicians and naturalists: Sir Isaac Newton and the Royal Society', in J. Z. Buchwald and I. B. Cohen (eds) (2000), *Isaac Newton's Natural Philosophy*, Cambridge, Massachusetts: MIT Press, pp. 77–102.

────── (2003), 'Isaac Barrow and the foundation of the Lucasian professorship', in Kevin C. Knox and Richard Noakes (eds) (2003), *From Newton to Hawking*, Cambridge and New York: Cambridge University Press, pp. 45–67.

Feisenberger, H. A. (1966), 'The libraries of Newton, Hooke and Boyle', *Notes and Records of the Royal Society of London* **21**, 42–55.

────── (ed.) (1975), *Sale Catalogues of the Libraries of Eminent Persons*, vol. 11, 'Scientists', London: Mansell [contains catalogue of Hooke's library].

Finlay, R and Shearer, B. (1986), 'Population growth and suburban expansion', in (q.v.) Beier and Finlay (eds) (1986), pp. 37–59.

Flamsteed, John (1975), *The Gresham Lectures*, ed. Eric G. Forbes, London: Mansell.

Foister, Susan (1996), 'Anthonis van den Wyngaerde's career as a topographical artist', in (q.v.) London Topographical Society (1996), pp. 1–4.

Foucault, L. (1847), 'Sur un horloge à pendule conique', *Comptes Rendus de l'Académie des Sciences* **25**, 154–60.

────── (1862), 'Sur une solution de l'isochronisme du pendule conique', *Comptes Rendus de l'Académie des Sciences* **55**, 135–6.

———— (1863), 'Expression générale des conditions d'isochronisme du pendule régulateur à force centrifuge', *Comptes Rendus de l'Académie des Sciences* **57**, 738–40.

Frank, R. G. (1975), 'Institutional structure and scientific activity in the early Royal Society', *Proceedings of the XIVth International Congress of the History of Science*, **4**, 82–101.

———— (1980), *Harvey and the Oxford Physiologists. Scientific Ideas and Social Interaction*, Berkeley and Los Angeles: University of California Press.

Fulton, J. F. (1961), *A Bibliography of the Honourable Robert Boyle F.R.S.*, 2nd edn, Oxford: Clarendon Press.

Gal, Ofer (1996), 'Producing knowledge in the workshop: Hooke's "inflection" from optics to planetary motion', *Studies in History and Philosophy of Science* **27**, 181–205.

———— (2002), *Meanest Foundations and Nobler Superstructures: Hooke, Newton and the Compounding of the Celestiall Motions of the Planetts*, Dordrecht, Boston and London: Kluwer.

Galison, Peter and Thompson, Emily. (eds) (1999), *The Architecture of Science*, Cambridge, Massachusetts: MIT Press.

Gaposchkin, Sergei (1963), 'Newton and Hooke', *Sky and Telescope* **25**, 14–5.

Gaukroger, Stephen (2001), *Francis Bacon and the Transformation of Early-Modern Philosophy*, Cambridge: Cambridge University Press.

Geraghty, Anthony (1997), [Review of Jeffery 1996], *Burlington Magazine* **139**, 336–7.

———— (2001), 'Edward Woodroofe: Sir Christopher Wren's first draughtsman', *Burlington Magazine* **143**, 474–9.

Gillispie, C. C. (ed.) (1970–80), *Dictionary of Scientific Biography*, 16 vols, New York: Charles Scribner's Sons.

Girouard, Mark (1978), *Life in the English Country House; a Social and Architectural History*, New Haven and London: Yale University Press.

Glanvill, Joseph (1661), *The Vanity of Dogmatizing: or Confidence in Opinions. Manifested in a Discourse of the Shortness and Uncertainty of our Knowledge and its Causes*, London.

Goidanich, Gabriele (1941), 'I primi documenti dell'esistenza dei funghi microscopici', *Bolletini Sta. Patol. Vegetale* **n.s. 21**, 318–31.

Golinski, J. V. (1989), 'A noble spectacle. Phosphorus and the public cultures of science in the early Royal Society', *Isis* **80**, 11–39.

Gooding, D., Pinch, T. and Schaffer, S. (1989), *The Uses of Experiment: Studies in the Natural Sciences*, Cambridge: Cambridge University Press.

Gough, H. J. (1935), 'Robert Hooke (1635–1703); a short appreciation', *Iron and Steel Industry* **8**, 373–5.

Gouk, Penelope (1980), 'The role of acoustics and music theory in the scientific work of Robert Hooke', *Annals of Science* **37**, 573–605.

———— (1982), 'Acoustics in the early Royal Society 1660–1680', *Notes and Records of the Royal Society of London* **36**, 155–75.

———— (1999), *Music, Science and Natural Magic in Seventeenth-century England*, New Haven and London: Yale University Press.

Gould, R. T. (1923), *The Marine Chronometer*, London: J. D. Potter.

Grew, Nehemiah (1681), *Museum Regalis Societatis, or A Catalogue & Description of the Natural and Artificial Rarities Belonging to the Royal Society and Preserved at Gresham Colledge*, London.

Gribbin, John (2003), *Science: a History*, London: Penguin Books.

Grubb, H. (1888), 'On the latest improvements to the clock-driving apparatus of astronomical telescopes', *Proceedings of the Institution of Mechanical Engineers* 31 July, 303–16.

Guicciardini, Niccolò (1999), *Reading The 'Principia': the Debate on Newton's Mathematical Methods for Natural Philosophy from 1687 to 1736*, Cambridge: Cambridge University Press.

Gunther, R. T. (ed.) (1930a), *Early Science in Oxford*, vol. 6, 'The life and work of Robert Hooke (part 1)', Oxford: The Author.

———— (ed.) (1930b), *Early Science in Oxford*, vol. 7, 'The life and work of Robert Hooke (part 2)', Oxford: The Author.

———— (ed.) (1931), *Early Science in Oxford*, vol. 8, 'The Cutler lectures of Robert Hooke', Oxford: The Author.

———— (ed.) (1935), *Early Science in Oxford*, vol. 10, 'The life and work of Robert Hooke (part 4)', Oxford: The Author.

———— (ed.) (1938), *Early Science in Oxford*, vol. 13, 'Robert Hooke's "Micrographia"', Oxford.

Gyssling, Walter (1917), *Anton Möller und seine Schule: ein Beitrag zur Geschichte der niederdeutschen Renaissancemalerei*, Strassburg: Heitz & Mündel.

H., R. (1660), *New Atlantis. Begun by the Lord Verulam, Viscount St Albans: and Continued by R. H. Esquire. Wherein is set forth a Platform of Monarchical Government* ... , London.

Hacking, Ian (1983), *Representing and Intervening; Introductory Topics in the Philosophy of Natural Science*, Cambridge: Cambridge University Press.

Hall, A. R. (1951a), 'Robert Hooke and horology', *Notes and Records of the Royal Society of London* **8**, 167–77.

———— (1951b), 'Two unpublished lectures of Robert Hooke', *Isis* **42**, 219–30.

———— (1957), 'Newton on the calculation of central forces', *Annals of Science* **13**, 62–71.

——— (1965), 'Galileo and the science of motion', *The British Journal for the History of Science* **2**, 185–99.

——— (1966a), *Hooke's Micrographia 1665–1965*, London: Athlone Press.

——— (1966b), 'Mechanics and the Royal Society 1668–70', *The British Journal for the History of Science* **3**, 24–38.

——— (1978), 'Horology and criticism: Robert Hooke', *Studia Copernicana* **6**, 261–81.

——— (1983), *The Revolution in Science 1500–1750*, London and New York: Longmans.

——— (1990), 'Beyond the fringe: diffraction as seen by Grimaldi, Fabri, Hooke and Newton', *Notes and Records of the Royal Society of London* **44**, 13–23.

——— (1992), *Isaac Newton, Adventurer in Thought*, Oxford: Blackwell.

——— (1996), 'Theory and responsibility in science and technology', *History of Technology* **18**, 1–12.

Hall, A. R. and Hall, M. B. (eds) (1962a), *Unpublished Scientific Papers of Isaac Newton*, Cambridge: Cambridge University Press.

——— (1962b), 'Why blame Oldenburg?' *Isis* **53**, 482–91.

Hall, A. R. and Westfall, R. S. (1967), 'Did Hooke concede to Newton?', *Isis* **58**, 403–5.

Hall, D. H. (1976), *History of the Earth Sciences during the Scientific and Industrial Revolution*, Amsterdam: Elsevier Scientific Publishing.

Hall, M. B. (1952), 'The establishment of the mechanical philosophy', *Osiris* **10**, 412–541.

——— (1965), 'Oldenburg and the art of scientific communication', *The British Journal for the History of Science* **2**, 277–90.

——— (1975), 'Science in the early Royal Society', in M. B. Crosland, (ed.) (1975), *The Emergence of Science in Early Modern Europe*, London and Basingstoke: Macmillan Press, pp. 57–77.

——— (1981), 'Salomon's House emergent: the Royal Society and co-operative research', in H. Woolf (ed.) (1981), *The Analytic Spirit*, Ithaca: Cornell University Press, pp. 177–94.

——— (1983), 'Oldenburg, the *Philosophical Transactions* and technology', in (q.v.) Burke (ed.) (1983), pp. 21–47.

Halley, Edmond (1937), *Correspondence and Papers*, ed. E. F. MacPike, London: Taylor and Francis.

Halliday, D. and Resnick, R. (1970), *Fundamentals of Physics*, New York: Wiley.

Hambly, E. C. (1987), 'Robert Hooke, The City's Leonardo', *City University* **2**, 5–10.

Hanson, Julienne (1989), 'Order and structure in urban design: the plans for the rebuilding of London after the Great Fire of 1666', *Ekistics* **334–5**, 22–42.

Hanson, J. M. (1990), 'Order and Structure in Urban Space: a Morphological Study of the City of London', unpublished PhD thesis, University of London.

Harris, Eileen (1990), *British Architectural Books and Writers 1556–1785*, Cambridge: Cambridge University Press.

Harris, Frances (1997), 'Living in the neighbourhood of science: Mary Evelyn, Margaret Cavendish and the Greshamites', in (q.v.) Hunter and Hutton (eds) (1997), pp. 198–217.

Hartley, Sir Harold (ed.) (1960), *The Royal Society: its Origins and Founders*, London: The Royal Society.

Harvey, J. (1987), *English Mediaeval Architects*, 2nd edn, London: Alan Sutton.

Harvey, P. D. A. (1993), *Maps in Tudor England*, London: The British Library.

Harwood, John (1989), 'Rhetoric and graphics in *Micrographia*', in (q.v.) Hunter and Schaffer (eds) (1989), pp. 119–47.

Helden, Albert van (1968), 'Christopher Wren's "De Corpore Saturni" ', *Notes and Records of the Royal Society of London* **23**, 213–29.

——— (1974), 'The telescope in the seventeenth century', *Isis* **65**, 38–58.

——— (1980), 'Huygens and the astronomers', in H. J. M. Boss, et al (eds) (1980), *Studies on Christiaan Huygens*, Lisse: Swets & Zeitlinger, pp. 147–65.

——— (1983), 'The birth of the modern scientific instrument', in (q.v.) Burke (ed.) (1983), pp. 49–84.

——— (1985), *Measuring the Universe: Cosmic Dimensions from Aristarchus to Halley*, Chicago: University of Chicago Press.

Henry, John (1983), 'Matter in Motion: the Problem of Activity in Seventeenth-century English Matter Theory', unpublished PhD thesis, Open University.

——— (1986), 'Occult qualities and the mechanical philosophy: active principles in pre-Newtonian matter theory', *History of Science* **24**, 335–81.

——— (1989), 'Robert Hooke, the incongruous mechanist', in (q.v.) Hunter and Schaffer (eds) (1989), pp. 149–80.

——— (2002), *Knowledge is Power; How Magic, the Government, and an Apocalyptic Vision Inspired Francis Bacon to Create Modern Science*, Cambridge: Icon Books.

Henry, Matthew (1712), *An Account of the Life and Death of Mr Philip Henry*, London.

Herivel, J. W. (1965a), 'Newton's first solution to the problem of Kepler motion', *The British Journal for the History of Science* **2**, 350–4.

—— (1965b), *The Background to Newton's 'Principia': a Study of Newton's Dynamical Researches in the Years 1664–84*, Oxford: Clarendon Press.

Herrmann, W. (1973), *The Theory of Claude Perrault*, London: Zwemmer.

Hesse, Mary (1964), 'Hooke's development of Bacon's method', in *Proceedings of the 10th International Congress for the History of Science*, Paris: Hermann, pp. 265–8.

—— (1966a), 'Hooke's philosophical algebra', *Isis* **57**, 67–83.

—— (1966b), 'Hooke's vibration theory and the isochrony of springs', *Isis* **57**, 433–41.

Heyman, Jacques (1998), 'Hooke's cubico-parabolical conoid', *Notes and Records of the Royal Society of London* **52**, 39–50.

Hide, Raymond (2001), 'Zenographic longitude systems and Jupiter's differential rotation', *Notes and Records of the Royal Society of London* **55**, 69–79.

Hill, C. P. (1988), *Who's Who in Stuart Britain*, London: Shepheard-Walwyn.

Hind, A. M. (1972), *Wenceslaus Hollar and His Views of London and Windsor in the Seventeenth Century*, New York: Benjamin Blom.

Hiscock, Walter George (1960), *Henry Aldrich of Christ Church*. Oxford: Christ Church.

Holwell, John (1678), *A Sure Guide to the Practical Surveyor in Two Parts*, London.

Hooke, Robert (1661), *An Attempt for the Explication of the Phænomena, Observable in an Experiment Published by the Honourable Robert Boyle, Esq; ... In Confirmation of a former Conjecture made by R. H.*, London.

—— (1665) *Micrographia: Or Some Physiological Descriptions of Minute Bodies Made By Magnifying Glasses With Observations and Enquiries thereupon*, London. Reprinted 1667. Reprinted in facsimile (undated), Boston & Stuttgart: Edition Medicina Rara. See also Gunter 1938 and Hooke 1998.

—— (1672–83), *Memoranda*, Guildhall Library, Corporation of London Ms. 1758. See also Hooke 1935.

—— (1674a), *An Attempt to Prove the Motion of the Earth from Observations made by Robert Hooke Fellow of the Royal Society*, London.

—— (1674b), *Animadversions On the first part of the Machina Cœlestis Of ... Johannes Hevelius ...*, London.

———— [anon] (1675), 'An account of the book, *Origin of Fountains*', *Philosophical Transactions* **10**, 447–50, 22 November.

———— (1676), *A Description of Helioscopes, and some other Instruments made by Robert Hooke, Fellow of the Royal Society*, London.

———— (1677), *Lampas: or Descriptions of some Mechanical Improvements of Lamps & Waterpoises Together with some other Physical and Mechanical Discoveries Made by Robert Hooke Fellow of the Royal Society*, London.

———— (1678a), *Lectures De Potentia Restitutiva, or of Spring Explaining the Power of Springing Bodies, to which are added some Collections ...*, London.

———— (1678b), *Lectures and Collections Made by Robert Hooke, Secretary of the Royal Society. Cometa containing ... Microscopium containing ...*, London.

———— (1679), *Lectiones Cutlerianæ*, London. See also Gunther 1931.

———— (1705), *Posthumous Works ... Cutlerian Lectures and other Discourses*, ed. Richard Waller, London. Reprinted, with an introduction by Richard S. Westfall (1969), New York: Johnson Reprint Corporation. Reprinted, in slightly reduced facsimile (1970), Hildesheim and New York: Georg Olms. Reprinted, with an introduction by T. M. Brown (1971), London: Frank Cass.

———— (1726), *Philosophical Experiments and Observations of the late Eminent Dr. Robert Hooke ...* ed. William Derham. London. Reprinted 1962, London: Frank Cass.

———— (1935), *The Diary of Robert Hooke 1672–1680*, ed. H. W. Robinson and Walter Adams, London: Taylor & Francis. Reprinted 1968, London: Wykeham Publications.

———— (1961), *Micrographia*, New York: Dover Books. Reprinted from Gunther 1938.

———— (1989), *Micrografía o Algunas Descripciones Fisiológicas de Los Cuerpos Diminutos Realizadas Mediante Christales de Aumento con Observaciones y Disquisiciones sobre Ellas*, ed. Carlos Solis, Madrid: Alfaguara.

———— (1998), *Micrographia*, CD ROM from Octavo at http://www.octavo.com/collections/projects/hkemic/index.html

Hoskin, M. A. (1982), 'Hooke, Bradley and the aberration of light', in M. A. Hoskin (ed) (1982), *Stellar Astronomy: Historical Studies*, Chalfont St Giles: Science History Publications, pp. 29–36.

Houghton, W. E. (1941), 'The history of trades: its relation to seventeenth-century thought, as seen in Bacon, Petty, Evelyn and Boyle', *Journal of the History of Ideas* **2**, 33–60.

Howard, Nicole (forthcoming), 'Robert Hooke's anatomy: beyond artificial wings', *Early Science and Medicine*.

Howgego, J. L. (1978), *Printed Maps of London circa 1553–1850*, 2nd edn, Folkestone: Dawson.

Howse, Derek (1970–71), 'The Tompion clocks at Greenwich and the dead-beat escapement', *Antiquarian Horology* **7**, 18–34, 114–33.

—— (1975), *Greenwich Observatory*, vol. 3, 'The buildings and instruments', London: Taylor and Francis.

Howse, Derek, and Finch, Valerie (1976), 'John Flamsteed and the balance spring', *Antiquarian Horology* **9**, 664–72.

Hull, Derek (1997), 'Robert Hooke: a fractographic study of Ketteringstone', *Notes and Records of the Royal Society of London* **51**, 45–55.

Hult, Jan (1977), 'Robert Hooke och hans Fjåderlag: ett 300-Årsminne', *Daedalus* **47**, 39–57.

Humphrey, D. (1931), *Intermediate Mechanics*, London: Longmans.

Hunter, Lynette and Hutton, Sarah (eds) (1997), *Women, Science and Medicine 1500–1700*, Stroud: Sutton Publishing.

Hunter, Michael (1975), *John Aubrey and the Realm of Learning*, London: Gerald Duckworth.

—— (1981), *Science and Society in Restoration England*, Cambridge: Cambridge University Press.

—— (1982), 'Reconstructing Restoration science: problems and pitfalls in institutional history', *Social Studies of Science* **12**, 451–66.

—— (1984), 'A college for the Royal Society: the abortive plan of 1667–8', *Notes and Records of the Royal Society of London* **38**, 159–86.

—— (1989), *Establishing the New Science: the Experience of the Early Royal Society*, Woodbridge: Boydell Press.

—— (1994a), *Robert Boyle by Himself and His Friends*, London: Pickering & Chatto.

—— (ed.) (1994b), *Robert Boyle Reconsidered*, Cambridge: Cambridge University Press.

—— (1994c), *The Royal Society and its Fellows 1660–1700: the Morphology of a Scientific Institution*, revised edn, Oxford: British Society for the History of Science.

—— (1995), *Science and the Shape of Orthodoxy*, Woodbridge: Boydell Press.

—— (2000), *Robert Boyle (1627–91): Scrupulosity and Science*, Woodbridge: Boydell Press.

—— (2003), 'Hooke the natural philosopher', in (q.v.) Bennett et al (2003), pp. 105–62.

Hunter, Michael and Littleton, Charles (2001), 'The work diaries of Robert Boyle: a newly discovered source and its internet publication', *Notes and Records of the Royal Society of London* **55**, 373–90.

Hunter, Michael, and Schaffer, Simon (eds) (1989), *Robert Hooke: New Studies*, Woodbridge: Boydell Press.

Hunter, Michael and Wood, P. B. (1986), 'Towards Solomon's House: rival strategies for reforming the early Royal Society', *History of Science* **24**, 49–108.

Hutchings, Robert (1992), *Physics*, Kingston, Surrey: Nelson.

Hutton, James (1785), 'Abstract of a dissertation read in the Royal Society of Edinburgh, upon 7 March and 4 April 1785 concerning the system of the earth, its duration and stability', facsimile (30 pp.) in G. W. White (ed.) (1970), *Contributions to the History of Geology*, vol. 5, Darien, Connecticut: Hafner.

——— (1788), 'Theory of the earth, or an investigation of the laws observable in the composition, dissolution and restoration of land upon the globe', *Transactions of the Royal Society of Edinburgh* **1**, 209–304.

Hutton, Sarah (1997), 'Anne Conway, Margaret Cavendish and seventeenth-century scientific thought', in (q.v.) Hunter and Hutton (eds) (1997), pp. 218–34.

Huygens, Christiaan (1888–1950), *Oeuvres Complètes*, 22 vols, ed. Société Hollandaise des Sciences, The Hague: Martinus Nijhoff.

Hyde, Ralph (1992), 'Ogilby and Morgan's City of London Map', in (q.v.) London Topographical Society (1992), pp. v–xii.

Iliffe, Rob (1992), ' "In the warehouse": privacy, property and priority in the early Royal Society', *History of Science* **30**, 29–68.

——— (1995), 'Material doubts: Hooke, artisan culture and the exchange of information in 1670s London', *The British Journal for the History of Science* **28**, 285–318.

Inwood, Stephen (2002), *The Man Who Knew Too Much. The Strange and Inventive World of Robert Hooke 1635–1703*, London: Macmillan.

Ito, Yushi (1988), 'Hooke's cyclic theory of the earth in the context of seventeenth-century England', *The British Journal for the History of Science* **21**, 295–314.

Jackson-Stops, Gervase (1980), 'Daniel Marot and the first Duke of Montagu', *Nederlands Kunsthistorisch Jaarboek* **31**, 244–62.

Jacques, David (2001), 'Garden design in the mid-seventeenth century', *Architectural History* **44**, 365–76.

Jardine, Lisa (1999), *Ingenious Pursuits: Building the Scientific Revolution*, London: Little, Brown & Co.

——— (2001), 'Monuments and microscopes: scientific thinking on a grand scale in the early Royal Society', *Notes and Records of the Royal Society of London* **55**, 289–308.

——— (2002), *On a Grander Scale: the Outstanding Career of Sir Christopher Wren*, London: HarperCollins.

———— (2003a), 'Hooke the man – his diary and his health', in (q.v.) Bennett et al (2003), pp. 163–206.

———— (2003b), *The Curious Life of Robert Hooke, the Man Who Measured London*, London: HarperCollins.

Jardine, Lisa, and Stewart, Alan (1998), *Hostage to Fortune: the Troubled Life of Francis Bacon*, London: Gollancz.

Jeffery, Paul (1996), *The City Churches of Sir Christopher Wren*, London: Hambledon Press.

Jeneman, H. R. (1985), 'Robert Hooke und die frühe Geschichte der Federwaege', *Berichte zur Wissenschaftsgeschichte* **8**, 121–30.

Johns, Adrian (1998), *The Nature of the Book. Print and Knowledge in the Making*, Chicago: Chicago University Press.

Johns, Henry (1989), 'Introduction to the maps', in (q.v.) Lobel (ed.) (1989), pp. 57–62.

Jones, E. L. (1951), 'Robert Hooke and *The Virtuoso*', *Modern Language Notes* **66**, 180–1.

Jones, P. E. (ed.) (1966), *The Fire Court*, vol. 1, 'Calendar to the judgements and decrees of the Court of Judicature appointed to determine differences between landlords and tenants as to rebuilding after the Great Fire', London: William Clowes.

Jones, P. E. and Reddaway, T. F. (1967), 'Introduction', in (q.v.) London Topographical Society (1967), pp. ix–xlii.

Jones, R. F. (1961), *Ancients and Moderns: a Study of the Rise of the Scientific Movement in Seventeenth-century England*, St Louis: Washington University Studies.

Jourdain, P. E. B. (1913), 'Robert Hooke as a precursor of Newton', *The Monist* **23**, 353–84.

———— (1914), 'The principles of mechanics with Newton from 1666–1679 and 1679–1687', *The Monist* **24**, 188–214 and 515–64.

———— (1915), 'Newton's hypothesis of ether and gravitation from 1672 to 1679', *The Monist* **25**, 79–106.

Kargon, R. H. (1971), 'The testimony of nature: Boyle, Hooke and the experimental philosophy', *Albion* **3**, 72–81.

Kassler, J. C. (1995), *Inner Music: Hobbes, Hooke and North on Internal Character*, London: Athlone.

Kassler, J. C. and Oldroyd, David (1983), 'Robert Hooke's Trinity College "Musick Scripts": his music theory and the role of music in his cosmology', *Annals of Science* **40**, 559–95.

Keller, Alex (1984), 'Has science created technology?', *Minerva* **22**, 160–82.

———— (1993), 'Technological aspirations and natural philosophy in seventeenth-century England', *History of Technology* **15**, 76–92.

Kent, Paul (2001), *Some Scientists in the Life of Christ Church, Oxford*, Oxford: Oxford University Press.

Kent, Paul and Chapman, Allan (eds) (2005), *Robert Hooke and the English Renaissance*, Leominster: Gracewing.

Kepler, Johannes (1619), *Harmonices Mundi Libri 5*, Linz: G. Tampachi. Reprinted 1969 in *Bibliotecha musica Bononiensis*, Sezione 2, no. 58, Bologna: Forni.

—— (1992), *New Astronomy*, translation of *Astronomia Nova* (1607) by William H. Donahue, Cambridge: Cambridge University Press.

Keynes, Sir Geoffrey (1960), *A Bibliography of Dr Robert Hooke*, Oxford: Clarendon Press.

King, Henry C. (1955), *The History of the Telescope*, London: Charles Griffin & Co.

Knellwolf, Christa (2001), 'Robert Hooke's *Micrographia* and the aesthetics of empiricism', in *The 17th Century* **16**, 177–200.

Knoop, D. and Jones, G. P. (1935), *The London Mason in the Seventeenth Century*, Manchester: Manchester University Press. Also published as *Ars Quatuor Coronatorum*, **48**.

Knowlson, James (1975), *Universal Language Schemes in England and France 1600–1800*, Toronto: University of Toronto Press.

Koyré, Alexandre (1950), 'A note on Robert Hooke', *Isis* **41**, 195–6.

—— (1952), 'An unpublished letter of Robert Hooke to Isaac Newton', *Isis* **43**, 312–37. Reprinted in Koyré (1965), pp. 221–60.

—— (1955), 'A documentary history of the problem of fall from Kepler to Newton', *Transactions of the American Philosophical Society* **45**, 329–95.

—— (1965), *Newtonian Studies*, Cambridge, Massachusetts: Harvard University Press.

Kroll, R. W. F. (1991), *The Material Word: Literate Culture in the Restoration and Early Eighteenth Century*, Baltimore: Johns Hopkins University Press.

Kubrin, D. C. (1968), 'Providence and the Mechanical Philosophy: the Creation and Dissolution of the World in Newtonian Thought', Cornell PhD thesis chapter 6.

Lancelloti, Secondo (1646), *L'Hoggidi, overo gl'ingegni non inferiori à'passati*, Venice: Guerigli.

Landauer, T. K. (1986), 'How much do people remember? Some estimates of the quantity of learned information in long-term memory', *Cognitive Science* **10**, 477–93.

Lang, Jane (1956), *Rebuilding St. Paul's after the Great Fire of London*. Oxford: Oxford University Press.

LeFanu, William (1990), *Nehemiah Grew: A Study and Bibliography of his Writings*, Winchester: St Paul's Bibliographies.

Lehmann-Haupt, H. (1973), 'The microscope and the book', *Festschrift für Clauss Nissen*, Wiesbaden, pp. 471–502.

Le Muet, Pierre (1663–64), *Manière de Bien Bastir Pour Toutes Sortes de Personnes*, Paris: chez Jean du Puis.

Leopold, J. H. (1976), '[Hooke's and Huygens's balance-spring inventions]', *Antiquarian Horology* **9**, 672–5.

Leybourne, William (1653, 1657, 1674, 1679 and 1722), *The Compleat Surveyor*, 1st, 2nd, 3rd, 4th and 5th edns respectively, London.

Lilley, Steven (1948), 'Robert Hooke and the modern music hall', *Discovery* **9**, 189.

Little, Brian (1975), *Sir Christopher Wren*, London: Robert Hale.

Lloyd, Claude (1929), 'Shadwell and the virtuosi', *Publications of the Modern Language Association of America* **44**, 472–94.

Lobel, Mary D. (ed.) (1989), *The British Atlas of Historical Towns*, vol. 3, Oxford: Oxford University Press.

Locke, John (1975), *An Essay Concerning Human Understanding*, ed. Peter H. Nidditch, Oxford: Clarendon Press.

—————— (1979), *Correspondence*, vol. 4, ed. E. S. de Beer, Oxford: Clarendon Press.

Loengard, J. S. (1989), *London Viewers and Their Certificates 1508–1558*, London: London Record Society.

Lohne, J. A. (1960), 'Hooke versus Newton: an analysis of the documents in the case of free fall and planetary motion', *Centaurus* **7**, 6–52.

London Topographical Society, The (1962a, b & c), *The Survey of Building Sites in the City of London after the Great Fire of 1666*, vols 3, 4 and 5, London: The London Topographical Society.

—————— (1964), *The Survey of Building Sites in the City of London after the Great Fire of 1666*, vol. 2, London: The London Topographical Society.

—————— (1967), *The Survey of Building Sites in the City of London after the Great Fire of 1666*, vol. 1, London: The London Topographical Society.

—————— (1992), *The A to Z of Restoration London (The City of London)*, London: The London Topographical Society.

—————— (1996), *Wyngaerde's Panorama of London circa 1544*, eds Sir Howard Colvin and Susan Foister, London: The London Topographical Society.

Long, Pamela O. (1991), 'Invention, authorship, "intellectual property", and the origin of patents: notes towards a conceptual history', *Technology and Culture* **32**, 846–84.

—————— (1999), ' Openness and empiricism: values and meanings in early architectural writings and in seventeenth-century experimental philosophy', in (q.v.) Galison and Thompson (eds) (1999), pp. 79–103.

Louw, H. J. (1983), 'The origin of the sash-window', *Architectural History* **26**, 49–72.

——— (1991), 'Window-glass making in Britain c.1660–c.1860 and its architectural impact', *Construction History*, **7**, 47–68.

——— (2003), 'The windows of Perrault's Observatory in Paris (1667–1683): the legacy of a proto-modern architectural inventor', *Construction History* **19**, pp. 19–46.

Louw, H. J. and Crayford, R. (1998), 'A constructional history of the sash-window c.1670–c.1725 part 1', *Architectural History* **41**, 82–130.

——— (1999), 'A constructional history of the sash-window c.1670–c.1725 part 2', *Architectural History* **42**, 173–239.

Low, D. A. (1946), *Heat Engines*, London: Longmans Green.

Lyell, Charles (1830), *Principles of Geology*, London: John Murray.

Lynch, William T. (2001), *Solomon's Child: Method in the Early Royal Society of London*, Stanford: Stanford University Press.

Lyons, Sir Henry (1944), *The Royal Society 1660–1940*, Cambridge: Cambridge University Press.

Lysacht, D. J. (1937), 'Hooke's theory of combustion', *Ambix* **1**, 93–108.

Mach, Ernst (1942), *The Science of Mechanics: A Critical and Historical Account of Its Development*, trans. Thomas J. McCormack, La Salle, Illinois: Open Court. Reprinted 1960.

MacIntosh, J. J. (1983), 'Perception and imagination in Descartes, Boyle and Hooke', *Canadian Journal of Philosophy* **13**, 327–52.

MacLeod, Christine (1988), *Inventing the Industrial Revolution. The English Patent System, 1660–1800*, Cambridge: Cambridge University Press.

Maddison, R. E. W. (1951), 'Studies in the life of Robert Boyle, 1', *Notes and Records of the Royal Society of London* **9**, 1–35.

——— (1969), *The Life of the Honourable Robert Boyle F. R. S.*, London: Taylor & Francis.

Malcolm, Noel (2002), *Aspects of Hobbes*, Oxford: Clarendon Press.

Manuel, Frank E. (1968), *A Portrait of Isaac Newton*, Cambridge, Massachusetts: Harvard University Press. Reprinted London: Frederick Muller Ltd, 1980.

Marot, Jean (c. 1660–70), *Recueil des Plans, Profils et Élévations de Plusieurs Palais, Chasteaux, Églises, Sepultures, Grotes et Hostels Bâtis dans Paris* [*Le Petit Marot*], Paris. Reprinted 1969, Farnborough: Gregg.

————— (1670), *L'Architecture Française* [*Le Grand Marot*]. Paris.

Marx, Karl (1954), *Capital – A Critique of Political Economy*, London: Lawrence & Wishart.

Masters, Betty R. (1974), *The Public Markets of the City of London Surveyed by William Leybourne in 1677*, London: The London Topographical Society.

Matthews, W. R. and Atkins, W. M. (eds) (1957), *A History of St Paul's Cathedral, and the Men Associated With It*, London: Phoenix House.

Matzke, E. B. (1943), 'The concept of cells held by Hooke and Grew', *Science* **98**, 13–14.

Mayo, Caroline (2001), 'Is the "A to Z of Restoration London" Accurate?', unpublished MSc dissertation, Department of Geomatic Engineering, University College London.

McConnell, Anita (1982), *No Sea Too Deep: a History of Oceanographic Instruments*, Bristol: Adam Hilger.

McKendrick, N. (1973), 'The role of science in the Industrial Revolution: a study of Josiah Wedgwood as a scientist and industrial chemist', in M. Teich and R. Young (eds) (1973), *Changing Perspectives in the History of Science; Essays in Honour of Joseph Needham*, London: Heinemann, pp. 274–319.

McKeon, Robert K. (1965), *Établissement de l'Astronome de Précision et Oeuvre d'Adrien Auzout, 2 fascicules*, Thèse présentée pour le Doctorat du Troisième Cycle, Université de Paris.

McKie, D. (1953) 'Flame and the flamma vitalis: Boyle, Hooke and Mayow', in E. A. Underwood (ed.) (1953), *Science, Medicine and History*, 2 vols, Oxford: Oxford University Press, pp. 469–88.

McKitterick, David (ed.) (1995), *The Making of the Wren Library, Trinity College, Cambridge*, Cambridge: Cambridge University Press.

McMath, R. R. and Mohler, O. C. (1960), 'Telescope driving mechanisms', in G. P. Kuiper and B. M. Middlehurst (eds) (1960), *Telescopes*, Chicago: University of Chicago Press, pp. 62–79.

Merritt, H. E. (1942), *Gears*, London: Pitman.

Merritt, J. F. (1998), 'Puritans, Laudians and the phenomenon of church-building in Jacobean London', *Historical Journal* **41**, 935–60.

Merton, R. K. (1970), *Science, Technology and Society in Seventeenth-century England*, New York: Howard Fertig, originally published in *Osiris*, **4**, 1938, pp. 360–632.

Metzger, Edward C. (1987), *Ralph, First Duke of Montagu 1638–1709*, Lewiston, New York: Edwin Mellen Press.

Meyer, F. (1930), 'Über die Entwicklung der astronomischen Instrumente im Zeisswerke "Jena"'. *Zeitschrift für Instrument-enkunde* **50**, 58–99.

Middleton, W. E. K. (1964), *The History of the Barometer*, Baltimore: Johns Hopkins University Press.

——— (1965), 'A footnote to the history of the barometer: an unpublished note by Robert Hooke', *Notes and Records of the Royal Society of London* **20**, 145–51.

——— (1966), *A History of the Thermometer and its Use in Meteorology*, Baltimore: Johns Hopkins University Press.

Middleton, William S. (1927), 'The medical aspect of Robert Hooke', *Annals of Medical History* **9**, 227–43.

Millington, E. C. (1945), 'Theories of cohesion in the seventeenth century', *Annals of Science* **5**, 227–43.

Mills, A. A., Hennessy, J. and Watson, S. (2003), 'Observations on the efficiency of gears', *Bulletin of the Scientific Instrument Society* **79**, 33–6.

Milne, Gustav (1986), *The Great Fire of London*, London and New Barnet: Historical Publications.

Montagu [Ralph, Duke of Montagu] (1709a), *The Court in Mourning. Being the Life ... of Ralph Duke of Montague, etc.*, London: J. Smith.

——— (1709b), 'Memoirs of the late Duke of Montagu', *The Monthly Miscellany, or Memoirs for the Curious* **3**, pp. 38–45 (February 1709) and pp. 77–82 (March 1709).

Montague, M. F. Ashley (1941), 'A spurious portrait of Robert Hooke', *Isis* **33**, 15–17.

More, L. T. (1944), *The Life and Works of the Honourable Robert Boyle*, Oxford: Oxford University Press.

Morgan, J. R. (1930–31), 'Robert Hooke (1635–1703) Part I', *Science Progress* **25**, 282–4.

Morgan, William (1682), *London &c Actually Survey'd*, London. Facsimile edn 1977, Lympne Castle, Kent: H. Margary, and London: Guildhall Library.

Moxon, Joseph (1703), *Mechanick Exercises, or the Doctrine of Handyworks*, originally published serially 1678–1700. Reprinted 1970, New York: Praeger; and 1975, Morristown, New Jersey: Astragal Press.

Moyer, A. E. (1977), 'Hooke's ambiguous presentation of Hooke's Law', *Isis* **68**, 266–75.

Mulligan, Lotte (1992a), 'Robert Hooke's "Memoranda": memory and natural history', *Annals of Science* **49**, 47–61.

——— (1992b), 'Robert Hooke and certain knowledge', *The Seventeenth Century* **7**, 151–69.

——— (1996), 'Self scrutiny and the study of nature: Robert Hooke's diary as natural history', *Journal of British Studies* **35**, 311–42.

Mulligan, Lotte, and Mulligan, Glen (1981), 'Reconstructing Restoration science: styles of leadership and social composition of the early Royal Society', *Social Studies of Science* **11**, 327–64.

Murat, I. (1984), *Colbert*, Charlottesville: University Press of Virginia.

Murdin, Lesley (1985), *Under Newton's Shadow: Astronomical Practices in the Seventeenth Century*, Bristol: Adam Hilger.

Nakajima, Hideto (1984), 'Two kinds of modification theory of light: some observations on the Newton-Hooke controversy of 1672 concerning the nature of light', *Annals of Science* **41**, 261–78.

———— (1994), 'Robert Hooke's family and his youth: some new evidence from the will of the Rev. John Hooke', *Notes and Records of the Royal Society of London* **48**, 11–16.

———— (2001), 'Astronomical aspects of Robert Hooke's scientific research', in G. Simon and S. Debarbat (eds) (2001), *Optics and Astronomy, Proceedings of the 20th International Congress of History of Science*, vol. 16, (Liege, 20–26 July 1997) Turnhout, Belgium: Brepols, pp. 161–6.

Nauenberg, Michael (1994a), 'Hooke, orbital motion, and Newton's *Principia*', *American Journal of Physics* **62**, 331–50.

———— (1994b), 'Newton's early computational model for dynamics', *Archive for History of the Exact Sciences* **46**, 221–52.

———— (1994c), 'Newton's *Principia* and inverse-square orbits', *The College Mathematical Journal* **25**, 212–22.

———— (1998), 'On Hooke's 1685 manuscript on orbital mechanics', *Historia Mathematica* **25**, 89–93.

———— (2000), 'Newton's Portsmouth perturbation method and its application to lunar motion', in (q.v.) Dalitz and Nauenberg (eds) (2000), pp. 157–94.

———— (2001), 'Newton's perturbation methods for three-body problem and their application to Lunar motion', in (q.v.) Buchwald and Cohen (eds) (2001), pp. 189–224.

———— (2003), 'Kepler's area law in the *Principia*: Filling in some details in Newton's proof of Proposition 1', *Historia Mathematica* **30**, 441–56.

Needham, Joseph (1959), *Science and Civilization in China*, vol. 3, Cambridge: Cambridge University Press.

Neufeld, M. W. (1927), 'Ein vorschlag zur herstellung künstlicher seider a.d.j. 1666 von Robert Hooke', *Kunstseide* **9**, 268.

Neville, R. G. (1962). 'The discovery of Boyle's law, 1661–2', *Journal of Chemical Education* **39**, 356–9.

Newton, Isaac (1687), *Philosophiae Naturalis Principia Mathematica*, London, 2nd edn 1713, 3rd edn 1726.

———— (1959–77), *Correspondence*, 7 vols, eds H. W. Turnbull, J. F.

Scott, A. R. Hall and Laura Tilling, Cambridge: Cambridge University Press.

——— (1967), *Mathematical Papers*, vol. 1, 1664–66, ed. D. T. Whiteside, Cambridge: Cambridge University Press.

——— (1969), *Mathematical Papers*, vol. 3, 1670–73, ed. D. T. Whiteside, Cambridge: Cambridge University Press.

——— (1974), *Mathematical Papers*, vol. 6, 1684–91, ed. D. T. Whiteside, Cambridge: Cambridge University Press.

——— (1989a), *De Motu Corporum in Gyrum*, 1684 manuscript, facsimile in (q.v.) Whiteside (ed.) (1989), pp. 3–11, translated with notes by (q.v.) Herivel (1965b), pp. 277–92 and by D. T. Whiteside in Newton (1974), pp. 30–91.

——— (1989b), 1684–5 manuscripts, facsimile in (q.v.) Whiteside (ed.) (1989), p. 20. Translation edited from (q.v.) Herivel (1965b), p. 301.

——— (1999), *The Principia*, trans I. B. Cohen and Anne Whitman, guide by I. B. Cohen, Berkeley, Los Angeles and London: California University Press.

Nichols, Richard (1994), *The Diaries of Robert Hooke, The Leonardo of London, 1635–1703*, Lewes, Sussex: The Book Guild.

——— (1999), *Robert Hooke and the Royal Society*, Lewes, Sussex: The Book Guild.

Nickles, T. (1990), 'Discovery', in R. C. Olby, et al, *Companion to the History of Modern Science*, London: Routledge, pp. 148–65.

Nicolson, M. H. (1935), 'The microscope and English imagination', *Smith College Studies in Modern Languages* **16**, no. 4.

——— (1956), *Science and Imagination*, Ithaca: Cornell University Press.

——— (1965), *Pepys' Diary and the New Science*, Charlottesville: University Press of Virginia.

Nicolson, M. H. and Mohler, N. M. (1937), 'The scientific background to Swift's "Voyage to Laputa" ', *Annals of Science* **2**, 299–334, abbreviated reprint in (q.v.) Nicolson (1956), pp. 110–54.

Niebauer, T. M., Sasagawa, G. S., Faller, E., Hilt, R. and Klopping, F. (1995), 'A new generation of absolute gravimeters', *Metrologia* **32**, 159–80.

Norman, C. A., Ault, E. S. and Zarobsky, I. F. (1938), *Fundamentals of Machine Design*, London: Macmillan.

O'Brien, G. W. (1970–80), 'Power, Henry', in (q.v.) Gillispie (ed.) (1970–80), vol. 11, pp. 121–2.

O'Connor, J. J. and Robertson, E. F. (2004), http://www-groups.dcs.st-and.ac.uk/history/Mathematics/Hooke.html

O'Donoghue, E. G. (1914), *The Story of Bethlehem Hospital From its Foundation in 1247*, London: T. Fisher Unwin.

Ogilby, John (1675), *Britannia, Volume the First: or, an Illustration of the Kingdom of England and Dominion of Wales: By a Geographical and Historical Description of the Principal Roads Thereof*, London.

Oldenburg, Henry (1965–86), *Correspondence*, 13 vols, eds A. R. and M. B. Hall, Madison: University of Wisconsin Press and London: Taylor & Francis.

Oldroyd, David (1972), 'Robert Hooke's methodology of science as exemplified in his "Discourse of Earthquakes"', *The British Journal for the History of Science* **6**, 109–30.

———— (1980), 'Some "Philosophicall Scribbles" attributed to Robert Hooke', *Notes and Records of the Royal Society of London* **35**, 17–32.

———— (1987), 'Some writings of Robert Hooke on procedures for the prosecution of scientific inquiry, including his "Lectures of Things Requisite to a Natural History" ', *Notes and Records of the Royal Society of London* **41**, 145–67.

———— (1989), 'Geological controversy in the seventeenth century: Hooke vs. Wallis and its aftermath', in (q.v.) Hunter and Schaffer (eds) (1989), pp. 207–33.

Olmsted, J. W. (1949), 'The "application" of telescopes to astronomical instruments, 1667–9', *Isis* **40**, 213–25.

Orton, T. and Roper, T. (2000), 'The role of mathematics in the teaching of science', *Studies in Science Education* **35**, 123–38.

Ottenheym, Koen (1989), *Philips Vingboons (1607–1678) Architect*, Zutphen: De Walburg Pers. See also Vingboons 1648 and 1674.

Oxford Dictionary of National Biography (ODNB), 56 vols (2004), eds H. C. G. Matthew and Brian Harrison Oxford: Oxford University Press.

Palladio, Andrea (1738), *The Four Books of Architecture*, trans. I. Ware, London. Originally published 1570 as *I Quattro Libri dell'Architettura*, Venice: appresso Domenico de' Franceschi.

Palter, Robert (1972), 'Early measurements of magnetic force', *Isis* **63**, 544–58.

Parker, S. (1666), *A Free and Impartial Censure of the Platonick Philosophie*, Oxford.

Patterson, L. D. (1948), 'Robert Hooke and the conservation of energy', *Isis* **38**, 151–6.

———— (1949), 'Hooke's gravitation theory and its influence on Newton. Part 1: Hooke's gravitation theory', *Isis* **40**, 327–41.

———— (1950a), 'Hooke's gravitation theory and its influence on

Newton. Part 2: the insufficiency of the traditional estimate ', *Isis* **41**, 32–45.

———— (1950b), 'A reply to Professor Koyré's note on Hooke', *Isis* **41**, 304–5.

———— (1951), 'Thermometers of the Royal Society', *American Journal of Physics* **19**, 523–55.

———— (1952), 'Pendulums of Wren and Hooke', *Osiris* **10**, 277–321.

———— (1953), 'The Royal Society's standard thermometer, 1663–1709', *Isis* **44**, 51–64.

Patterson, T. S. (1931), 'John Mayow in contemporary setting', *Isis* **15**, 47–96.

Pavlow, A. P. (1928), 'Robert Hooke, un évolutionist oublié du 17e siècle', *Palæobiologica* **1**, 203–10.

Pelseneer, Jean (1929), 'Une lettre inédite de Newton', *Isis* **12**, 237–54.

———— (1931), 'Un journal inédit de Hooke', *Isis* **15**, 97–103.

Pepys, Samuel (1972–86), *Diary*, 11 vols, eds R. C. Latham and William Matthews, London: Bell & Hyman.

Perez-Gomez, A. (1993), 'Introduction', to a new translation of Claude Perrault's *Ordonnance for the Five Kinds of Columns after the Method of the Ancients*, Santa Monica: Getty Center.

Perks, Sydney (1922), *The History of the Mansion House*, Cambridge: Cambridge University Press.

———— (1927), *Essays on Old London*, Cambridge: Cambridge University Press.

Perrault, C. (1700), *Recueil de Plusieurs Machines de Nouvelle Invention, Ouvrage Posthume*, Paris: Jean Baptiste Coignard.

Petzet, M. (1967), 'Claude Perrault als Architekt des Pariser Observatoriums', *Zeitschrift für Kunstgeschichte* **30**, 1–54.

Picard, Lisa (1997), *Restoration London*, London: Weidenfeld and Nicholson.

Picon, A. (1988), *Claude Perrault ou La Curiosité d'un Classique*, Paris: Picard.

———— (1992), *French Architects and Engineers in the Age of Enlightenment*, Cambridge: Cambridge University Press.

———— (1999), 'Architecture, science and technology', in (q.v.) Galison and Thompson (eds) (1999), pp. 309–38.

Polyani, Michael (1983), *The Tacit Dimension*, Gloucester, Massachusetts: Peter Smith.

Pope, Alexander (1965), *The Poems*, ed. John Butt, London: Methuen.

Porter, Roy (1977), *The Making of Geology: Earth Science in Britain 1660–1815*, Cambridge: Cambridge University Press.

———— (2000), *Enlightenment; Britain and the Creation of the Modern World*, London: Allen Lane.

Porter, Roy and Rousseau, G. S. (1998), *Gout: the Patrician Malady*, New Haven and London: Yale University Press.

Porter, Stephen (1996), *The Great Fire of London*, Stroud: Sutton Publishing.

Powell, Anthony (1963), *John Aubrey and his Friends*, new edn, London: Mercury Books.

Powell, Thomas (published anonymously) (1661), *Humane Industry: or, a History of most Manual Arts*, London: Herringman, Henry.

Power, Henry (1664), *Experimental Philosophy*, London.

Power, M. E. (1945), 'Sir Christopher Wren and the "Micrographia" ', *Transactions of the Connecticut Academy of Arts and Sciences* **36**, 37–44.

Price, D. J. de S. (1957), 'The manufacture of scientific instruments', in C. Singer (ed.) (1957), *History of Technology*, vol. 3, Oxford: Oxford University Press, pp. 620–47.

Pugliese, P. J. (1982), 'The Scientific Achievement of Robert Hooke, Method and Mechanics'. PhD thesis, Harvard University, Ann Arbor Michigan and London: Microfilms International.

—— (1989), 'Robert Hooke and the dynamics of motion in a curved path', in (q.v.) Hunter and Schaffer (eds) (1989), pp. 181–205.

—— (2004), 'Hooke, Robert (1635–1703), natural philosopher', in (q.v.) *Oxford Dictionary of National Biography*, (2004), vol. 27, pp. 951–8.

Pumfrey, Stephen (1991), 'Ideas above his station: a social study of Hooke's curatorship of experiments', *History of Science* **29**, 1–44.

—— (1995), 'Who did the work?', *The British Journal for the History of Science* **28**, 131–56.

Purver, Margery (1967), *The Royal Society: Concept and Creation*, London: Routledge & Kegan Paul.

Pyle, Andrew (ed.) (2000), *Dictionary of Seventeenth-Century British Philosophers*, Bristol: Thoemmes Press.

Rahman, A. (1957), 'Biography and science' [review of 'Espinasse (1935)], *Science Culture* **22**, 551–3.

Raman, V. V. (1972), 'Background to Newtonian gravitation', *Physics Teacher*, **10**, 439–42.

Ranalli, G. (1982), 'Robert Hooke and the Huttonian theory', *Journal of Geology* **90**, 319–25.

Rappaport, Rhoda (1986), 'Hooke on earthquakes: lectures, strategy and audience', *The British Journal for the History of Science* **19**, 129–46.

—— (1997), *When Geologists were Historians 1665–1750*, Ithaca: Cornell University Press.

Rasmussen, S. E. (1960), *London the Unique City*, abridged, Harmondsworth: Penguin Books. Originally published 1934, first English edition 1937, London: Jonathan Cape.

Ravetz, Jerome R. (1971), *Scientific Knowledge and its Social Problems*, Oxford: Clarendon Press.

Reddaway, T. F. (1940), *The Rebuilding of London after the Great Fire*, London: Jonathan Cape. Reprinted with minor changes 1951, London: Edward Arnold.

Richards, Graham (1992), *Mental Machinery. Part 1,The Origins and Consequences of Psychological Ideas from 1600 to 1850*, London: The Athlone Press.

Richards, P. W. (1981), 'Robert Hooke on mosses', *Occasional Papers of the Farlow Herbarium* **16**, 137–46.

Rigaud, Stephen (ed.) (1841), *Correspondence of Scientific Men*, 2 vols, Oxford: Oxford University Press. Reprinted 1965, Hildesheim: George Olms.

Robinson, H. W. (1938), 'Gleanings from a library: 1. A note on the early minutes', *Notes and Records of the Royal Society of London* **1**, 92–4. Reprinted as 'Hooke's pocket watch', *Annals of Science* **4** (1939), 322–3.

—— (1949), 'Robert Hooke as surveyor and architect', *Notes and Records of the Royal Society of London* **6**, 48–55.

Rosenfeld, L. (1927), 'Le théorie des couleurs de Newton et ses adversaires', *Isis* **9**, 44–65.

Rossi, Paolo (1970), *Philosophy, Technology and the Arts in the Early Modern Era*, New York: Harper and Row.

—— (1984), *The Dark Abyss of Time: the History of the Earth and the History of the Nations from Hooke to Vico*, English translation, Chicago: University of Chicago Press.

Rossiter, A. P. (1935), 'The first English geologist Robert Hooke (1635–1703)', *Durham University Journal* **28**, 172–81.

Rostenberg, Leona (1989), *The Library of Robert Hooke; the Scientific Book Trade of Restoration England*, Santa Monica: Modoc Press.

Rouse Ball, W. W. (1893), *An Essay on Newton's 'Principia'*, London and New York: Macmillan.

Royal Commission on Historical Monuments (RCHM) (1924), vol. 'Westminster Abbey', London: RCHM.

Rudwick, Martin (1972), *The Meaning of Fossils: Episodes in the History of Geology*, London: Macdonald & Co.

Ruestow, Edward G. (1996), *The Microscope in the Dutch Republic: the Shaping of Discovery*, Cambridge: Cambridge University Press.

Ruffner, J. A. (1966), 'The Background and Early Development of

Newton's Theory of Comets', PhD thesis, Indiana University, chapter 6.

Russell, D. (1997), *Scenes from Bedlam*, London: Baillère Tindall.

Russell, J. L. (1964), 'Kepler's laws of planetary motion 1609–1666', *The British Journal for the History of Science* **2**, 1–24.

Sabra, A. I. (1967), *Theories of Light from Descartes to Newton*, London: Oldbourne.

Salmon, Vivian (1974), 'John Wilkins's Essay (1668): critics and continuators', *Historiographia Linguistica* **1**, 147–63. Reprinted in Salmon, V. (1979), *The Study of Language in Seventeenth-century England*, Amsterdam: John Benjamins B.V., pp. 191–206.

Salzman, L. F. (1952), *Building in England Down to 1540*, Oxford: Oxford University Press.

Sargeaunt, John (1898), *Annals of Westminster School*, London: Methuen.

Saunders, Ann (1997), 'The second Exchange 1669–1838', in (q.v.) Saunders (ed.) (1997), pp. 121–35.

—— (ed.) (1997), *The Royal Exchange*, London: The London Topographical Society.

Saunier, C. (1867), *Treatise on Modern Horology in Theory and Practice*, trans. J. Tripplin and E. Rigg, London: Tripplin and Rigg.

Savot, Louis (1624), *L'Architecture Françoise des Bastimens Particuliers*, Paris: S. Cramoisy.

Scala, Gail Ewald (1974), 'An index of proper names in Thomas Birch, "The History of the Royal Society" ', *Notes and Records of the Royal Society of London* **28**, 263–329.

Schaffer, Simon (1987), 'Godly men and mechanical philosophers: souls and spirits in Restoration natural philosophy', *Science in Context* **1**, 55–85.

—— (1989), 'Glass works: Newton's Prisms and the Uses of Experiment', in David Gooding Trevor Pinch and Simon Schaffer (eds) (1989), *The Uses of Experiment: Studies in the Natural Sciences*, Cambridge: Cambridge University Press, pp. 67–104.

—— (1998), 'Regeneration: the body of natural philosophers in Restoration England', in Christopher Lawrence and Steven Shapin (eds) (1998), *Science incarnate: historical embodiments of natural knowledge*, Chicago: University of Chicago Press, pp. 83–120.

Schneer, Cecil J. (1954), 'The rise of historical geology in the seventeenth century', *Isis* **45**, 256–68.

—— (1960), 'Kepler's New Year's gift of a snowflake', *Isis* **51**, 531–45.

Schofield, John (ed.) (1987), *The London Surveys of Ralph Treswell*, London: The London Topographical Society.

Scull, A. (1996), *Masters of Bedlam*, Princeton: Princeton University Press.

Serlio, Sebastiano (1584), *I Sette Libri dell'Architettura*, Venice. Facsimile edn 1978, Forni: Sala Bolognese.

Shadwell, Thomas (1966), *The Virtuoso*, ed. M. H. Nicolson and David Rodes, London: Edward Arnold.

Shapin, Steven (1988a), 'The house of experiment in seventeenth-century England', *Isis* **79**, 373–404.

—— (1988b), 'Robert Boyle and mathematics: reality, representation and experimental practice', *Science in Context* **2**, 23–58.

—— (1989), 'Who was Robert Hooke?', in (q.v.) Hunter and Schaffer (eds) (1989), pp. 253–85.

—— (1994), *A Social History of Truth; Civility and Science in Seventeenth-Century England*, Chicago: Chicago University Press.

—— (1996), *The Scientific Revolution*, Chicago: Chicago University Press.

—— (2003), [Review of Inwood 2002], *London Review of Books*, 6 March 2003.

Shapin, Steven and Schaffer, Simon (1985), *Leviathan and the Air-pump. Hobbes, Boyle and the Experimental Life*, Princeton: Princeton University Press.

Shapiro, Alan (1973), 'Kinematic optics: a study of the wave theory of light in the seventeenth century', *Archive for the History of Exact Sciences* **11**, 134–266.

Sheepshanks, R. (1836), 'On a clock for giving motion in Right Ascension to equatorial instruments', *Monthly Notices of the Royal Astronomical Society* **3**, 40–6.

Sheppard, F. H. W. (ed.) (1960), *Survey of London*, vol. 29, 'The Parish of St James Westminster', London: The Athlone Press.

Shirley, John W. (1983), *Thomas Harriot: A Biography*, Oxford: Clarendon Press.

Siemens, C. W. (1866), 'On uniform rotation', *Philosophical Transactions of the Royal Society of London* **156**, 657–70.

Simpson, A. D. C. (1981), 'The Early Development of the Reflecting Telescopes in Britain', unpublished PhD thesis, Edinburgh University.

—— (1984). 'Newton's telescope and the cataloguing of the Royal Society's repository', *Notes and Records of the Royal Society of London* **38**, 187–214.

—— (1989), 'Robert Hooke and practical optics: technical support at a scientific frontier', in (q.v.) Hunter and Schaffer (eds) (1989), pp. 33–61.

Singer, B. R. (1976), 'Robert Hooke on memory, association and perception', *Notes and Records of the Royal Society of London* **31**, 115–31.

Singer, Charles (1955), 'The first English microscopist, Robert Hooke', *Endeavour* **14**, 12–8.

Slaughter, M. M. (1982), *Universal Languages and Scientific Taxonomy in the Seventeenth Century*, Cambridge: Cambridge University Press.

Smith, E. H. (1994), *Mechanical Engineer's Reference Book*, London: Butterworth Heinemann.

Smith, Maurice, (2000), *The Father of Modern Science and an 'Unsung' Hero*, http://www.microscopy-uk.org.uk

Soo, L. M. (1998), *Wren's 'Tracts on Architecture' and Other Writings*, Cambridge: Cambridge University Press.

South, Robert (1717), *Twelve Sermons and Discourses on Several Subjects and Occasions*, London.

Speake, C. C., Niebauer, T. M., McHugh, M. P., Keyser, P. T., Faller, E., Cruz, Y., Harrison, J. C., Mäkinen, Jaako and Beruff, R. B. (1990), 'Test of the inverse-square law of gravitation using the 300-m tower at Erie, Colorado', *Physical Review Letters* **65**, 1967–71.

Spedding, J., Ellis, R. and Heath D. (eds) (1870), *The Works of Francis Bacon*, vol. 4, 'Novum Organum', London: Longmans and Company.

Sprat, Thomas (1667), *The History of the Royal Society of London for the Improving of Natural Knowledge*, London. Reprinted J. I. Cope and H. W. Jones (eds) (1959), St Louis: Washington University Press, and London: Routledge and Kegan Paul.

Steele, Richard (1714), *The Lover*, **27**, 27 April, London.

Steno, Nicolaus (1669), *De Solido Intra Solidum Naturaliter Contento Dissertationis Prodomus*, Florence. English version with notes by J. G. Winter (ed.) (1916) New York: Macmillan.

Stephenson, Bruce (1987), *Kepler's Physical Astronomy*, Princeton: Princeton University Press.

Stevenson, Christine (1996a), 'Robert Hooke's Bethlem', *Journal of the Society of Architectural Historians* **55**, 254–75.

—— (1996b), *Medicine and Magnificence; British Hospital and Asylum Architecture 1660–1815*, New Haven and London: Yale University Press.

—— (2005), 'Robert Hooke, monuments and memory', *Art History* **28**, 43–73.

Stimson, Dorothy (1948), *Scientists and Amateurs: a History of the Royal Society*, New York: Henry Schuman.

Stoesser, Alison (1997), 'Robert Hooke and Holland: Dutch Influence on Hooke's Architecture', 3 vols, (unpublished dissertation), Doctoraalscriptie Bouwkunst Rijksuniversiteit Utrecht.

————— (2000), 'Robert Hooke and Holland: Dutch influence on his architecture', *Bulletin KNOB; Bulletin van de Koninklijke Oudheidkundige Bond* **99**, 121–37.

————— (2003), 'The influence of Dutch classicist architects on the works of Robert Hooke, scientist and architect', in Juliette Roding et al (eds) (2003), *Dutch and Flemish Artists in Britain 1550–1800, Leids Kunsthistorisch Jaarboek* **13**, pp. 189–206.

Stow, John (1720), *A Survey of the Cities of London and Westminster ... Brought Down from the Year 1633 ... to the Present Time by J. Strype*, 2 vols, London.

Stroup, A. (1990), *A Company of Scientists: Botany, Patronage, and Community at the Seventeenth- Century Parisian Academy of Sciences*, Berkeley: University of California Press.

Stubbe, Henry (1659), *Sundry Things From Severall Hands Concerning the University of Oxford*, London.

Summerson, John (1963), 'The mind of Wren', in John Summerson (1963), *Heavenly Mansions*, New York: Norton, pp. 51–86.

Summerson, Sir John (1990), 'Christopher Wren: why architecture?', in Sir John Summerson (1990), *The Unromantic Castle and Other Essays*, London: Thames & Hudson, pp. 64–8.

————— (1993), *Architecture in Britain 1530–1830*, 9th edn, New Haven and London: Yale University Press.

Symonds, R. W. (1952), 'Robert Hooke and Thomas Tompion', in *Illustrated Catalogue to British Clockmakers' Heritage Exhibition*, London: Science Museum.

Tanford, Charles and Reynolds, Jacqueline (1995), *A Travel Guide to Scientific Sites of the British Isles*, Chichester: Wiley.

Taylor, E. G. R. (1937a), 'The geographical ideas of Robert Hooke', *Geographical Journal* **89**, 525–8.

————— (1937b), 'Robert Hooke and the cartographical projects of the late seventeenth century (1666–1696)', *Geographical Journal* **90**, 529–40.

————— (1940), 'The *English Atlas* of Moses Pitt' 1680–83', *Geographical Journal* **95**, 292–9.

————— (1950), 'The origins of continents and oceans: a seventeenth-century controversy', *Geogrpahical Journal* **116**, 193–8.

————— (1954), *The Mathematical Practitioners of Tudor and Stuart England 1485–1714*, Cambridge: Cambridge University Press.

Thompson, Sir Edward M. (undated), *History of the British Museum*, unpublished manuscript, British Library Add. MS. 52292.

Thomson, Gladys S. (1940), *The Russells in Bloomsbury 1669–1771*, London: Jonathan Cape.

Thurley, Simon (1998), *The Whitehall Palace Plan of 1670*, London: The London Topographical Society.

Timbs, John (1898), *Clubs and Club Life in London*, London: Chatto and Windus.

Tipping, H. Avery (1924a), 'Ragley Hall Warwickshire I and II', *Country Life*, 22 March, 438–45 and 29 March, 476–82.

Toomer, Gerald James (1996), *Eastern Wisedome and Learning*, Oxford: Clarendon Press.

Tozer, E. T. (1990), 'Discovery of an ammonoid specimen described by Robert Hooke', *Notes and Records of the Royal Society of London* **44**, 3–12.

Turnbull, Herbert Westren (1939), *James Gregory Tercentenary Memorial Volume*, London: G. Bell & Sons.

Turner, A. J. (1973), 'Mathematical instruments and the education of gentlemen', *Annals of Science* **30**, 51–88.

—— (1974), 'Hooke's theory of the earth's axial displacement: some contemporary opinions', *The British Journal for the History of Science* **7**, 116–70.

—— (1994), 'Learning and language in the Somerset Levels: Andrew Paschall of Chedsey', in W. D. Hackmann and A. J. Turner (eds) (1994), *Learning, Language and Invention*, Aldershot and Paris: Variorum and Société Internationale de l'Astrolabe, pp. 297–308.

Turner, G. L'E. (1980), *Essays on the History of the Microscope*, Oxford: Senecio Publishing Co. Ltd.

—— (1981), *Collecting Microscopes*, London: Studio Vista.

Turner, H. D. (1956), 'Robert Hooke and theories of combustion', *Centaurus* **4**, 297–310.

—— (1959), 'Robert Hooke and Boyle's air pump', *Nature* **184**, 395–7.

Van Campen: see Campen, Jacob van.

Van Eerde: see Eerde, Katherine S. van.

Van Helden: see Helden, Albert van.

Vingboons, Philips (1648), *Afbeelsels der Voornaemste Gebovwen uyt alle die Philips Vingboons Geordineert Heeft part 1*, Amsterdam: The Author and Johannes Vingboons, facsimile in (q.v.) Ottenheym (1989), pp. 185–226.

—— (1674), *Tweede Deel van de Afbeeldsels der Voornaemste Gebovwen uyt alle die Philips Vingboons Geordineert Heeft part 2*, Amsterdam: The Author, facsimile in (q.v.) Ottenheym (1989), pp. 227–70.

Walker, H. (1952), 'Worm gear design', *The Engineer* **194**, 110–14.

Walker, William (1655), *A Treatise of English Particles*, London.

Wallis, Helen (1994), 'Navigators and mathematical practitioners in Samuel Pepys's day', *The Journal of Navigation* **47**, 1–19.

Walpole, Horace, Earl of Orford (1826–28), *Anecdotes of Painting in England*, 5th edn, 5 vols, London: John Major.

Ward, G. R. M. (trans.) (1845–51), *Oxford University Statutes*, 2 vols, London.

Ward, John (1740), *The Lives of the Professors of Gresham College*, London.

Ward, Ned (1927), *The London Spy*, ed. A.L. Hayward, London: Cassell.

Wattie, Margaret (1937), see 'Espinasse 1937.

Webster, Charles (1963), 'Richard Towneley and Boyle's Law', *Nature* **197**, 226–8.

———— (1965), 'The discovery of Boyle's Law and the concept of elasticity of air in the seventeenth century', *Archive for History of the Exact Sciences* **2**, 441–502.

———— (1970–80), 'Towneley, Richard', in (q.v.) Gillispie (ed.) (1970–80), vol. 13, pp. 444–5.

———— (ed.) (1974), *The Intellectual Revolution of the Seventeenth Century*, London: Routledge & Kegan Paul.

Welch, Charles (1893), *History of the Monument*, London: Corporation of London.

Westfall, Richard S. (1962a), 'The development of Newton's theory of colour', *Isis* **53**, 339–58.

———— (1962b), 'Newton and his critics on the nature of colours', *Archives Internationales d'Histoire des Sciences* **15**, 47–59.

———— (1963), 'Newton's reply to Hooke and the theory of colours', *Isis* **54**, 82–96.

———— (1966), 'Newton defends his first publication', *Isis* **57**, 299–314.

———— (1967), 'Hooke and the law of universal gravitation', *The British Journal for the History of Science* **3**, 245–61.

———— (1969), 'Introduction' in reprint of (q.v.) Hooke (1705), New York: Johnson Reprint Corporation.

———— (1970–80), 'Hooke, Robert', in (q.v.) Gillispie (ed.) (1970–80), vol. 6, pp. 481–8.

———— (1971a), *Force in Newton's Physics: the Science of Dynamics in the Seventeenth Century*, London: Macdonald and New York: American Elsevier.

———— (1971b), *The Construction of Modern Science: Mechanisms and Mechanics*, New York and Chichester: Wiley.

———— (1980), *Never at Rest; a Biography of Isaac Newton*, Cambridge: Cambridge University Press.

———— (1983), 'Robert Hooke, mechanical technology and scientific investigation', in (q.v.) Burke (ed.) (1983), pp. 85–110.

Westman, R. S. (1980), 'The astronomer's role in the sixteenth century: a preliminary study', *History of Science* **18**, 105–47.

Wetenhall, Edward (1678), *Of the Gift and Duty of Singing to God*, Dublin.

Whiteside, Derek T. (1964), 'Newton's early thoughts on planetary motion: a fresh look', *The British Journal for the History of Science* **2**, 118–37.

———— (1970a), 'Before the *Principia*, the maturing of Newton's thoughts on dynamical astronomy, 1664–1684', *Journal for the History of Astronomy* **1**, 5–19.

———— (1970b), 'The mathematical principles underlying Newton's *Principia Mathematica*', *Journal for the History of Astronomy* **1**, 116–38.

———— (ed.) (1989), *The preliminary manuscripts for Isaac Newton's 1687 'Principia', 1684–1685*, Cambridge: Cambridge University Press.

———— (1991), 'The prehistory of the *Principia* from 1664 to 1686', *Notes and Records of the Royal Society of London* **45**, 11–61.

Whitrow, G. (1938), 'Robert Hooke', *Philosophy of Science* **5**, 493–502.

Wilchinsky, Z. (1939), 'The theoretical treatment of Hooke's law', *American Physics Teacher* **7**, 134.

Wilkins, John (1668), *An Essay Towards a Real Character and a Philosophical Language*, London.

Williams, E. (1956), 'Hooke's law and the concept of the elastic limit', *Annals of Science* **12**, 74–83.

Willmoth, Frances (1987), 'John Flamsteed's letter concerning the natural causes of earthquakes', *Annals of Science* **44**, 23–70.

———— (1993), *Sir Jonas Moore; Practical Mathematics and Restoration Science*, Woodbridge: Boydell Press.

Wilson, C. A. (1970), 'From Kepler's laws, so-called, to universal gravitation: empirical factors', *Archive for the History of Exact Sciences* **6**, 89–170.

Wilson, Catherine (1995), *The Invisible World: Early Modern Philosophy and the Invention of the Microscope*, Princeton: Princeton University Press.

Wilson, L. G. (1960), 'The transformation of the ancient concept of respiration in the seventeenth century', *Isis* **51**, 161–72.

Winn, James Anderson (1987), *John Dryden and His World*, New Haven and London: Yale University Press.

Wing, Vincent (1665), *Examen Astronomiæ Carlinæ*, London.

Wittkower, Rudolph (1982), *Art and Architecture of Italy 1600 to 1750*, 5th edn, New Haven and London: Yale University Press.

Wolpert, Lewis (1992), *The Unnatural Nature of Science*, London: Faber and Faber.

Wood, P. B. (1978), 'Francis Bacon and the "Experimentall Philosophy": a Study in Seventeenth-century Methodology', MPhil thesis, University of London, chapter 3.

———— (1980), 'Methodology and apologetics. Thomas Sprat's "History of the Royal Society" ', *The British Journal for the History of Science* **13**, 1–26.

Woodbridge, Kenneth (1986), *Princely Gardens: the Origins and Development of the French Formal Style*, London: Thames and Hudson.

Woodhead, J. R. (1965), *The Rulers of London 1660–1689*, London: London & Middlesex Archaeological Society.

Woodruff, L. C. (1919), 'Hooke's *Micrographia*', *American Naturalist* **53**, 247–64.

Woodward, John (1695), *An Essay Towards a Natural History of the Earth ...*, London: Ric. Wilkin. Reprinted 1978, New York: Arno Press.

Worsley, Giles (2004), 'Taking Hooke seriously', *The Georgian Group Journal* **14**, 1–25.

Wren, Christopher (jun.) (ed.) (1750), *Parentalia, or Memoirs of the Family of Wrens*, London. Reprinted 1965, Farnborough: Gregg Press.

Wren Society (1924–43), *Wren Society Publications*, 20 vols, Oxford: Oxford University Press for the Wren Society.

Wright, Michael (1989), 'Robert Hooke's longitude timekeeper', in (q.v.) Hunter and Schaffer (eds) (1989), pp. 63–118.

Young, Elizabeth and Wayland (1956), *Old London Churches*, London: Faber and Faber.

Young, C. (1930), 'Driving and controlling mechanism of the 36-inch reflecting telescope of the Royal Observatory, Edinburgh', *Journal of Scientific Instruments* **7**, 264–67.

Notes

Introduction

1   Inwood 2002; Bennett et al. 2003; Cooper 2003b; Jardine 2003b. See also Pugliese 2004.
2   Kent and Chapman (eds) 2005 and Chapman 2005.
3   For full details here and herafter, see the entries under these authors in the bibliography.
4   See Hooke 1998.
5   Hooke 1989.
6   Harwood 1989; Dennis 1989; Wilson 1995; Ruestow 1996.
7   Johns 1998, pp. 428–34; for example, Shapin 1996; Jardine 1999.
8   Cooper 2004.
9   Wright 1989. A more recent exception is Chapman 2005. Another recent example, notable for its popular appeal, is volume 5 of a magazine of science for adults published in Japan in 2004 by Gakken. The magazine, accompanied by a box containing components of Hooke's microscope, gives detailed instructions on how to assemble a scaled-down replica of Hooke's microscope and how to use it to examine many of the objects illustrated in *Micrographia*. See www.gakken.co.jp
10 See Hunter in Bennett et al 2003.
11 Howard (forthcoming).
12 Worsley 2004.
13 On Hooke's ideas on music, see also: Kassler and Oldroyd 1983; Kassler 1995.
14 For further comments on this topic, see Hunter in Bennett et al 2003, pp. 145–50.
15 See Tanford and Reynolds 1995, p. 110.
16 Patterson 1950a, p. 44.

Chapter 1

1   Newton 1687; reprinted London: William Dawson & Sons (undated); revised 2nd edition, 1713; 3rd edition, 1726; third edition translated by Andrew Motte, *The Mathematical Principles of Natural Philosophy*, 2 vols (London: Benjamin Motte, 1729); reprinted with an introduction by I. Bernard Cohen (London: Dawsons of Pall Mall, 1968); revised by Florian Cajori, *Sir Isaac Newton's Mathematical Principles of Natural Philosophy and His System of the World*, 2 vols. (Berkeley: University of California Press, 1962; reprinted New York: Greenwood Press, 1969). See also: Chandrasekhar 1995; Cohen 1971; Guicciardini 1999; Newton 1999.
2   Symptomatic of the neglect of Hooke and his legacy is that he is virtually alone among the great scientists of the past for whom no extant portrait exists.
3   Hunter and Schaffer 1989; Andrade 1950, 1954; 'Espinasse 1956.
4   Gunther 1930a, 1930b, 1931, 1935 and 1938; reprinted 1968–69, London: Dawsons of Pall Mall.

5   Mach 1942, p. 230.
6   Rouse Ball 1893.
7   Pelseneer 1929; Koyré 1952, reprinted in Koyré 1965.
8   Centore 1970; Cohen 1980, 1981, 1985; Hall, A. R. 1983; Patterson 1949, 1950a; Westfall 1967, 1971a, 1980; Whiteside 1964, 1970a, 1970b.
9   Dugas 1955 pp. 331–56, 1958 pp. 353–72.
10 Hooke 1678a. Also in Gunther 1931, pp. 331–56.
11 Bennett et al 2003; Cooper 2003b; Drake 1996; Gal 2002; Inwood 2002; Jardine 2003b; Nichols 1994; Pugliese 1982.
12 Newton 1959–77, vol. 2, p. 297.
13 Westfall 1980, p. 383.
14 Newton 1959–77, vol. 2, pp. 435–7.
15 Cohen 1971, p. 293; see also Lohne 1960, pp. 48–9.
16 Nauenberg 1994b.
17 Nauenberg 1994a, 1998; see also Pugliese 1989, pp. 200–4.
18 Newton 1989a. For a discussion see Whiteside 1991.
19 Descartes 1983, plate ii, p. 290.
20 Huygens 1888–1950, vol. 16 'Percussion Etc' [1929] pp. 253–301: 'De Vi Centrifuga' [1659]. For Newton see: Herivel 1965b, pp. 192–8; Hall 1957.
21 Nauenberg, 1994b.
22 Quoted in Brackenridge 1995, p. 63; also quoted with some variations in Herival 1965b, p. 130.
23 Newton 1959–77, vol. 2, pp. 307–8.
24 Nauenberg 1994b.
25 James Crompton (1648–94), an astronomer who was elected as a Fellow of Jesus College, Cambridge, in 1672.
26 Newton 1959–77, vol. 2, p. 361.
27 Nauenberg 1994b; Brackenridge and Nauenberg 2002.
28 Nauenberg 2000, 2001.
29 Brackenridge 1995, pp. 217–8; Chandrasekhar 1995, p. 115. Without justification Chandrasekhar claims that 'these simple relations must have escaped him [Newton] during the two years when he was under extreme pressure of writing the *Principia*; and that they became transparent to him during his "lonely voyages", in the leisure of his London years.'
30 Nauenberg 1994b.
31 Nauenberg 2003.
32 Reproduced in Whiteside 1991, p. 13.
33 Quoted in Newton 1999, p. 444.
34 Hooke 1705, p.xxviii. Also in Gunther 1930a, p. 67.
35 Hooke 1674a; reprinted in Gunther 1931, pp. 1–28; reported in 1674 *Philosophical Transactions* 9, 12–3.
36 See Hooke's 'A Discourse of the Nature of Comets [1682]', in Hooke 1705, pp. 184–5.
37 Patterson 1949, 1950a.
38 Giovanni Alfonso Borelli (1608–79), Italian physicist and astronomer who published *Theoricæ Mediceorum Planetarum ex causis physicis deductæ* in 1666 in which he supposed that a centrifugal tendency acted on a planet and counterbalanced the gravitational attraction of the Sun.
39 Ismael Bouillaud (Ismaelis Bullialdi [Bullialdus], 1605–94), French librarian, priest and eminent astronomer and mathematician who published *Astronomia Philolaica* in 1645 based upon Copernicus's and Kepler's discoveries.
40 Newton to Halley, dated 20 June 1686 in Newton 1959–77, vol. 2, p. 438.
41 Halley to Newton, dated 22 May 1686 in Newton 1959–77, vol. 2, p. 431.
42 Nauenberg 1994b.

43 Quoted in Cajori, *Newton's Mathematical Principles*, p. 550 (see note 1 above).

44 Lohne 1960; Arnol'd 1990.

45 Marcus Marci (1595–1667), Bohemian physician and professor of medicine at the University of Prague (1620–60) who published *De proportione motus* in 1639 describing his theory and experiments on collisions of bodies, and *Thaumantias liber de arcu coelesti* in 1648 reporting his researches on optics.

46 A. R. Hall 1983, p. 303.

47 A. R. Hall 1983, p. 314.

48 Quoted in French in Rouse Ball 1893, p. 69: 'servent à faire voir quelle distance il y a entre une verité entrevue et une verité demontreé ...'. Rouse Ball cited as his source Stephen Peter Rigaud, *Historical Essay on the First Publication of Sir Isaac Newton's Principia* (Oxford: Oxford University Press, 1838), p. 66, which has been reprinted with an Introduction by I. Bernard Cohen (New York and London: Johnson Reprint Corporation, 1972), p. 66.

49 See Hooke's 'Motion in a Curve. A Statement of Planetary Movements as a Mechanical Problem [1666]', in Gunther 1930a, pp. 265–8.

50 See Hooke's 'A Discourse of the Nature of Comets [1682]' in Hooke 1705, p. 179.

51 Hooke 1705, p. 167.

52 Pugliese 1989, p. 202.

53 Newton 1989a.

54 Pugliese 1989, pp. 203, 200, 204.

55 Nauenberg 1994a, pp. 331–50.

56 Ibid.

57 Pugliese believes that Newton's *De Motu* was not 'generally known to members of the Royal Society prior to the appearance of his *Principia*,' the 'principal argument' being 'the total lack of discussion of its contents'; see Pugliese 1989, p. 203. Likewise, Mordechai Feingold, who is familiar with the history of the Royal Society, also believes that Halley did not circulate Newton's *De Motu* to members of the Royal Society (private communication 9 January 2004).

58 Newton 1959–77, vol. 2, p. 405.

59 Newton 1959–77, vol. 2, p. 442.

60 When the *Principia* was published in 1687, most of its readers, among whom were some of the best mathematicians in Europe, had considerable difficulties in understanding its contents and in particular the significance of Kepler's area law. For example, the French mathematician Pierre Varignon (1654–1722) assumed different laws for the time evolution of orbital motion, such as those proposed by the English astronomer Seth Ward (1617–89) and the Italian-French astronomer Giovanni Domenico Cassini (1625–1712): see Guicciardini 1999, pp. 202–5. Therefore it is revealing that Hooke recognized that Newton's proof of Kepler's area law in his *De Motu* was based upon his own principles of planetary motion.

61 Quoted in Herival 1965b, p. 278.

62 Ibid.

63 Quoted in Nauenberg 1994a, p. 347.

64 See: Hooke's 'A Statement of Planetary Movements [1666]' Gunther 1930a, pp. 265–267; Birch 1756–7, vol. 2, pp. 90–2.

65 Quoted in: Gunther 1930a, p. 265; Birch 1756–7, p. 91.

66 Armitage 1950 and Hall 1983, pp. 302–304.

67 See Hooke's 'Statement of Planetary Movements [1666]' in Gunther 1930a, p. 266.

68 Gunther 1930a, p. 267.

69 Ibid.

70 Richard S. Westfall commented in a letter to me of 22 January 1995, that 'your tracing of the ellipse is indeed quite remarkable. I have been willing, apriori, to assert with confidence that anything half so precise was impossible.' His remark

underscores the importance of repeating often-neglected historical experiments to understand their significance in shaping theoretical concepts.

71   Ibid.

72   Newton 1959–77, vol. 2, pp. 304–6; figure and quotation on p. 305.

73   The precession of the apsides (auges) arises because for noncircular motion the trajectory of a conical pendulum does not lie in a plane. The precession can be readily calculated for small eccentricities of the orbit.

74   Newton 1959–77, vol. 2, p. 305.

75   Nauenberg 1994a.

76   In his sixth Cutler Lecture, which he published in 1678, Hooke deciphered his anagram, *ceiiinosssttuu*, presented two years earlier, which translates to *ut tensio sic vis* (as the extension so the force); see Gunther 1931, pp. 333–4. It is not generally recognized that Hooke was able to obtain the correct phase–space relation between velocity and position for the harmonic oscillator, shown in a graph in a beautiful frontispiece of his paper. He also showed that the period of the spring was independent of amplitude, but he did not obtain the correct dependence of amplitude and velocity on time.

77   See Hooke's 'Gravity, [1666]' in Gunther 1930a, pp. 256–9.

78   The idea to demonstrate the motion of the earth by observing stellar parallax can be traced back to the ancient Greeks.

79   Hooke 1674a, p. 2; also in Gunther 1931, p. 2.

80   Gunther 1930a, p. 343.

81   After a few months, Hooke observed a displacement in the expected position of Gamma Draconis, but he tells us that unfortunately the objective lens of his telescope accidentally broke and he therefore discontinued his observations; see Hooke 1674a, p. 24 and Gunther 1931, p. 24. The English astronomers James Bradley (1693–1762) and Samuel Molyneux (1689–1728) repeated Hooke's observations in 1725 with a better telescope and discovered that the observed displacements could not be due to parallax, but they were unable to interpret them. By 1727, however, after erecting another telescope and continuing his observations, Bradley found the explanation as due to the finite velocity of light, which the Danish astronomer Ole Römer (1644–1710) had determined in 1676. Bradley thus was able to establish the motion of the Earth, finally accomplishing Hooke's *Attempt to Prove the Motion of the Earth from Observations*. See 'A Letter from the Reverend Mr. James Bradley *Savilian Professor of Astronomy at Oxford, and F.R.S. to Dr.* Edmund Halley, Astronom. Reg. &c. *giving an Account of a new discovered Motion of the* Fix'd Stars', *Philosophical Transactions* **35** (1727), 637–61; reprinted in *Miscellaneous Works and Correspondence of the Rev. James Bradley, D.D. F.R.S.* (Oxford: Oxford University Press, 1832; reprinted New York and London: Johnson Reprint Corporation, 1972), pp. 1–16.

82   Hooke 1674a, pp. 1–28; reported in *Philosophical Transactions* **9** (1674), 12–3.

83   I have substituted the names of the planets for the accepted symbols for them that Hooke used.

84   Hooke 1674a, pp. 27–8.

85   Gunther 1930a, pp. 22–3.

86   Cooper 2003b.

87   Newton 1959–77, vol. 2, p. 297.

88   Pelseneer 1929, p. 244.

89   Newton 1959–77, vol. 2, p. 309.

90   D. T. Whiteside quoted Hooke without however indicating that Hooke was referring to an experimental observation relevant to Newton's diagram, remarking only that: 'Inadequate or no, even such relatively unsophisticated reasonings [Newton's] were above Hooke's head and he could only compliantly answer …' (Newton 1974, p. 12). I have shown, however, that Newton's

reasonings were far from unsophisticated and instead demonstrated a remarkable theoretical understanding of the motion of a body moving under the action of a constant attractive central force, in good agreement with Hooke's observations (Nauenberg 1994b).

91 Newton 1959–77, vol. 2, p. 309.
92 Ibid.
93 Ibid.
94 Newton 1959–77, vol. 2, p. 313.
95 Newton 1959–77, vol. 2, pp. 300, 302.
96 Newton 1959–77, vol. 2, p. 301.
97 Newton 1959–77, vol 2, p. 298.
98 Hooke 1674a.
99 Newton 1959–77, vol. 2, pp. 446–7.
100 'A True state of the Case and Controversy between Sr Isaac Newton & Dr Robert Hooke as to the Priority of that Noble Hypothesis of Motion of the Planets about the Sun as their Centre', undated manuscript, Trinity College Library, Cambridge. Reproduced in Gunther 1935, pp. 56–60; on p. 60.
101 Hooke 1674a.
102 Henry Oldenburg, Secretary of the Royal Society, published extracts of Huygens's and Cassini's letters commenting on Hooke's tract in *Philosophical Transactions* **9** (1674), 91–2. Newton's correspondence with Hooke and Halley makes clear that he also had become familiar with Hooke's tract.
103 Quoted in Gunther 1935, p. 98. I thank Niccolò Guicciardini for translating the Latin into English.
104 Newton 1959–77, vol. 2, p. 309.
105 Ibid.
106 Newton 1959–77, vol. 2, pp. 435–6.
107 For example, Newton 1959–77, vol. 2, pp. 435–40.
108 Newton 1959–77, vol. 2, pp. 441–5.
109 Edward Paget (1656–1703?), Fellow of Trinity College, Cambridge, who was appointed as Mathematical Master at Christ's Hospital and was elected as a Fellow of the Royal Society in 1682.
110 Newton 1959–77, vol. 2, pp. 444–5.
111 Newton 1959–77, vol. 2, p. 447.
112 Newton 1959–77, vol. 2, p. 308.
113 Nauenberg 1994b. For Newton's work see: Newton 1967, pp. 252–5; Newton 1969, pp. 151–9.
114 Quoted in Cohen 1971, p. 293.
115 Newton 1959–77 vol. 2, p. 442.
116 Ibid.
117 Nauenberg 1994a.
118 Ibid; Nauenberg 1998.
119 Hooke 1705, pp. 184–5.
120 The handwriting is that of Charles Hayes, a self-taught mathematician who wrote a textbook on the differential calculus under the title *A treatise on fluxions* that was based in part on l'Hôpital's textbook (D. T. Whiteside, private communication, 1993.
121 Guillaume François Marquis de l'Hôpital, *Analyse des infiniment petits pour l'intelligence des lignes courbes* (Paris: l'Imprimerie Royale, 1696).
122 Gottfried Leibniz, 'Nova methodus pro maximis et minimis, itemque tangentibus, quae nec fractas nec irrationales quantitates moratur, et singulare pro illis calculi genus', *Acta Eruditorum* [Leipzig] **10** (1684), 467–73; reprinted in C. I. Gerhardt, *Leibnizens mathematische Schriften*, Band I, zweite Abtheilung (Halle: H. W. Schmidt, 1858), pp. 220–6; reprinted *Mathematische*

Schriften, Band V (Hildesheim and New York, Georg Ohms Verlag, 1971), pp. 220–6.

123   'A True state of the Case and Controversy between Sr Isaac Newton & Dr Robert Hooke as to the Priority of that Noble Hypothesis of Motion of the Planets about the Sun as their Centre', undated manuscript, Trinity College Library, Cambridge. Reproduced in Gunther 1935, pp. 56–60.

124   Quoted in Patterson 1949, p. 329.

125   Ibid.

126   Nauenberg 1994b.

127   Ibid.

128   Pelseneer 1929.

129   Newton 1974, vol. 6, pp. 149–52.

130   Nauenberg 1994b.

131   Quoted in Brackenridge 1995, p. 63.

132   Nauenberg 1994b.

133   Hooke to Newton, 24 November 1679, in Newton 1959–77, vol. 2, p. 297.

Chaper 2

1   Newton 1959–77, vol. 2, p. 313 dated 17 January 1680.

2   Gal 2002.

3   *Micrographia*, 'Preface', xi–xiii.

4   'Cæterum totum cœli Planetarij Spatium vel quiescit (ut vulgo creditur) vel uniformiter movetur in directum et perinde Planetarum commune centrum gravitatis ... vel quiescit vel una movetur. Utroque in casu motus gravitatis inter se ... eodem modo se habent, et eorum commune centrum gravitatis respectu spatij totius quiescit, atque adeo pro centro immobili Systematis totius Planetarij haberi debet. Inde vero systema Copernicæum probatur a priori. Nam si in quovis Planetarum situ computetur commune centrum gravitatis hoc vel incidet in corpus Solis vel ei semper proximum erit. Eo Solis a centro gravitatis errore fit ut vis centripeta non semper tendat ad centrum illud immobile, et inde ut planetæ nec moveantur in Ellipsibus exacte neque bis revolvant in eadem orbita. Tot sunt orbitæ Planetæ cujusque quot revolutiones, ut fit in motu Lun? et pendet orbita unaquaæque ab omnium Planetarum motibus conjunctis, ut taceam eorum omnium actiones in se invicem. Tot autem motuum causas simul considerare et legibus exactis calculum commodum admitentibus motus ipsos definire superat ni fallor vim omnium humani ingenii. Omitte minutias illas et orbita simplex et inter omnes errores mediocris erit Ellipsis de qua jam egi.' (Newton 1989b).

5   Hooke 1674a, pp. 27–8.

6   Newton 1959–77, vol. 2, p. 297.

7   Gal 2002, p. 20.

8   Birch 1756–57, vol. 2, p. 91, entry for 23 May 1666.

9   Gal 2002, pp. 21–2.

10   Birch 1756–57, vol. 2, p. 91, entry for 23 May 1666.

11   Descartes 1983, part 2, article 39.

12   Ibid.

13   Descartes 1983, part 3, article 30.

14   Descartes 1983, part 3, article 46.

15   In his 17 January 1680 letter to Newton (Newton 1959–77, vol. 2. p. 309) Hooke gets Kepler's area law wrong. In a 1666 lecture on gravitation to the Royal Society (Birch 1756–57, vol. 2, p. 70) he ascribes to Kepler his own view on the subject.

16 Kepler 1992, part 3, Chapter 32, p. 376.
17 Kepler 1992, p. 89 (summaries of chapters).
18 Wing 1665, p. 5.
19 Hooke 1665, p. 219.
20 Hooke 1665, p. 222.
21 Hooke 1665, p. 227.
22 Hooke 1665, p. 227, square parenthesis in the original.
23 Birch 1756–57, vol. 2, p. 70.
24 Kepler 1992, p. 119.
25 Kepler 1619, book 3, axiom 7, p. 146.
26 Newton 1959–77, vol. 2, p. 309.
27 Ibid.
28 Ibid, italics added.
29 Herivel 1965b, p. 301.
30 Hooke 1705, pp. 279–450. See also Drake 1996, pp. 159–365.
31 Hooke 1705, p. 290.
32 Hooke 1705, p. 291.
33 Hooke 1705, p. 322.
34 Hooke 1705, p. 291.
35 Hooke 1665, p. 227.
36 Birch 1756–57, vol. 2, p. 91.
37 Hooke 1674a, p. 26.
38 Newton 1959–77, vol. 2, p. 313.
39 Newton 1959–77, vol. 2, p. 306.
40 Birch 1756–57, vol. 2, p. 91.
41 Birch 1756–57, vol. 2, p. 92.
42 Ibid.
43 Birch 1756–57, vol. 2, p. 89 and *Philosophical Transactions* vol. 1 (1666), 263–89.
44 Birch 1756–57, vol. 2, p. 89.
45 Herivel 1965b, p. 301.

Chapter 3

1   Shapin 1989; Drake 1996; Inwood 2002; Bennett et al 2003; Cooper 2003; Jardine 2003b.
2   Hunter and Schaffer 1989, pp. 1–2.
3   Scala 1974, p. 295.
4   Helden 1968, p. 220 and Simpson 1989, p. 34, note 2.
5   Helden 1974.
6   Bonellli and Helden 1981, pp. 21 and 39.
7   Birch 1756–57 vol. 2, p. 74.
8   For example Bonelli and Helden 1981, p. 4, note 2.
9   Oldenburg 1965–86, vol. 3, pp. 248–59.
10 Oldenburg 1965–86, vol. 3, pp. 347–9 and ibid, plate 3, following p. 346. The original illustration by Hooke is Bibliothèque Nationale, Paris, MS N.a.L. 1641, fol. 10r.
11 Oldenburg 1965–86, vol. 4, pp. 443–9.
12 Oldenburg 1965–86, vol. 7, pp. 139–42.
13 See also Nakajima 2001, pp. 165–6.
14 Shapin and Schaffer 1985, p. 32.
15 Helden 1974, p. 38.
16 Hooke 1665, pp. 241–2.

17   Hooke 1665, pp. 242–6.
18   Hooke 1665, between pp. 242 and 243.
19   Hooke 1665, sig. e1r-e2v and Schema 1, Fig. 3.
20   Hooke 1665. sig. e2r.
21   Helden 1974, pp. 53–4.
22   Helden 1980, pp. 156–7.
23   Birch 1756–57, vol. 2, p. 139.
24   Hooke 1665, p. 237. Hooke continued: by this Instrument each Observer should, at Certain prefixt times observe the Moon or other Planet, in, or very near, the Meridian.
25   Rigaud 1841, vol. 2, pp. 33–59.
26   Bennett 1989, p. 22.
27   Bennett 1989, p. 25.
28   Hooke 1674b, p. 9.
29   Howse 1975, pp. 17–8, 75–9.
30   Hooke 1674a, see especially pp. 23 et seq.
31   Birch 1756–57, vol. 3, pp. 10–5.
32   Westfall 1962a.
33   Nakajima 1984, Birch 1756–57, vol. 3, p. 13.
34   Birch 1756–57, vol. 3, p. 12.
35   Birch 1756–57, vol. 2, p. 152.
36   Birch 1756–57, vol. 3, p. 1.
37   Simpson 1981, p. 111.
38   Newton 1959–77, vol. 1, p. 3.
39   Oldenburg 1965–86, vol. 9, pp. 116–20.
40   Simpson 1981, p. 82.
41   Bennett 1989, p. 49.
42   Turnbull 1939, p. 249.
43   Simpson 1981, p. 149.
44   Helden 1974, p. 49.

Chapter 4

1   Hooke 1665, Preface, sig. b1r.
2   Hooke 1705, pp. 62–3.
3   For example, in one of his 'Lectures concerning Navigation and Astronomy', he says that a standard foot measure was 'agreed upon by a Club of our Mathematical Instrument-makers, of whom Mr. Elias Allen was the chief' (Hooke 1705, p. 457).
4   Hooke 1705, p. 19.
5   Hooke 1705, pp. 19–20.
6   Hooke 1665, sig. b2r&v.
7   Oldenburg 1965–86, vol. 2, p. 384.
8   Hooke 1705, p. 15.
9   Pepys 1972–86, vol. 6, p. 18.
10   Power 1664.
11   Hooke 1665, sig. f2v – also 'the Ingenious Physician Dr. Henry Power' (Hooke 1665, sig. g2v).
12   Hooke 1705, p. 483.
13   Hooke 1705, p. 558.
14   Hooke 1705, p. 452.
15   Hooke 1665, p. 144.
16   Hooke 1679, p. 59.

17   Hooke 1665, pp. 44, 46, 60, 62.
18   Hooke 1679, p. 90.
19   Royal Society Classified Papers, vol. 20, f. 58.
20   Dickinson 1970, p. 8.
21   Hooke 1678a, p. 24.
22   Hooke 1665, sig. g2r.
23   Bennett 1973, p.144.
24   Hooke 1679, p. 9.
25   Hooke 1679, p. 41.
26   Hooke 1679, p. 38.
27   Hooke 1679, p. 55.
28   Hooke 1679, pp. 79–80.
29   Hooke 1679, p. 43.
30   Hooke 1679, p. 49.
31   Hooke 1679, p. 43.
32   Hooke 1679, p. 49.
33   Hooke 1679, p. 48.
34   Hooke 1679, p. 49.
35   Hooke 1679, p. 50.
36   Hooke 1679, p. 65.
37   Hooke 1679, p. 74.
38   Hooke 1679, p. 69.
39   Hooke 1679, p. 102.
40   Birch 1756–57, vol. 1, pp. 288–9.
41   Hooke 1665, sig. a2v.
42   Hooke 1665, sig. b1r.
43   Pepys 1972–86, vol. 5, pp.32–3.
44   Pepys 1972–86, vol. 5, p. 25.
45   Hooke 1705, p. 39.
46   Hooke 1705, p. 63.
47   Hooke 1665, pp. 151–2. At the same Royal Society Council Meeting as Wren promised to think of experiments to entertain the king, Hooke was instructed to prepare his hygroscope for the same purpose (Birch 1756–57, vol. 1, pp. 271–2).
48   Hooke 1665, p. 2.
49   Hooke 1665, pp. 189–90.

Chapter 5

1   Hooke 1674b.
2   Hooke 1679; Gunther 1930 p. 428 and plate 2.
3   Needham 1959, p. 367–82.
4   Brahe 1946; Bouillin 1994.
5   Bennett 1980.
6   King 1955.
7   Patterson 1952; Pugliese 1989.
8   Huygens (1888–1950), vol. 6, p. 167; vol. 16, p. 242; vol. 17, p. 133.
9   Halliday and Resnick 1970.
10   Pugliese 1989.
11   Siemens 1866; Low 1946, pp. 318 ff.
12   Saunier 1867.
13   Moxon 1970.
14   Humphrey 1931, p. 123.
15   Mills et al 2003.

16   Merritt 1942; Walker 1952; Smith 1994.
17   Norman et al 1938.
18   Sheepshanks 1836; Foucault 1847, 1862, 1863; Grubb 1888; Meyer 1930; Young 1930.
19   Young 1930.
20   Low 1946; McMath and Mohler 1960.

Chapter 6

1   Arnol'd 1990, p. 12.
2   Gribbin 2003, p. 149.
3   Smith 2000.
4   Westfall 1970–80, vol. 6, p. 484.
5   Chapman 1996, p. 245.
6   Westfall 1983, p. 90.
7   Jardine 1999, pp. 50–2.
8   Patterson 1949, 1950a; Pugliese 1982; Nauenberg 1994a; Gal 1996.
9   Patterson 1948.
10   Westfall 1983.
11   Pugliese 1982.
12   Gunther 1930a, pp. 267–9, 285–6 and 352.
13   Hooke 1705, p. 549.
14   Moyer 1977 p. 270.
15   Westfall 1983.
16   Bennett 1986, p. 7.
17   Inwood 2002, p. 402.
18   Gunther 1935, pp. 1–50.
19   Hooke 1665, pp. 10–22.
20   Hooke 1665, schem: IIII.
21   Centore 1970.
22   Gal 1996.
23   Gunther 1930a, pp. 91–4.
24   Centore 1970; Pugliese 1982.
25   Gunther 1930a, p. 104.
26   Hooke 1665, pp. 33–44 and schem: IIII.
27   Hooke 1665, schem: IIII.
28   Gunther 1931, p. 155–208 and Tab. I facing p. 208.
29   Gunther 1931, p. 165 and Figure 6.5 here.
30   Gunther 1931, p. 208 and Tab. II on facing page.
31   Westfall 1983, p. 97.
32   Gunther 1931, p. 167.
33   Gunther 1931, p. 166.
34   Gunther 1930b, pp. 435 and 438.
35   Gunther 1930a, pp. 292–6 and Figure 6.6 here.
36   Gunther 1930, pp. 295–6.
37   Gunther 1931, p. 168, Tab: 2 facing p. 208, and Figure 6.7 here.
38   Hooke 1935, pp. 182–3.
39   Hooke 1705, pp. 563–7.
40   Hooke 1705, p. 565, Tab: XIII and Figure 6.8 here.
41   Westfall 1983.
42   Westfall 1983, p. 98.
43   Patterson 1948.
44   Westfall 1983.

45   Gal 1996.
46   Westfall 1971, p. 45; Sarton according to Hall 1996, p. 2; Hall as reported by McKendrick 1973, p. 282; Hall 1996, p. 6; Dear 2001; Ravetz 1971, p. 39; Polanyi 1983, p. 88.
47   Bronowski 1951, pp. 29–35; Polanyi 1983, pp. 66–8; Hunter 1981, pp. 64–5.
48   Hacking 1983; Gooding et al 1989; Nickles 1990; McKendrick 1973, pp. 292 et seq; Keller 1993, p. 85; Keller 1984, p. 165; Bennett 1986, pp. 24–5.
49   Hutchings 1992, p. 121; Dobson et al 1997, p. 31.
50   Arons 1990, p. 17; Orton and Roper 2000, p. 128.

Chapter 7

1   Hooke 1705, pp. 138–48.
2   Richards 1992, p. 69.
3   Singer 1976; Inwood 2002, pp. 328–32.
4   See Boyle's 'A short Memorial of some Observations made upon an Artificial Substance, that shines without any precedent Illustration' quoted by Gunther 1931, pp. 273–82.
5   Golinski 1989, p. 20.
6   Gunther 1931, p. 319.
7   Landauer 1986.
8   Sprat 1667, p. 113.
9   Parker 1666, p. 76.
10   Shapin and Schaffer 1985, p. 70.
11   Hesse 1966a, p. 69.
12   Richards 1992, pp. 66–9.
13   Draaisma 2000.
14   Draaisma 2001.

Chapter 8

1   Hooke 1705, p. xxvi.
2   Schaffer 1998.
3   Hooke 1705, p. 134.
4   Biswas 1967.
5   Hooke 1675, p. 447. See also Birch 1756–57, vol. 3, p.222; Gunther 1930b, p.433.
6   Hooke 1665, p. 2. See also Glanvill 1661, p. 100.
7   Mulligan 1992a; Richards 1992; Draaisma 2000.
8   Hooke 1705, p. 140.
9   Hooke 1665, Preface.
10   Ibid.
11   Hooke 1705, sig. A2r.
12   Hooke 1705, p. 6.
13   Hooke 1705, p. 18.
14   Hooke 1705, p. 21.
15   Hooke 1705, p. 34.
16   Hooke 1705, p. 63.
17   Wilkins 1668; Salmon 1974; Turner 1994.
18   Hooke 1726, pp. 26–8.
19   Published in Hunter and Wood 1986.
20   Iliffe 1992.
21   Bennett 1980, 33–48.

22   Hunter and Wood 1986, p. 237.
23   Shapin 2003; MacLeod 1988, p. 41.
24   Westfall 1980; Schaffer 1989.
25   Iliffe 1992.
26   Lancellotti 1646, p. 457; Gyssling 1917, p. 21.
27   Beckmann 1782, p. 126; Marx 1954, p. 403.
28   Sprat 1667, p. 398.
29   Iliffe 1992, p. 31.

Chapter 9

1   Hooke 1705, pp. 279–450.
2   Woodward 1695, p. 47.
3   Drake 1996, pp. 87–95; Drake 2005, pp. 75–94.
4   Hooke 1705, p. 313.
5   Westfall 1970, pp. 481–8.
6   Drake 1996, pp. 83–5.
7   Ito 1988.
8   Hooke 1705, p. 313.
9   Hooke 1705, p. 334.
10   Hooke 1705, p. 293.
11   Drake and Komar 1981.
12   Schneer 1960.
13   Davies 1964.
14   Hooke 1705, p. 291.
15   Hooke 1705, p. 433.
16   Hooke 1705, p. 411.
17   Lyell 1830, pp. 31–5.
18   Drake 1996, pp. 104–11.
19   Hooke 1705, p. 435.
20   Pavlow 1928, p. 203 (author's translation).
     The original text is:
         'Il paraît étrange de parler d'un évolutionniste, ayant vécu à une époque, où
         ni l'anatomie comparée ni la paléontologie n'existaient encore, à une époque
         où Scheuchzer, décrivant le squelette d'une salamandre fossile géante, le
         prenait pour le squelette d'un homme antédiluvien; quand on prenait des
         dents fossils de requin pour des langues d'oiseau pétrifiées (glossopetræ);
         quand Aldobrandi, dans sa fameuse et volumineuse Zoologie, décrivait et
         reproduisait une quantité de dragons, tous imaginaires, comme ayant
         réellement existé, et dessinait, à côté de chaque exemplaire, la plante ou
         l'espèce d'herbe, dont l'animal s'était nourri.'
21   Hooke 1705, p. 322.
22   Hooke 1705, p. 327.
23   Drake 1996, p. 53.
24   Drake 1981; idem 1996.
25   Hutton 1785; idem 1788.
26   Steno 1669.
27   Drake 1996.
28   Cooper 2003b, p. 72.
29   Aubrey 1949a, pp. 242–245.
30   Hooke 1665, p. 80.
31   Rossiter 1935.

Chapter 10

1   Gunther 1935; Hooke 1935.
2   'Espinasse 1956.
3   More 1944.
4   Wren 1750.
5   Colvin 1995.
6   Westfall 1980.
7   Andrews et al 1997; O'Donoghue 1914; Russell 1997; Scull 1996; Stevenson 1996a.
8   Knoop and Jones 1935.
9   Harvey 1987; Salzman 1952.
10   Lang 1956.
11   Alberti 1988.
12   McKitterick 1995.
13   Heyman 1998.

Chapter 11

1   For Bedlam see Stevenson 1996a, pp. 254–75; for the Monument see Cooper 2003b, pp. 200–5 and Stevenson 2005.
2   For the City churches see Jeffery 1996, especially Chapter 9. For Hooke's collaboration with Wren see Jardine 2002, pp. 294–306 and Cooper 2003b, pp. 188–92.
3   For other examples of Hooke's use of European models, with emphasis on the Dutch, see Stoesser 2003, pp. 189–206.
4   For Hooke's relations with Wren see: Jardine 2002, passim; idem 2003b, pp. 14–5, 80–1, 150–4 and 173–4. For the collaboration of Hooke and Wren on canalizing the Fleet Ditch see Cooper 2003b, pp. 164–71.
5   These posts are mentioned in the receipt of payment for the Babers Field plot by William Russell and his wife, Rachel Vaughan; see the document in Caygill and Date 1999, Fig. 1. Ralph Montagu (1638–1709) was the son of the third Baron Montagu of Boughton, to whose title he succeeded in 1683. Between 1666 and 1678 he was Ambassador to France four times. In 1689 he was created Viscount Monthermer and Earl of Montagu and in 1705 Duke of Montagu (information from: Sir E. M. Thompson's *History of the British Museum*, unpublished, British Library Add. MS. 52292, fol. 45r; Cokayne (ed.) (1910–59) vol. 9, pp. 106–7. A recent biography of Montagu is Metzger 1987.
6   The choice location was much praised by Stow 1720, vol. 2, p. 85: 'Great *Russel Street*, a very handsome large and well built Street, graced with the best *Buildings* in all *Bloomsbury*, and the best inhabited by the *Nobility* and *Gentry*.'
7   Montagu had his public audience with Louis XIV on 27 April 1669, 'which for a distinguishing Mark of Honour he [Montagu] had in his Most Christian Majesty's Bed-Chamber, and even within the Rails round the Bed, where the King stood to receive him' (Montagu 1709a, p. 3). During his stay in Paris 'the Magnificence of his Table was answerable to the Grandeur of his Attendance' (ibid).
8   See Summerson 1993, especially pp.182–4 for Wren's visit to Paris in 1665–66 and the impressions he gained there; see also Jardine 2002, pp. 239–47 and in particular her quote from *Parentalia* on pp. 241–2: 'the Louvre for a while was my daily object, where no less than a thousand Hands are constantly employ'd … Which altogether make a School of Architecture, the best probably, at this Day in *Europe*'.

9 Wren had been appointed Surveyor on Sir John Denham's death in 1669 (Jardine 2002, p. 295). The City's parochial churches rebuilding programme followed the Rebuilding Act of 1670 (Jardine 2002, pp. 295–6; Jeffrey 1996, p. 31). Wren became architect for St Paul's by the royal warrant of 12 November 1673: see Jardine 2002, pp. 289–90 for the text of the warrant. My thanks also to Lisa Jardine for the perceptive comment on Montagu as client.

10 Montagu was there from 1646–47 until at least 1649, when he contributed a poem to *Lachrymae Musarum*. My thanks to Eddie Smith, Westminster School, for this information. Hooke attended from around 1650–55 (see Chapter 14 here). Wren was also an Old Boy of Westminster, having attended between 1641 and 1646 (Jardine 2002, pp. 50 and 53).

11 Hooke 1935. The manuscript version in Guildhall Library (Hooke 1671–83) covers a slightly longer period. It has no pagination.

12 Hooke 1935, p. 115. Flamsteed was appointed in 1675 (Jardine 2002, pp. 308–10).

13 Or 'Mountacue' (Hooke 1935 passim).

14 The last entry relating to Montagu in Hooke's *Diary* is for 25 August 1682 (Guildhall Library MS. 1758).

15 Hooke first mentions the 'Italian painter', that is, Antonio Verrio, on 13 February 1675 (Hooke 1935, p. 147). Other artists apparently involved were Robert Streater, who painted the ceiling of Wren's Sheldonian Theatre, and Caius Cibber, who was responsible for the decorative panel on the Monument and the figures of Raving and Melancholic Madness for Bedlam. Hooke mentions Streater in his Diary on 10 April 1675 (Hooke 1935, p. 158) and 5 September 1676 (Hooke 1935, p. 248) and Cibber on 3 August 1675 (Hooke 1935, p. 173). Perhaps Streater was involved in some of the painted interior decoration and Cibber in the decoration of the chimney-pieces. For Streater see Summerson 1993, pp. 116–7 and for Verrio see Summerson 1993, pp. 125–6. The first reference to the garden is on 21 May 1675 (Hooke 1935, p. 162) where Hooke talks of 'designing the ground'. Hooke discussed the levelling of the court and a 'sinking garden' on 17 January 1676 (Hooke 1935, p. 212). On 15 April 1676 Hooke mentions his design for a semicircular terrace or 'tarras' and fountain with semicircular steps (Hooke 1935, p. 226). Robinson and Adams's note on 'tarras', (Hooke 1935, p. 226) as an ingredient in material like cement, is not meaningful in this context.

16 Hooke 1935, p. 134.

17 19 May and 24 July 1675 (Hooke 1935, pp. 161 and 170, respectively).

18 For dinner see Hooke 1935, p. 175 (17 August 1675). For pictures see, for example, Hooke 1935, p. 176 (21 August 1675 – the naked woman picture) and Hooke 1935, p. 250 (20 September 1676 – Venus and Adonis). For books see Hooke 1935, p. 250 (21 September 1676) and Hooke 1935, p. 332 (5 December 1677).

19 For the Earl of Oxford see Hooke 1935, p. 223 (28 March – 1 April 1676). For France see Hooke 1935, pp. 244–5 (24 and 31 July 1676).

20 Hooke 1935, p. 149 (20 February 1675).

21 'all that peice or parcell of land lying in a feild commonly called or knowne by the name of Babers Feild scituate lying and being in the parish of St Gyles in the Feilds in the county of Middlesex containeing by admeasurement seaven Acres and Twenty perches now inclosed separated or divided from the rest of the feild by a brick-wall ...', which was sold for £2610 (Thompson undated, fol. 309r and Caygill and Date 1999, p. 8).

22 The deed of sale states that the purchaser undertook 'to erect and new-build one faire and large messuage and dwelling house fitt for him the said Ralph Mountagu and his family to inhabitt, composed of an uniforme building

together will all convenient stables, coach-houses, and other out offices, suitable to the said mancion or dwelling house; and further, shall alsoe keepe fenced in with a brick wall the residue of the said peice of ground and shall make thereout a convenient Courtyard, and on the back part thereof shall have space sufficient for convenient Gardens and Walkes...' (Thompson undated, fols. 309v–310r).

23   Thomson 1940, p. 65.

24   For Russell's visits to the site see Hooke 1935, pp. 162 and 165 (22 May and 17 June 1675, respectively) and for Hooke's visit to Southampton House see Hooke 1935, p. 166 (29 June 1675).

25   Evelyn 1955, vol. 4, pp. 344–5. The '*Corridore*' is the colonnade on the inside of the street screen.

26   Moxon 1975, p. 264 gives the relevant text of the Act as follows: 'Be it further Enacted, That all Houses of the fourth sort of Building, being Mansion Houses, and of the greatest bigness, not fronting upon any of the Streets or Lanes as aforesaid; the number of the Stories, and the Height thereof, shall be left to the discretion of the Builder, so as he [the mansion house] exceeds not four Stories'.

27   Lady Northumberland, Montagu's wife, in writing to her half-sister Rachel Russell on 11 February 1675, mentions 'no less than three [models], that are big enough for [her daughter] Miss Ann, to walk in'. Cited from *The Letters of Rachel, Lady Russell*, vol. 1 (1853), p. 23 by Thompson undated, p. 51.

28   Hooke had purchased Vingboons and Le Muet on 9 November 1674 (Hooke 1935, p. 129). Vingboons was published in two parts: the first in 1648 with the title *Afbeelsels der Voornaemste Gebovwen ...* and the second in 1674 wth the title *Tweede Deel van de Afbeeldsels der Vornaemste Gebovwen ...* [*Second Part of the Illustrations of the Finest Buildings ...*]. The spelling variation 'afbeeldsel' is replicated in the title pages of the respective parts. For further editions, see Ottenheym 1989, pp. 179–80. Although Hooke only bought his Marot on 23 March 1675, he was certainly aware of it before this, as is clear from his design (Hooke 1935, p. 154). The first edition of Le Muet was published in 1623, and the second edition in 1647. The latter was published again in 1666. The two Marots were published between 1660 and 1670.

29   First pointed out by Downes 1966, p. 57.

30   The accuracy of Morgan's depiction can be amply demonstrated by later portrayals of the screen, such as, for example: Colen Campbell's engraving in *Vitruvius Britannicus*, published in 1715; drawings by John Buckler made in 1828, (British Library Add. MS. 36370, ff. 31–35); and drawings by George Scharf made in the 1840s, now in the British Museum.

31   Palladio, for example, had shown alternating pediments on the second floor of the Palazzo Montano Barbarano (Palladio 1738, book 2, plate 16), and Serlio had illustrated alternating pediments on dormer windows on a villa (Serlio 1584, book 7, p. 105).

32   Ottenheym 1989, p. 193, Fig. 4.

33   For example, see Vingboons's illustration of Joseph Deutz's house (Ottenheym 1989, p. 261, fig. 55).

34   The *Diary* entries for 24 July and 17 August 1676 (Hooke 1935, pp. 244 and 246, respectively) indicate that there were changes in the appearance of the screen and entrance.

35   Great Russell Street had been cut through to Tottenham Court Road in 1664 by Montagu's father-in-law, the Earl of Southampton, to provide better access to Southampton House (Thomson 1940, p. 46). It was already known by its present name in 1674 (Thomson 1940, p. 60).

36   Palladio 1738, book 2, plate 44.

37   Van Campen's designs for the Town Hall were engraved by Jacob Vennecool (Van Campen 1661).
38   Montagu 1709b, p. 80.
39   For 'salon' Evelyn uses the term 'the Great Roome' (Evelyn 1955, vol. 4, p. 344, entry for 10 October 1683).
40   For a discussion of the 'formal' plan and its use at Vaux le Vicomte, see Girouard 1978, p. 126. Marot also illustrated the plan (Marot c. 1670, no plate number).
41   Evelyn 1955, vol. 4, p. 345.
42   Evelyn 1955, vol. 4, p. 344.
43   The first edition of 1624 with the illustration on p. 113 was listed in the auction catalogue of Hooke's books (Rostenberg 1989, p. 177).
44   McKitterick 1995, p. 41.
45   I am indebted to Tony Spence for confirming that excavations in the British Museum's forecourt have revealed that the east end of the colonnade from the street screen had infilled inverted arches and also his observation that the brick earths on gravel and glacial clays would otherwise not have been strong enough to support the structure.
46   Harris 1990, p. 325 mentions Hooke's encouragement. Moxon 1975, p. 256 cites Hooke's application and the reason for it.
47   The 'sashes' are mentioned for the first time on 21 October 1678 (Hooke 1935, p. 381). One was blown down on 2 February 1680 (Hooke 1935, p. 437).
48   This development is discussed fully by Louw and Crayford 1998, pp. 82–130 (with reference to Montagu House on pp. 110–2) and idem 1999, pp. 173–239.
49   Boyceau 1638, p. 71 points out that square or oblong beds were best because their straight lines 'rendent les allées longues et belles et leur donnent une plaisante perspective'.
50   Jacques 2001, particularly pp. 371 and 374.
51   Hooke 1935, pp. 212 and 226.
52   As at Balleroy, see Blunt 1993, fig. 165, p. 204.
53   Israel Silvestre's print of Liancourt's garden, 1655, gives a good illustration of this (Woodbridge 1986, p. 140, fig. 145).
54   Entries for 5 November 1679 and 10 October 1683 in Evelyn 1955 vol. 4, pp. 184 and 344, respectively.
55   On 28 November 1677, 21 October 1678 and 26 November 1678 (Hooke 1935, pp. 330, 381 and 386, respectively).
56   Entry for 10 October 1683 in Evelyn 1955, p. 344.
57   See for example the Heaven and Hell Room on the Burghley House website, www.stamford.co.uk/burghley/heaven.htm
58   Wittkower 1982, Chapter 14.
59   There are many references. Two examples will serve to illustrate: on 24 May and 1 December 1676 (Hooke 1935, pp. 234 and 260, respectively).
60   Evelyn 1955, vol. 4, p. 344 and Walpole 1826–28, vol. 3, p. 170.
61   For confirmation of this view see Caygill and Date 1999, p. 10.
62   The drawing is in the British Library (Add. MS. 5238, fol. 56) and is reproduced on the website www.roberthooke.org.uk/batten6.htm
63   Recent monographs on Puget make no mention of such a visit. See for example Chancel 1997.
64   See Jardine 2003b, pp. 3–9 for a description of Hooke's conflict with Newton and Cooper 2003b, pp. 82–5 for a consideration of Hooke's contribution to Newton's ideas.
65   Jackson-Stops 1980, p. 245. Although the rebuilding project was begun in 1687, the main block was only completed after Montagu's return to favour under William III in 1689.

66 Ellis 1829, vol. 1, p. 25 values the loss of the property at £40 000 and the contents at £6000. Cornforth 1992, p. 22 quotes a letter of 5 December 1680 from Barillon, the French Ambassador in England, indicating that Louis XIV had paid Montagu a pension. Another theory holds that Louis was willing to finance half of the reconstruction if French architects and artists were employed. Cornforth 1992, p. 22, note 20 cites Dussieux as the source of this information, but Dussieux himself points out that he had copied the information from a translation of Walpole's *Anecdotes of Painting* (Dussieux 1876, p. 267). Walpole indeed relates this story and adds that the purpose 'was to teach the English, how a perfect palace should be constructed and embellished' (Walpole 1826–28, vol. 3, pp. 170–1).

Chapter 12

1 Rossi 1970; Houghton 1941; Long 1999.
2 Spedding, Ellis and Heath 1870, pp. 257–8.
3 Herrmann 1973, pp. 13–4; Murat 1984, pp. 161–70.
4 Summerson 1963, pp. 51–86.
5 Hooke 1705, pp. 18 and 329; Kroll 1991, pp. 113–34.
6 Batten 1936–37, p. 87.
7 Summerson 1963, p. 62.
8 Picon 1992.
9 Iliffe 1995.
10 Hunter 1989, p. 313.
11 Long 1999, pp. 85–9.
12 Hunter 1989, p. 294.
13 Spedding, Ellis and Heath 1870, p. 271.
14 Hooke 1705, p. 330.
15 Hunter 1989, p. 305.
16 Perrault 1700; Herrmann 1973, pp. 12–5; Picon 1988, pp. 95–102.
17 Louw 1983, p. 55; idem 2003.
18 Picon 1988, pp. 184–7; Berger 1993, pp. 65–74.
19 Picon 1999, pp. 312–3.
20 Grew 1681, pp. 361–3.
21 Blondel 1675–83, book 6, Chapter 7.
22 Heyman 1998.
23 Colvin and Newman 1981, p. 50.
24 Jardine 2002, p. 423.
25 Campbell 2002.
26 Bendry 1995.
27 Louw and Crayford 1998; idem 1999.
28 Moxon 1975, p. 257.
29 Hooke 1935, p. 175.
30 Spedding, Ellis and Heath 1870, pp. 265–70.
31 Gunther 1931, pp. 100–1.
32 Inwood 2002, p. 372.
33 Louw 1991, p. 48.
34 Inwood 2002, p. 410.
35 Gunther 1931, p. vii.
36 Perez-Gomez 1993, p. 16.
37 Perez-Gomez 1993, p. 37.
38 Soo 1998, pp. 196–241.
39 Bennett 1972.
40 Summerson 1990, pp. 64–8.

41 Soo 1998, p. 216.
42 Inwood 2002, pp. 113–4, 179–80 and 377–8.
43 Ehrlich 1995; Bennett 1986; Helden 1983.
44 Galison and Thompson 1999.
45 Petzet 1967; Picon 1988, pp. 197–223.
46 Picon 1988, pp. 206–12; Stroup 1990, pp. 43–5; Petzet 1967; Louw 2003.
47 Jardine 2002, pp. 307–15; Inwood 2002, pp. 186–9.
48 Hunter 1989, pp. 156–81.
49 Jardine 2002, pp. 315–21.
50 Campbell 2002; Jardine 2002, pp. 321–7.
51 Clark 1964, pp. 328–33; Batten 1936–37, pp. 89–90.

Chapter 13

1 Hunter and Schaffer 1989, p. 1.
2 Shapin 1994, p. 156.
3 I treat the broader issue in Feingold 1996.
4 Shapin 1989, p. 256.
5 Shapin 1989, p. 253.
6 Shapin 1994, pp. 164–5 and note 18; p. 166.
7 Shapin 1989, p. 277.
8 Aubrey 1949b, p. 139; De Morgan 1885.
9 Shapin 1989, pp. 256–7 and 260.
10 Shapin 1989, p. 259.
11 For Hooke's social world, see Iliffe 1995.
12 Evelyn 1955, vol. 3, pp. 369–70.
13 Shapin 1989, pp. 268–9.
14 Shapin 1994, p. 398.
15 Aubrey 1898, vol. 1, p. 121.
16 Boyle 1999–2000, vol. 12, p. 92 where the young man was tentatively identified as John Mayow. For Boyle's protégés see Maddison 1969.
17 Shapin 1989, pp. 256 and 263.
18 For biographical information: Inwood 2002; Jardine 2003b.
19 Cooper 2004.
20 Westfall 1980, pp. 70 and 73–4.
21 Jardine 2003b, pp. 24–6, 54–5 and 65.
22 Aubrey 1898, vol. 1, p. 410.
23 Jardine 2002, Chapter 2.
24 Aubrey 1898, vol. 1, p. 411.
25 Shirley 1983, pp. 209–11, and passim; Malcolm 2002, pp. 5–6 and 24.
26 Cooper 2005.
27 Boyle 1999–2000, vol. 1, p. 159.
28 Boyle 1999–2000, vol. 3, pp. 45 and 83–93; Davis 1994.
29 Hunter 1989, p. 22; Birch 1756–57, vol. 1, pp. 123–4.
30 Hooke is included in the original list of 20 May 1663 of those 'received, admitted, and ordered to be registered fellows of the Royal Society' (Birch 1756–77, vol. 1, p. 239). The 3 June minute regarding his election as fellow was part of exempting him of all charges (Birch 1756–77, vol. 1, p. 250).
31 For the Gresham affair, see Cooper 2003b, pp. 36–9.
32 Cutler attempted to renege on his promise and Hooke was forced to litigate. See Hunter 1989, Chapter 9.
33 *The Record of the Royal Society*, 4th edn, London: The Royal Society, pp. 296–8.

34 Pumfrey 1991, p. 13.
35 Ward (trans.) 1845–51, vol. 1, pp. 277–8 and 281–2; Pumfrey 1991, p. 13. For the Savilian and Lucasian professorships, see Feingold 1994; idem 2003.
36 Pumfrey 1991, p.17; Birch 1756–57, vol. 2, p. 452.
37 Wren 1750, p. 260.
38 Sprat 1667, p. 434.
39 I shall address the issue in full in my forthcoming *History of the Royal Society.*
40 Oldenburg 1965–86, vol. 2, p. 235.
41 Royal Society Early Letters W.3.6.
42 Shapin 1989, p. 265; Oldenburg 1965–86, vol. 2, pp. 605 and 610. For the land-carriage project, see Hunter 1989, pp. 88–9.
43 Shapin 1994, pp. 291–300.
44 Huygens 1888–1950, vol. 3, pp. 285–7; Oldenburg 1965–86, vol. 2, pp. 126, 444; Royal Society, Boyle Papers, vol. 27, p. 13 – online as part of the edition of Boyle's workdiaries, workdiary 21, entry 222 at http://www.livesandletters. ac.uk/wd
45 Shapin 1994, p. 393.
46 Shapin 1994, p. 392; Birch 1756–57, vol. 3, p.78.
47 Hooke 1665, sig. b1r&v.
48 Shapin 1989, p. 264.
49 Locke 1975, pp. 9–10.
50 Aubrey 1898, vol. 1, p. 411.
51 Sprat 1667, p. 397; Hooke 1665, sig. g2r.
52 Newton 1959–77, vol. 3, pp. 359–60.
53 Henry 1989, p. 176.

Chapter 14

1 Sprat 1667.
2 The most often quoted statistic is that 13 bishops were the product of Busby's Westminster. The historian of the Royal Society, Bishop Thomas Sprat, was said to 'have thanked God that though he was not educated at Westminster, yet he became a Bishop'. The histories of the School often highlight those whose talents have shone in the arts or as statesmen, but some further indicators of the breadth of the talent that the School nurtured are that before Busby's death 24 Old Westminsters had joined the Royal Society, including four Presidents (Hoskyns, Montagu, Wren and Wyche); nine had become members of the Royal College of Physicians; there were botanists (Plukenet, Uvedale and Courten) and at least one chemist (Freind).
3 Wetenhall 1678, Introduction reads:
'To the Learned and truly Venerable, Dr. Richard Busby, My ever Honoured Master. Sir, I rather prefix this Recognition to the ensuing Discourse, than to either of the other in its company, because, Sir, it was truly the sense I had of Your piety, which first operated towards the Reconciling me to Church-Musick. I came to You with prejudices (very unreasonable, such as commonly all prejudices are) against it: The first Organ I ever saw or heard, was in Your House, which was in those days a more regular Church than most we had publickly. I then thus judged, if a man of such real Devotion, I knew You to be of, would keep an organ for sacred use, even when it was interdicted and of dangerous consequence, there was certainly more reason than I apprehended.'
See also Bodleian MS Rawlinson D 216 (wrongly ascribed to William James in early catalogues, but in fact the diary of Under Master Thomas Vincent, correctly ascribed by J. B. Whitmore) for the first four months of 1655. Many of the names used by Vincent are still obscure in that they are often Latinized surnames or

nicknames. On 30 January an ambassador and one of the Members of Parliament were at Busby's house to hear music. On 18 March Busby fetched Vincent and took him to *Philomelus* where Vincent heard Busby and others singing; they took the Protector's Organist back to supper.

4 Covenant signatories in a MS of the Busby Trustees in Westminster Abbey Muniments.

5 Steele 1714.

6 Alexander Pope wrote in book 4 of *The Dunciad*:
'When lo! A Spectre rose, whose index-hand
Held forth the Virtue of the dreadful wand;
His beaver'd brow a birchen garland wears,
Dropping with infant's blood, and mother's tear.
O'er ev'ry vein a shudd'ring horror runs;
Eton and Winton shake thro' all their Sons.
All flesh is humbled, Westminster's bold race
Shrink, and confess the Genius of the place;
The pale Boy-Senator yet tingling stands,
And holds his breeches close with both his hands'.
(Pope 1965, pp. 773–4.)

7 Henry 1712, p. 5.

8 South 1717, p. 48.

9 See Winn 1987, app. B for an excellent modern translation and, uniquely, a single volume containing all three documents.

10 Cranston 1957, p. 23 has a list of Locke's expenditure for Michaelmas 1649.

11 The range of titles is too large to list here, but it inevitably includes inter alia, Ptolemy: *Magna Construcionis (Almagest)*, 1559; Kepler: *Epitome Astronomiae Coppernicanae*, 1635; Gassendus: *Institutio Astronomica, cui accesserunt Galilei Nuntius Sidereus, et Johanis Kepleri Dioptrice*, 1653.

12 'I have hopes the Algebra will take well. One of Dr Busby's Scholars had one of me Friday last and He told me the Doctor did highly extoll it and read it to them usually every night: and all that have it do like it.'
Out of Moses Pitt's letter to Mr Brancker dated 2 June 1668 (British Library Birch Additional MS. 4398, fol. 196).

13 Hooke 1705, p. iii.

14 In the Busby Library is to be found Ravius's *A Discourse of the Orientall Tongues* (1649), which may well have been a precursor to Busby's grammar.

15 Cranston 1957, p. 27.

16 Evelyn 1850–52, vol. 4, p. 352, entry for 11 May 1661.

17 In this I concur with Toomer 1996, pp. 265–8, who discusses the subject at some length, though the proof is fundamentally based on lack of evidence of earlier indications. For the quotation concerning Hooper later in the sentence see *Dictionary of National Biography* vol. 9, p. 1196. I have been unable to trace its source.

18 Rostenberg 1989.

19 There are of course notable exceptions, for example: William Taswell, a Busby lecturer in Hebrew at Christ Church; and Humphrey Prideaux, the first Busby Lecturer in Hebrew, who has a claim as an Arabist from his research for his *Life of Mahomet*.

20 Gunther 1935, p. 263. Entry for 31 July 1693.

21 Evelyn 1850–52, vol. 4, p. 352, entry for 13 May 1661.

22 Walker 1655.

23 Thomas Vincent's Diary (Bodleian MS Rawlinson D 216). Entries for 1 and 11 January and 28 February 1655.

24 From a MS of the Busby Trustees in Westminster Abbey Muniments. Also listed

are: 'An Harpsicon: An old Lute: A Bass Violl: A many prick'd lessons &c for Vocals and Instrumentall Musick.'

25 Hiscock 1960, p. 3.

26 Including, for example, Ubaldus's *Mecanicorum Liber* (1615) and Gilbert's *De Magnete* (1600).

27 Hooke 1705, p. xxvi.

28 Wren 1750, p. 182.

29 Ibid.

30 From a MS of the Busby Trustees in Westminster Abbey Muniments.

31 Though no exactly contemporary reference to kite-flying at the School exists, in *The True Domestick Intelligence* for Friday 30 January 1680 is a brief note:

'London, Jan 27, 1680: It is reported that several Schools in and about London have petitioned his Majesty, that he will be pleased to give them the late Petitions to make Kites of; which if granted, it is supposedt the Westminster Scholars will have them, as being particularly his Majesties favour.'

32 Dickinson 1970, p. 27.

33 Stubbe 1659 (British Library Thomason Tract E 988/25).

34 Christ Church Oxon Archives, Dp ii c1 fol. 75.

35 Westminster School Archives, A3/65: a paper by W. P. Holmes arguing that Henry Purcell was the recipient of one of these scholarships.

36 Nakajima 1994, pp. 11–6.

37 'So I with them to Westminster by coach, the Cofferer telling us odd stories: how he was dealt with by the men of the church at Westminster in taking a lease of them at the King's coming in; and perticularly the devilish covetousness of Dr Busby.' (Pepys 1972–86, vol. 8, pp. 118–9.)

38 MS *In Libro Depositinn: fo: 99: usq fo: 109:* [produced for] *Sir Thomas Trevor Knight. His Maj[ties] Attornie Generall.* Busby Trustees Collection, Westminster Abbey Muniments.

39 Westminster Abbey Muniments 43112. The list is broken into three forms. The names include parentage and age. So for example it includes: Henry Ardern, aged 13, elected to Trinity College, Cambridge in 1659 aged 18; Martin Hill, aged 14, who was admitted sizar to St John's College, Cambridge, aged 16 in May 1656; and George Hooper, aged 15, who was born in 1640. Many others' biographical details are unknown. It is not possible to judge when in the year such a list might have been compiled, nor for what reason, and therefore there could be some inaccuracy in the ages. However no pupil in the list whose date for going up to university is known (19 of them) arrived before 1655.

40 Hooke 1705, p. iii.

41 Gunther 1935, p. 128. Entry for 11 June 1689.

42 British Library Birch Addtional MS 4292, fol. 84; 4292, fol. 87; 4293, fol. 85.

43 'My Lord Bacon whom I therefore quote because he is the most rationall of all the opposers of Aristotle & the rest are but dwarfes to this Giant' (British Library Birch Additional MS 4292, fol. 87).

44 Locke 1979, letter 1471. To Edward Clarke.

45 'Received from Sir J Frederick a green staff of governor of Christs hospitall, gave 1sh'. (Hooke 1935, p. 14, entry for 23 November 1672.)

46 'Read 3⁴ hour Lecture, in the hall Paget & 2 other men and 40 children.' (Gunther 1935, p. 118, entry for 2 May 1689.)

47 For example: 'tea with Dr Busby, he told me of a Mathemat. teacher.' (Gunther 1935, p. 244, entry for 29 May 1693.)

48 For example: 'A Westminasterian here about Barometer and Thermometer' (Hooke 1935, p. 303, entry for 23 July 1677); and 'Dined with Dr Busby. Tompion & Aturbury junr [probably Francis Atterbury, one of Busby's pupils

and subsequently Dean of Westminster] squeezing & Diamt Watches' (Gunther 1935, pp. 91–2, entry for 22 January 1688).

49   'Sept 9 1687 Munday Septemb 9 At Dr Gales house by Pauls Schoole met Deane Lloyd, Dr Gale, Doctor Pell, Mr Hooke, Mr Pitt.' (British Library Birch Additional MS 4279, fol. 202.) This is part of the collection of Pell's papers that were found in Dr Busby's house at his death and subsequently ended in the British Library.

50   Westminster Abbey Muniments Chapter Minutes 12 April 1695, where he is incorrectly recorded as Dr Richard Hooke.

51   Westminster Abbey Muniments Chapter Minutes.

52   'Ordered unanimously the Mr Plukenet bee discharged his Office of Clerk of the Workes for grosse Negligence & manifest ignorance & great suspicion of fraud in the execution there of' (Westminster Abbey Muniments Chapter Minutes, 16 January 1684.) See also Hooke 1935, p. 434 entry for 30 December: 'From Busby 5 Guinnys [gold]. Plucknet cunning.'

53   Royal Commission on Historical Monuments 1924, plate 178.

54   'Agreed with Bates for Dr. Busby for 35sh. per Square for framing, raising rales, scaffold for roof; 15sh. per square for bricketting, finding all but boords – With mason for 10d superficial all without walls.' (Hooke 1935, p. 403, entry for 13 March 1679.) See also Royal Commission on Historical Monuments 1924, plate 164.

55   'Recd then in full of all demands whatever for & concerning the laying black & white Marble in the Quire & Providing Materials of all kind for the same, ten pounds, which with several former sums received, makes in All one hundred fifty one pounds & fifteene shillings. And I do hereby exonerat Dr Richd Busby, who hath fully paid & dischargd the said summes to mee from all or any molestation, claime, or demand from any person or Persons, whatsoever In witness whereof I have unto subscribe my name & sett my seale. Tho: Plukenett In the presence of John Gee, Tho. Knipe.' (Westminster Abbey Muniments 66915, 20 December 1677.)

56   Westminster Abbey Muniments 66887 gives the date of 1681 from Tufnell's bill.

57   Gunther 1935, p. 252. Entry for 22 June 1693.

58   Westminster Abbey Muniments 44099, 44154.

59   Wren Society (1924–43) vol. 11, plates 1, 2 and 3 show the state of the North Porch, the Rose Window and Solomon's (Galilee) Porch in 1659: Wren's survey, Dickinson's design.

60   British Library Sloane MS 4062 fol. 229.

61   British Library Sloane MS 1009 fol. 144 and Westminster Abbey Muniments 66914.

62   Sheppard 1960, p. 109.

63   Westminster Abbey Muniments Chapter Minutes 12 December 1685.

64   Gunther 1935, p. 189, entry for 20 February 1690.

65   Westminster Abbey Muniments Chapter Minutes 3 June 1693.

66   British Library Sloane MS 1039, fol. 123.

Chapter 15

1   Indeed, the slavish obsession with Newton's activities in a period when the implications of the *Principia* were not generally understood is not without a taint of whiggery.

2   British Library Sloane MS 4024, transcribed and edited by Gunther 1935.

3   These deserve much closer attention than they have heretofore been given. I thank Michael Hunter for urging me to comment on this vast and jumbled 'treasure trove' of material, which includes a number of unpublished lectures

referred to elsewhere in this paper. Some items are merely abstracts, transcriptions or translations of works Hooke was studying. Also included are letters, a few astronomical observations, even a Gresham lecture. Some of the earlier material may bear directly on the question of Hooke's efforts to solve the problem of planetary motion. A list of these papers published in Keynes 1960 is not without errors. See also Hunter 1989, p. 333.

4 Gunther 1935, p. 74.

5 Gunther 1935, p. 73.

6 A total of 14 letters between Hooke and Newton after Oldenburg's death are to be found in Newton (1959–77) consisting of six from the autumn of 1677 to the late spring of 1678, and eight between November 1679 and December 1680. The latter constitute the exchange over mechanics. Few are noted by Hooke in his *Diary*, but we find, under 5 December 1679, 'wrote to Mr. Newton', and for 9 December 1679, 'Sent letter to Newton, Beal' (Hooke 1935, pp. 432–3).

7 The earlier *Diary* (Hooke 1935) spans the period August 1672 to the last day of December 1680, but fragments at each end remain unpublished. Most of the later diary (British Library Sloane MS 4024) was published in Gunther 1935. In addition there are several small fragments, October 1681 to September 1683, and 1 June 1695, in British Library Sloane MS 1039, covering about three months in 1695. The final fragment (Gunther 1930b, p.759) for 1 June 1695, just before Hooke's 60th birthday, is in a much more fleshed-out narrative style, for example: 'I stayd with Mr. Blount and Mr. Hally from 8 to neer 12 a'clock, then went and dined at the Roman in Queen Street, with Sir Christopher Wren, Mr. Blount, and his cozen Mr. Aldersey … ' Whether there was/is more to the diary, is beyond our knowledge. The later diary as it exists in the Sloane manuscripts begins on 1 November 1688, suggesting either the initiation of a new book or, alternatively, a new resolution. That portion concludes on 9 March 1690, not quite a year and a half later. It resumes on 5 December 1692 and a review of what else we know of Hooke's life from the Royal Society's archives, shows nothing that might offer an explanation. Similarly, the final entry on 8 August 1693 gives no clue that writing will not resume the next day. Altogether an enigma.

8 I count 20 or so allusions to health issues, not including numerous references to 'headake'. The most serious would seem to be when he wrote that he was 'Much out of order and stopd in breathing' (Gunther 1935, p. 211, entry for 3 February 1693). A month later he writes 'excused my not coming pp [post prandium – after the mid-day meal] when he should have visited a construction site (Gunther 1935, p. 219, entry for 3 March 1693).

9 He uttered the same cry in January 1689 and in February 1693. Evidently the dreary winters had something to do with his mood.

10 Hooke 1705, p. xxiv.

11 Newton 1959–77, vol. 2, pp. 297–300.

12 We speak here of Hooke's 'The Laws of Circular Motion' manuscript in Trinity College Library, Cambridge (MS O.11a.1/16). This appears, rather innocuously, in the list of manuscripts at Trinity (O.11a) in Keynes' Hooke bibliography.

13 Newton 1959–77, vol. 3, p. 42, dated 15 September 1689.

14 See also Hooke's 'A True State of the Case and Controversy Between Sir Isaac Newton and Dr. Robert Hooke …' published in facsimile in Gunther 1935, pp. 56–60.

15 Almost a year earlier, on 9 January 1689, a meeting day, Hooke had raised the issue with those present at Jonathan's after the meeting; he records 'Agreed by all' (Gunther 1935, p. 89), but in his diary entry for 27 November 1689 Hooke wrote 'I propounded Collections. Hill found tricks: voted against me' (Gunther 1935, p. 167).

16 Royal Society Council Minutes for 27 November 1698 and 22 October 1690.

17   *Royal Society Journal Book*, 1 April 1691.
18   The Secretaries in this period were Thomas Gale, who served between 1685 and 1693, and Richard Waller, 1687–1709. But it was Halley, as Clerk, who was principally responsible for the *Transactions* between 1686 and 1692, the period in question, but only four numbers were published in the years 1688–92. Halley also edited the *Transactions* between 1714 and 1719, when he was Secretary.
19   See Chapter 14 here.
20   An almost exact contemporary of Hooke, Steno repudiated science before he reached the age of 30 (in 1667). See Chapter 9 here.
21   *Royal Society Journal Book* (copy) entry for 19 February 1690.
22   *Royal Society Journal Book*, entry for 10 July 1689. The record states that it took 7 seconds for the sound to travel from the Tower to Gresham College (a distance of 1000 yards according to Ogilby and Morgan's map) therefore '... the Motion of sound is about 143 yards in a second, and that 12 seconds answers to the distance of a Mile'. The approximate value of the speed of sound through the air is about 340 metres (372 yards) per second. The error is hard to explain on the basis of the scanty evidence. The distance of 1000 metres from Ogilby and Morgan's map is correct to about 10 metres and the time interval between seeing the flash and hearing the explosion could be easily measured to half a second: the error to be expected is therefore of the order of 10%.
23   *Royal Society Journal Book*, 19 July 1693.
24   Gunther 1935, p. 128.
25   Based on the absence of his voice from the *Royal Society Journal Book* and his name from Hooke's regular lists of members present.
26   Here, of course, I refer to the words of whomever was taking minutes for the *Journal Book*; Gale and Waller were the Secretaries throughout this period.
27   A 'Lambeth doctorate' of Physick, awarded him by his friend Tillotson, which entitled him to put M.D. after his name.
28   Though Hooke's last *Philosophical Transaction* was in 1702, he had not published anything really new since 1688. In all, he only had 21 papers published in the organ of the Royal Society, in nearly 40 years (Keynes 1960, pp. 56–7). But only four numbers were published in the years 1687–92.
29   Hoskins had been President for one year, 1682–3, following Wren.
30   To the extent that Hooke's lists are complete, there appear to have been no more than about a dozen or so present, and sometimes fewer.
31   Gunther 1935, p. 226.
32   Hooke 1705, p. xxvi.
33   The Royal Society resumed meeting after its summer recess in late October, by which time Hooke was well enough to attend all or most meetings well into the following spring. Of course, he did not have to travel far.
34   Hooke 1705, p. xxvi.
35   Ibid.
36   We surmise, without evidence.
37   See Chapter 11 here.
38   These attributions are not without controversy, but seem very probable. See Jeffrey 1996.
39   To which we can add Ragley Hall and Willen Church, in the countryside.
40   Hooke 1705, p. xxviii.

Chapter 16

1   It received the imprimatur of the Royal Society on 23 November 1664.
2   Huygens's father had sent him some extracts from the book – presumably

without illustrations. Although Christiaan duly wrote to the Royal Society, under whose official auspices the work appeared, he already had some reservations about the author of *Micrographia*. He confided to his father, privately, that Hooke was neither amiable, nor a good enough mathematician for his activities in any field to be taken seriously by Christiaan: 'Thanks for the extracts from Hooke [*Micrographia*] I know him very well. He understands no geometry at all. He makes himself ridiculous by his boasting.' (Huygens 1888–1950, vol. 5, p. 240.)

3   13 February 1665. Huygens 1888–1950, vol. 5, p. 236.

4   Huygens 1888–1950, vol. 5, p. 245.

5   On Huygens's annotations of his copy see Barth 1995.

6   See the letter of thanks sent by Auzout to Sir Constantijn Huygens (Huygens 1888–1950, vol. 5, pp. 179–80). I accept McKeon's redating of this letter: 'Auzout, en effet, en renvoyant un livre d'anglais que Constantyn Huygens lui avait prêté, lui écrivit une lettre de remerciement [Huygens 1888–1950, vol. 5, pp. 179–80]. Les editeurs de Huygens suppose qu'il s'agissait d'un livre écrit par Boyle et que la lettre avait été écrite vers la fin de 1664.' (McKeon 1965, fascicule 2, p. 212.)

7   5 June 1665 '... Je receus il y a quelques jours une lettre de M. de Zulichem qui me mandoit que vous aviez trouvé aussi bien que moy quantité de bonnes choses dans le livre de Hook, il me temoignoit aussy une grande passion pour le microscope de M. de Monconnis don't vous aures appris la mort, mais on ma dit que son fils le vouloit vendre 15 pistoles' (*Codex Hugenianus*, Universiteit-bibliotheek, Leiden).

8   Auzout proposed setting up the Observatory in the dedicatory letter to Louis XIV which prefaced his *L'Ephéméride du comète de 1664* (Paris, 1665): 'C'est un des principaux desseins de la Compagnie des Sciences et des Arts, qui n'attend plus que la protection de Vostre Majesté pour travailler puissament à la perfection de toutes les Sciences & de tous les Arts utiles. Son Projet est si grand & pourra estre si glorieux à l'Estat, & si utile au Public, s'il est executé dans toute son etenduë, qu'il est impossible de n'estre pas persuadé que Vostre Majesté qui a des desseins si vastes & si magnifiques ne l'approuve & ne le favorise, & ne la puis asseurer que toutes les Nations voisines sont depuis quelque temps dans une attente incroyable d'un si bel établissement.' (Dedicatory letter to the King, unpaginated.) With the support of, among others, Colbert and Huygens (who was awarded a substantial salary by the King in 1664, and moved to Paris in 1666) the Observatory was built and began functioning in 1667.

9   Hooke 1665, fols e1r-v. 'It seems the most easie, because with one and the same Tool may be with care ground an Object Glass, of any length or breadth requisite, and that with very little or no trouble in fitting the Engine, and without much skill in the Grinder. It seems to be the most exact, for to the very last stroke the Glass does regulate and rectifie the Tool to its exact Figure; and the longer or more the Tool and Glass are wrought together, the more exact will both of them be of the desir'd Figure. Further, the motions of the Glass and Tool do so cross each other, that there is not one point of either Surface, but has thousands of cross motions thwarting it, so that there can be no kind of Rings or Gutters made either in the Tool or Glass.'

10   Such a printed report is equivalent, in the period, to a priority claim, preceding an application for patent.

11   *Lettre à Monsieur l'Abbé Charles, sur la Ragguaglio di nuove Osservationi da Giuseppe Campani* (Paris, 1665). See also note 26.

12   Auzout and the Royal Society (that is, the Secretary, Oldenburg) had been corresponding since early January 1665, following the publication of Auzout's *l'Ephéméride du comète de 1664* (Paris, 1665). See Oldenburg 1965–86, vol. 2,

pp. 341 and 359–68. The *Journal des sçavans* began publication in January 1665, but ceased after three months. It began again in January 1666. Thus Auzout's published letters may well have been intended for publication in the *Journal*, where indeed a review of the Campani book (probably by Auzout) was eventually published in January 1666.

13　Oldenburg 1965–86, vol. 2, pp. 383–410.

14　Oldenburg 1965–86, vol. 2, p. 384. For Hooke's disclaimer see Hooke 1665 fol. a2v: 'The Rules you have prescrib'd your selves in your Philosophical Progress do seem the best that have ever yet been practis'd. And particularly that of avoiding Dogmatizing, and the espousal of any Hypothesis not sufficiently grounded and confirm'd by Experiments. This way seems the most excellent, and may preserve both Philosophy and Natural History from its former Corruptions. In saying which, I may seem to condemn my own Course in this Treatise; in which there may perhaps be some Expressions, which may seem more positive then your Prescriptions will permit: And though I desire to have them understood only as Conjectures and Quaeries (which your Method does not altogether disallow) yet if even in those I have exceeded, 'tis fit that I should declare, that it was not done by your Directions.' See also Hooke 1665, fol. blr: 'If therefore the Reader expects from me any infallible Deductions, or certainty of Axioms I am to say for my self, that those stronger Works of Wit and Imagination are above my weak Abilities; or if they had not been so, I would not have made use of them in this present Subject before me: Wherever he finds that I have ventur'd at any small Conjectures, at the causes of the things that I have observed, I beseech him to look upon them only as doubtful Problems, and uncertain ghesses, and not as unquestionable Conclusions, or matters of unconfutable Science. I have produced nothing here, with intent to bind his understanding to an implicit consent.'

15　This was a common admission by continental readers of *Micrographia*. By early the next century an abridged edition had been produced to satisfy the non-English speaking market, omitting most of the text, but reproducing all the plates.

16　Oldenburg 1965–86, vol. 2, p. 420.

17　'I am very glad that we shall soon see your learned Mr Wren here. I fear that he will not find our Company in very good shape, but if he sees nothing very splendid here at least we shall learn much from him' (Oldenburg 1965–86, vol. 2, p. 429).

18　Boyle 2001, vol. 2, p. 87.

19　Huygens 1888–1950, vol. 5, pp. 503–6. Moray continues ominously (for Hooke): 'When you wish to know the details Mr Oldenburg knows sufficient to communicate them, which could well save you effort, time and expense.'

20　13 September 1664 (*Codex Hugenianus*, Universiteitbibliotheek, Leiden).

21　A feature of print epistolary controversies is that they tend deliberately to efface other correspondents and letter exchanges, which are contributing extra information to the exchange spotlighted by publication.

22　For the tone of these letters, at least in the early days of the correspondence, see the first letter sent by Moray, 31 May 1661: 'Monsieur Vous devez sçavoir combien de satisfaction J'ay <eue> en l'honneur de Votre conuersation, si, du moins vous vous souvenez de ce que Je Vous en ay tant de fois dit. Mais Vous aurez de la peine à Vous imaginez combien Votre lettre m'a apporté de joye. Vous m'y faites Voir non seulement que Vous m'aimez, mais aussi que Vous croyez que Je Vous aime. En bonne foy, Vous ne Vous y trompez point de tout. Ce n'est pas moy seul qui fut ravi d'apprendre que Vous estes heureusernent arrivé a La Haye. Tout ceux que Vous m'auez nommez, et tout le reste de nostre Societé, y prennent autant d'interest que moi mais ces Messieurs De Bronker,

Neal, Slingsby, et Boile sont satisfaits de la souciance que Vous avez d'eux, à un point qui me donne presque de la Jalousie. Voilà assez de cette sorte de langage. Je crois que nostre amitié, est desja si bien fondé, qu'il ne sera plus besoin de nous entretenir de civilitez.' (*Codex Hugenianus*, Universiteitbibliotheek, Leiden.)

23 This is confirmed by the fact that on 2 November 1664 Hooke was admonished to 'endeavour to have his new instrument for grinding optic-glasses ready against the next meeting' (Birch 1756–57, vol. 1, p. 483).

24 McKeon 1965, fascicule 2, pp. 209–10: 'Huygens, à qui le frère de Campani avait envoyé le *Regguaglia* [Huygens 1888–1950, vol. 5, pp. 96–7] on donna un bref compte rendu dans une lettre à Moray: "Il [Campani] se vante d'une nouvelle manière de faire des verres par le moyen d'un tour, et sans autrement se servir de forme" [Huygens 1888–1950, vol. 5, p. 109, 19/8/64]. Moray répondit: "Quant à la façon des verres par le moyen d'un tour, Monsieur Hooke nous en a proposé une invention il y a 5 ou 6 mois [précisément 7/5/64] qui semble n'être pas contemptible quoiqu'on ne l'a pas encore mise en pratique. Vous saurez ce que c'est si Vous le désirez" [Huygens 1888–1950, vol. 5, p. 116, 13/9/64]. Deux mois plus tard il fournissait plus de détails à Huygens: "Je crois vous avoir devant dit que Monsieur Hooke nous a proposé il y a plusieurs mois, un èspece de tour pour faire des verre pour les télescopes sans se servir d'aucune forme ou moule. Son invention est, de placer le verre sur le bout d'un bâton qui tourne sur deux pivots, puis avoir un cercle de fer placé sur le bout d'un autre baton qui tourne de la même façon, en sorte que le bord du cercle couvre le centre du verre, puis appliquant le cerele au verre en sorte que les deux batons fassent tel angle qu'il désire, à mesure que l'angle est grand ou petit il fait la superficie du verre d'une section d'une grande sphère ou d'une petite" [Huygens 1888–1950, vol. 5, p. 135, 7/11/64]'.

25 Huygens 1888–1950, vol. 5, p. 156 (see McKeon 1965, fascicule 2, pp. 111–2).

26 This interest in Campani's techniques for making high-accuracy telescopes formed part of a larger debate about the Copernican theory of planetary motion, and the Inquisition's attitude towards it. See for instance the review of Auzout's *Lettre à Monsieur l'Abbé Charles, sur la Ragguaglio di nuove Osservationi da Giuseppe Campagni* (Paris, 1665) in the *Journal des sçavans* of 11 January 1666: '[Auzout] dit que les observations de Campani sur les Planetes de Saturne & de Jupiter, & celles qu'il a faites luy-mesme vont à conformer l'opinion de Copernic, pour laquelle il pretend que plusieurs Sçavans se seroient declarez, sans le Decret de l'Inquisition de Rome, qui l'a condamnée. Neantmoins il soûtient que ce Decret ne les doit pas empescher de le faire, parce qu'il n'est que provisionnel, & ne condamne pas absolument la Doctrine de Copernic. Aussie monstre-il qu'elle ne s'accorde pas moins avec les principes de Religion, qu'avec ceux de la Philosophie' (p. 20).

27 See McKeon 1965, fascicule 2, p. 211: 'Huygens répondit à Moray par le prochain courrier qu'il approuvait cette méthode proposée par Hooke et pour lui Campani l'employait également la méthode. Il se demandait toutefois si cette invention pouvait être réalisée de la manière envisagée par Hooke: "… je ne pense pas que ce soit le moyen de faire rien de bon [d'appliquer le cercle de fer au bout d'un baton et le verre à un autre], mais je m'imagine que le cercle ne doit servir que pour doucir, et perfectionner la figure du verre après qu'on l'a lui a fair prendre dans une forme" [Huygens 1888–1950, vol. 5, p. 148, 21/11/64]'.

28 Huygens 1888–1950, vol. 5, p. 174, dated 25 November 1664 (McKeon 1965, fascicule 2, p. 112).

29 'Méthode du cercle. qu'il n'importe pas quoique le verre devienne de plus grande sphère et que la forme étant donnée imparfaite se perfectionne

nécessairement par le cercle' (Huygens 1888–1950, vol. 5, p. 198, minute of a letter dated 15 November 1665).

30   On 2 January 1665 Huygens wrote to Moray impatiently asking for more information about Hooke's working model of the lathe. He described how, in his own trials, he did better by keeping the circle fixed, keeping 'le verre sur le cercle, … mais le cercle sur le verre immobile que pourtant il tournait un peu de temps en temps' (Huygens 1888–1950, vol. 5, p. 186).

31   Here, as in the case of the balance-spring watch, we have the issue of Huygens – eager for recognition in the new Paris Académie – absorbing technical detail gathered from informants in London, and incorporating it in his own scientific instruments without acknowledgement. This is precisely the period during which Hooke later accused Oldenburg and Moray of having leaked details of his balance-spring watch to Huygens, and Huygens having adapted his own prototype watches accordingly.

32   This was not the only 'leak' of Hooke's lens-grinding machine. On 13 November 1664 Oldenburg wrote to Hevelius: 'A new way of polishing lenses exactly is being worked upon by a certain famous Englishman [Hooke], a fellow of the Royal Society, which is soon to be examined and tested. It consists in this: by means of one of those machines of the same kind [as Campani's] one can work such glasses as may be used in telescopes of any desired length both more accurately and more speedily than hitherto has been done. I assure you that you shall receive good news of it in my next letter, God willing' (Oldenburg 1965–86, vol. 2, p. 306).

33   Oldenburg 1965–86, vol. 2, p. 441–2.

34   Boyle 2001, vol. 2, p. 493.

35   Boyle 2001, vol. 2, pp. 610–11.

36   Oldenburg 1965–86, vol. 2, p. 474. The original is bound in the back of a copy of Auzot's *Réponse de Monsieur Hooke* in the British Library.

37   Oldenburg 1965–86, vol. 2, p. 516 (Author's translation).

38   Oldenburg 1965–86, vol. 2, p. 447.

39   Oldenburg 1965–86, vol. 2, p. 448. On 3 August Oldenburg also wrote to Hevelius: 'What a certain Englishman has undertaken for the improvement of telescopes has not yet succeeded as he wished. Almost all our studies are languishing at the present time and almost all members of our philosophical assembly are so dispersed, because of the pestilential infection raging amongst us. … Almost the whole of our Society is now scattered throughout Britain; with a very few others I remain in London despite the plague, fortifying myself with God's providence and the best medicaments against the plague that I can buy.' (Oldenburg 1965–86, vol. 2, pp. 452–3.)

40   The Halls' annotations to the letters in Oldenburg 1965–86 treat Hooke's contribution consistently as if it were an ill-conceived and botched project, and as if Auzout were self-evidently correct in all his criticisms.

41   Oldenburg 1965–86, vol. 2, p. 83. Wren's position was presumably not helped by the fact that he had recently had to concede Huygens's superior talent as an observational and theoretical astronomer, when Huygens's model for the rings of Saturn was demonstrably more plausible than the one Wren had himself come up with.

42   On 1 July 1665 Auzout wrote to Oldenburg: 'Je me rejouis de ce que nous verrons icy dans peu votre savant M. Wren. Je crains quil ne trouve pas notre compagnie en fort bon etat, mais sil ne voit pas icy grande chose du moins nous aprendrons beaucoup de luy.' (Oldenburg 1965–86, vol. 2, p. 428.)

43   Boyle 2001, vol. 2, pp. 504 and 517.

44   Oldenburg 1965–86, vol. 2, pp. 294 and 297.

45   My own view is that this review is by Auzot, though it might be by Justel.

Index